Dana Facaros & Michael Pauls

CORSICA

'If you are in search of authentic *corsitude*,
it's to the heart of the island you must go,
into its tallest mountains and villages
where the sea is only a distant rumour,
seen only from the highest heights.'

CADOGANguides

1 Col de Punticella
2 Aiguilles de Bavella

3

3 Porto
4 Bastia harbour at dusk

5 Bonifacio
6 Ajaccio, sign
7 Ajaccio, port
8 Bonifacio

9 Olmeto-Plage

10 Filitosa
11 Ajaccio

12

13

14

15 Porto-Vecchio
16 Penta-di-Casinca
17 Restaurant sign

18 The Calanche de Piana

About the authors

Dana Facaros and **Michael Pauls** have written over 30 books for Cadogan Guides. They have lived all over Europe with their son and daughter, and are currently ensconced in an old farmhouse in southwestern France with a large collection of tame and wild animals.

Acknowledgements

The authors would like to thank everyone who has worked on this guide, especially the many kind and helpful staff of Corsica's tourist offices.

Contents

Cadogan Guides
2nd Floor, 233 High Holborn,
London WC1V 7DN
info@cadoganguides.co.uk
www.cadoganguides.com

The Globe Pequot Press
246 Goose Lane, PO Box 480, Guilford,
Connecticut 06437–0480

Copyright © Dana Facaros and Michael Pauls
    2001, 2006

Cover photographs © John Miller
Photo essay © John Ferro Sims and John Miller
Maps © Cadogan Guides, drawn by Maidenhead
    Cartographic Services Ltd
Art Director: Sarah Gardner
Managing Editor: Natalie Pomier
Editor: Linda McQueen
Editorial Assistant: Nicola Jessop
Proofreading: Daphne Trotter
Indexing: Isobel McLean

Printed in Italy by Legoprint
A catalogue record for this book is available
    from the British Library
ISBN-10: 1-86011-326-5
ISBN-13: 978-1-86011-326-0

The author and publishers have made every effort
to ensure the accuracy of the information in this
book at the time of going to press. However, they
cannot accept any responsibility for any loss,
injury or inconvenience resulting from the use of
information contained in this guide.

Please help us to keep this guide up to date. We
have done our best to ensure that the information
in this guide is correct at the time of going to press.
But places and facilities are constantly changing,
and standards and prices in hotels and restaurants
fluctuate. We would be delighted to receive any
comments concerning existing entries or omis-
sions. Authors of the best letters will receive a
Cadogan Guide of their choice.

Introduction

01

I believe, if I could again visit Corsica, I might recover.

last words of James Boswell (1740–95)

Boswell knew: Corsica is like a shot of adrenaline straight to the heart. Just being there makes a body feel more alive, steeped in the Mediterranean sun, surrounded by the Fauvist red and pink of the granite, warmed by a clear turquoise sea, the spicy perfume of the *maquis* filling the lungs. And just head inland and another, equally bracing world awaits, a majestic Corsica of snowcapped mountains, rushing rivers, waterfalls, and towering forests. Here and there silent villages filigreed with mist cling to impossible crags; wild flowers explode into bloom in one of the least polluted environments in Europe. The ancient Greeks, who knew scores of islands from their travels, called Corsica 'the most beautiful'. It is also, by any reckoning, one of the most mysterious and compelling, an island that people are rarely satisfied to visit once. Some wouldn't go anywhere else.

Many visitors treat Corsica like a beautiful woman, too mesmerized by the fascinating surface to dig into the contents; yet on Corsica the contents are rich. On several occasions, the Ile de Beauté has been a stage for genius: for the first portraitists in Europe, who left the startling statue-menhirs of Filitosa; for Paoli's precocious democractic experiment that (among other things) gave women equality and the vote some 200 years before they would get it again under the French state; and for a compelling, all-star cast of tragically flawed, over-ambitious heroes and villains who colour its history, culminating in Napoleon.

This history has made Corsica a complicated, often contradictory place. Although the vast majority of Corsicans want more say over their own destiny, they are content to remain citizens of France; while condemning the plague of nationalist violence and racketeering, they are grateful that the bombing of holiday villas has kept their coasts from suffering the concrete-coated, car-choked fate of the Côte d'Azur. The Corsican Resistance, the Maquis, was famous in the war, and today Corsicans, determined to keep their island the way they like it, have resisted much of what passes for progress and globalization. Big corporations have been put on notice that they aren't welcome: Corsica is one of the last McDonald's-free zones in the world.

There's a word, '*corsitude*', for the island's essential difference, its attitude. Cuteness, quaintness and the easy flattering charms of Corsica's Italian neighbours are alien to it; an obsequious or bubbly Corsican is an oxymoron. 'It depends on those who pass whether I am a tomb or a treasure, where I keep silent or speak,' as Paul Valéry (who had Corsican origins) put it. *Corsitude* evokes introspection, pride, a quiet dignity tinged with fatalism, prone to mystery and the otherworldly, as if the island's terrifying beauty, its lonesome pines and winds whispering in the *maquis*, had cast a spell over its inhabitants. Where Corsicans are most readily expressive is in music, especially their polyphonies, songs so haunting and archaic that they make your hair stand on end – for this is music born from the granite, from the faith that Corsica has kept with itself, from a long-ago faraway that most of us can scarcely imagine.

A Few Facts to Get You Started

Corsica lies 190 miles/300km southeast of Marseille, but only 50 miles/80km from the Tuscan coast (Pisa ruled Corsica in the Middle Ages, and the island is economically drawing close to Tuscany again). At 3,360 square miles/8,700 square kilometres, it is less than half the size of Wales or about the same size as Puerto Rico, making it the fourth largest island in the Mediterranean, after Sicily, Cyprus and Sardinia, but by far the most vertical. Except for the narrow eastern plain, the whole island is mountainous, from the foothills on the coast to the ice-gouged peaks of the central range. Of these the tallest is **Monte Cinto** (8,810ft/2,685m), second only to Etna on the Mediterranean islands, while five other peaks rise over 7,500ft/2,250m. On either side of the central spine, Corsica is striped with alternating ridges and river valleys; on the western coast these terminate in four broad gulfs, while the north is distinguished by the long, mountainous finger of Cap Corse. Forests cover a quarter of the land, and most are protected as part of the 1,390 sq mile/3,600 sq km Parc Régional, which encompasses 75 miles/120km of pristine coast – the longest protected stretch in Europe.

The central mountains neatly divide Corsica into its two traditional and very distinct halves, each speaking its own dialect of Corse, the island's native language, which is close to medieval Italian. The north and east is 'this side of the mountains', *Diqua dei Monti*, and historically it has been the more 'civilized' half, the *Terre des Communes/ Terra dei Comuni*, populated by an independent-minded peasantry whose frequent rebellions had a strong flavour of natural, un-ideological socialism. The south and west, 'beyond or that side of the mountains' or *Dila dei Monti*, was the untamed, vendetta-ridden *Terre des Seigneurs/Terra dei Signori*, 'Land of the Lords', the battleground of Corsica's feudal barons who fought the Aragonese, the Genoese and the French, but most of all each other.

In 1970 Corsica was made an administrative region, the Collectivité Territoriale de Corse (CTC). In 1974 the island, originally all part of *département* 20, was divided into two, the *département* of **Haute Corse** (the old *Diqua dei Monti*) with its seat at Bastia, hence the 2B you see on the number plates, and the *département* of **Corse du Sud** (*Dila dei Monti*), with the capital in Ajaccio (2A). Within these two *départements* are no fewer than 360 *communes*, each with a mayor and administrative responsibilities.

One incontestable fact about the Corsicans is that there are not too many of them, at least on Corsica, even though a worldwide head count of people of Corsican origin is said to number around a million, including 500,000 in metropolitan France alone. At the last count a mere 272,000 (40 per cent of them 'foreign', i.e. mostly from mainland France, including former French colonists from Algeria) share the island with 100,000 sheep, 32,000 goats (the island has its own distinct breed, the Capra Corse), 30,000 wild boar and over two million tourists a year, who come mainly in July and August. Two-thirds of them never leave the coast. Corse du Sud is the least populated *département* in France and Haute Corse follows fast on its heels. There are far more Corsicans on the continent than on the island (one is actress/model Laetitia Casta, the current 'Marianne' of France); if someone ever tries to trick you in a trivia contest,

Chapter Divisions

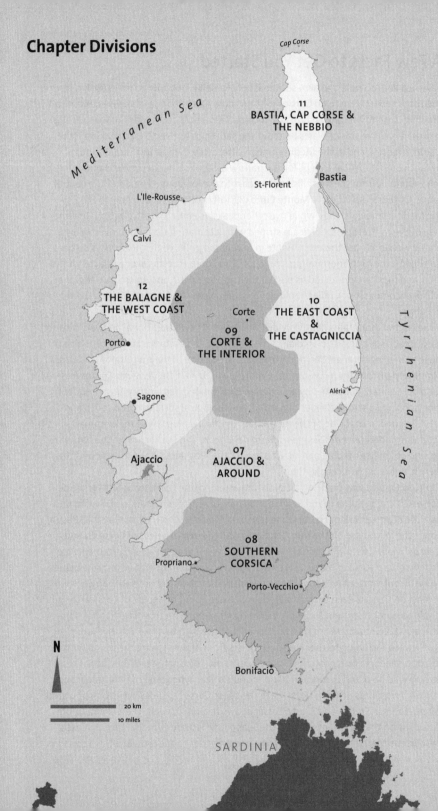

Cap Corse

11
BASTIA, CAP CORSE &
THE NEBBIO

Mediterranean Sea

St-Florent

Bastia

L'Ile-Rousse

Calvi

12
THE BALAGNE &
THE WEST COAST

Corte

10
THE EAST COAST
&
THE CASTAGNICCIA

09
CORTE &
THE INTERIOR

Tyrrhenian Sea

Porto

Sagone

Aléria

07
AJACCIO &
AROUND

Ajaccio

08
SOUTHERN
CORSICA

Propriano

Porto-Vecchio

N

20 km
10 miles

Bonifacio

SARDINIA

remember that Marseille, with an estimated 300,000 Corsicans, is the largest 'Corsican' city in the world. Of those Corsicans who have stayed put, almost half live in Ajaccio and Bastia, a large percentage employed by the state or in the tourist industry. The traditional agricultural economy and pastoral economies are beginning to make a comeback, however, after decades in decline, and it's there that many young people on the island are pinning their hopes.

Where to Go: A Guide to the Guide

For its size, Corsica is staggeringly diverse. Palm-lined **Ajaccio**, Napoleon's birthplace and the seat of Corsica's regional government, is the 'Frenchest' of Corsica's towns; it has the bulk of its museums and souvenirs of the Bonapartes, including a surprising collection of Italian Renaissance paintings left by Napoleon's uncle. Ajaccio's gulf is laced with fine sandy beaches towards the Iles Sanguinaires, where there are some lovely walks, but especially towards and beyond Porticcio; and yet in less than an hour you can be in the bosom of the mountains, at Bastelica or Zicavo.

Southern Corsica gets the most tourists. Although Propriano, the big resort south of Ajaccio, doesn't have much in the character department, its wooded gulf has more excellent beaches, and it lies near the truly lovely and fascinating prehistoric site of Filitosa, with Corsica's finest statue-menhirs. Stern granite Sartène, just inland, is atmospheric, the keeper of old traditions, while becoming the next big thing in Corsican wines. At the southern tip of the island, Bonifacio, with its tall houses piled on sheer white cliffs overlooking Sardinia, is one of the most striking towns in the entire Mediterranean. Just up the east coast, the most popular resort on the island, Porto-Vecchio, draws ferryboatloads of Italians to its dreamy beaches, top-notch hotels, great restaurants and nightlife. A few miles above begins the lovely Forêt de l'Ospedale, and it's only a short drive to the wild granite pinnacles of the Col de Bavella, one of Corsica's celebrated beauty spots. The mountain villages of the Alta Rocca just inland make great bases for walks into this lovely, deeply wooded corner of the island; one, Levie, is near the Casteddu de Cucuruzzu, Corsica's second most important megalithic site.

Spectacularly set **Corte**, in the **interior of the island**, was Paoli's capital and is today the seat of Corsica's university and its spanking new museum. On all sides are mountains and gorges, racing rivers (many with natural pools for bathing), forests, sublime views and a whole network of paths to explore, including the walk up the idyllic Val Restonica to the Lac de Melo. Or drive up the awe-inspiring, rocky waste of the Scala di Santa Regina to the high plateau of the Niolo and make the trek to the pretty Lac de Nino, or drive through a steep canyon to the remote Valle d'Asco and up into the forests and highest mountains, to the edge of *mouflon* and eagle country.

The island's (relatively) flat **east coast**, where Corsica keeps most of its clementine groves, is lined with sandy beaches. The highlight here is Aléria, the ancient capital of the Greeks and Romans and the star cultural attraction with its museum full of Attic vases; its lagoon is the source of most of Corsica's oysters. For anyone in search of *la Corse profonde*, roads from the coast delve inland to remote, seldom-explored mountain micro-regions such as the Boziu and Fiumorbo. To the north is the beautiful **Castagniccia**, the most extensive chestnut forest in the Mediterranean, crisscrossed by narrow roads and mule paths, leading to tiny villages and big Baroque churches, recalling the days when this was the most densely populated rural area of Europe.

Bastia, the bustling business end of Corsica, offers the piquant charms of its old port and its Genoese citadel. From here you can make a loop around the tiny hamlets of **Cap Corse**, the narrow, steeply mountainous peninsula that resembles a giant finger pointing towards Genoa. 'The island in the island', as it's called, was always the one place on Corsica that made its living from the sea, and is dotted with 19th-century 'American mansions' built by its sons who struck it rich in the Caribbean. The northern tip is covered by a lovely path called the Sentier des Douaniers, while lobsters star in the seafood restaurants of Centuri-Port. Convivial St-Florent, 'Corsica's St-Tropez', makes a great base for visiting the wine region and beautiful Romanesque churches of the **Nebbio**, centred around Patrimonio; boats or a path from St-Florent will take you into the wild Désert des Agriates, with a long stretch of undeveloped coast and some of Corsica's best beaches.

The northwest of Corsica is called the **Balagne**, a lovely land of fertile hills known as the Garden of Corsica, once famous for its millions of olive trees. Most people stay in the port-beach resorts of L'Ile-Rousse and Calvi, the latter just trailing Porto-Vecchio as the island's most popular destination, with some of Corsica's finest hotels and restaurants, and a calendar of festivals and cultural events that extends well into the autumn. Inland, the heartland of the Balagne has several looping necklaces of lovely *villages perchés* (Pigna, Sant'Antonino, Speloncato, Montemaggiore, etc.), each under the tower of a Baroque church; part of the Balagne's current revival has involved attracting artisans to set up workshops in the villages, so it's one of the best places for shopping in Corsica as well.

The remarkable red granite Golfe de Porto on the **west coast** south of Calvi is so stunning that UNESCO has made it a World Heritage Site, encompassing the Réserve Naturelle de Scandola and the Calanches de Piana, wonders rivalled just inland from Pian by the Gorge of Spelunca and magnificent Laricio pine Forêt d'Aitone. Further south, the nicest resort in the Golfe de Sagone is Cargèse, Corsica's Greek town, within easy striking distance of some fine beaches. Inland you can make the walk up to the pretty mountain Lac de Creno, while to the south towards Ajaccio is the beautiful if rather empty Cinarca, fief of Corsica's medieval gangsters and last refuge of its bandits.

History

Corsica's earliest years are difficult to trace. The archaeological record is incomplete, and very little was written about the island; then, as now, Corsica, in spite of its location in the centre of the western Mediterranean, existed only on the fringes of European consciousness. The Greeks called it *Kyrnos*, after a city state in Asia Minor, while the name *Corsica* itself seems to be Phoenician, meaning perhaps 'wooded island'. What little information ancient writers had to hand, they turned into mythology. Pausanias, for example, records that two sons of 'Libyan Hercules', Sardus and Kyrnos, conquered and settled Sardinia and Corsica. Rarely are such stories without at least a grain of truth; behind Pausanias' account is the shadow of one of the mysterious 'sea peoples', the Shardana, who threatened the powerful Egyptian empire, perhaps from Libya, before making their presence felt over the islands of the western Mediterranean, and giving their name to Sardinia.

8000–3000 BC
Neolithic and Chalcolithic: Corsicans Make Pots and Pans but Have No Need for Tinkers

The first Corsicans may well have hopped over from Sardinia, which was settled half a million years ago, or they may have come by way of Tuscany. So far the oldest artefacts discovered date back to *c*. 8000 BC and tell of a **Neolithic** culture that had the usual axes, 'cardial' pottery (decorated with imprints of a shell called a cardium), arrowheads and the like, all stylistically close to finds in Tuscany. A tomb at **Curacchiaghju** yielded evidence of the island's earliest trade import – diamond-hard obsidian from Monte Arci in Sardinia, dated to 6610 BC. Corsica's first known **settlements** (Curacchiaghju, Strette on Cap Corse, and Basi in the lower Taravo valley) were protected by natural rock shelters. They had domesticated animals – cattle, *mouflons* and goats – and were also hunters, gatherers and fishers; they made bowls, and probably ate a lot of soup. No agricultural tools were found, and defence of the settlements doesn't seem to have been a consideration either. The oldest skeleton, the 'Lady of Bonifacio' (now in the museum at Levie), discovered at Araguina, goes back to 6610 BC and shows that the dead were buried with a degree of ceremony. By the next millennium, Corsica's population had reached an estimated 3,000.

The centuries passed, and the pots improved. In the 4th millennium BC the **Basi** culture produced original glazed ware, decorated with fine vertical lines in relief. Farming began in earnest as the population grew and became more settled; the first stone huts appeared, along with grindstones and pestles, not only for grain but for toasted acorns, which were eaten when nothing else was on the menu. The appearance of loom weights suggests a revolution in fashion from pelts to woven wool, and a new kind of pot arrived, shallow with perforated walls, identical to ones found in Sardinia, the Balearics and Lipari that may have been used for draining the curds and whey for cheese. Burials took place in **hypogeum tombs**, in natural openings in the granite called *taffoni* that the Corsicans, even in historical times, regarded as sacred.

Copper slowly made its way into the local repertoire of useful items (Corsica has at least smidgens of all 400 known minerals, with the exception of gold and diamonds). The Proto-Corsicans were in close contact with their Proto-Sard and Proto-Tuscan cousins, who may have taught them metalworking; Terrina, the most important **Chalcolithic** site, has a number of different pottery styles, suggesting trade or perhaps intermarriage. But there is also a noticeable increase in **arrowheads**, suggesting that these exchanges may not always have been friendly.

3000–1800 BC
Menhirs with Personality

A great change came in around 3000 BC, with an invasion, or perhaps an early form of cultural and religious evangelism. All we know is that the urge and skill to erect **megalithic** buildings filtered down from Provence to Corsica, through Sardinia, en route to North Africa. A preoccupation with death, or life after death, was already present, as new, elaborate burial techniques were adopted to honour the dead. What the Corsicans really excelled at were **menhirs**; over 500 have been found on the island, a density no other place in the Mediterranean can equal.

The island went through several distinct megalithic phases. At first, bodies were interred in underground *cists* or stone chest tombs, which were marked by circles of simple menhirs, as at Settiva. In the second stage, *c.* 2500 BC, the dead were buried under classic, above-ground table-style dolmens, and menhirs were aligned around them. These are smoother and more refined stones, with the outline of a head; sometimes they look more phallic than anthropomorphic. The 258 stones at **Pagliaghju** near Sartène form the most important alignment in the Mediterranean.

In the next phase, the menhirs acquired definite heads and well-defined shoulders. This anthropomorphizing happened in places near Corsica as well, at Pontrémoli in Tuscany, at Laconi on Sardinia and St-Pons-de-Thomières in Languedoc, where the menhirs have faint indications of eyes and noses, breasts and weapons. But the Corsicans went a step further, and *c.* 1700 BC created the **statue-menhirs**. These are individualistic portraits, faces that stare literally out of the night of time; the most famous figure, known as **Filitosa IX**, has well-defined eyes, nose, mouth and chin. Who they were meant to depict is an open question. Some have suggested they are images of the deceased, chiefs or warriors, whose presence or protection was still required from beyond the grave.

The next stage, at Filitosa and Scalsa-Murta, depicts the new arrivals, or at least the advent of new technology: **warriors** with bronze swords, daggers, and helmets with curious peaks. One theory is that the helmets once had horns, like those of their Sardinian neighbours. Recent dating techniques have pushed back the date of Corsica's first fortified villages, the *casteddi* (singular *casteddu*) to the late Neolithic period as well. Chances are that immigrations and invasions occurred throughout the centuries.

1500–6th Century BC
The Bronze Age Torréens

The arrival of the **Bronze Age**, not a happy event for any native Mediterranean peoples, seems to have been particularly rough on Corsica. Throughout the second millennium BC, the peaceful agricultural erectors of menhirs had to contend with an upsurge in aggression from newcomers with a new religion, leather clothes and metal weapons. Roger Grosjean, the doyen of Corsican archaeologists, called the island's new Bronze Age culture the **Torréen**, after one of their sites in the village of Torre near Porto-Vecchio. At one point they may have come courtesy of Sardinia, or the Balearics, or perhaps even from further afield. The Torréens gradually pushed the indigenous people north over the mountains, where they continued to make their last few unarmed statue-menhirs.

In Egypt, the state records at the time of the Torréens refer to a people called the **Shardana**, who, as depicted on the temple Medinet-Habu, look rather like the armed statue-menhirs at Filitosa, with horned helmets. The Shardana fought in the employ of Egypt at the great Battle of Kadesh in 1299 BC against the Hittites, and later manned the bodyguard of the Pharaohs. In 1236–1223 and 1198–1166 BC, however, they changed sides and reappear in the Egyptian chronicles as invaders, part of the aggregation of troublemakers the Egyptians called the '**Sea Peoples**', which included the Akkaiwasha (Achaeans, or Mycenaeans), the Tyrrennoi (Etruscans) and the Sikels of eastern Sicily. The Sea Peoples slashed their way around the shores of the eastern Mediterranean, then used the Nile Delta as a base for a full-scale assault on Egypt that ultimately failed: reliefs in Egyptian tombs show them attacking the fleet of Ramses III in 1190 BC; they also show Shardana soldiers and their allies brought into Egypt as prisoners of war. Grosjean's theory is that the Shardana are the same as the Torréens and Bronze Age Sards – at any rate, the latter were certainly in close contact with the Mycenaeans and may have picked up some tips on building stone vaults.

Whatever their origins, it was under the Torréens that Corsica's *casteddi* came into the general architectural current of the Bronze Age, with their cylindrical beehive structures known as *torres*, related to the *nuraghi* of Sardinia, the Mycenaean *tholos* tombs, and the Balearic *talayots*, sharing characteristics such as corbelled roofs and entrance corridors (*dromos*). No one knows quite what the *torres* and their various galleries and central chambers (*cella*) were for: cult purposes (occasionally human ashes have been found inside), temples of fire, defence (many are in strategic positions that look out over the coast), occasional shelters (ceramics have been found inside them), or even food storage. Some were inhabited into the Iron Age.

565 BC–AD 500
Newcomers Galore

During their great period of expansion in the 8th–6th centuries BC, the **Greeks** founded colonies and trading counters wherever they could in the western

Mediterranean. One of these was at Alalia (565 BC) on Corsica's east coast. The founders came from **Phocaea** in Asia Minor, the same folk who founded Marseille, and they were so taken with Corsica that they nicknamed it *Kalliste*, 'the most beautiful'. Alalia was the first real urban settlement on the island, and although the Greeks introduced the Mediterranean staples – wheat, wine and olives – they had little if any influence on most of the island, where the people went about their business more or less as before, hunting, gathering, farming and herding. But if the majority of Corsicans remained blithely unaware that they had company, the main players in the western Mediterranean, the Etruscans and Carthaginians, were appalled to find these cuckoos nesting in their sphere of influence, and in 540 they combined their fleets to attack the Greeks in the Battle of Alalia. The Greeks stubbornly held fast, and founded at least one other colony on the island, Portus Syracusanus, by Porto-Vecchio.

The Greeks remained until the **Carthaginians** added Corsica to their growing empire in 280 BC, just in time for the **Romans** to snatch it from them in 259 BC during the Punic Wars. Compared to the Romans, the Greeks, Etruscans and Carthaginians were mere adventurers, content to hold a few coastal bases and leave the inaccessible interior to its own devices. The Romans wanted it all, and of course they got it. With their accustomed doggedness they battered the wild Corsican mountaineers into submission, violently crushing revolt after revolt until finally pacifying the island in 115 BC, at the price of half the population dead or enslaved. Ancient writers fail to agree on whether the Corsica they subdued had been a communal Garden of Eden or a den of beasts. All accounts do agree, however, that the freedom-loving Corsicans made useless slaves, though apparently they did better as fighters in Rome's legions.

The inhabitants of this island live on the honey and meat that their country offers in abundance. They live together according to just and humane laws, as opposed to the ways of all other barbarians. Whoever first finds a beehive in the mountains or in the hollow of a tree never has to fight over its possession. Owners never lose their flocks, all of which have been given distinct marks, even if no one watches over them. As for the rest, in all the events of their lives, they cultivate the practice of justice.
Diodorus Siculus, *Universal History, Book V, Chapter 79* (58 BC)

These populations, confined to their mountains and reduced to brigandage, are more ferocious than wild beasts. This one can easily verify without even leaving Rome, as Roman generals often descend on the island, suddenly attack some of their fortresses, and bring back a large number of slaves. One can then observe the strange appearance of these fierce men, like animals of the forests or brutalized like beasts that cannot bear to live in servitude. If they resign themselves to not dying, they so weary their masters by their apathy or indifference that they make them regret the few coins they spent to buy them.
Strabo, *Geography, Book V, chapter 4* (early 1st century AD)

It wasn't an entirely one-sided relationship. Rome may have brought 'civilization' to Corsica, but Pliny the Elder claimed that the Corsicans introduced the Romans to such pleasures as baths in wild asses' milk mixed with arbutus honey.

After the conquest was complete, the usual Roman public works programme followed. In 93 BC, Marius sent colonists to found a new capital, Mariana (south of Bastia) while his rival Sulla made Alalia (now Aleria) into a military base in 81 BC. Although many colonists were given smallholdings, most of the good land went to the wealthy and was divided into big *latifundia* plantations with slaves and serfs. The emperors seemed to be fond of it, and separated it adminstratively from Sardinia and put it directly under their rule. The population soared to 130,000. The native Corsicans who survived learned to speak Latin; the island's resources were thoroughly exploited and the eastern plain became an important source of grain (although there wasn't much left over to export to Rome). But Cap Corse exported wine, and the Balagne its olive oil; the forests yielded cork and beeswax, and the lagoons their much-loved oysters. In the 2nd century AD the Christianization of the island began, though some of the more isolated parts of the interior held out against it until 1100.

500–1077
Vandals, Byzantines, Lombards, Saracens and Italians

Hard times followed the decline of Rome, as new waves of seaborne invaders drove the Corsicans into the interior. The **Vandals**, true to their name, stayed just long enough to wreck everything – Alalia/Aleria was wiped off the map after a millennium of civilized life – until they were driven off to North Africa by the **Byzantines** under Belisarius in 534. By then the Vandals were Christians, but heretical Arian ones, so they exiled all the orthodox bishops they found in Africa to Corsica, where they helped to spread the faith and give the island its quota of early saints. But as the wars dragged on, the Greeks found Corsica impossible to keep; the **Ostrogoths** took over (549–553), and later Pope Gregory the Great did all he could to keep the Byzantines from returning. Next, in 725, came the truly barbarous **Lombards**, soon to be masters of Italy. When the **Franks** under Pépin the Short defeated the Lombards in 754, Corsica was promised to the pope, a donation ratified by Pépin's son **Charlemagne**.

These arrangements looked nice on paper, but from the early 8th to the 9th century Muslim pirates contested with mercenary Tuscans for real control of the island. The coastal, Christianized populations took refuge on the mainland or inland, while Corsica's medieval chronicler, Giovanni della Grossa, recounts that the **Moors** held sway for 166 years under six kings – Lanza Incisa, Musi, Ferrandino, Scalabro and Nugolone, father and son. The large number of 'Moorish' topographical names on Corsica, especially of mountains and interior areas, would seem to confirm the deep impression they made. Only today most scholars, after a close reading of Grossa, believe that by 'Moors' he meant **pagans** just as they did in the *Chanson de Roland* (where the infidel 'Moors' of the story were really pagan Basques). Because of Corsica's isolation during that dangerous period, many Corsicans apparently reverted to paganism (or 'reverted to Saracenism', as Grossa put it).

It took three expeditions to free the island (or take it back from the pagans), one led by a **Count Burchard** in 807, the next one in 825 by **Bonifacio II**, the Marquis of

Ugo Colonna and the Curse of the Cinarchesi

Ninth-century Corsica is a place where history and legend are as entangled and sticky as overcooked spaghetti. According to the chronicler Giovanni della Grossa, a member of one of the greatest aristocratic families in Rome, Ugo Colonna, joined a faction battling Pope Leo III and his successor Stephen IV. When it became clear that Charlemagne (a firm supporter of the papacy) wasn't going to stand for any of this, Colonna and the others submitted to the pope, who promised to forgive them if they wrested Corsica from the Moors. Ugo Colonna set out with 1,000 foot-soldiers and 200 knights and took the island, and in reward was not only forgiven by the pope but made Count of Corsica. Many historians doubt whether Ugo Colonna ever existed, and believe the whole story was cooked up by the Corsican warlords to polish up their lineage. Yet, in Corte, the ruins of a palace – perhaps Ugo Colonna's – were discovered exactly where Giovanni della Grossa described it.

The story goes on to tell that the descendants of Ugo Colonna's son Cinarca, known as the Cinarchesi, ruled the west and sometimes all of Corsica from their fief over the Golfe de Sagone. Although the most powerful and talented lords of the island, the Cinarchesi as individuals were dogged by tragic flaws. Giovanni della Grossa pinpoints the moment when things started going wrong, in the year 1000, when the Cinarchesi lord, Count Arrigo Bel Messere ('Harry the Handsome'), renowned across the island for his justice, was killed in Ocana when he got caught up in a local feud. A voice, recounts della Grossa, could be heard all across the island:

E morto il conte Arrigo Bel Messere, / E Corsica sarà di male in peggio.

(Count Arrigo Bel Messere is dead / And Corsica will go from bad to worse.)

Tuscany, appointed guardian of Corsica by Charlemagne's son Louis the Pious, and the last by Bonifacio's son **Albert**. The pope sent five bishops and granted the victors fiefs in Corsica: the Savelli of Rome became counts of the Balagne, and the Obertenghi of Genoa were given much of the rest of the *Diqua dei Monti'*, the northeastern half of the island. Still it would be a while before the 'Moors' surrendered for good (*see* p.193).

1077–1284
The Pisans and the Giudice di Cinarca

The Dark Ages continued darkly as local chieftains struggled to take control and make their power hereditary. Meanwhile, close at hand, the **Republic of Pisa** was making a name for itself, growing rich from trade in the eastern Mediterranean. In 1077, Pope Gregory VII put Pisa in charge of the unruly island's administration; in 1091, Urban V made Corsica a fief of the Archbishop of Pisa. The Pisans divided the island into some 300 *pieves* or parishes, and brought a degree of peace and prosperity that Corsicans hadn't experienced since the *pax romana*. The most lasting reminders of Pisan rule are the Romanesque churches scattered across the island, many of which doubled as courts of law and adminstrative centres. All were well built – even the tiniest, most remote parish church, lost in the *maquis* miles from the nearest road, is made of carefully dressed stone. Many of the smaller ones are similar, as if teams of Pisan builders stamped them out from a basic template; the most elaborate are multicoloured, in stripes or chequerboard patterns, and some have strange, wonderful sculptural decoration over the portal and windows or simply stuck on the wall.

Through the 12th and 13th centuries, Corsica became a pawn in the struggle between Pisa and its rapidly rising rival, **Genoa**. In 1113, in a bid to settle things once and for all, the pope gave the Genoese the bishoprics of Mariana and Nebbio (St-Florent) and invented a third bishopric, Accia, in the *Diqua dei Monti*, to equal the three Pisa held in the south (Ajaccio, Aléria and Sagone), the *Dila dei Monti*. But Genoa wanted more, and gained footholds at Bonifacio (1187) and Calvi (1268), then chased the Pisans out altogether in 1284, after defeating them decisively at the **Battle of Meloria**.

Corsican history, however, is more than recounting a parade of occupiers, none of whom ever held the island without meeting stiff resistance from the Corsicans themselves. Outsiders would grab the island for political or economic advantage, but rarely win hearts or minds. Mountain villages were nests of proud and independent spirits, although seldom tuned to the same cause; rivalries between local barons and families were often just as fierce as any hatred for the occupier. The first and perhaps greatest local baron, the one who became the paragon for Corsican patriots to come, was **Sinucello della Rocca** of the house of Cinarca. Sinucello started his career in the mid-13th century fighting for Pisa but, while he was away, a kinsman who supported Genoa took over his lands. It was while he was re-establishing control over his estates that the famous incident at **Olmeto** took place (*see* p.103); afterwards, Sinucello grew rich and powerful by playing Pisa and Genoa off against each other, collecting bribes from both while putting the squeeze on his Corsican rivals. Yet when he saw a chance, in the twilight of Pisan rule, he acted *for* Corsica, governing the island under a liberal constitution that curbed the power of his own class and acting with such a fine sense of justice that the people called him the 'Judge', the **Giudice di Cinarca**. His most lasting legacy was the setting up of popular assemblies, the *consulte*, that gave a voice to all Corsicans (male ones, anyway), and helped instil in Corsicans their precocious respect for republican virtues. The wily Genoese, however, found ready allies in Corsican nobles miffed at the loss of their former power, and after Pisa's defeat at Meloria in 1284 Sinucello found himself bereft of his old ally. Gradually pushed back to his old domains in the southwest, old and blind, he was betrayed by a bastard son who handed him over to Genoa, where he was thrown in a prison to die, nearly 100 years old.

1284–1729
Property of the Bank of St George

> One cannot know Corsican history without regretting that Shakespeare
> never heard of its tales.
> > Dorothy Carrington

Under Genoese rule, events would be dominated by a series of 'great men', hoping to boot out the foreign oppressors and become the next Giudice and Count of all Corsica

– bold leaders and patriots, although not always of the most idealistic sort (some were little better than gangsters). As writer Dorothy Carrington noted in the mid-20th century, any of their lives would make a stirring romance or tragedy. History records no fewer than 16 making the bid for the great prize, and if none succeeded in emulating the Giudice di Cinarca's life, most managed to copy his death, in a Genoese prison, betrayed by a jealous neighbour or kinsman before finally climbing to the top.

The **Corsican lords** themselves were often just as oppressive. In 1358, a popular revolt led by **Sambuccio d'Alando** broke out in the *Diqua dei Monti* against them, leading to their ousting and the establishment of the '*Terra dei Comuni*' – a progressive colonial government with a charter providing for universal suffrage, equality and communal ownership of land. The Genoese for their part encouraged the planting of figs, olives, vines and chestnuts to make the island more self-sufficient; in 1584 this would become a mandatory chestnut, olive, fig and mulberry tree per family per year. The results of this programme are still visible in the chestnuts of the Castagniccia and the olive groves of the Balagne; the hoped-for silk industry, however, never really took off.

The Corsicans of the more archaic south and west of the island, the *Dila dei Monti*, refused to be converted into peasants; in spite of Genoese penalties they remained transhumant shepherds, or simply emigrated. As opposed to the *Terra dei Comuni*, the *Dila dei Monti* was the *Terra dei Signori*, where the Cinarchesi and their rivals continued to reign as feudal bosses, each man up in his mountain castle, squeezing taxes from the peasants, hoping to raise another army against Genoa.

Their internal bickering opened the way for an invasion by the **Aragonese**. Aragon had become involved in Corsican affairs back in 1297, when **Pope Boniface VIII**, at loggerheads with Genoa, transferred sovereignty of Corsica and Sardinia to Aragon. Aragonese attempts to take what they thought was coming to them throughout the 14th century were repulsed by Genoa, and by the fact that all parties, Genoa, Aragon, and Corsica, were slowed down by the **Black Death** in 1347–8.

Aragon kept a hand in the game by supporting the Cinarchesi lords, in particular **Vincentello d'Istria**, a descendant of the Giudice, who single-handedly succeeded in clearing Corsica of the Genoese, save only their great strongholds of Calvi and Bonifacio. In 1420 **Alfonso of Aragon** arrived with his fleet to help capture the last two hold-outs from Genoa, but abandoned the cause when he received word of a better offer: Jeanne II of Naples, under threat from her Bourbon husband, was asking him to defend her lands in exchange for becoming her heir. As lord of nearly all Corsica, Vincentello looked good for a while: he made Corte his capital, reformed the clergy, kept taxes low, and was supported by the *consulte* and the rural captains. The pope, the Tuscans and even the Genoese (grudgingly) recognized Corsican autonomy. But then Vincentello became a victim of his own flaws; a violent, sensuous man, he raped one noble girl too many, and lost his supporters. In 1434 they let him fall into the hands of the Genoese, who took him back to Genoa and publicly lopped off his head.

A period of anarchy, feudal struggles and casual atrocities followed. Then, in one of those rare events in history that cast a clear light on the motives of nations and take some of the romantic glow off the past, the Genoese farmed out Corsica in 1453 to their national **Bank of St George** for exploitation. Unlike banks today, this one had its own army, and one of its first acts was to rebuild the island's fortresses and begin the chain of watchtowers that surrounds Corsica; the Bank also founded the city of **Ajaccio** to keep an eye on the Cinarchesi. Pope Nicholas V granted it the right to appoint Genoese bishops to all of Corsica's sees, an insult to the local clergy that would turn them into Corsican patriots as well. The Bank of St George's military rule and wars with the feudal barons of the *Dila dei Monti* resulted in an almost total breakdown of social order, as well as the near extinction of the nobility; the last Cinarchesi lord, **Rinuccio della Rocca**, fought the Bank from 1502 until he too was killed in 1511. Plagues added to the island's woes, and thousands of Corsicans were forced to emigrate to survive, but the Genoese and their Bank finally won.

At least, they thought they had. Here yet another larger-than-life Corsican patriot-adventurer takes the stage – **Sampiero Corso** (*c.* 1498–1567), a humble shepherd who rose to become a great military leader on the continent, mostly in the employ of the king of France. Sampiero's career signalled the first French involvement on the island, when he helped France seize Corsica for a short period in the 1550s (*see* pp.94–5), mainly to niggle Genoa and her new ally Spain – only to have the French give it back to Genoa without too much fuss in 1559 with the **Treaty of Cateau-Cambrésis**. Sampiero earned his nickname, 'the most Corsican of the Corsicans', by refusing to accept European *realpolitik*, returning to boot out the hated Genoese on his own (with the secret help of Catherine de' Medici). He nearly succeeded, though he too was betrayed, ambushed and murdered by his Corsican enemies in the employ of the Genoese. Outside Corsica, Sampiero's memory lives on in a strange way: after he strangled his noble wife with his own hands, the story became current throughout Europe. It was the one tale Shakespeare *did* hear of, and he turned it into *Othello*.

After Sampiero, Corsica was too exhausted to resist any further. In 1562, the Republic of Genoa dismissed the Bank of St George and took over direct rule of the island. This was no bonus: Corsicans call the 1600s the '**Century of Iron**'. Yet while the Genoese behaved despotically, and kept a firm grip on the bishops, they were content to leave Corsicans in charge of local administration. On the positive side, the Genoese continued their policies of promoting the island's agriculture, but they strictly limited trade, all of which had to go through Genoa. The corruption of the officials worsened, and bred resentment and injustice, and the **vendetta** (*see* pp.34–6) flourished as never before. This was also the time of religious revival, especially of the **confraternities** (*see* pp.28–9), present in Corsica since the 14th century: they commissioned most of the paintings on the island. Baroque churches went up, often in small villages, and the island even produced a saint, the Franciscan reformer **St Théophile of Corte** (1676–1740).

1729–55
The War for Independence

The local nobility may have been rendered more or less impotent, but a new force was rising in Corsica: the *bourgeoisie*, many of them important landowners who had profited from Genoese agricultural policies, and who had attended university in Italy, experiencing first hand what life was like without a colonial oppressor. At the same time Genoa, like its paymaster Spain, was in decline; its weakness and decadence were suddenly brought home in 1729, when a rebellion over taxes broke out in the Boziu, and the villagers managed to send the Genoese packing with their tails between their legs. Word spread, other fed-up villagers took action, and the Genoese would never control the interior again.

The first struggle for independence in modern times was under way. In January 1731, an assembly, gathered in Corte, declared Corsica's independence, and elected a triumvirate of primates, one of whom was **Dr Giacinto Paoli**. Genoa appealed to Emperor Charles VI, and his troops made the patriots sue for a settlement in 1732. But no sooner were they gone than the rebellion broke out again; independence was declared – again – in 1735, complete with the first constitution of any modern democracy, and 'Dio Vi Salvi Regina', a hymn to the Virgin, was made national anthem. Genoa burned Corsica's harvest, hoping to starve the population into submission.

The subsequent war took on a note of *opéra bouffe* with the strange interlude of **Théodore von Neuhof** (*see* p.190), one of the most remarkable con artists in a century of talented swindlers. In 1736, when the Genoese were blockading the coast and Corsican guerillas controlled most of the island, this charming and eccentric German hustler turned up in the Castagniccia with a new suit, a supply of leather boots, munitions and well-crafted lies about 'connections' in the great courts of Europe. With the promise of more goodies to come, he talked the Corsicans into crowning him King Théodore I. Surprised by the ease of his conquest, Neuhof assumed full regal trappings, and waited for the next stroke of luck. It never came. Finally, realizing that his subjects' sense of humour might have its limits, King Théodore decided to depart – by night, of course, disguised as a priest. He spent his last years in Soho, London, where he is remembered in Soho Square with a plaque.

Genoa next appealed to **France** for aid against the rebels. France already fancied Corsica, like a nice bit of cake, and readily agreed to send troops to quash the patriots. They did so decisively in 1739, under the ruthless **Marquis de Maillebois**. Many of the leaders, including Dr Giacinto Paoli, went into exile. Genoa was back in control, at least on paper, until a new pair of actors entered the scene: **Britain** and **Piedmont-Sardinia**, whose king up in Turin was flexing his muscles. The two arrived on Corsica in 1743, during the **War of the Austrian Succession**, ostensibly to help the Corsicans but with the idea of dividing the island among themselves. British warships bombarded Bastia, which was attacked by land by a Corsican force supported by the king of Sardinia; Bastia surrendered, but the Sardinian-supported Corsicans quarrelled with local patriots and the Genoese got Bastia back. The British navy bombed it again in 1748, but the French once again came to Genoa's rescue. They hung around this time and set up an administration under the Marquis de Cursay; the Genoese, alarmed by his success, manipulated De Cursay's downfall, and the French withdrew in 1752.

Meanwhile, the *consulte* (the popular assemblies first set up by the Giudice di Cinarca) were meeting across Corsica, coming up with various constitutional solutions, and various generals to lead them. As the French departed, another constitution was written, and **Dr Gian'Pietro Gaffory** of Corte was made *generalis-simo*, only to be assassinated through Genoese machinations the next year. His four successors, one of whom was Clemente Pascoli, eldest son of Dr Giacinto Paoli, were unable to agree amongst themselves, and at Clemente's suggestion they summoned his younger brother Pasquale, who had accompanied their father to Naples and attended university there, and was serving as a sub-lieutenant in the Neapolitan army, to return to Corsica and lead them.

1755–96
Paoli, the 'Nation Corse' and the Anglo-Corsican Kingdom

I have a certain presentiment that one day this little island will astonish Europe.
Jean-Jacques Rousseau, *The Social Contract*, 1769

Pasquale Paoli was 30 years old when he was declared General of the Corsican Nation in 1755 and, although not really up to snuff as a commander (Clemente, the famous sharpshooter, was the military man), he was one of the most remarkable politicians of the Enlightenment. In 1755, he wrote a progressive constitution based on the sovereignty of the people and separation of powers as proposed by Montesquieu's 1748 *De l'Esprit des lois*. He invited Rousseau to come to the small but uncorrupted *tabula rasa* of Corsica to help; Rousseau declined, but suggested a visit to his young friend James Boswell. Paoli fostered education and public works, and set up a printing press, mint and arms factory. He made his capital at Corte, under the walls of d'Istria's citadel, and founded a free university there, and built a new port at L'Ile-Rousse as a counter to Calvi, which couldn't be wrenched from the Genoese. He even came close to eliminating the vendetta by impartially executing all murderers (*see* p.195).

In a time before expressions such as 'self-determination' had any meaning, always squeezed for money, beleaguered and besieged by the Genoese and their French allies, opposed by Corsicans notables who hated his ideals of equality, Paoli didn't really stand a chance. When his little homespun navy ran the Genoese blockade to liberate the nearby island of Capraia, the Genoese finally threw in the towel – only to sell the island to Louis XV in the **Treaty of Versailles** in 1768 for the paltry sum of two million lire, to pay back a debt. 'One doesn't know whom to hate more, the one who sold us or the one who bought us,' Paoli raged. 'Let us confound them in our hate since both have treated us with equal disdain.' He called all able-bodied Corsicans to arms, but, as Dorothy Carrington put it, his defiance was on the scale of Cuba declaring war on the USA – 100,000 impoverished Corsicans, taking on the 22 million citizens of the richest and most powerful state in Europe. The French army came to collect, and defeated the Corsicans at Ponte Novo in 1769. Paoli took refuge in England. Corsica became a French possession on 15 May 1769, and three months later Letizia Bonaparte gave birth in Ajaccio to her second son, Napoleon (or 'Nabulion' as he was registered), with the wish that her baby boy would be 'the avenger of Corsica'.

But the fairy who heard Letizia's wish was thrown a curve ball when her husband Carlo changed his mind and chummed up with the French. The Comte de Marbeuf, then governor of Ajaccio, appointed him to represent the Corsican nobility at Versailles. Thanks to Marbeuf's good offices (it is said he had an affair with the beautiful Letizia while Carlo was away), young Napoleon, a gifted maths student, was given a scholarship to a military academy in Brienne. He wasn't the only Corsican to find hope in France; fired by the Revolution's promises of liberty, equality and brother-hood, Corsicans petitioned the Convention to give them equal rights with the rest of France (this still-strong republican spirit of equality is behind all the arguments against giving the island any kind of special autonomous status today), and in November 1789 Corsica was made an integral part of France.

Ironically, on the same day, France lifted a ban on political exiles that allowed Paoli to return to Corsica after 21 years in England. He was hailed as a hero, and at first he loyally toed the line with the new regime as head of the Corsican National Guard. But disillusionment set in, and by 1793, during the Terror, Paoli was in trouble again, suspected of moderation, and summoned to Paris where he would be guillotined. So once again he declared Corsican independence; his supporters rallied around '*U Babbu di a Patria*' (The Father of the Nation). But it was too late: many Corsicans (including the Bonapartes) were already committed to the Revolution.

Nor were the powers of Europe ready to let such a strategic island govern itself and Paoli, knowing this, secretly turned to his second homeland – Britain. Having recently been booted out of Toulon by Napoleon, the British were on the lookout for a new Mediterranean base, and after sending Sir Gilbert Elliot, a relative of William Pitt, to scout it out, they agreed to Paoli's proposal. The British cleared the last French troops from the island – it was in this skirmish that Nelson had his close call in Calvi, and was left blind in one eye. A new constitution in 1794 granted Corsica a good deal of autonomy, but disappointed Paoli and his supporters when Elliot instead of Paoli was made viceroy. Since Paoli was now in a real jam, with a price on his head in France, there was little he could do about it.

Elliot had the best intentions in the world. He was fond of Corsica, whose moun-tains reminded him of his native Scotland, and he liked the Corsicans, although he never really understood them. ('These people are an enigma,' he fretted, particularly specifying Paoli's 'strong tendencies to democracy'.) In 1795, at Elliot's urging, the rest-less Paoli was retired to London with a fat pension, and in 1796 the troops of Madame Bonaparte's baby boy forced the British out of Corsica without a fight. Corsica has been incontrovertibly French ever since.

1796–1943
French Fantasies, Colonial Realities

The French are powerless against the nature, manners, and passions of the Corsicans.
A. C. Pasquin Valéry

After all the hopes kindled in the 18th century, Corsica's history until quite recently is a sad tale of neglect, economic stagnation and widespread emigration. The Corsicans accused Paris of paying more attention to France's foreign colonies than to the island in its own backyard, and they were right. Little was done to integrate the island into the wider European economy, while a lack of effective law enforcement and justice led to the continuation of the code of honour, vendettas and banditry (*see* pp.34–7).

Although by 1830 a new steamer service provided an overnight service to Ajaccio from Marseille. The first Frenchman to pay much attention to Corsica was Prosper Mérimée, who came to Corsica as Inspector of Historical Monuments in 1839; he travelled with a caravan and two local guides, and afterwards produced two highly influential books. One, the *Notes d'un voyage en Corse*, includes his opinions on the island's art (he liked the megalithic and Romanesque, but didn't care for the Baroque). The second book was *Colomba*, a harrowing tale of vendetta egged on by an anti-heroine, based on a true story in the village of Fozzano near Sartène.

Mérimée's tales brought over French romantics by the boatload: aristocrats and writers such as Dumas and Flaubert, and later such painters as Léger and Matisse. A trip to Corsica briefly eclipsed even the Grand Tour of Italy in popularity, although it wasn't the island's beauty that attracted the first travellers, but rather an idealized vision of the island as a throwback to the classical age: its Roman virtue, its Athenian democracy, its Homeric hospitality, its Spartan sobriety. By the 1870s the first hotels were being built around Ajaccio's famously clement coast as winter resorts for the French, Germans and especially the British, who lay about being slightly melancholy in winter gardens; they were numerous enough to support an Anglican church.

The French built the island's first railways, linking Ajaccio to Bastia in 1894, but otherwise did little to help. The population dropped steadily with each decade, although not all the Corsicans were leaving to seek their fortune in Marseille or the Caribbean. Following Napoleon's lead, many found a home in the service of the state – so many that, by the time the **First World War** began, Corsicans made up a fifth of the French army. Some 40,000 – of a total population of 320,000 – never returned.

Corsicans also made up a quarter of France's colonial officials, and held a dispropor-tionate number of administrative posts in metropolitan France; they earned a reputation for toughness that sometimes slipped into brutality. French philosopher Simone Weil, in her posthumously published *L'Enracinement* (*The Need for Roots*, 1949) was one of the first to note that this was a queasy two-way disease:

> *Corsica is an example of the danger of contagion implicated in uprooting [*déracine-ment*]. After having conquered, colonized, corrupted and let rot the people of this island, we have submitted to them in the form of police prefects, policemen, adjuncts, school monitors, and other functions of this sort, and in these capacities they have treated the French in turn as a population more or less conquered.*

Yet Corsican toughness can be a blessing. Although Vichy-appointed *préfets* were put in charge of Corsica at the start of the **Second World War**, the Axis sent an Italian force to occupy the island in 1942, after the Allies starting landing in North Africa. It took some 80,000 troops – one soldier for every two Corsicans, they said, and that included the women and children. Nevertheless, Corsica soon had the strongest and most effective resistance movement in France, numbering some 12,000 and domi-nated by the communists. The **Maquis** – the name given to the French underground as a whole by the Allies – originated here, from the thick Mediterranean scrub where outlaws had found cover for centuries. In December 1942, the Maquis was contacted by the Special Operations Europe agents in North Africa; agent Andrew Croft, a former polar explorer, trained the Corsicans in sabotage and equipped them with explosives. The submarine *Casabianca*, captained by Jean L'Herminier, made perilous voyages from Algeria to supply arms and agents, alerting the Maquis to drop-offs by cryptic messages broadcast over the BBC.

When Mussolini was pushed out and the Badoglio government surrendered in 1943, tens of thousands of Italian troops were left stranded on Corsica, and many fled to join the Maquis. But rather than fight them the few German forces on Corsica (and on Sardinia) evacuated through Bastia, liberating this corner of France far more quickly than De Gaulle had expected, not to mention without his input – hence it rarely makes the history books. But while Bastia was in the streets celebrating its liberation on 4 October 1943, the city was bombed by the American air force; like De Gaulle, they hadn't expected liberation to happen so quickly, and tragically caused the worst damage that the island suffered in the entire war. But the US Army stayed long enough on Corsica to do it a favour as well; the DDT they sprayed made possible the resettlement of coastal plains that had been malarial since the fall of Rome.

1943–Present
Corsica Celebrates its Entry into the Modern World with a Fit of Madness

...a desire to affirm its own identity, if only it knew how.
Jonathan Fenby, *On the Brink*

By 1945 the population of Corsica had fallen to 150,000 – halved in 30 years not only by conflict but a mass rural exodus. The French government finally gave some attention to economic development in Corsica. **Tourism**, which had begun in earnest in the 1930s with the publication of the first mountain guidebook and organized excursions to beauty spots such as Cap Corse, the Col de Bavella, and the Calanches de Piana, was encouraged, with new roads and airports. For the most part, however, Paris's approach has been a rather simple-minded one of laying **subsidies** on everything from boat fares to fuel prices. Corsica gets proportionally more government money than anywhere in France – 60 per cent of its total income; for better or worse, the island has gone from being a colony to the slightly more exalted status of ward of the state.

The 1970s saw the beginning of what the Corsicans call the *riacquistu*, the 're-acquisition' of everything Corsican: the language, which was being forgotten by the young; the haunting traditional music of polyphonic voices and age-old instruments; and, even noisier, a political movement for autonomy or even independence. This had its roots in the 1960s, partly in the discontent of farmers and in government scandals, and in resentment over the special favours shown by the government to the *pied-noir* refugees (17,000 arrived on Corsica in 1962 after the war in Algeria). Add to these a growing number of French holiday-home builders and retirees, and many

Corsicans feared they would soon become a minority in their own land. In 1975, then-prime minister Jacques Chirac ordered an unnecessarily rough police response on a *pied noir*-owned wine estate in Aléria, which the Corsicans had occupied as a demonstration (*see* p.178). This more than anything galvanized support for the nationalist movement; the **FLNC**, the Front de la Libération Nationale de la Corse, was founded the following year.

No one familiar with Corsican history was surprised when the movement rapidly turned violent: the clans who had resisted the Genoese since the 14th century, with their age-old vendettas, were ready to resist the French. The 1980s was a great decade for **bombings** (as many as forty at a stretch), both on the island and against government facilities all over France, as the FLNC found both fun and profit in manipulating Paris. Some give them credit for the reopening of the university at Corte in 1981.

The next bombing target was non-Corsican-owned holiday homes (always, it must be said, while unoccupied). Nationalism was the excuse, but the real incentive was often good old-fashioned extortion. Corsica has always had its gangland life, like the fellows who briefly made Marseille drug supplier to the world. Somewhere along the line the mobs and the nationalists merged, while the banned FLNC exploded into an array of splinter groups, all posing in the woods around a campfire at night for favoured news cameras, wearing ski masks and sub-machine guns, all raising hand-sewn flags that look much the same. There is no serious reason to doubt that most are deeply into rackets, everything from heroin to fruit machines. Much of the time they fight over turf; over a hundred of them have died in the past three decades.

All this became clear in the course of the 1990s. In 1993 a nationalist activist was assassinated after denouncing the corruption in the movement (in 1996, his wife, **Laetitia Sozzi**, founded the movement **Manifeste pour la Vie** to protest against the violence). And in 1997, the nationalist leadership's involvement in racketeering was further exposed when **François Santoni**, head of **Cuncolta** (the political wing of the 'FNLC Canal Historique') and his girlfriend, the lawyer Marie-Hélène Mattei, were found to have been behind a bombing at the Spérone Golf Course in Bonifacio after the owner, Jacques Dewez, failed to pay up. But then, for many people, the killings suddenly went too far. On 6 February 1998, the tough but popular *préfet* (the *de facto* governor of the island) **Claude Erignac** was shot in Ajaccio – the first *préfet* in France to be killed since the Resistance leader Jean Moulin was tortured to death by the Nazis in 1943. The island went into shock, and to everyone's surprise, even the FLNC condemned the murder; the prime suspect, goatherd **Yvan Colonna**, a member of a radical fringe group, disappeared in the *maquis*, hidden in the age-old codes of honour and silence (*see* pp.34–7).

Despite the outpouring of public sympathy, the French government lost it when the replacement *préfet*, **Bernard Bonnet**, was implicated in April 1999 in the *affaire de la paillote*, when a team of police commandos under his direct orders was caught burning a beach-shack restaurant illegally erected on a beach near Ajaccio. Bonnet was imprisoned, the state was discredited, and the nationalists on the rebound won 24 per cent in the subsequent elections.

Over the past 30 years, in short, the French have learned to love Corsica as much as the British love Northern Ireland. Nationalist strategy has always been to keep the pressure on Paris, wheedling concessions to keep up their popularity at home. Even Corsicans adamantly opposed to their politics grudgingly credit the nationalists with keeping Corsica out of the clutches of developers and outsiders who would exploit her; some 70 per cent of her coasts are still natural. On the Côte d'Azur, the number is 4 per cent.

The Socialist government under **Lionel Jospin** came up with a controversial package to give Corsica a certain amount of autonomy, devolving issues of culture, regional development, education, agriculture and infrastructure to the Corsican assembly, but in 2002 France's highest court declared it unconstitutional; in republican France, no one gets special treatment. Next it was the Gaullists' turn, and they've come up with a more republican plan: devolve similar powers to *all* the French regions. **Nicolas Sarkozy**, then the tough law-and-order Minister of the Interior, made Corsica the test case for the plan – in the face of a good deal of opposition, even on the right, which feared the plan would weaken the central government. Nor did all the separatists jump for joy: 'We will not see Corsica, a historic nation that once enjoyed full sovereignty, lumped in with some uniform and general decentralisation programme for the whole of France,' sniffed **Jean-Guy Talamoni**, leader of the **Corsica Nazione** and member of the region's assembly. But Sarkozy, inspired by a visit to the Scottish parliament, was certain that it would be a perfect model for Corsica.

A **referendum** in July 2003 offered voters the chance to eliminate the current two *départements*, 2A and 2B, and their current regional council, in favour of a single territory represented by a unified assembly of 91 (with parity for women, an innovation in this very macho society). Although the fiery and ambitious Sarkozy came to Corsica eight times to campaign for votes, hoping to put a feather in his political cap, the referendum failed, with just under 51 per cent voting *non*. Several reasons were proposed: separatists were angered by the announcement, 48 hours before the vote, of the capture of their Robin Hood, Yvan Colonna (*see* p.36), accusing the police of indulging in an outrageous piece of political theatre. In Bastia, the vote was 70 per cent negative after Emile Zuccarelli, the city's charismatic mayor, came out against it, saying he wouldn't support anything that tried to placate the separatists. The island's numerous retirees feared for their pensions, and bureaucrats, not only those working in the *départements* but also in the offices of the island's 360 *communes* (many with only a dozen people), were afraid of job cuts. Nationalists reacted to the vote by blowing up four holiday homes.

Meanwhile the French government is thinking again, while taking a new hard line against separatists, going after them on extortion rather than terrorist charges. Even Jean-Guy Talamoni was arrested (causing island-wide protests) in a big sweep in 2004. In March 2005, in a big show trial in Paris, **Charles Pieri**, the feared leader of the **FLNC-UC** (Union des Combattants), and 21 others, including members of his family, were found guilty of using a security firm and a cleaning agency between 1993 and 2003 to blackmail and fleece French holiday companies such as Club Med and Nouvelles Frontières. Pieri was condemned to a 10-year prison term, and the FLNC-UC furiously announced the end of its 15-month ceasefire. Talamoni was acquitted, and returned to a hero's welcome staged by 3,500 supporters.

Poll after poll suggests that, while Corsicans do want to preserve their special identity, and consider themselves Corsican before they consider themselves French, they don't want outright independence – a recent survey found only 13 per cent in favour. There is a realization that the issue is becoming less important under the new Europe. In spite of the referendum, devolution continues apace: since 1992 the responsibilities and funds of the CTC (Collectivité Territoriale de Corse) have increased more than threefold, and in 2005 will include infrastructure and education. They are aware that musical groups such as the Cantu U Populu Corsu and I Muvrini have done a far better job of promoting Corsica's cause in France than the *clandestins* with their balaclavas and plastic explosives.

Whatever the politicians may do and say, there is a grass-roots revolution happening in Corsica. The island is gaining rather than losing population – in fact, in the past few years, demographic growth has surpassed the French average. Young Corsicans are either staying at home or moving back, in love with the unspoiled natural beauty of their island, but returning equipped with the Internet to stay linked to the rest of the world, and degrees in the latest agricultural techniques and equipment. They produce exquisite olive oil (before the Second World War and the subsequent huge fires in the Balagne, Corsica was the second-largest producer in the world), AOC wines, cheese, honey, fruit, *charcuterie* and vegetables. They also respect how fragile the beauty is, and note the economic limits and environmental impact of traditional summer tourism; increasingly they are looking towards the Italian *agriturismo* model, which offers strung-out urban visitors a taste of rural authenticity as well as delicious meals. Corsica's future may well lie in its deepest roots, in its ability to maintain its soul against all odds. And although Sarkozy's vision of a Scottish Corsica was rejected in the referendum, the success of regional governments in the EU does look like an increasingly attractive option, perhaps even some day soon.

Aspects of *Corsitude*

03

A Wild Nature: From *Maquis* to *Mouflon*

Corsica, so vertical that it has three climatic zones (Mediterranean, mountain and alpine), is the greenest and best-watered island in the Mediterranean, as well as one of the least touched by pollution. Some 2,830 species of flora cover it, including, to the delight of botantists, 175 endemic plants – an abundance of sun-drenched flora that has become the basis of a new industry in essential oils.

The vegetation Corsica is best known for is the **maquis**, a thick scrub of oak, juniper, thorn, heather and wild herbs and flowers grows up to 20ft high in places and covers nearly half of the island, lending it its distinct lemony, peppery, musky perfume. Even though it likes to encroach on abandoned farmland, the *maquis* is not without its good points: it produces a mass of beautiful flowers, especially in March, and it shelters a range of small song birds. *Maquis* herbs are used to season grilled meats, and bees transform its flowers into delicious honey that varies dramatically according to season; the honey from one shrub, the arbutus or strawberry tree, is the most prized of all and was said by the ancient Romans to be the elixir responsible for the remarkable longevity of the Corsicans. Other *maquis* shrubs are the fragrant yellow broom; the even more perfumed myrtle, whose leaves, flowers and blueish-black berries go into perfumes and liqueurs; bay, rosemary, and lentisk (or mastic) with little leaves and red or mauve berries; and cistus, with rather greyish leaves and pink or white flowers that last only a day from April to July. Asphodel with its long stalks and white flowers is common in spring on overgrazed land, so common in fact that Corsicans of the diaspora who have forgotten their origins are said to 'no longer recognize the asphodel' ('un' cumnosce più l'albucciu'). As monotonous as the dense green thicket of *maquis* can seem at times, the people who know it best – the hunters – need only the tiniest sign to know exactly where they are and never get lost.

In spring, Corsica runs amok with **wild flowers**; among the usual varieties are 50 species of orchid, violets (the symbol of the Bonapartist party) and, in the mountains, tufty Corsican hellebore, a species unique to this island and Sardinia. During the summer drought, the most interesting plants are by the shore, among them pretty sea holly with blue flowers, white sea daffodil, and orange or lilac Hottentot fig. In October, after the first rains, crocuses and purple cyclamens carpet the hills.

In spite of the fires that plague Corsica, much remains of the old **forests** that once covered the island. The most impressive of these are the great stands of endemic Laricio pines, elegant conifers unique to Corsica with distinctive pyramid tops, which only grow at altitudes over 3,000ft. Standing up to 180ft, with trunks measuring 7ft in diameter, they were prized as masts by the Genoese; some of the very oldest ones, up to 800 years old, grow in the Forêt d'Aitone. At lower altitudes you'll find parasol pines, big-coned maritime pines, plane trees, cork oaks (blood-red where their bark has been flayed, for export to Sardinia's bottle-top factories), beeches, and two non-natives that have prospered: olives, introduced by the ancient Greeks, and the eucalyptus, introduced under Napoléon III to drain the malarial coast. Nor is the biggest forest on Corsica natural: the **sweet chestnuts** of the Castagniccia, planted under the Genoese, although much diminished by fires, parasites and neglect, still make up the largest chestnut forest in Europe. In autumn the trees put on one of the best colour displays in the Mediterranean.

Besides the usual cast of Mediterranean creatures – boars (half of whom have now interbred with the wild pigs), rabbits, hedgehogs, weasels, tortoises, mosquitoes, and buzzing cicadas – Corsica, like many large isolated islands, has its share of rare or unique fauna, some of which it shares only with neighbouring Sardinia. Perhaps the most peculiar is the now-extinct **Lagomys** or *Prolagus corsicanus*, a hare-like creature the size of a large rat, and a favourite dish of Neolithic Corsicans; caches of gnawed Lagomys bones have been found at a number of sites. The ancient Greeks called the islets between Corsica and Sardinia the *Cuniculariae*, the 'rodent islands', suggesting that a few may have survived into historical times.

Today Corsica is the only known home of the *sitelle*, the Corsican **nuthatch** or *pichjarina* (*Sitta whiteheadi sharpe*), a little bird first noted by English naturalist John Whitehead in 1883, and recognizable for its habit of walking down pine trunks head-first; curiously, its nearest cousins live in the forests of Canada and Mongolia. At least ten pairs of **lammergeiers**, or bearded vultures (*altore*), the rarest and largest bird of prey in Europe, live in the highest mountains of the Niolo, floating high overhead on 8ft wingspans, looking for dead animals and their bones, which they drop from heights to break open for the marrow; because flocks have diminished, officials of the Parc Régional now put out dead sheep for them to feed on. Some 30 pairs of **golden eagles** (*acula*) live in the mountains, while **ospreys** (*alpana*) with their mighty talons, the only big bird of prey to live exclusively off fish, were reduced to four nesting couples in 1970 when the Parc Régional took action to protect them; now there are nearly 30 pairs in the Réserve Naturelle de Scandola. The rare **Andouin's gull** nests off Cap Corse, but more common is a big species of gull, the **Goéland Leucophée**, or 'port rat' according to the locals. At night you'll hear the monotonous whistle of a tiny **Scops owl** (*ciocciu*) who lives in the *maquis*. Other uniquely Corsican creatures are the **trout**, the *truite macrostigma*, named for the large 'stain' on its sides, and the **discoglose**, the Corsican frog, plus a unique **snail** that lives in the Ricanto, the **Tyrrhenian wall lizard**, and the island's own **salamander**, with a yellow stripe down its back. Not unique to the island, but common, are the big **geckoes** which do their bit to keep your *gîte* bug-free, and growing numbers of **Hermann's tortoises** (*cupulatta*) There are no poisonous snakes, although the slender, striped **whip snake** (*sarpu*), which likes to bask in the sun, may bite if surprised.

With its long curling horns that form a circle around its head, the **mouflon** (*muvra*), Europe's only species of wild sheep, is the totem animal of Corsica, perhaps because of its very unsheeplike independence. *Mouflons* were brought to Europe from Anatolia during the great Neolithic agricultural revolution *c.* 9,000 years ago. At some point they undomesticated themselves and took to the high mountains, avoiding people as much as possible. Usually they roam in groups of four to ten, taking turns standing guard, and emitting a shrill whistle when danger approaches; they leap fearlessly across abysses, knowing that if they trip and fall on their heads their horns and skulls are hard enough to protect them from the blow (the fact that many of them actually don't survive used to help to keep the bearded vultures in business).

Numbered in their thousands in the early 1900s, *mouflons* were hunted nearly to extinction until they were protected in 1956; today there are about 1,000 left, most of them on the slopes of Monte Cinto, as park officials work, without any great success, to re-establish them across their old mountain haunts. They are hard to see – the best place to sight one is at the Maison du Mouflon in the Asco gorge (*see* p.172). The hunters did bag the last Corsican **deer** (*Cervus elaphus corsicanus*) in the 1960s, but since then individuals of the same species from Sardinia were reintroduced in 1985 and have been bred at reserves in Quenza and Casabianda.

Polyphony, Confraternities, Music and Dance

One of things Corsicans do best is sing, and there are few places in Europe where traditional music has made such a determined stand against the terror of modern pop. Well over a hundred singers have made recordings (by percentage of population, that's one out of every 260, which must be a record in itself), and there are some 80 groups across the island who perform regularly, often for their own pleasure. And nearly all of these sing or have sung polyphony, which one leading singer has called the 'Corsican blues'.

Polyphony ('many voices') is a musical 'texture', rather like a fugue, formed by several different melodic voices, as opposed to most modern western music that has just one voice (monophony) or a dominant melody accompanied by chords (homophony). Some say polyphonies may well be pre-Christian, and it's certainly true that they have a powerful archaic quality, derived from their use of parallel fifths (which were first described in the 9th century, but sound far older). In Corsican polyphony there are three voices: *a segunda* (the lead), *u bassu* (the accompaniment) and *a terza* (the highest voice, for the ornament), but, as Corsicans will argue, there's a fourth voice as well, the 'Angels' Part' that happens magically when they sing together. Dorothy Carrington commented that at no other time are Corsicans 'as united in their apartness, their insularity' as when they sing polyphonies. Listen to them in a little granite chapel in a mountain village, or even in the back of a bar, the singers huddled together, cupping their ears and closing their eyes in concentration, and the haunting strangeness and beauty of their music can give you goosebumps.

Polyphony was kept alive over the centuries in Corsica thanks to the Franciscans and the lay confraternities they founded, beginning in the 13th century. Open to anyone from lord to shepherd, the confraternities were dedicated to singing contemplative and devotional songs, and, as laymen back then were not allowed to participate in the liturgy, the Franciscans invented 'para-liturgies' for them to use in their chapels – many of which, especially in the Counter-Reformation, were acoustically designed for *a cappella* singing. And each had its own chants, in Latin or Tuscan, some of immense musical complexity, according to the few traces that have survived (they were rarely written down, as few Corsicans could read music; even today they nearly always learn polyphonies by ear). It was said a member of one confraternity could identify another with his eyes closed, just by hearing their songs. They performed mystery plays in front of the church, on the *parvis*; they also (as they continue to do today) sang in saint's day and Holy Week processions, and, ever since the Black Death in the 14th century, sang the Mass for the Dead. Alongside all the liturgical songs, however, there grew up a large body of polyphony *paghjella*, or secular songs, sung in Corsican.

Outlawed by the Revolutionary government in 1790, the confraternities made a comeback in the 19th century, only to suffer a serious setback when the reforms of Pius X in 1903 banned polyphony music and chants in favour of choral music sung by parishioners. Although the clergy was hostile, a number of Corsican confraternities refused to give up their ancient songs, although many would suffer from a sheer lack of participants after the rural exodus and two world wars. By 1945, only two confraternities (Sermanu near Corte and Rusiu in the Castagniccia) still sang Latin/Tuscan polyphonies. The reforms of Vatican II seemed to put the last nail in the coffin – until 1972, when 40 musicians from all across the island united to form Canta u Populu Corsu ('the Corsican people sing'), led by Corsica's leading singers and composers, Ghjuvan-Paulu Poletti and Petru Guelfucci, and it wasn't long before polyphony became synonymous with the *riacquistu* of Corsican culture. Canta u Populu Corsu made the first recordings, and gave birth, directly or indirectly, to nearly all the current groups on the island, many of whom mix tradition with creativity, composing new polyphony in response to current issues that touch Corsica – hence the term 'the blues' – often with traditional instruments and sometimes even electronics. Among the best-known are I Muvrini ('The Little *Mouflons*'), famous all over France and beyond for their high energy world music sound (though they return every year and perform in tiny villages); A Filetta, sponsors of the Calvi polyphony festival; the Nouvelles Polyphonies Corses, a group of men and women who produced the first Corsican record to go platinum after they performed in the opening ceremonies of the Albertville Winter Olympics; Bastia-based I Chjami Aghjalesi; plus Tavagna, Caramusa, Voce di Corsica, Tempus Fugit and Diana di l'Alba. The most purist is Ghjuvan-Paulu Poletti's Chœur d'Hommes de Sartène, dedicated to traditional sacred music, for alongside the revival of polyphony there has been a revived interest in confraternities among the young, and several were re-founded in the 1990s.

Other ancient traditions are kept alive as well; one, often heard at weddings and holidays, is the verbal sparring match called *chjam' è risponde*, in which two contestants improvise and chant verses on daily events, the prize going to whoever sings the best and comes up with the wittiest remarks; they are one of the features at Casamaccioli's festival of A Santa di U Niolu (*see* p.166). Other songs range from serenades (*u serinatu*, for the newly wed), lullabies (*berceuse*), war songs (*a paladina*) and *tribbiera* (peasant song) to the weird *lamenti*, sung over the dead (when the bandit Pietri was killed in 1886, he thoughtfully had on his person a collection of *lamenti* ready for his mourners, written half in ink, half in his own blood).

Instrumental music plays less of a role, but some of the Corsican instruments themselves are as old as the hills: the three–five-hole goathorn flute (*pifana*), the reed recorder (*pirula or cialambella*), the bagpipes (*caramusa*), the Jew's harp (*riberbula*) which is said to come from the Iron Age, the mandolin, the four-string fiddle and the cithern, *cetera*, with eight double strings, similar to a medieval Tuscan lute, of which only twelve examples existed by the 1970s; today they are made again in Pigna in the Balagne, an important centre of the island's musical renaissance.

Until the 19th century, Corsican prudery forbade couples' dances, but there were many traditional group dances such the *tarantella* and others with names that betray their origins, such as the *marsilliana*, *monferina* and *tarascone*. The most spectacular footwork was reserved for the legendary *Moresca*, a combination of narration, theatre and war dance in costume and bells in which everyone in a village would join in, each playing a certain role. This was one of several Mediterranean 'Moorish' dances popular from the 12th century on that came to Britain as morris dancing. At the climax of the *Moresca*, 160 costumed dancers would split into two camps and mimic a battle, typically Ugo Colonna's 9th-century triumph over the Saracens. *Morescas* on other subjects were also popular: Tasso's *Gerusalemme liberata* was a favourite, and lasted over four hours. Although not on the same scale as the polyphonies, there has been a revival in traditional dancing, especially to fiddle music, especially at the late July *FestiBallu* in Corte – not to be missed if you're anywhere in the vicinity.

The Moor's Head

You only have to be in Corsica for about five minutes before encountering the *testa nera*, or Moor's head, which Pasquale Paoli put on the flag of independent Corsica in 1762. Local legends have grown up over the years to explain why: some say it represents the expulsion of the Saracens in the shadowy 9th century, others say it's a Moorish king captured in battle, or the head of Moor who tried to abduct a Corsican girl but was slain by her fiancé. The roots of the *testa nera*, however, go back to the Knights Templars. The Templars were founded in 1118 by a Catalan named Hugues de Payen, whose shield bore three black heads. In Arabic the root of the word 'understanding' is the same as the root for 'black' or 'collier' and the Moor's head was used by those esoteric knights as a shorthand for wisdom. The Moor's head was brought back by the Crusaders to England, where it gradually lost its meaning to become a favourite pub sign. Elsewhere, by the 15th century, the Moor's head (often blindfolded) had become a symbol of exclusion and otherness; it appears now and then in the art of the period, perhaps most strikingly on the banners of the defeated Persian pagans in Piero della Francesca's famous frescoes on the *Legend of the Cross* in Arezzo.

The medieval Catalan kings of Aragon had a close relationship with the Templars; the greatest of them, Jaume the Conqueror, was their pupil, and placed the Moor's head on his shield. Thus in the 14th century, when Pope Boniface VII granted the 'kingdom of Corsica and Sardinia' to Aragon, Barcelona's cartographers at once marked them with a Moor's head. Aragon did capture and rule Sardinia (and leave it a flag with not one but four Moors' heads), but it never managed to take Corsica from Genoa. Yet the pope's gift was never revoked: one of Spanish king Juan Carlos' titles is 'King of Corsica'.

Because Corsica is dedicated to the Virgin, the first insurgents in 1735 adopted a white flag of the Immaculate Conception. But it was the Moor's head on a Spanish map that caught the fancy of Théodore von Neuhof, Corsica's king for a day (*see* p.190), and he had it minted on his coins and engraved on his portraits. Paoli, when elected General of the Nation, made the *testa nera* the flag and arms of Corsica in 1762, but raised the blindfold as a symbol of the awakening of the Corsican people.

Saints and Shamans

Converted early on, perhaps by St Paul himself, the Corsicans have never wavered from the pope's camp, apart from a short-lived fling with heresy in the Middle Ages. The entire island is dedicated to the Virgin Mary; she appeared on the first flag of independent Corsica in 1735 and her polyphonic hymn, *Dio vi salvi Regina*, was (and is) the island's national anthem. The transcendent Judaeo-Christian God is something of a neglected stranger, but the Corsicans have compromised to allow his Son a starring role at Easter. Although church attendance has dropped in recent years, devotion rooted in the land and tradition (as in the revival of the confraternities, *see* p.29, and the pilgrimages to rural shrines) is still very much alive.

Like any rural people, Corsicans help the year along with a cycle of rituals and festivals. Some customs predate Christianity, and others are old superstitions, with which the Church, for its own reasons, did little to interfere. Corsican clerics never sought an iron grip over their people, and more often than not they supported the islanders' struggles against their oppressors; some of the most determined fighters against the Genoese and French have been priests. The War of Independence against Genoa was declared at the Franciscan convent of Orezza, while the island's bishops gathered to produce a document legitimizing the revolt.

On **New Year's Day**, village children have the task of renewing bonds that may have soured between families over the preceding year. As no one can refuse children, they go from door to door with wishes that the next year might be better and they are thanked and given sweets and fruit in return; bad luck awaits any household that gives them nothing. At **Epiphany**, besides the *galette des Rois* introduced from France, a Corsican must eat lasagne or face the consequences: '*Pasque Pifania, à ch'ùn face lasagne/Tuttu l'annu si lagna*' ('Anyone who doesn't make lasagne for Epiphany will complain the whole year long').

Candlemas or *Ciriola* (2 February) is the signal for better weather; during Mass, the faithful carry blessed candles home, taking great care to keep them alight along the road to keep bad luck from the family. *Ciriola* is associated with **Carnival**, where things are topsy-turvy; hence the Groundhog Day theory prevalent in Corsica, that fine weather that day means more winter, and a rainy day means spring is just around the corner. Other Carnival traditions and dances have all but died out, although young men in some villages still go out and about one evening before Lent for a *Birba*, rather like Hallowe'en trick-or-treating. The *birba* itself is a long cane with a fork attached to it. If they find a door closed to them or insufficient salami, fritters or wine on offer, they sing imploring verses, assuring the hosts that not to feed them will make the devil furious. If that doesn't work, they threaten the household with their *birba*. If the door remains closed in spite of all their cajoling and threatening in verse, they lambast it with curses. A popular one is:

Quante petri c'é in stu muru,/Quanti peli ha vostru mulu/Tante zecche a u vostru culu!

(As many stones as there are in this wall,/and as many hairs as there are on your mule,/may you have as many ticks up your ass!)

The spring rites of **Easter** are deeply felt across the island. Before Palm Sunday people gather palm fronds to make crosses for their homes, and a bier is prepared to receive the effigy of the dead Christ, decorated with flowers, candles and little trays of pale wheat shoots, a custom that goes back to the ancient Greeks, who called them 'gardens of Adonis'. On Good Friday, the confraternities, led by their elected priors, make their processions, passing through the Stations of the Cross or the small chapels that stand on the edge of every Corsican village. Many processions trace a spiral, the *granitula* (the 'snail') in strict single-file outside the church; as it slowly unwinds, the confraternity enters the church. The *granitula* goes straight back to Neolithic times: the spiral is the simplest form of labyrinth, symbolizing the return to the origin of life and the progression from death to rebirth.

Holy Saturday is the occasion for a good spring clean, the *pulizzia di Pasqua*, which includes the burning of the palm crosses of the previous year and perhaps a new coat of whitewash on the walls. Easter Sunday itself passes rather uneventfully (perhaps because in Corsica the dead never seem really dead anyway), while Easter Monday is the occasion for a picnic and cakes decorated with eggs called *campanili* or *caccavelli*.

Traditionally the first eggs laid on **Ascension Day** in May are kept in the house over the next year and never rot (or so they say), while keeping away lightning; sailors' wives put the egg in the window during storms to calm the waves, and if someone falls ill the magic egg is brought to the bedside. The patron saint of shepherds, **St Anthony of Padua**, has his day on 13 June; little breads called *paniotti* are blessed by the priest and distributed among family, friends and even the flock to usher in prosperity and fertility; if a house was on fire, throwing on *paniotti* would extinguish the flames. The patron saint of farmers, **St John the Baptist**, has his day near the summer equinox. In the old days, the traditional bonfires for St John are also the occasion for adolescents to formalize childhood friendships, each becoming one another's *compà* or *cummà* (godfather or godmother), as they hold hands and leap over the fire together, swearing undying friendship – a rare chance in a tradition-bound society for an individual to choose his or her own friends.

Besides the **Assumption of the Virgin** (15 August), the summer calendar was devoted to fairs and pilgrimages in Mary's honour; the most important survivor takes place at Casamaccioli in the Niolu (*see* pp.166–7), complete with a *granitula* procession, on 8–10 September. The **harvest** was so important that a truce was declared between feuding families; breakers of the peace would be held to account by all-powerful *parolanti*, or mediators, who would punish them by burning their fields or houses.

According to traditional Corsican belief (influenced in no small way by a history full of invasions and vendettas), the whole world outside the family was filled with harmful and jealous spirits. **Malevolent forces** roamed across the land: dolmens were forges of the devil, or homes of ogres; menhirs were the tombstones of infidels; the *orri* – natural shelters eroded by the wind in granite – were the haunt of the undead.

Invisible witches or *streghi* would sneak into a house at night to suck a baby's blood; *acciatori* hung about in the dark waiting to chop off the heads of unwary travellers. **Eagles**, perhaps a more immediate threat, were kept away with a spell, an *intu di l'acula*, cast by shepherds on Christmas Eve. If a baby received a **compliment**, a mother could only avert trouble by calling down God's blessing or by making the sign of the 'horns' over the child with her fist, or even by spitting on it. Certain people could cast the **evil eye** (the *occihju*), sometimes without even knowing it, and the only cure was to go to the village 'evil eye remover', the *encantatora* or *signatora*, usually a woman, who had inherited the gift of exorcism from her mother. She would say a prayer and make the sign of the cross over a bowl of water before dropping hot olive oil into it. If the drops remained separate and round, it proved that there was no evil eye; if they coalesced, the operation had to be repeated an odd number of times until they no longer did, and the patient was relieved of the curse.

Although often contradicted by their religious beliefs, Corsicans have long held an ancient Mediterranean gut belief in destiny. **Second sight** was something of a national trait, given to children if their godparents mispronounced or omitted one word of the baptismal rite; even Pasquale Paoli, a true son of the Enlightenment, told Boswell that he often dreamed of events before they occurred (he foresaw the guillotining of his friend, the mayor of Paris). This gift, or curse, was seen as a sneak preview of the **dream world**, where events were all acted out and decided by a destiny that humans could never avoid, instead only playing out their roles like shadow puppets.

Destiny, however, gave some people a startling active role in the dream world. When the Saracens occupied Corsica, they called the inhabitants 'wizards', perhaps referring to the shamans known as ***mazzeri*** or *culpatori*, whose peculiar habits led writer Dorothy Carrington to call them 'dream hunters of the soul' (*see* **Further Reading**). *Mazzeri* – ordinary people in the daytime, marked only by their fascinating gaze – felt (or rather feel, as there are said to be a couple of dozen still in Corsica) alive only at night in their dreams when, armed with sticks and stones, they hunted for souls. The rules of the dream sport demanded that they attack the first creature they came across, even if they knew the animal was really the soul of a person they loved. If wounded by the *mazzeri*, the victim in real life fell ill; if killed, he or she would die within the year. All deaths in a village would be attributed to the dream hunts of the *mazzeri*, but, because they were only playing their roles in the shadow world of destiny, they were never blamed, either. Once a year, on 31 July , all the *mazzeri* would join forces at the centre of the island in a pan-Corsican battle for souls (*see* p.154).

Napoleon once said 'death is a state of the soul', and it's a state the Corsicans have always taken very seriously. As in other isolated corners of the Mediterranean – the Mani in the Peloponnese is one – archaic funeral rites were still practised into the mid-20th century: there were histrionic displays of grief; despairing laments for the dead improvised by the *voceratrices,* women who specialized in dirges; women held hands and danced a circular *caracollu* around the bier during the wake; food offerings for the departed were left beside graves. In the same spirit, there was an awareness that the dearly departed were never far away. 'In Corsica, your dead never leave you alone,' as Joseph Conrad quoted his mariner friend Dominique Cervoni: the night was filled with ghosts, who appeared alone or gathered for funerals, sometimes as guardians of a family, but more often to warn or punish the living, or demand vengeance like Hamlet's father. On 2 November the Corsicans light enormous candles in their family tombs, and believe in general that this is the night when the dead come back on a tour of inspection. Families would leave out milk and chestnuts to appease them, and in the morning check the hearth for footprints in the ashes.

Vendettas and Bandits

One mustn't judge Corsican morals by our little European ideas. Here a bandit is generally the most honest man in the region.
Gustave Flaubert

Along with '*maquis*' as a synonym for the Resistance, the word *vendetta* is Corsica's only contribution to the English language. Its practice goes back to Homeric times, and has at its root an extraordinary sense of honour, perceived within a person as the ideal of self-worth but, just as importantly, perceived without by one's neighbours. As possibilities for wealth and advancement were limited on the island, honour was a person's most prized possession, to be defended at all costs. What made Corsica such an extreme case was pinpointed by Dorothy Carrington: 'Pride, antique hubris; the worst part of honour. A foreigner is always liable to underestimate this trait in the Corsican character because he is simply unable to believe that pride in such dimensions can exist.' Corsican history is striped with the comet-tails of proud men burned up by their tragic destiny, in which the vendetta nearly always played a leading role.

Along with pride, history and geography conspired to make Corsica fertile ground for the blood feud. Although the Genoese governor Giorgio Doria eventually produced civil and criminal statutes for the island in 1571, it was common knowledge even then that judges invariably decided in favour of whoever paid the highest bribe. Up in their mountain valleys, Corsicans could rely only on their own clans to maintain the law and preserve their honour; as a correlation, any taint was felt by all the family (up to the degree of third cousin was the unwritten rule), who would act as a unit to settle scores with the entire family of the transgressor. Crime, in fact, was always low because the penalty was severe and implacable: death. Vendettas often led to the total extinction of a family, and as such acted as the perfect deterrent to sheep-rustling, rape, adultery or disputes of even the most trival kind – dozens have died after a quarrel that began over a tree cut down or a straying donkey.

A unique feature of the vendetta, compared to the blood feuds of other nationalities, is that Corsicans, from their enormous pride, would never accept blood money in exchange for a life. As a result, Corsica was deadly: during the worst period, between 1682 and 1714, the annals record 28,715 violent deaths (out of a population of 120,000) which made the odds of being killed in a vendetta roughly one in 150, enough to make the South Bronx in the 1970s seem like a Sunday school.

'It's a form of suicide,' as a Corsican once told Dorothy Carrington, especially as vendettas were often provoked on purpose. Women, who were expected to remain not only virgins but literally untouched by any man before marriage, were often the cause. All a man had to do was approach a girl in a crowded public place (often as she was leaving Mass) and pull off her headscarf, an act called the *attacar*. Everyone around would cry out, '*Disonorata! Disonorata!*' ('Shamed! shamed!') and it was understood that the girl, even if she violently resisted the *attacar*, had to marry the culprit at once or die a spinster, or see her family embroiled in a bloody vendetta.

Not surprisingly perhaps, women took a leading role in perpetuating the vendetta, in spite of the perverse results that more often than not brought about the death of their husbands, brothers or sons. A mother would bring her children to the corpse of their murdered father, stick her finger in the wound, and with the blood make the sign of the cross on her little one's brows with terrible imprecations for vengeance. The shirt of the victim, stained with blood and torn by stilettos, would be hung on the wall; when the body was laid out on the kitchen table, the plaintive *lamenti* sung to mourn a natural death would be replaced by the bloodcurdling wails of the *voceru*, demanding vengeance, reaching a frenzy while the other women tore their hair and garments and plunged their nails into their breasts till they drew blood, crying, '*De sangue sentu una sete/Di morte sentu una brama*' ('I have a thirst for blood/I have a hunger for death'). As they sang, the men in the next room grimly kept time, banging their rifle butts against the floor.

To show that the family was in a state of war, they let their hair and beards grow, and boarded up the windows and doors of their house, so that the only entrance was by ladder. From then on no one was safe. Men went to church armed to the teeth, never knowing when they might be ambushed; in a vendetta all means to an end were good. Men who failed to exact revenge were publicly scorned and humiliated by their families and neighbours (a state called *ribeccu*) until they did the deed.

Because nearly every family in Corsica had enemies, the Genoese exploited the vendetta time and time again to rid themselves of troublesome rebels, usually offering the killers money and a new life in Genoa where they might escape revenge. Pasquale Paoli came the closest to eradicating the scourge by impartially executing all vendetta killers, including one of his own cousins, then razing their houses and erecting a 'pillar of infamy' on the site. His attempt to undermine the old concepts of honour ended with the coming of the French, and it wasn't long before the Corsicans were back to settling their own scores again, often against the 'invaders'. The French responded with hideous tortures and executions, but to little effect, as men involved in a vendetta expected to die anyway. Yet as times became more settled (by the late 19th century the murder rate dropped to under 50 a year), the French *literati* found the vendetta and the whole ideal of honour fascinating as a primitive yet rather noble relic of antiquity. Two key works were Prosper Mérimée's bestselling *Colomba*, inspired by a real-life vendetta in Fozzano in the 1860s, and the more romantic *Les Frères Corses* by Alexandre Dumas, an outlandish swashbuckling tale of vengeance undertaken by Siamese twins parted at birth.

Banditry was the natural offshoot of the vendetta. Short of the complete extermination of a family, a vendetta could at least come to a hiatus when a man vanished into the *maquis* after murdering the enemy who dishonoured his family. The word 'bandit' in this case harks back to the original sense of the word, as in 'banned' from society: as everyday brigands became more common in the 19th century, those who killed because of pride and duty became known as *bandits d'honneur*. In the *maquis* their families would supply them with food, and they were protected from their enemies or the police by an implacable law of silence. *Bandits d'honneur* became folk heroes, the tragic embodiments of the Corsican ideal; Victorian-era travellers would come to visit them in their hideaways, and usually left deeply impressed by their conversation. Some bandits were famed for their piety; several churches, especially in the Castagniccia, have charmingly naïve works of art sculpted by bandits. They even had a patron saint, Pancrace.

The noble and pious bandits, however, were a minority; most were desperadoes who terrorized the population. Some, like Théodore Poli, 'King of the Mountains' (*see* p.267), or the Bonelli brothers of Bocognano (*see* p.150), enjoyed a certain cult status for their Robin Hood-type exploits against the French *gendarmes*. After the First World War, as Corsica came into closer contact with the rest of Europe, the *bandit d'honneur* became a rarity; personal possessions replaced personal honour, and bandits took to large-scale criminal activity, imposing 'taxes' on the population in exchange for protection. As the violence increased, the Corsicans tired of them, and the French Army was able to wipe out the last bandit, André **Spada**, sending him to Bastia to be guillotined in 1935; officially, the last vendetta ended in the 1960s.

Last bandit? Well, not quite. In July 2003, the French police finally bagged goatherd Yvan Colonna, the suspected assassin of Préfet Claude Erignac in 1998 (*see* **History**, p.22) and the most wanted man in France, in an old stone barn near Porto-Pollo. Eight of Colonna's colleagues were captured the year after Erignac's death, but for years nothing the police did – interviewing every separatist on the island, examining the records of eight million phone calls, searching throughout metropolitan France and South America – brought them any closer to the man they believed actually pulled the trigger. On Corsica, Colonna acquired the mythic status of the bandits of yore – and the chief inspector began to suspect that, just like those bandits, Colonna was hiding right under their noses in the *maquis*. His family were put under surveillance and were spotted taking an unexplained walk on a cold, rainy day. It was noticed that the fugitive's friends often turned off their mobile phones when walking in the woods. Searches were made of hundreds of isolated huts and barns in the area and in several they found stacks of recent newspapers. Infra-red cameras were installed in these barns, and Colonna was spotted talking to his goats (a known habit of his), and arrested the next evening, without resistance. The fact that it occurred only days before the referendum on autonomy designed by French minister Nicolas Sarkozy (*see* p.23) didn't play well – the police were accused of having known where Colonna was hiding all along and saved his capture for a piece of theatre just before the vote.

The French police then began to round up everyone suspected of lending aid and succour to Colonna while he was on the run, sparking off demonstrations. In Ajaccio, thousands came out wearing T-shirts saying 'We all gave shelter to Yvan!' In Olmeto and Propriano, there were angry protests condemning this French intrusion on the most fundamental pillars of the Corsican soul – the tradition of hospitality and the

code of honour. At the time of writing Colonna waits in prison in Paris, claiming inno-
cence and awaiting trial.

Napoleon

Men of genius are meteors destined to be consumed in lighting up their century.

Napoleon, age 22

It can be awkward for proud nationalists when your world conqueror, the one who brought your country its greatest triumphs and territories, comes from outside. Alexander the Great came from Macedonia, a place that 4th-century BC Athenians disdained as barbaric, even though Alexander made it his business to spread Hellenism from Egypt to India; as a pupil of Aristotle, he may even have performed his *mission civilatrice*, as the French would have called it, with some sincerity.

Alexander, however, was the son of a king. Napoleon, who brought France to its pinnacle of *gloire*, was the first great self-made man of modern times. Born just three months after Genoa sold Corsica to France, he would spread republican virtue like hard butter on the flabby, decadent bread of Europe's aristocracy. Many thinking people, inspired by Lafayette's *Declaration of the Rights of Man*, cheered him on as the great liberator of Europe; Beethoven dedicated his Third Symphony, the *Eroica*, to him. Yet Napoleon, who declared that every one of his soldiers carried 'a marshal's baton in his knapsack', was too Corsican to really trust anyone outside his clan; ironically, not long after France took control of Corsica, Corsicans, all named Bonaparte, took control of France and much of Europe.

Napoleon's Corsican hubris also led to trouble. Alexander's followers had been put off when he declared himself a god, and although Napoleon didn't go quite so far and only made himself an emperor, the effect was similar. Beethoven angrily crossed off his symphony's dedication when he heard the news, although Goethe, the wise man of Europe, who personally met Napoleon, could still write in 1811:

What centuries have dimly meditated
His mind surveys in brightest clarity;
All that is petty has evaporated,
Here nothing is of weight save earth and sea.

Like Alexander, Napoleon was a brilliant opportunist and propagandist for himself, twisting the truth every which way in his bulletins from the front ('to lie like a bulletin' was a proverbial expression in the French army) and finding painters to immortalize his acts, lending him imperial gravity (Alexander favoured artists who made him look like a sun god). Both were obsessive. 'The terror he inspires is inconceivable. One has the impression of an impetuous wind blowing about one's ears when one is near that man,' wrote Madame de Staël after a weekend in his house.

Napoleon's father Carlo had been one of Pasquale Paoli's greatest supporters, but Bonaparte *père* lost little time in going over to Corsica's new French owners, with equal dedication; Paoli himself, as he went into exile, told Carlo that his first duty was to take care of his growing family. Yet Napoleon, sent away from home at the age of nine on a scholarship to a French military academy (where he was teased for being Corsican), grew up as an ardent Corsican nationalist and admirer of Paoli: 'Frenchmen, not satisfied with having robbed us of all that we cherished, you have also corrupted our morals,' he wrote indignantly. He began a history of Corsica, but never finished it because he kept changing his mind on how it should end. Then Carlo died in 1785 when Napoleon was only 15, leaving him to support his large family as a lieutenant.

The Revolution changed everything. When Napoleon returned to Ajaccio in 1789, he was shocked to see how backward Corsica was, how the *ancien régime* on the island hadn't budged; he gave fiery speeches at the local Jacobin club. When Paoli broke with Paris and once again declared Corsican independence in 1793, Napoleon and his followers started a civil war; Paoli sentenced him and all the Bonapartes to 'perpetual execration and infamy'. Napoleon's last visit to Corsica was in the dead of night, to take the whole clan to France, never to return.

Although now his bitter rival, Paoli would remain a role model to Napoleon. He was the general of the nation, but he was also a law-giver, someone who had taken the blank slate of Corsica's government and created a new idealistic order. Napoleon, already hungry for power, would do the same as Paoli, but for all of Europe. He would create a brave new world order. Perhaps the essential difference just never occurred to Napoleon: that Paoli had been, not a conqueror, but a liberator of his homeland, a man who ruled with his co-citizens' consent.

In some ways Boney was insignificant, neglected little Corsica's revenge on France. A million and a half Frenchmen died in his Grande Armée, but *la gloire* was addictive, and as the 19th-century Gallic banana republic tried to recapture it, it became clear that Napoleon was far too important to give up. Even while he was still alive on St Helena (where he was fond of comparing himself to Prometheus Bound or even to Jesus Christ) his rehabilitation was under way, first with his memoirs, which inspired the Parisians to finish his Arc de Triomphe. In 1840, Louis-Philippe orchestrated the return of his remains from St Helena and installed them in an outrageous bombastic tomb in the Invalides (it all backfired; rather than shed reflected *gloire* on Louis-Philippe, it made him look punier than ever). Then another Napoleon, nephew of the first, was given a try and led a Second Empire legendary for its corruption; after its fall, the diaries of Napoleon's other confidants on St Helena, not meant for publication but much more revealing of his cynicism, were published. But faded *gloire* is better than no *gloire*, and the tomb is too heavy to move. The Russians got it right when they embalmed Lenin, the easier to slip him out the back door.

Napoleon's somewhat ambivalent status as a French hero and role model for totalitarians explains, in a small way, France's long neglect of his native island; it was awkward to be reminded of his strong Corsican accent, his fringe origins, and how he put France, once the most populous and powerful country in Europe, into the second division. Besides, Napoleon himself began the policy of Corsian neglect when he himself appointed an oppressive governor, General Morand, who suspended all constitutional rights on the island – perhaps necessary, as many Paolists regarded Boney as a traitor. Nevertheless, the Corsicans who followed him were among his most loyal supporters; he remembered 21 of them in his will. Ajaccio, his home town, has since forgiven him and loves playing the part of the *ville impériale*; the rest of the island makes a few *euros* selling bottles of drink with his picture on the label.

The Corse Language

Next to nothing is known of the original Corsican language. The Greek colonists called it incomprehensible, while Seneca, who studied it during his exile in Corsica in AD 41–9, speculated that it was related to Iberian, a non-Indo-European language, possibly proto-Basque. With the Roman conquest, it was replaced by Latin and evolved into Corse or Corsu, a language close to medieval Tuscan; Italians who visit the island are enchanted when they hear Corsicans nattering away in a language close to that of Dante. Unlike many minority languages in Europe, however, Corsu is alive and well; some 86 per cent of the island's native Corsican population speak it fluently on a regular basis, while nearly all understand it.

Writing, however, came late; in fact the illiteracy and isolation of most of the population guaranteed that the language would evolve relatively untainted. All official texts were printed in Italian until the 1780s, and all educated Corsicans continued to write in that language, until French was imposed in earnest in the mid-1800s.

Corsu is a language rich in proverbs, and one says '*Una lingua si cheta, un populu si more*' ('A language silenced is a people who die'). Back in the 1960s, just as French TV and radio saturated the last remote mountain valleys, the Corsicans began to feel as if they were dying indeed. As the main thrust of the cultural *riacquistu*, they started to demand official recognition for Corsu – only to come up against the wall of the French constitution, which declares that French is the only official language of the République.

Even so, Paris over the years has slowly relaxed its linguistic grip on its minorities. Since 1974 Corsu has had the status of a *langue régionale*, and the number of publications, dictionaries, radio and television broadcasts in Corsu have increased ever since. A major stumbling block, however, is that, like the Corsicans themselves, Corsu resists standardization, with its markedly different dialects: you have Northern Corsu, or *lingua suprana*, spoken around Bastia and Corte, and Southern Corsu, *lingua suttana*, spoken around Sartène and Porto-Vecchio – and in northeastern Sardinia. In Ajaccio they speak a transition between the two, *lingua mizana*; in Calvi and Bonifacio, the old Genoese outposts, the dialect is close to Ligurian. The dialects share 80–90 per cent of the same words, but have different syntax and usage – making Corsu a nightmare for those who want to teach it in school, with rules and textbooks.

Although the constitution has prevented France from ratifying the 1992 European Charter for Regional or Minority Languages, things continue to happen 'unofficially.' In April 2001, the Minister of Education, Jack Lang, came out and admitted that since Napoleonic times the French government had systematically repressed regional languages, and announced that France would support bilingual education and recruit bilingual teachers in public schools. In Corsica, this has only supported a growing trend: today 30,000 schoolchildren are taught or have some of their lessons in Corsu,

Glossary of Terms

bocca: mountain pass

cala: cove

calanca: creek or ravine, under the cliffs

capu: cape

casa: house

casatorre: a stronghold where people could take refuge in times of trouble

castagnu: chestnut tree

castellu or *casteddu*: fortified Bronze Age settlement

cella: the room inside a torre or central monument

cima: peak

fiume: river

fiumicellu: stream

foce: high mountain pass

funtana: spring or fountain

lau or *lavu*: lake

licettu: oak forest

orriu (pl. *orii*): a shelter under a boulder, often bricked in, used for storage. The word is believed to derive from the Latin *horreum*, 'granary'

piana: plateau

pinetu: pine wood

piscia: waterfall

serra: mountain range

stagnu: pond or pool

surgente: spring

taffoni: crevices, hollows or pits eroded in the granite, often used as shelters in prehistoric times

teghie: roof 'tiles' made of thin plates of schist, sometimes granite

torre: tower

students can study it as a living language, and the University of Corte offers a course in it as well.

As you'll notice on the road signs (nationalists diligently black out whatever French names the hunters haven't blown to bits), Corsu has a nice symmetry to it – there's a *u* (pronounced oo as in boo) or an *a* (or 'the') at the beginning of most words, and an *u* or an *a* at the end. Although the Italians, backed by their own dozens of dialects, have little trouble pronouncing it, be warned that things are rarely pronounced as they are spelt: 'Porto-Vecchio', for instance, turns into 'Portu-Vek'; Castagniccia is pronounced 'Castagneetch.' Corsican words also dominate on maps; the short glossary in the box above may help.

Food and Drink

04

Although gourmets never list it among the great culinary regions of France, Corsica is worth a visit just for its food. Its clear rivers and seas, its sunny, unpolluted Mediterranean and mountain climates and soils uniquely influence its produce: this is what the French call *terroir*, and you can really taste it. Free-range lamb, kid and veal are grazed on mountain herbs; fish, prawns and spiny lobster are plucked out of the clear sea; running free in the chestnut forests and *maquis*, pigs make excellent *charcuterie*. Corsica produces all of France's clementines and nearly all of the rest of its citrus fruit, as well as figs, kiwis and exotic fruits. The olive oil and wine are excellent; hazelnuts and almonds are making a comeback, as well as chestnuts, once known as the 'bread tree' of Corsica and still used in a hundred different ways (*see* p.188). The emphasis on freshness means that dishes are seasonal, and many say the best time to dine in Corsica is in the autumn and winter.

Although agriculture has expanded, in particular in terms of goods aimed at the higher end of the market, farmers have yet to meet the demand. Although local markets are a good place to find genuine local produce, you can go a step even better by visiting the producer. Four regions – I Trè Vaddi (the Gravona, Prunelli and Cruzinu valleys), the Balagne, Castagniccia and central Corsica – have established *Routes des Sens Authentiques*, listing producers who welcome visitors. Most ask that you ring a day ahead: for contact details, see *www.corsica-terroirs.com*.

Corsican Specialities

Brocciu and Some Other Cheeses

Usually cheese comes near the end of the food list, but in pastoral Corsica it holds pride of place. A staple of the diet since Neolithic times, today two-thirds of the annual 2,500 tons of cheese produced are from ewe's milk (*brebis*), the rest from goat's milk (*chèvre*), flavoured with the *maquis* (Corsican cows are for raising veal). The lion's share of milk goes into making **brocciu** (pronounced *brootche*), the cheese most emblematic of Corsica. AOC since 1983, *brocciu* is a light fresh cheese, similar to ricotta but with more character, made from goat or ewe's whey, usually eaten fresh within 48 hours of its production (and no longer than five days, which makes it difficult to export), or salted, drained and ripened. It can end up in everything: soup, *beignets* or omelettes; stuffed in pasta, fish, vegetables; for breakfast with salt and pepper or jam, or as a dessert; in *eau-de-vie*; in fig jam; or baked in a *fiadone* or cheesecake. When Napoleon's mother lived in Rueil-Malmaison near Paris, she had such a hankering for *brocciu* that she had Corsican goats brought over to graze on her lawns and give her a supply, only it wasn't the same without the *maquis* and, in particular, the nitrogen-rich asphodels that give the milk its distinctive taste. Fresh *brocciu* is available only from November to early July; the rest of the year it is *demi-sec* (half-dried), *passu* (cultured), made from powdered milk, or else chefs make do with *brousse*, a far less distinctive *fromage frais* made from cow's milk.

Corsica makes excellent 'real' cheeses, too, and they're no namby-pambies; if well aged, they 'walk', as the French say. Although some shepherds sell their milk to the

Cheese Regions

Certain regions of Corsica are especially known for their cheese:

Niolu: Exclusively a *fromage fermier*, a soft cheese with a washed crust made high up on the Niolo plateau.

Venacu: Flat cylinders of sheep's and/or goat's cheese with an orangey crust. Usually consumed *affiné* on the cheeseboard, it can be grated on pasta when well aged.

Bastelicacciu: From the Gravona and Prunelli valleys, a soft white sheep's cheese made in winter when the flocks are down in the plain, and always eaten fresh.

Sartinese: A pressed goat's or sheep's cheese with a dry crust made all over the south of Corsica, mostly by home-based producers. This is a *fromage de garde*, that Corsicans would keep over the winter; kept long enough it decays into tangy *casuminadu* or *casgiu merzu*, its texture 'whipped' by live maggots or cheese-hoppers. It's appreciated by connoisseurs, but don't expect to find it in a shop!

Calinzana: A square goat's or sheep's cheese with a washed crust made around Calenzana, with a piquant taste. *Calinzana* is eaten either fresh, *primaticciu*, after five or six months, or *vecchju*, after 10 months, as a delicacy.

Société Roquefort rather than trying to reach EU levels of hygiene in their mountain *bergeries*, many now produce their own individual farmhouse cheeses (*fromages fermiers*), which have to be made according to traditional methods by shepherds, using only the milk from a single herd. Individual character therefore predominates, so much so that Corsican cheeses are sold under the name of the producer. A great place to try many of them is at the Venaco cheese fair, *A Fiera di U Casgiu*, in early May.

Corsican cheeses are often served with fig compote or melon to soften their pungency; the combination is delicious. For more, see the Corsican cheese trade association's site, *www.fromages-corse.org*.

Olive Oil

Corsican olive oil, the island's top export in the 19th century and a fundamental ingredient in its cuisine, is making a recovery from the 20th-century abandonment and fires that wreaked havoc on the groves of the Balagne (the chief growing region), although production is still less than a quarter of what it was in the 1800s. Recently granted its AOC papers at Oliu di Corsica, Corsican olive oil stands out for its yellowy gold colour and distinctive sweet, nutty-peppery taste. Three main varieties of olives are used – Ghjermana, Sabina and Zinzala; all three are grown at the prize-winning Domaine de Marquiliani in Aléria (*see* p.179), one of the leading lights in the renaissance of Corsica's liquid gold.

Charcuterie

Corsica's middle name is *charcuterie*. On the hoof, in its finest form it comes from semi-wild free-range Corsican black pigs and boars, foraging on *maquis* herbs, acorns, barley, corn and chestnuts. By modern agricultural standards they are slaughtered late (between 14 and 36 months), but this is when their meat is at its most flavoursome. What the Corsicans don't do is make enough of it for the demand, and some

85–90 per cent of *charcuterie corse* is industrially made, in the Corsican style, from pigs imported from the mainland. The pricier but tastier real McCoy, aged in naturally cool cellars, may be found in restaurants that make their own, or in boutique shops with the *authentica* label; plans are in the works to make that into an AOC label, with all the concomitant guarantees of origin and authenticity.

Served with olives, platters of *charcuterie* are the island's favourite starter: you'll find thin slices of **prizuttu** (ham, usually chestnut-smoked and aged up to three years to acquire its distinctive hazelnut flavour); **coppa** (salted and peppered pork loin); **salamu** (dried salami); **lonza** (preserved fillet of pork, served in paper-thin slices); and, if you're lucky, the most Corsican of them all, **figatellu**, a little pig liver sausage marinated in wine, pepper and garlic, 'as simple and rustic in appearance as a Corsican mountain', served dried and raw, or fresh and *sautéed*, or grilled with chestnut *pulenta* or, perhaps best of all, over an open fire so the excess fat drips off, then stuffed into a sliced baguette. There are also two fresh sausages destined for the grill: **salcicetta** and **sangui** (spicy black pudding). **Panzetta**, like streaky bacon, is a favourite with fried eggs.

Soups, Pasta and Other Starters

'Either eat your soup or jump out of the window,' say the Corsicans, who know what's good for you. If the island has one all-round classic dish, it would have to be the thick and hearty bean and vegetable soup of the mountains, **suppa corsa/soupe corse**, a meal in itself that includes dried beans, chickpeas, garden vegetables, herbs, onions, garlic, olive oil, cabbage, potatoes and a ham bone or slices of *figatellu* for flavour. Any restaurant near the coast will serve **suppa di pesce/soupe de poisson**, dark and garlicky, accompanied by croutons, grated cheese and a *rouille* of red peppers crushed with garlic and olive oil. Corsican *bouillabaisse*, **aziminu**, combines fish, shellfish, crustaceans and squid, flavoured with *pastis*, fennel and pepper; Cap Corse has been making it longer than elsewhere and has some of the best. In winter and spring you'll find **minestra di brocciu/soupe au brocciu**, made with mint and chard; others are **suppa d'erbiglie/soupe d'herbes**, made from greens and herbs, and **suppa di castagne/soupe de chataignes**, made with chestnuts, leeks, onions and bones.

The popularity of pasta in Corsica betrays centuries of Italian rule. Favourites are cannelloni or less often ravioli filled with *brocciu* and herbs, served in a tomato sauce, or spaghetti with lobster. In the north, *storzapreti* (priest-chokers) are a legacy of the Genoese: little balls of spinach and chard, poached and served with grated cheese. Omelettes with *brocciu* are a vegetarian standby, as are courgettes, aubergines or artichokes filled with *brocciu*. Little pies, such as *inciulate* or *chaussons*, packed with chard and onion, or pumpkin or cheese, or mashed potato (*sciacci*) or even pork or boar pâté, can be a starter or just a snack, while many restaurants do *beignets* filled with dried cod, leeks, onions, courgettes, or *brocciu*.

Game

Corscians are avid hunters, to put it mildly, and in autumn and winter game rules the menu – partridge, hare, quail, pigeon, thrush and duck star in many dishes. One Corsican classic, **blackbird pâté** (*pâté de merle*) flavoured with myrtle, was an old favourite of Alice B. Toklas, but (supposedly) is illegal now, and made with starlings (*sansonnets*) instead. But the star of the show is **wild boar** (*cignale*), bagged by the village *chasse* to end up in terrines, sausages, pâtés, *civets*, *en daube*, or in lasagne.

Seafood

Although Corsica is surrounded by crystal seas swarming with fish, it was never a big part of the islanders' traditional diet; like their neighbours, the Sards, the Corsicans were shepherds and landlubbers, at Lent sticking to the dried cod delivered in shiploads by the Genoese, as well as sardines and sometimes anchovies and mackerel. Tourists like fish, however, and the seas have been overfished in past few decades (the number of fish caught is half what it was in the 1980s); now some 200 fishermen bring back what they can in a day, and usually sell the catch at the quay direct to restaurants. The usual Mediterranean denizens of the deep star on menus along the coast, often in restaurants owned by fishermen. Special mention must be made of the *langoustes* (spiny lobsters) around Calvi and Cap Corse, and Corsica's *oursins* (sea urchins), generally considered among the finest in the Mediterranean, but edible only from November to March; they're in such demand as a pasta sauce (*crème aux oursins*) or in omelettes that swimmers hardly ever step on them any more. On the east coast, meaty **mussels** and **oysters** are farmed in the Etangs de Diane and d'Urbino. In the mountains **trout** features on the menu, often prepared *à la corse*, fried with garlic and vinegar or filled with *brocciu*.

Meat

On the island of shepherds, **lamb** (*agnellu*) is the favourite meat, usually grilled or roasted, or prepared *en perbronata*, a sauce of tomatoes and peppers, or in a stew (*tianu*). **Kid** (*cabrettu*) is popular as well, especially at Christmas; roasted with oregano or stewed and spicy in the classic *cabrettu a l'istrettu* or marinated in vinegar and spices in *misgiscia*, then roasted or mixed in a ragoût. Kid and lamb also feature in *stifatu*, a classic Sunday dish, marinated in white wine, stuffed with bacon and *cèpes*, served with macaroni and covered with grated cheese. Corsica's free-range **veal** (*vitellu*) is tasty and served in a variety of ways, including a ragoût with olives, cabbage, peas, tomatoes, peppers and potatoes. *Tripette*, or tripe in tomato sauce, is another favourite. In autumn, look for side dishes with wild mushrooms – Corsica has plenty, and there are several guides available.

Desserts and Other Sweet Things

I morti incù i morti / E'i vivi incù e fritelle
(The dead with the dead / And the living with the doughnuts)
old Corsican saying

Corsicans often finish dinner with a piece of fruit, but they also have some desserts you won't find elsewhere. Special mention must be made of *fritelli* – doughnuts that are an obsession of New England proportions: they can be sweet and round, made of chestnut or wheat flour or filled with *brocciu*, or with apples flavoured with citron.

A whole range of desserts come from **chestnuts**: *parfaits* and flans; **pisticchini** (chestnut soufflé); chestnut crêpes filled with preserved citron (*cédrat confit*) and set alight with *eau-de-vie*; **torta castagnina**, a flat cake made of chestnut flour and ground walnuts; and **migliacci** (or **falculelli**), soft biscuits with *brocciu* baked on chestnut leaves. *Brocciu* also figures in the classic **fiadone**, a cheese tart flavoured with lemon, and in *brioche*-like **campanili**. **Canistrelli**, hard biscuits made with olive oil and honey and flavoured with aniseed or lemon, are delicious dipped in wine.

Don't pass up a chance to try Corsican **honey**, prized since ancient Roman times as the 'honey of honeys', especially the white honey from the Valle d'Asco; in 1999 it was even sent up into space, to supply the Mir space station. It is the only honey in France to have AOC status. There are six distinct AOC varieties: spring honey, spring *maquis* honey, chestnut honey (quite strong), *maquis* honey, summer *maquis* honey and autumn *maquis* honey, as well as special honeys from asphodel, clementine blossoms and arbutus. The Corsicans are also master jam-makers, mixing and matching figs, clementines, lemons, almonds and chestnuts.

Drink

Water

Corsica's tap water, from its mountain streams, is the best in France, but it also bottles its four different mineral waters. There are two still ones: trendy Saint-Georges (one of the few mineral waters without a trace of nitrates) in a pale blue bottle designed by Philippe Starck, and the more common Zilia from the Balagne; and two sparklers, Acqua Corsa and the fabled iron-rich Orezza, served at some of France's top restaurants (*see* p.193).

Wine

One glass of Corsican wine and I climb Stromboli
old Tuscan proverb

Although the Corsicans themselves aren't big drinkers, wine-making on Corsica has a long history. Introduced by the Greeks in Alalia in the 6th century BC, vines thrived on the combination of the granite-schist soil and constant sun moderated by mountains and sea; in later years even Virgil the connoisseur praised the wine of the Balagne. Then came centuries of trouble, before the vineyards prospered again under the Genoese, who in 1572 ordered every landowner to plant four vines and ten fruit trees. The rules were that the wine they made could only be sold to Genoa, where the locals developed such a taste for it that they continued to import it even after Corsica became French. But as the proverb suggests, it was rustic, explosive stuff.

After the 19th-century phylloxera epidemic that decimated French vines, the renewal of the local wine industry only really took off with the beginning of tourism; in the 1960s, French-Algerian *pieds-noirs* repatriated along Corsica's east coast seized on this ready summer market, producing vast quantities of rough table wine on 80,000 acres of land. When it was discovered that certain growers were cheating to increase production even further, and giving Corsican wine a bad reputation, the resulting scandal had repercussions far beyond the world of wine (*see* p.178).

Since those dark days, however, the island's wines have since undergone a major renaissance and are probably better than they've ever been. Led by fabled grower Antoine Arena in Patrimonio, Corsica's 350 wine-makers in the past two decades have uprooted over three-quarters of the 'easy' high-yield vines used for *vin de table* and replanted much smaller *domaines* with superior, low-yielding varieties; from 80,000 acres cultivated in the 1970s, today only 18,000 acres are under vines.

Wine Regions

Ajaccio (Clos Capitoro, Comte Peraldi, Clos d'Alzeto): Famous for its *sciaccarellu*, here designated a cru, producing excellent rosés and harmonious reds that improve with age. Clos Capitoro's rare Corsican *blanc de blanc* won a gold medal in Paris in 1998. A new producer to look out for is Ornasca, which bottled its first wines in 1995 and has already won accolades.

Patrimonio (Arena, Orenga de Gaffory, Leccia, Clos de Bernardi, Cordoliani, Gentile, Paoli, Clos Signadore): The oldest AOC district on Corsica, and the only one on limestone rather than granite. The main grape is *niellucciu*, producing powerful, well-structured red wines; Patrimonio's fruity whites, fresh rosés and excellent muscats, made from teeny-tiny grapes, have graced papal tables in the past.

Corse-Sartè (San Michele, Saparale, Pero Longo, San Armettu, Fiumicicoli): From Sartène, very much the up-and-coming wine area, recognized with top prizes in Paris for their very distinguished *sciaccarellu* reds of great character; these were Napoleon's favourite, and there are plenty of people today who agree.

Calvi (Clos Reginu, Clos Columbu, Orsini): Produces equal amounts of reds and rosés from *sciaccarellu*, with a fine bouquet, and whites reminiscent of Graves. In the Middle Ages, Calvi's *vermentinu* was reserved for bishops and monasteries. Orsini's rosé is an excellent match for garlicky dishes such as *soupe de poisson*.

Coteaux de Cap Corse (Clos Nicrosi): From a mere 75-acre growing area, excellent reds that can take ageing, but the peninsula is especially known for its delicate flowery, perfumed whites made from *vermentinu*.

Muscat de Capi Corsu: A handful of growers in the same region also produces a highly prized golden muscat, on pocket-sized plots – well worth tracking down.

Corse-Figari: the southernmost vine region in France grows distinctive wines on an arid windy plateau with mostly *sciaccarellu*, although some of the best are the white wines from the Domaine de Tanella. Look for traditional Corsican grape varieties, such as Carcajolu Neru.

Corse-Porti-Vechju: Known for elegant reds from *sciaccarellu* with percentages of *niellucciu* that age well (Torraccia's organically grown Cuvée Oriu in particular), plus cracking rosés and dry and exceptionally fruity whites.

Corse: Essentially the wines from the fertile east coast and valley of Golo, and here too there are major improvements that have all but wiped out the memory of the former plonk: much of the *grenache*, *cinsault* and *carignan* is being replaced with *niellucciu* and *vermentinu*, with very encouraging results.

Under the general AOC Corse umbrella there are eight *appellations d'origine contrôlée*, which now account for a third of the total production. Thirty varieties are grown, but three 'Corsican' grapes dominate. Granite-loving **sciaccarellu** (or *schiuchita-jolu*, literally 'crunchy') is unique to the island, similar to *pinot noir*, and makes clear red wines and rosés with hints of pepper, raspberry and coffee. **Niellucciu**, similar to sangiovese, the prime Chianti grape, was introduced by the Genoese in the 13th century, and is the grape that makes Patrimonio great, producing intense, gamey red wines perfumed with the flowers of the *maquis* and forest fruits. Both can take considerable ageing. **Vermentinu**, a relative of malmsey, yields excellent dry white wines with a floral, almond bouquet and a high alcohol content. For a complete list of producers, see *www.vinsdecorse.com*. For the names to trust, *see* box, p.47.

The common toast in Corsica is *'A vostra saluta'*, and *'Grazie tantu'* is the response. Old-school traditionalists shake the last few drops in their glass on to the ground, as an offering to the gods.

Beer

It's hit the beer-drinking world by storm: **Pietra**, an artisanal beer made from toasted chestnut flour and brewed since 1996 at Furiani, now one of France's biggest independent breweries. It's exported all over the world, and in many places has achieved cult status. The brewery makes three kinds, the dark amber Pietra (6%) and the blond ale Serena (4.8%), with a slight lemony aftertaste, and Colomba (5%), a prizewinning white unpasteurized (hence cloudy) beer flavoured with *maquis* herbs; they are so different that chefs have begun creating new recipes that make use of their distinctive flavours. There's also a new light beer, Torra, flavoured with arbutus or myrtle.

Whisky

There's also something new to look for: Corsican whisky. Pietra and the Mavella distillery have combined forces to make **P&M** whisky, using malt from chestnut flour, and maturing it in old Patrimonio muscat barrels. A second Corsican whisky is **Altore**, currently distilled from three malts in Scotland and brought to Corsica to age in Patrimonio barrels, although there are plans to move everything to Corsica.

Apéritifs and Liqueurs

Corsica has some classic *apéritifs*. Sweet muscat from the Cap is made into **Cap Corse** by Mattei, a vermouth-like tipple, with quinquina, oranges and herbs from the *maquis*. **Pastis**, the classic aniseed tipple of the south is also popular: look for local labels **Casanis** and the new competition, called **Mannarini**. Also look for *vins de fruit*, made from macerating fruit (especially peaches and clementines) in wine, as well as an excellent range of sweetish liqueurs from fruit and herbs, that some drink as *apéros*, and some as a *digestif*: **bonapartine**, from oranges and tangerines; **limonocinu corsu** (like *limoncello*) or the more powerful **cédratine**, made from *cédrats* or citrons; **liqueur de myrte**, with myrtle; or **liqueur Orsini** made from chestnuts.

The classic *digestif*, however, is **eau-de-vie** or *acquavita*, made from wine, and Corsica (especially Mavella) makes excellent ones, sometimes again flavoured with fruits.

French Menu Decoder

Also *see* Corsican specialities (pp.42–6).

Hors-d'œuvre et Soupes (Starters and Soups)

amuse-gueule appetizers
assiette assortie plate of mixed cold *hors-d'œuvre*
bouchées mini *vol-au-vents*
bouillabaisse famous fish soup of Marseille
bouillon broth
charcuterie mixed cold meats, salami, ham, etc.
consommé clear soup
crudités raw vegetable platter
potage thick vegetable soup
velouté thick smooth soup, often fish or chicken

Poissons et Coquillages (Crustacés) (Fish and Shellfish)

anchois anchovies
anguille eel
bar sea bass
barbue brill
baudroie anglerfish
belons flat oysters
bigorneau winkle
blanchailles whitebait
brème bream
bulot whelk
cabillaud cod
calmar squid
colin hake
congre conger eel
coques cockles
coquillages shellfish
coquilles St-Jacques scallops
crabe crab
crevettes grises shrimp
crevettes roses (gambaru) prawns
cuisses de grenouilles frogs' legs
darne slice or steak of fish
daurade (muvone, uchjonu) sea bream
denti dentex
écrevisse freshwater crayfish
escargots snails
espadon (spadone, pesciuspada) swordfish
esturgeon sturgeon
flétan halibut
friture (frittura) whitebait/deep-fried fish
fruits de mer seafood
gambas giant prawns

gigot de mer a large fish cooked whole
grondin red gurnard
hareng herring
homard Atlantic lobster
huîtres (ostrice) oysters
lamproie lamprey
langouste (arigosta) spiny lobster
langoustines Dublin Bay prawns
limande lemon sole
lotte monkfish
loup (rangola, luvazzu) sea bass
maquereau mackerel
merlan whiting
mérou (lucerna) grouper
morue salt cod
moules mussels
muge mullet
murène moray eel
oblade silver bream
oursin sea urchin
pagel/pageot sea bream
palourdes clams
poulpe (polpu) octopus
praires small clams
raie (raza) skate
rascasse scorpion fish
requin shark
rouget (triglia/russiciu) red mullet
sabre (sciabula) scabbard or cutlass fish
sar silver bream
saumon salmon
St-Pierre John Dory
seiche cuttlefish
telline tiny clam
thon tuna
truite trout

Viandes et Volailles (Meat and Poultry)

ailerons wings
biftek beefsteak
blanc breast or white meat
blanquette stew of white meat, thickened with egg yolk
bœuf beef
boudin blanc sausage of white meat
boudin noir black pudding
brochette meat (or fish) on a skewer
caille quail
canard, caneton duck, duckling
capre kid
carré the best end of a cutlet or chop.
cervelle brains
chair flesh, meat
chapon capon

cheval horsemeat

civet meat (usually game) stewed in wine and blood sauce

cœur heart

confit meat cooked and preserved in its own fat

côte, côtelette chop, cutlet

cuisse thigh or leg

dinde, dindon turkey

entrecôte ribsteak

épaule shoulder

faisan pheasant

faux-filet sirloin

foie liver

frais de veau veal testicles

fricadelle meatball

gésier gizzard

gibier game

gigot leg of lamb

graisse or *gras* fat

grillade grilled meat, often a mixed grill

grive thrush

jambon ham

jarret knuckle

langue tongue

lapereau young rabbit

lapin rabbit

lard (lardons) bacon (diced bacon)

lièvre hare

magret de canard breast of duck

marcassin young wild boar

moelle bone marrow

mouton mutton

museau muzzle

noix de veau (agneau) topside of veal (lamb)

oie goose

os bone

perdreau or *perdrix* partridge

petit salé salt pork

pieds trotters

pintade guinea fowl

plat-de-côtes short ribs or rib chops

porc pork

pot au feu meat and vegetables cooked in stock

poulet chicken

poussin baby chicken

quenelle poached dumplings made of fish, fowl or meat

queue de bœuf oxtail

ris (de veau) sweetbreads (veal)

rognons kidneys

rosbif roast beef

rôti roast

sanglier wild boar

saucisses sausages

saucisson dry sausage, like salami

selle (d'agneau) saddle (of lamb)

steak tartare raw minced beef, often topped with a raw egg yolk

tournedos thick round slices of beef fillet

travers de porc spare ribs

tripes tripe

veau veal

venaison venison

Légumes, Herbes, etc. (Vegetables, Herbs, etc.)

ail garlic

aïoli garlic mayonnaise

algue seaweed

aneth dill

anis anise

artichaut artichoke

asperge asparagus

aubergine aubergine (eggplant)

avocat avocado

basilic basil

betterave beetroot

blette Swiss chard

bouquet garni mixed herbs in a little bag

cannelle cinnamon

céleri celery

céleri-rave celeriac

cèpes ceps, wild boletus mushrooms

champignons mushrooms

chanterelles wild yellow mushrooms

chicorée curly endive

chou cabbage

chou-fleur cauliflower

ciboulette chives

citrouille pumpkin

clou de girofle clove

cœur de palmier palm heart

concombre cucumber

cornichons gherkins

courgettes courgettes (zucchini)

cresson watercress

échalote shallot

endive chicory (endive)

épinards spinach

estragon tarragon

fenouil fennel

fèves broad (fava) beans

flageolets white beans

fleurs de courgette courgette flowers

frites chips (French fries)

genièvre juniper
gingembre ginger
haricots (rouges, blancs) (kidney, white) beans
haricot verts green (French) beans
jardinière with diced garden vegetables
laitue lettuce
laurier bay leaf
lentilles lentils
(épis de) maïs sweetcorn (on the cob)
marjolaine marjoram
menthe mint
mesclun salad of various leaves
morilles morel mushrooms
navet turnip
oignons onions
oseille sorrel
panais parsnip
persil parsley
petits pois peas
piment pimiento
poireaux leeks
pois chiches chickpeas
pois mange-tout sugar peas or mangetout
poivron sweet pepper
pomme de terre potato
potiron pumpkin
primeurs young vegetables
radis radishes
riz rice
romarin rosemary
roquette rocket (arugula)
safran saffron
salade verte green salad
salsifis salsify
sarriette savory
sarrasin buckwheat
sauge sage
seigle rye
thym thyme
truffes truffles

Fruits et Noix (Fruit and Nuts)

abricot apricot
amandes almonds
ananas pineapple
banane banana
bigarreau black cherries
brugnon nectarine
cacahouètes peanuts
cassis blackcurrant
cédrat citron
cerises cherries
citron lemon
citron vert lime

(noix de) coco coconut
coing quince
dattes dates
figues (de Barbarie) figs (prickly pear)
fraises (des bois) (wild) strawberries
framboises raspberries
fruit de la passion passion fruit
grenade pomegranate
groseilles redcurrants
lavande lavender
mandarine tangerine
mangue mango
marrons chestnuts
mirabelles mirabelle plums
mûre (sauvage) mulberry, blackberry
myrtilles bilberries
noisette hazelnut
noix walnuts
noix de cajou cashews
pamplemousse grapefruit
pastèque watermelon
pêche (pêche blanche) peach (white peach)
pignons pine-nuts
pistache pistachio
poire pear
pomme apple
prune plum
pruneau prune
raisins (secs) grapes (raisins)
reine-claude greengage plums

Desserts

Bavarois mousse or custard in a mould
biscuit biscuit, cracker, cake
bombe ice-cream dessert in a round mould
bonbons sweets, candy
brioche light sweet yeast bread
charlotte sponge fingers and custard cream
   dessert
chausson turnover
clafoutis baked batter pudding with fruit
compote stewed fruit
corbeille de fruits basket of fruit
coulis thick fruit sauce
coupe ice cream: a scoop or in cup
crème anglaise egg custard
crème caramel vanilla custard with
   caramel sauce
crème Chantilly sweet whipped cream
crème fraîche slightly sour cream
crème pâtissière thick custard cream filling for
   pastries, made with eggs
gâteau cake
gaufre waffle

glace ice cream
madeleine small sponge cake
miel honey
mousse 'foam': frothy dessert
parfait frozen mousse
profiteroles choux pastry balls, often filled
   with chocolate or ice cream
sablé shortbread
savarin a filled cake, shaped like a ring
tarte, tartelette tart, little tart
truffes chocolate truffles
yaourt yoghurt

Fromage (Cheese)
(fromage de) brebis sheep's cheese
chèvre goat's cheese
doux mild
fromage blanc yoghurty cream cheese
fromage frais a bit like sour cream
fort strong

Cooking Terms and Sauces
bien cuit well-done steak
à point medium steak
saignant rare steak
bleu very rare steak

aigre-doux sweet and sour
aiguillette thin slice
à la jardinière with garden vegetables
au feu de bois cooked over a wood fire
au four baked
beignets fritters
à la broche roasted on a spit
chaud hot
cru raw
cuit cooked
diable spicy mustard or green pepper sauce
émincé thinly sliced
en croûte cooked in a pastry crust
en papillote baked in buttered paper
épices spices
farci stuffed
feuilleté flaky pastry
fourré stuffed
frais, fraîche fresh
frappé with crushed ice
frit fried
froid cold
fumé smoked
galette flaky pastry case or pancake
garni with vegetables
(au) gratin topped with breadcrumbs
grillé grilled
haché minced

médaillon round piece
moutarde mustard
pané breaded
pâte pastry, pasta
paupiette rolled and filled thin slices of fish
   or meat
pavé slab
piquant spicy hot
poché poached
salé salted, spicy
sucré sweet
tranche slice
à la vapeur steamed

Miscellaneous
addition bill (check)
beurre butter
confiture jam
couteau knife
crème cream
cuillère spoon
fourchette fork
huile (d'olive) (olive) oil
nouilles noodles
œufs eggs
pain bread
pâte pastry, pasta
poivre pepper
sel salt
sucre sugar
vinaigre vinegar

Boissons (Drinks)
bière (pression) draught beer
(demi) bouteille half-bottle
chocolat chaud hot chocolate
café coffee
café au lait white coffee
café express espresso coffee
café filtre filter coffee
citron/orange pressé(e) fresh lemon/orange
   juice served with water and sugar syrup
demi 25cl draught beer 37.5cl wine/
   champagne
eau (minérale, non-gazeuse/plate or *gazeuse)*
   (mineral, still or sparkling) water
glaçons ice cubes
infusion, tisane herbal tea
jus juice
lait milk
pression draught
thé tea
verre glass
vin blanc/rosé/rouge white/rosé/red wine

Travel

Getting There

Although there are direct and charter flights from the UK, from most other points your best bet is to fly to Paris, Marseille or Nice and from there catch a cheap domestic flight to Corsica. If you would like to combine your journey with a short Mediterranean ferry trip, look into flights to Marseille, Genoa or Nice.

By Air

Corsica has four **airports**, at Ajaccio, Bastia, Calvi and Figari (in the south by Bonifacio), and flying there directly from the UK, even in high season (Easter and summer), works out cheaper than the costs of overland transport and the ferries.

From the UK and Ireland

At the time of writing, the only **scheduled flights** to Corsica are to Bastia from London Gatwick on British Airways on Tues, Thurs and Sun from spring till mid-October. During the same period there are direct charters to Corsican airports, nearly always on a Sunday.

Regular scheduled flights out of season involves changing planes at a French airport – usually Paris, Nice or Marseille.

From the USA and Canada

There are frequent flights to Paris, the gateway to France, on most of the major airlines, as well as direct flights from New York to Nice on Delta and Air France, where you can get either a connecting flight or a ferry.

Airline Carriers

UK and Ireland

Air France, t 0870 142 4343, *www.airfrance.co.uk.*
British Airways, t 0870 850 9850, *www.ba.com.*
GB Airways, t 0870 850 9850, *www.gbairways.co.uk.*
easyJet, t 0905 821 0905, *www.easyjet.com.* To Nice or Marseille, from Luton, Stansted, Gatwick, Newcastle, Bristol, Liverpool or Belfast.
Jet2.com, t 0871 226 1737, *www.jet2.com.* To Nice from Manchester and Leeds Bradford.
BMI, t 0870 6070 555, *www.flybmi.com.* London Heathrow and Nottingham East Midlands to Nice, and charters to Corsica.
Ryanair, t 0906 270 5656, *www.ryanair.com.* London Stansted to Genoa, for a ferry.
Aer Lingus, t 0818 365000, *www.aerlingus.com.* Dublin or Cork to Nice or Marseille.

Websites
www.cheapflights.co.uk
www.expedia.co.uk
www.lastminute.com
http://travel.kelkoo.co.uk
www.opodo.co.uk

USA and Canada
Air Canada, t 888 567 4160 (Canada), **t** 800 268 0024 (USA), *www.aircanada.ca.*
American, t 800 433 7300, *www.aa.com.*

Air France, t 800 237 2747, *www.airfrance.us* (Canada **t** 800 667 2747, *www.airfrance.ca*).
Alitalia, t 800 223 5730, *www.alitaliausa.com* (Canada *www.alitalia.ca*).
British Airways, t 800 AIRWAYS, *www.ba.com.*
Continental, t 800 231 0856, *www.continental.com.*
Delta, t 800 241 4141, *www.delta.com.*
United, t 800 538 2929, *www.united.com.*
Virgin Atlantic, t 800 821 5438, *www.virgin-atlantic.com.*

Websites
www.cheapflights.com
www.courier.org (courier flights)
www.ebookers.com
www.expedia.com
www.traveldiscounts.com
www.travelocity.com
http://travel.priceline.com

Charters and Discounts

Charter Flight Centre, t 0845 045 0153 *www.charterflights.co.uk.*
Flights4less, t 0871 222 3432, *www.flights4less.co.uk.*
Holiday Options, t 0870 013 0450. *www.holidayoptions.co.uk.* Flight-only options.
Trailfinders, 194 Kensington High St, London W8, **t** (020) 7937 1234, *www.trailfinders.co.uk.*
Western Air, t 0870 330 1100, *www.westernair.co.uk.*

From Mainland France to Corsica

Air France, t 0802 802 802, *www.airfrance.fr.*
Flies year-round from Paris Orly to Ajaccio, Bastia and Calvi.

CCM Air, t 04 95 29 05 09, *www.aircorsica.com,* *www.ccm-airlines.com.* Links Corsica's four airports to Bordeaux, Lille, Lyon, Marseille, Toulouse, Nantes and Strasbourg. Good fly/drive discounts.

Ollandini, t 04 95 23 92 91, *www.ollandini-voyages.fr.* Specialists in flights to Corsica, plus hotels and other deals.

By Land and Sea

Getting to the Ports: By Train

If you hate flying and driving, France's high-speed **TGVs** (*trains à grande vitesse,* see *www.tgv.com*) offer an attractive alternative for getting from Paris to Marseille or Nice, although if you take the **Eurostar** (**t** 08705 186 186, *www.eurostar.com*) from London you'll have to change trains in Paris. TGVs shoot along at an average of 170mph, and the journey from Paris Gare de Lyon to Marseille (11 daily) now takes only 3hrs 10mins. For Toulon or Nice, you'll have to change in Marseille. Costs are only minimally higher on a TGV. People under 26 are eligible for a 30 per cent discount on fares and there are other discounts if you're 60 or over. For other special offers, advance reservations and car hire information, *see www.voyages-sncf.com.*

Rail Europe UK, 178 Piccadilly, London W1, **t** 08708 371 371, *www.raileurope.co.uk.*

Rail Europe USA/Canada t 877 257 2887 (USA), **t** 800 361 RAIL (Canada), *www.raileurope.com.*

Getting to the Ports: By Coach

The most excruciating way to get from the UK to the south of France, short of crawling on your hands and knees, is by **National Express Eurolines** coach, **t** 08705 80 80 80, *www.eurolines.com.* Tickets are available from any National Express office. There are four journeys a week to Marseille (19hrs); prices are from around £99 return.

Getting to the Ports: By Car

Marseille is the closest port to Corsica if you're driving, 1,100km from Calais. The various *autoroutes* will get you south fastest but be prepared to pay some €70 in tolls; the N7 south of Paris takes much longer, but costs nothing and offers great scenery.

A car entering France must have its registration and insurance papers, and if you're coming from the UK or Ireland the dip of the headlights must be adjusted to the right. Carrying a warning triangle is mandatory. Driving in the mountains of Corsica can be rough on a car, and it's important that everything (especially the brakes!) is in top nick. Drivers with a valid licence from an EU country, Canada, the USA or Australia no longer need an international licence.

The **ferry** to mainland France is a good option by car or with children (aged 4–14 get reduced rates; under-4s go free). Fares vary according to season and demand (these days, annoyingly, the brochures will only print a rough 'price guide'). The most expensive booking period runs from the first week of July to mid-August; other pricey times include Easter. Book as far ahead as possible and keep your eyes peeled for special offers.

Putting your car on a **Eurotunnel** train (**t** 08705 35 35 35, *www.eurotunnel.com*) is

Channel Ferry Companies

Brittany Ferries, t 08703 665 333, *www.brittanyferries.com.* Sailings from Portsmouth to Caen (6hrs) and St-Malo, from Poole to Cherbourg (4½hrs), and from Plymouth to Roscoff (6hrs).

Condor Ferries, t 0845 243 5140, *www.condorferries.co.uk.* Sailings from Weymouth and Poole to St-Malo.

Hoverspeed, t 0870 240 8070, *www.hoverspeed.co.uk.* Seacats Dover–Calais (35mins), Folkestone–Boulogne (55mins), Newhaven–Dieppe (2hrs).

Norfolkline, t 08708 70 10 20, *www.norfolkline.com.* Dover to Dunkerque, but for cars only, not foot passengers.

P&O Ferries, t 08705 20 20 20, *www.poferries.com.* Portsmouth to Le Havre (5½hrs) and Dover to Calais (45mins).

SeaFrance, t 08705 711 711, *www.seafrance.com.* Dover to Calais (1½hrs).

Speed Ferries, t 08702 200 570, *www.speedferries.com.* Dover to Boulogne.

Transmanche, t 0800 917 1201, *www.transmancheferries.com.* Newhaven to Dieppe.

perhaps a more convenient way of crossing the Channel. It takes only 35mins from Folkestone to Calais, and there are up to four departures an hour 365 days of the year. If you travel at night (10pm–6am), it will be slightly cheaper. The price for all tickets is for each car less than 6.5m in length, plus the driver and passengers. **French Motorail** (**t** 08702 415 415, *www.raileurope.co.uk/frenchmotorail*) is a comfortable but costly option for travelling on from Calais that involves putting your car on the train. Services run from May to September from Calais to Nice. Prices for four travelling are over £1,000 return.

For breakdown cover in France contact the **AA**, **t** 0800 085 2840, *www.theaa.com*, or **RAC**, **t** 0800 550 550, *www.rac.co.uk*.

By Ferry from France and Italy

You can sail to Corsica from France or Italy (which is three times closer to the island and much cheaper), and buy tickets online for nearly all companies at *www.aferry.co.uk*.

If you plan to sail in July or August, especially from France, book as soon as possible. Times range from the 12hr overnight ferries from Marseille to Bastia to a mere 2hrs 45mins on the NGV from Nice to Bastia. When choosing a destination port, remember that Corsican roads are very winding, and it takes about five hours to drive from Calvi to Ajaccio. Prices vary widely according to season (red – the highest – to white, green and blue periods).

Entry Formalities

Passports and Visas

Holders of EU, US, Canadian, Australian, New Zealand, Hong Kong and Japanese passports do not need a visa to enter France for stays of up to three months, but everyone else still does; contact your nearest French consulate.

If you intend to stay longer, non-EU citizens need a *carte de séjour*. Apply for an extended visa before leaving home, a complicated procedure requiring proof of income, etc. You can't get a *carte de séjour* without the visa. Apply for the *carte de séjour* at the *mairie*.

Customs

Those arriving from another EU country do not have to declare goods imported into France for personal use. Customs will be likely to ask questions if you buy in bulk, e.g. more than 3,200 cigarettes or 400 cigarillos, 200 cigars or 3kg of tobacco; plus 10 litres of spirits, 90 litres of wine and 110 litres of beer.

Travellers from outside the EU must pay duty on goods worth more than €175 imported into Corsica.

Travellers from the USA are allowed to take home, duty-free, goods to the value of $800, including 200 cigarettes or 100 cigars; plus one litre of alcohol. You're not allowed to bring back absinthe or Cuban cigars.

Ferry Companies

SNCM (in France), **t** (+33) (0)8 25 88 80 88, *www.sncm.fr*. Sailings from Marseille, Toulon and Nice to Bastia, Ajaccio, Calvi and Ile-Rousse, plus Porto-Vecchio and Propriano in season. Owned by the state and committed to public year-round service, but heavily indebted and may be partially privatized – hence the strikes that left thousands of tourists stranded on Corsica in September 2005. Ask about the economical *Tarif Plein Soleil*, which offers the best fares, at certain times of the year. SNCM also runs the **NGVs** (*Navires à Grande Vitesse*) that take only 2hours 45mins from Nice to Calvi.

CMN, **t** (+33) (0)8 01 20 13 20, *www.cmn.fr*. CMN carries freight as well as cars and people (they have a range of cabins as well).

Night sailings year-round out of Marseille to Ajaccio, Bastia and Propriano, continuing twice a week to Porto Torres (Sardinia).

Corsica Ferries, **t** (+33) (0)4 95 32 95 95 (in Bastia), or Viamare Travel in London, **t** 0870 410 6040, *www.corsicaferries.com*. Fast ferries in summer from Nice, Livorno, Toulon and Savona to Bastia; from Nice and Toulon to Ajaccio; from Toulon and Nice to L'Ile-Rousse; from Nice and Savona to Calvi.

Moby Lines, **t** (+49) 6111 4020, *www.mobylines.com*. The ferries with the big blue whales on their sides sail from Genoa and Livorno to Bastia, and from Santa Teresa di Gallura in Sardinia to Bonifacio.

Medmar Linee Lauro, **t** (+39) 081 551 3352, *www.medmargroup.it*. Links Naples to Palau (Sardinia) and Porto-Vecchio.

Getting Around

Public transport on Corsica is limited, so you'll need a car, motorbike, bicycle or a good pair of walking boots to get around.

By Train

Information, t 04 95 32 80 60.

The Chemins de Fer Corses is a one-metre narrow-gauge railway of 1888, run by a little train known as a *micheline*, nicknamed the *Trinighellu*, or 'Trembler'. The line is a marvel of engineering, and well worth a ride just for the scenery: dramatic ravines and mountains. There's a 158km route from Bastia to Ajaccio (4 trains a day, out of season only 2 a day, and none on Sunday) with a branch from Bastia to Calvi, changing at Ponte Leccia. The train is a walker's best friend, with stations at the junctions of paths in the Parc Naturel Régional in Corte and Vizzavona, but in summer you will need to arrive early to get a seat. At the time of writing, there may be delays, as a massive 11-year renovation is under way that will increase the number of trains and cut the Ajaccio–Bastia journey to 3hrs.

By Bus

A sometimes confusing array of private bus companies serves the main towns of the coast and interior, but not with any great frequency; most Corsicans have cars, and schedules tend to be aimed at getting students to school. In the summer season services are more frequent, but it's best to ring the companies first; local phone numbers are listed throughout the text of this guide.

By Car

Driving is the easiest way to see Corsica, but it has its drawbacks: pricey petrol and narrow mountain roads pitted with potholes that are usually empty in May and October but become nightmarish in July and August, especially the narrow, bendy, vertiginous ones. Consider tooting a warning as you approach. Another hazard for the pottering tourist is the native Corsicans, who have an Italian-style video-game approach behind the wheel. When they breathe down your neck, slow down and signal to the right at the first opportunity to let them overtake. Other hazards include an extraordinary number of animals – cows, sheep, goats, dogs, pigs, donkeys, wild boar, chickens, kittens and dogs – you name it, they're just around the bend. **Signposting** can be non-existent or misleading (die-hard nationalists not only blacken the French name of towns, or shoot it full of holes, but occasionally even turn signs the wrong way), so bring a good map.

Speed limits are 110km/69mph on dual carriageways; 90km/55mph on other roads; 50km/30mph in an 'urbanized area' (once you pass a white sign with a town's name on it and until you pass another sign with the town's name barred). Fines for speeding begin at €200 and can be astronomical if you fail the breathalyser. If you wind up in an **accident**, the procedure is to fill out and sign a *constat amiable*. If your French isn't sufficient to deal with this, hold off until you find someone to translate for you so you don't accidentally incriminate yourself. If you have a **breakdown** and are a member of a motoring club, ring them; if not, ring the police.

Always give **priority to the right** (*priorité à droite*) at any intersection – unless you're on a motorway or on a road with a yellow diamond 'priority route' sign. Although no longer part of the *code de la route*, this French anachronism can cause accidents. When you get lost in a city, the *toutes directions* or *autres directions* signs are 'Get Out of Jail Free' cards.

Petrol stations keep shop hours (most close Sunday and/or Monday) and are rare in rural areas, so check your fuel supply before planning any forays into the mountains.
Route planner: *www.mappy.fr.*
Autoroute information: *www.autoroutes.fr.*

Car Hire

If you mean to hire a car on Corsica, book one in advance, either on the Internet or in a fly/drive or package deal: a basic car starts at €180 a week. The minimum age for hiring a car is either 21 or 25, the maximum 70. Local numbers are listed throughout the text of this guide.

By Motorcycle

Motorcycles are one of the most popular means of getting around Corsica, although prices for hiring any bike over a 80cc scooter (the minimum oomph you'll need to get over the mountains) is nearly as expensive as car hire. This is mostly because of insurance, and it may not even cover you if you crash or the bike is stolen, although rental charges do include third party insurance and a helmet. Note, too, for most you'll need to have driven for at least two years; for larger models you'll need to have a motorcycle licence and be at least 23 years old. Try: **Corse Moto Evasion**, *www. corsicamoto.com*; **Corse Moto Services, t** 04 95 70 12 88, *www.corse-moto-service.com*; **Corsica Moto Rent**, *www.rent-car-corsica.com*.

By Bicycle

Cycling spells more pain than pleasure in most French minds, and this is especially true in Corsica. Even if you're fit, beware that roads can be excruciatingly narrow and not in the best repair. May and mid-September are the best months for a cycling holiday (not too hot and not too busy), although you'll need to pack rain gear.

Air France and British Airways carry bikes free from Britain. Other airlines will carry them as long as they're boxed and are included in your baggage weight. French trains with a bicycle symbol in the timetable carry bikes free; ferries carry them free or for a minimal charge. Bicycle and mountain bike (VTT) hire shops exist in larger towns.

Holiday Companies

In the UK

Corsican Affair, t (020) 7385 8438, *www.corsi canaffair.co.uk*. Apartments, hotels and villas.

Corsican Places, t 08701 605 744, *www.corsica. co.uk*. Properties with sporty options.

Direct Corsica, *www.directcorsica.com*. Special interest tours including the Castagniccia and walks, plus all kinds of accommodation.

Exodus, t 0870 240 5550, *www.exodus.co.uk*. Trekking and walking holidays.

French Golf Holidays, t (01277) 824100, *www. frenchgolfholidays.com*. For Sperone.

Inntravel, t (01653) 617788, *www.inntravel. co.uk*. A wide choice of walking holidays.

KE Adventure, t (01768) 773966, *www. keadventure.com*. Guided treks.

Mark Warner, t 0870 770 4227 *www. markwarner.co.uk*. Family holidays.

Nature Trek, t (01962) 733051, *www.naturetrek. co.uk*. Birdwatching and botanical walks.

Sherpa Expeditions, t (020) 8577 2717, *www. sherpa-walking-holidays.co.uk*. Self-guided walks and escorted GR20 treks.

Simply Travel, t (020) 8541 2205, *www.simply- travel.com*. Tailor-made 'Discovering Corsica' tours, hotels and self-catering properties.

Simpson Travel, t (020) 8392 5851, *www. simpson-travel.com*. Villas with pools, boutique hotels and rural retreats.

Tall Stories, t (01932) 252 002, *www.tallstories. co.uk*. Small-group active holidays in Corsica for all levels of expertise.

VFB Holidays, t (01242) 240310, *www.vfbhols. co.uk*. Fly-drive holidays.

Voyages Ilena, t (020) 7924 4440, *www. voyagesilena.co.uk*. Upscale villas and hotels.

The Villa Company, t (01756) 770 100, *www. villa-holiday-company.co.uk*. Choice of villas.

Hooked on Cycling, t (01501) 744 727, *www. hookedoncycling.co.uk*. Self-guided tours of Cap Corse and the Castagniccia.

World Walks, t (01242) 254353, *www.world walks.com*. Self-guided treks including GR20.

In the USA

Adventure Center, t 800 228 8747, *www. adventurecenter.com*. Guided walking tours.

Bike Riders Tours, t 800 473 7040, *www. bikeriderstours.com*. The name says it all.

Club1, t (866) 722 5821, *www.club1travel.com*. Singles' flotilla holidays around Corsica.

Headwater, t 800 567 6286,*www. headwater.com*. Walking holidays.

J World, t 800 666 1050, *www.jworld-sailing. com*. Bareboat sailing holidays.

Kalliste Tours, t (831) 438 0907, *www.kalliste tours.com*. Cultural, history, chestnut tours.

Sailing Paradise, t 1 888 864 7245, *www. sailingparadise.com*. Sail around Corsica.

Wayne and Sue's Adventures, t (877) 283 3551, *www.waynesue.com*. Hiking on the GR20.

In Australia

Walkabout Gourmet, t (03) 5159 6556, *www. walkaboutgourmet.com*. 'Soft' walking tours with an emphasis on food.

Practical A–Z

06

Climate

Corsica has a fine climate, one of the sunniest in France, perfect for growing olives, tangerines and grapes by the coast while snow powders the mountains. The visiting season runs from **April to October**, and, if you have the luxury of choosing, April, May and September are the very best months – in spring the *maquis* and wild flowers are in bloom, and days are nearly always bright and sunny, but the island is not intolerably hot, nor as crowded as in July and August. Although the highest passes may be blocked with snow into Easter, by **May** it's warm enough to swim; by mid-May you can hike in the mountains, although it can rain, and still snow in the higher reaches. **August**, when France and Italy are all on holiday, is the single worst month, when everything is crowded, temperatures, humidity and prices soar and afternoon electrical storms can make the mountains dangerous. Things calm down considerably by **September**. In **October** the weather is tradi-tionally mild on the coast and warm enough for days on the beach. Torrential downpours can happen at any time, but especially in the autumn. Most resort hotels close after October and don't re-open until Easter or later.

Winters are misty and moisty, although you can have a pretty good time in Ajaccio and points south, or walk the Mare a Mare Sud path (*see* p.72) and probably have it all to your-self. Gourmets will find many of Corsica's specialities – the game, chestnuts and more – at their peak in late autumn and winter.

Like all Mediterranean islands, Corsica's weather is influenced by the **winds**: the south-westerly *libeccio*, warm herald of rain; the hot and dry *sirocco* from North Africa, from the southeast; the *mistral* or *maistrale*, the cold and often powerful wind from the northwest; the *tramuntana* (or the *cracale* or the *grégal*) from the northeast; and the *levante* from the east.

Consulates and Embassies

UK: British Consulate-General, 24 Avenue de Prado, 13006 Marseille, **t** 04 91 15 72 10, *www.fco.gov.uk.*
USA: Consulate-General, 12 Place Varian Fry, 13086 Marseille, **t** 04 91 54 92 00, *www. amb-usa.fr/marseille/default.htm.*
Canada: Canadian Embassy in France, Ambassade du Canada, 35 Avenue Montaigne, 75008 Paris, **t** 01 44 43 29 00, *www.amb-canada.fr*; also 10 Rue Lamartine, 06000 Nice, **t** 04 93 92 93 22.
Ireland: 4 Rue Rude, 75116 Paris, **t** 01 44 17 67 00, *http://foreignaffairs.gov.ie/irishembassy/ France.htm.*
Australia: 4 Rue Jean Rey, 75015, Paris, **t** 01 40 59 33 00.

Crime and the Police

Police **t** 17

Although violence in Corsica is rare against tourists, thefts and car break-ins do happen and it's a good idea to insure valuables. Report thefts at the nearest police station or *gendarmerie*, if only to get the bit of paper you need for an insurance claim. If your passport is stolen, contact the police and your nearest consulate (*see* above) for emergency travel documents. If your credit cards are stolen, call the emergency numbers given on p.65. Carry photocopies of your passport, driver's licence, etc.; it makes it easier when reporting a loss.

By law, the police in France can stop anyone anywhere and demand an ID, so be prepared. You'd have to very unlucky to run into the CRS

Jan	Feb	Mar	April	May	June	July	Aug	Sept	Oct	Nov	Dec
Average Monthly Highs in °C (°F)											
13 (55)	14 (56)	15 (59)	17 (63)	20 (70)	24 (75)	27 (81)	27 (81)	25 (77)	21 (71)	17 (63)	14 (56)
Average Monthly Water Temperatures in °C (°F)											
13 (55)	13 (55)	13 (55)	14 (56)	16 (63)	20 (70)	24 (75)	25 (77)	23 (72)	21 (71)	18 (66)	15 (59)
Average Monthly Hours of Sunshine											
133	139	191	225	278	316	369	333	265	210	148	124

Calendar of Events

Corsicans have abandoned many of their traditional festivals, but have introduced new ones with an emphasis on culture. Note that this list is hardly exhaustive and can change from year to year; double-check listings in *Corse-Matin* and on local tourism sites.

January
Late Jan Mediterranean dance festival, Ajaccio

February
Festival of Italian film, Bastia
Clementine fair, Antisanti
A Tumbera, fair dedicated to traditional pig-killing festivities, with cooking contests, Renno (near Vico)

March
Spanish film festival, Bastia
Archaeology and history days, Calvi
Festival of the Sea, Bastia
18 *Notre-Dame de la Miséricorde*, Ajaccio
Festa di l'Oliu Novu, olive oil fair, Ste-Lucie-de-Tallano
Oursinade L'Ile-Rousse: a massive sea urchin-slurping festival

April
Festival of Comic Strips, Bastia
Week of British Cinema, Bastia
Chestnut Fair, Piedicroce
Second Sun Wine and cheese festival, Cauro
Holy Thurs *A granitula* spiral procession (*see* p.32), on the knees, Borgo and Canari
Easter *A Merendella* in Castagniccia; Easter fair at Piedicroce
Easter Orthodox rites at Cargèse, with rifles

Good Friday *U Catenacciu*, Sartène; Processions of the Five Orders in Bonifacio and San-Martino-di-Lota; Procession of the Black Christ, Bastia; procession *a granitula* in Calvi, also in Corte, Orezza and Erbalunga
Easter Mon Fair at Porto-Pollo

May
Festa di a Brocciu A day dedicated to Corsica's favourite cheese, Piana
1–2 *A Fiera di u Casgiu*, cheese festival, with competitions, music, etc., Venaco
Tour de Corse rally
I Pescadori in Festa, fishermen's festival, Ajaccio
Fiera di u Mare, sea festival, Solinzara
Festival des Arts Sonnés, concerts and street theatre, circuses, etc., Corte
Festival Ile Danse, contemporary dance, Ajaccio
Festival Folklorique, Bastia
Festimare, sea festival, Ile-Rousse
Nautival, sea festival, Macinaggio
Ascension Festival des 3 Cultures, Calvi
Medieval days, Bonifacio, celebrating the visit in 1541 by Charles V; costumes, music, dance and flag-throwing
La Route du Sud, cycling race in southern Corsica

June
2 Processions, races and more in honour of St Erasme, patron of fishermen, at Calvi, Ajaccio and Bastia
Les Voix du Lazaret, world music singing festival, Ajaccio
Jazz festival, Calvi
Photography Biennale (even years, Bastia)
Vivre la Corse en Velo, 600km cyclefest over six days

(*Compagnies Républicaines de Sécurité*), the national mobile swat teams you'll see rumbling around on Corsica to fight terrorism.

The drug situation is the same in France as anywhere in the West: soft and hard drugs are widely available, and the police only make an issue of victimless crime when it suits them (your being a foreigner just may rouse them to action). Smuggling any amount of marijuana into the country can mean a fine or prison term, and there's not much your consulate can or will do about it.

Disabled Travellers

When it comes to providing access for all, rugged, sparsely populated Corsica is hardly in the vanguard, and mountain or water sports for the disabled, catered for elsewhere in France, have yet to arrive, although, fingers crossed, it will change in the very near future. Newer hotels, apartments, *gîtes* and restaurants, however, are accessible to visitors with disabilities and SNCM ferries take passengers in wheelchairs (although they ask that you tell them when you buy a ticket).

La Nuit du Conte, storytelling, Vero

12–13 *Cavall'in*, regional horse fair, Corte, with a horse show, jumping, parades, markets and all-night music

23 *San Ghjuvà*, or St John's Day, traditional music, Corte; patron saint festival at Bastia

July

Nuits de la Guitare, Patrimonio, big international music festival

Estivoce, International singers and Corsicans, often together, in Pigna and the Balagne

Au Son des Mandolines, Ajaccio, the world's biggest mandolin festival

Fête du Livre Corse, L'Ile-Rousse

Calvi on the Rocks, rock festival, Calvi

Polyphonies de l'Eté, concerts in July and August, Ajaccio

Tutti in Piazza FestiBallu, popular dance festival, Corte

Cap Corse wine fair, Luri

Mediterranean Trophy sailboat races, from Corsica to northern Sardinia and back

Grand Raid Inter-Lacs. Gruelling foot race around seven lakes, Corte

First weekend Re-enactment of the changing of the governors, with pageantry, costumes, flag-throwing and drums, Bastia

10–11 *Fiera di San Petru*, traditional craft fair, with *chjam'è risponde* competitions, events and music, Lumio.

13 Foire de la Pierre, stone fair and fireworks, Lumio

14 Fireworks, parties, *batailles des fleurs* and celebrations for Bastille Day; usually horse races at Zonza

17–18 Olive fair, Montemaggiore, held in an olive grove, devoted to olives and their oil

Mid-month *Relève du Gouverneur de Bastia*

Sorru in Musica, 10 days of classical concerts at Vico and around

24–28 *Festa di u mare*, Santa Severa, boat races and carnival, all in honour of the sea

Ile Mouvante, Sant'Antonino. Two intensive weeks of arts, theatre, dance and music.

August

1 Pilgrimage up Monte San Petrone and Mass, Campana

1–2 Procession of the Brotherhoods and Festival of the Convent, Vico

5 Pilgrimage of Notre-Dame des Neiges, Bavella

Theatre Festival of Haute Corse, Giussani

Film Festival of the Rural World, Lama

Fêtes de Samperu Corsu, Bastelica

Festa Antica, Aléria, ancient Roman fun and games, fair, parades, music and fireworks

Porto Latino, Latin music festival, St-Florent

Traditional music festival, Sermano

Festival de Musique (jazz and guitar mostly), Erbalunga

Boziorando Via Romana, 50km race along mule paths in the Boziu region

Foire de l'Ane, donkey fair, Sant'Antonino

Almond fair, Aregno

Festa di u Legnu e di a Furesta, wood and forest fair, Vezzani, with lumberjack contests, chain saw sculptures and more

Hazelnut fair, Cervioni

Fiera di Filitosa, agricultural fair

Crafts fair, Baracci

Rencontres de Musiques Classiques et Contemporaines, Calenzana. Six nights of concerts

14 *Fête de l'Hospitalité*, Sartène

Specialist Organizations

UK

RADAR, 12 City Forum, 250 City Rd, London EC1V 8AF, **t** (020) 7250 3222, *www.radar.org.uk*.

Holiday Care Service, 7th floor, Sunley House, 4 Bedford Park, Croydon, CR0 2AP, **t** 0845 124 9971, *www.holidaycare.org.uk*.

Tripscope, The Vassall Centre, Gill Avenue, Bristol, BS16 2QQ, **t** 08457 58 56 41, *www.tripscope.org.uk*. Offers expert advice on every aspect of travel for elderly and disabled travellers.

Can be Done, **t** (020) 8907 2400, *www.canbedone.co.uk*. Specialist holidays.

USA and Canada

Mobility International USA, PO Box 10767, Eugene, OR 97440, USA, **t**/TTY (541) 343 1284, *www.miusa.org*.

SATH, 347 5th Avenue, Suite 610, New York NY 10016, **t** (212) 447 7284, *www.sath.org*.

Emerging Horizons, *www.emerginghorizons.com*. An international subscription-based online (or mailed) quarterly travel newsletter for people with disabilities.

13–15 *Fêtes Napoléoniennes*, Ajaccio, big birthday party for the Little Corporal, with parades, spectacles and fireworks
15–18 Assumption festivities, Calvi and Bastia
28–29 Trials for sheep dogs and pointers, Casamaccioli

September

U Settembrinu di Tavagna, international music festival in the villages of the Castagniccia
Festival d'Art Lyrique, Canari
Vivre la Corse en Velo, 600km cycle fest over six days (as in June)
Rencontres de Chants Polyphoniques, Calvi
6–8 Festival of *A Santa di U Niolu*, one of the oldest and best festivals on the Island, with traditional songs and ancient country fair, Casamaccioli
8 The Virgin's birthday: pilgrimage to Notre-Dame de Lavasina, Lavasina; *fête de Notre-Dame* and stuffed aubergines, Bonifacio; *fêtes* in Ste-Lucie-de-Moriani and Notre-Dame de la Serra, Calvi
Corsica Raid Adventure, Porticcio: teams compete in a variety of sports over a week; considered the best in Europe
Crafts fair, Porto-Vecchio
Festa di u Ficu, fig festival, Peri
Festi acqua, water festival, Propriano
Journées Napoléoniennes, Ajaccio, a special do for the Napoleonically obsessed, with costumes, films, scholarly debates, torchlight parades, collectables, books, actors and sound-and-light shows
Third Saturday La Paolina, 72km marathon from L'Ile-Rousse to Morosaglia
Last weekend *Mele in Festa*, honey fair, Murzo

October

Festiventu, Calvi, a popular event on the subject of the wind: new energy technologies, sports, culture and science
Musicales, Bastia, dedicated to all kinds of music, from Baroque opera to pop
U Festivale di u Filmu Arte Mare, Mediterranean film festival, Bastia
Journées Montagnes, between Ajaccio and Corte: cinema, songs, etc.
4 St Francis' day, celebrated at the Couvent San Damiano in Sartène with a recently revived 19th-century choral Mass.
International Chess Open, Bastia

November

1 Day of the Dead Mass, sung *a paghjella*, in Sermano
Chestnut fair, Evisa, with mushrooms, too
Festival du Film Espagnol, Spanish film festival, Ajaccio
Tour de Corse-Rallye de France, four days, all on asphalt – the last leg of the FIA World Championship Rally
Last weekend Apple and local products fair, Bastelica

December

Festival International de la BD, Ajaccio. Comic strip festival.
Fiera di a Castagna, Chestnut fair, Bocognano. A big winter get-together attracting tens of thousands of people, specializing in the variety of dishes made from chestnut flour, although general agricultural products and crafts are well represented too.
Christmas Christmas fair, Bastia

Eating Out and Bars

Restaurants on Corsica generally serve food between 12 noon and 2pm and in the evening from 7 to 10pm, some with later summer hours. Most offer a choice of **set menus** (sometimes including the house wine, *vin compris*), and the price of these, indicated throughout the text, gives an idea of comparable cost even if you order *à la carte*, which is invariably more expensive. If service is included it will say *service compris* or s.c.; if not, *service non compris* or s.n.c.

When looking for a restaurant, home in on the one place crowded with locals. Don't overlook hotel restaurants, some of which are absolutely top notch. To avoid disappointment, call ahead in the morning to reserve a table, especially at the smarter restaurants, and especially in the summer. Don't pass up a chance to dine at one of Corsica's famous *auberges*, where for a set price you get a traditional feast of six or seven courses.

Bars and cafés (which often do sandwiches and simple meals or *formules*) tend to remain open throughout the day. The prices are

> ## Restaurant Prices
>
> In the big cities only, as well as giving the actual set menu prices (*see* p.63), this guide divides restaurants into price categories as follows. Restaurants within hotels are the same price range as the hotel unless stated.
>
> *very expensive* over €60
>
> *expensive* €30–60
>
> *moderate* €15–30
>
> *inexpensive* under €15

progressively more expensive depending on whether you're served at the bar (*comptoir*), at a table (*la salle*) or outside (*la terrasse*). If you order *un café* you'll get a small black espresso, unless you ask for a *grand*; for milk, order *un crème*; for decaffeinated, ask for a *déca*.

Many cafés also do continental breakfasts, a good bet if what your hotel offers is expensive or boring. *Chocolat chaud* (hot chocolate) is usually good; if you order *thé* (tea), you'll get a nasty ordinary bag and the water will be hot rather than boiling. An *infusion*, or herbal tea, is kind to the all-precious *foie*, or liver, after you've over-indulged. Besides the usual French spirits, wines, beers and mineral waters, Corsica produces a range of its own, including the Pietra brewery's answer to Coke: Corsica Cola, sold across the island.

For more about eating and drinking in Corsica, including local specialities, wines and a menu decoder, *see* **Food and Drink**, pp.41–52.

Health and Insurance

Ambulance (SAMU) t 15
Police and ambulance t 17
Fire t 18

According to the UN, France has the best healthcare system in the world. Local hospitals or clinics are the place to go in an **emergency** (*urgence*). Doctors take turns going on duty at night and on holidays: ring one to listen to the recorded message to find out what to do. To be on the safe side, always carry a phone card or, better yet, a cell phone if you're going off the beaten track.

If it's not an emergency, **pharmacists** are trained to administer first aid and dispense advice for minor problems. In rural areas there is always someone on duty if you ring the bell; at weekends, town pharmacies are open on a rota and addresses (*pharmacie de garde*) are posted in their windows and in the local newspaper.

Before purchasing **travel insurance**, non-European nationals should check their health insurance schemes back home to see if they're covered in France.

E111 forms for EU nationals have been replaced by the **European Health Insurance Card** (EHIC) which will give the bearer access to the state healthcare scheme and public hospitals in all EU countries. Like the old system, the card is available for UK residents free (apply at post offices, online at *www.dh. gov.uk/travellers* or by calling t 0845 606 2030). Unlike the E111 forms, however, you'll need to apply for a card for every member of the family (you'll need passports and national insurance numbers). The EHIC must be stamped and signed to be valid, and the card must be renewed every 3–5 years.

In France, expect to pay up front for any treatment or prescription, then apply for a refund of part of the costs. Ensure that the doctor or dentist you consult is *conventionné* (within the French national health system). He or she will give you a signed statement of the treatment given (*feuille de soins*) for refund purposes. You will be charged for the treatment, as well as for any prescribed medicines, and the amount(s) should be shown on the *feuille*. When getting prescribed medicines, the pharmacist will return your prescription and you should attach it to the *feuille* in order to claim a refund. Medicine containers also carry detachable labels (*vignettes*), showing the name and price of the contents. If the pharmacist hasn't already done this, stick these in the appropriate place on the *feuille*, and sign and date the form at the end.

Send your application for a refund to the nearest health insurance office (*Caisse Primaire d'Assurance-Maladies* or CPAM) while you are still in France. The refund will be sent to your home address, but it may be subject to a bank charge. This refund process normally takes around two months. Around 70 per cent of standard doctors' and dentists' fees are refunded, and between 35 per cent and 65 per cent of the cost of most prescribed medicines.

You must also pay for outpatient treatment in hospitals and then claim a refund from the CPAM. For in-patient treatment, however, the hospital doctor will issue you with a certificate (*attestation*). The hospital should then send a *Notice of Admission – Acceptance of Responsibility* (*Avis d'admission – prise en charge*) form to the local CPAM office along with your EHIC. If not, you should send it yourself. If you are treated in an approved state hospital, the CPAM will pay 75 per cent or more of the cost direct to the hospital. You pay the balance. You must also pay a fixed daily hospital charge (*forfait journalier*). The 25 per cent balance and the *forfait journalier* are non-refundable.

To avoid nasty surprises, buy a **travel insurance** policy before leaving home that covers theft and losses and will 'top-up' your medical refund to 100 per cent and cover the costs of repatriation if necessary. Check to see if it covers extra expenses in case you get bogged down in airport strikes. Many of the larger credit card companies offer some free travel insurance (for health and theft, etc.) if you use them to book a package holiday.

Beware that accidents resulting from 'dangerous sports' are rarely covered by ordinary insurance, and if you mean to walk the GR20 or dive, you may need even more. For detailed, updated health information on travelling abroad, see the website of the Centres of Disease Control, *www.cdc.gov*.

Media

If you want to get a feel for local news or find out about local events, especially local crime, pick up the daily *Corse-Matin*, *www.corse-matin.com*. All the other French national papers are widely on sale, and in the larger towns and resorts you'll find the *International Herald Tribune* and a selection of British dailies.

Radio can be especially interesting in Corsica: the mountains are so high that your car radio is likely to change stations around every bend; one minute it's in French, then Italian, and around another bend, Spanish.

Although many of the lower priced hotels in Corsica have **TV**s, not many have satellite, so a holiday can be a good excuse to not know what's going on back home. There is, however, French and Italian programming, and half an hour of regional Corsican news at 7.30pm on France 3.

Money and Banks

Euros come in denominations of €500, €200, €100, €50, €20, €10 and €5 (banknotes) and €2, €1, 50 cents, 20 cents, 10 cents, 5 cents, 2 cents and 1 cent (coins).

The wide acceptance of **credit cards** and **ATM machines** (*distributeurs de billets*) for withdrawing cash make them by far the most convenient way of carrying cash, although there are a few things to note. Although it's always wise to have some cash on hand, you'll probably come out ahead by using your card to pay when you can rather than taking out loads of cash from the machine and paying the percentage/commission charges. On the other hand, note that many British credit cards lack the microchip required to work automatic machines such as petrol station pumps. Also note that to prevent fraud, your credit card company may refuse payment in an Italian shop because it's an 'unusual' purchase that deviates from your normal buying habits; it may be wise to let your bank know that you are travelling abroad and may be doing some 'unusual' purchasing.

In Corsica, however, it must be said smaller establishments (especially chambres d'hôtes and *fermes-auberges*) tend to accept only cash and that ATMs are few outside the main towns. Visa (*Carte Bleue*) is by far the most widely recognized credit card, followed by MasterCard, and American Express.

If your **card is lost or stolen** in France, ring the Interbank service (for Visa, MasterCard, Carte Bleue or Eurocard call **t** 08 36 69 08 80; for American Express, **t** 01 47 77 72 00; for Diners Club, **t** 01 49 06 17 50). They will block it. The police will provide you with a certificate called the *Récépissé de déclaration de vol* to give to your bank or insurance company.

Banks are generally **open** 8.30am–12.30pm and 1.30–4pm; they close on Sunday, and most close either on Saturday or Monday as well. **Exchange rates** vary, and nearly all take a commission of varying proportions.

Opening Hours, Museums and National Holidays

In Corsica, **shops** open at 8 or 9am, and close down for lunch from 12 noon to 2pm, with

French National Holidays

1 January New Year's Day
Easter Sunday Mar or April
Easter Monday Mar or April
1 May *Fête du Travail* (Labour Day)
8 May VE Day, Armistice 1945
Ascension Day usually end of May
Pentecost (Whitsun) and following Mon
   beginning of June
14 July Bastille Day
15 August Assumption of the Virgin Mary
1 November All Saints' Day
11 November First World War Armistice
25 December Christmas Day

later hours in the summer; food shops may not open until 4 or 5pm. Everything shuts down on Sunday and Monday, although *boulangeries* and food shops are usually open on Sunday mornings, and grocers and *super-marchés* may open on Monday afternoon.

Museums close for lunch as well, and often all day on Monday or Tuesday, and sometimes for all of November or the entire winter. Hours change with the season: longer summer hours begin in May or June and last until the end of September – usually. Most close on national holidays and give discounts if you have a student ID card, or are an EU citizen under 18 or over 65 years old.

Churches are usually open all day, or closed all day and only open for Mass. Sometimes notes on the door direct you to the *mairie*, bar or someone's house where you can pick up the key. If not, ask around.

On French national holidays, banks, shops and businesses close, although bakeries and food shops may be open in the mornings.

Post Offices, Telephones and E-mail

Directory enquiries t 12
International directory enquiries t 3212

Known as the *La Poste*, and easily discernible by a stylized blue bird on a yellow background, **post offices** are open in the cities Monday–Friday 8am–7pm, and Saturday 8am until 12 noon. In villages, offices may not open until 9am, break for lunch, and close at 4.30.

Nearly all **public telephones** have switched over from coins to *télécartes*, which you can purchase at any post office or news-stand for €8 for 50 *unités* or €16 for 120 *unités*. In bars you'll often find coin-gobbling phones that don't give change.

The French have eliminated area codes, giving everyone a 10-digit telephone number. However, if **ringing France from abroad**, drop the first 'o' of the number after the international dialling code 33. For **international calls from France**, dial oo followed by the country code (UK 44; US and Canada 1; Ireland 353; Australia 61; New Zealand 64), and then the local code (often minus the o).

You'll find **Internet cafés** in the major resorts and towns; most hotels now have access, and will usually let you check your e-mail.

While all three French **mobile phone** providers – Orange (partially owned by France Telecom), SFR, and Bouygues Telecom – are represented on Corsica, your mobile may well not work in more remote areas of the island; US cellphones won't be compatible unless they have tri-band technology.

The down side of taking your cellphone to France is the huge roaming charges you'll pay to receive and make calls. Before leaving home, contact your provider to find out what international services they offer or check *www.oo44.co.uk, www.SIM4travel.com, www.textbay.net* and *www.uk2abroad.com*. Some phones can make use of local providers by changing the SIM card, which requires 'unlocking' your phone from its UK network, do-able in shops in France (check first to see if it's necessary by trying someone else's card in your phone). The Orange SIM card you need is called a *mobicarte*.

Shopping

Although some of the flashier resorts (Porto-Vecchio, Calvi, Bonifacio) have Côte d'Azur-like boutiques and shops selling tourist tat and bric-a-brac, you can also find traditional goods as well: Corsican hand-made knives with horn handles, ceramics, woodwork, or items in stone, wool and coral (especially in Ajaccio and Bonifacio). A signposted route, *A Strada di l'Artigiani*, through the villages of the Balagne will take you to wine-growers, honey-producers, potters, jewellers and more (*see* p.239). Other suggestions: CDs of traditional music, wine, liqueurs and food (nearly every town has a *produits corses* grocer selling honey, jams, sweets, *charcuterie*, olive oil, liquors).

Thanks to tax concessions, alcohol and tobacco are cheaper than on the continent, so you can at least stock up on your vices for less. If you've missed out, purchase Corsican goodies online from home. Try:
La Table Corse: *www.latablecorse.com*
Corsica Produits: *www.corsicaproduits.com*.

Sports and Outdoor Activities

If you love the great outdoors, you'll love the Mountain in the Sea, whether you're a Sunday stroller or ready to take on the GR20, the most gruelling long-distance path in Europe. Corsica is one of the few Mediterranean islands where rivers flow all year; it even has a permanent 'glacier'. A third of the land area is a regional natural park, and there are 76 sites listed on the Natura 2000 programme.

Yet five out of six visitors never leave the island's lovely beaches. Some 1,000km long, Corsica's coast is by any measure the most beautiful and the least developed in France, and nearly all Corsicans (except the developers) are happy to keep it that way.

Before setting out on any adventures, however, it's essential to consult the **weather forecast** (*météo*), even in the dog days of August. Afternoon storms can strand you on mountain peaks, heavy rains can turn rivers into dangerous torrents, and changing winds can spell disaster at sea.

France Météo, t 08 92 68 02 20, €0.34/a minute, has up-to-the-minute reports (in French).

Diving

Crystal-clear unpolluted seas, dramatic sea bed and wealth of flora and fauna make Corsica one of the top places to dive (*la plongée*) in Europe, especially around Bonifacio, Scandola, Ajaccio, Cargèse, the Désert des Agriates, Calvi and Propriano, but even on the sandy east coast you're never far from a diving centre. Nearly all will teach you if you've never dived before (you'll need a certificate of good health from your doctor); courses to get you the first level of certificate that you need will take about five days and cost around €200. It's also important to wait a day or so if you've just flown in or come down from the high mountains.

Qualified diving centres are listed in the text; for a list of all 84 centres on Corsica visit the site of the **Comité Régional Corse de la Fédération Française d'Etudes et de Sports Sous-Marins**, *http://perso.wanadoo.fr/gjl/crc*. In July and August you need to book your dives; in June and September, however, the water temperatures are very comfortable, too. Two books to whet your appetite are *La Corse Sous-Marine* and *Mes 50 Plus Belles Plongées en Corse*, both by Georges Antoni.

Kayaking/Canyoning

Corsica's numerous rivers are among the most exciting for white-water sports, whether beginners or experts seeking Class V and VI thrills over dramatic turbulent runs, boulders and wild waterfalls. The season for big-thrill-seeking kayakers is relatively short – March and April during the snow melt, when the waters thunder down the ravines; among the most exciting are the Tavaro, Gravona, Golo and the scariest of all, the Fium'Orbo, with its rapids, vertical 30ft/9m drops that leave the paddler suspended in the air. For more on the rivers, in English, see *http://perso.wanadoo.fr/gjl/crc/nev.html*.

Canyoning, or following a river on its course down the mountains, has become especially popular in recent years, requiring both climbing skills and swimming. Specialist firms supply the necessary wet suits, ropes, helmets and other equipment (*see* box overleaf); the Alta Rocca rivers by Bavella, Calanches de Piana, the gorges by Bonifato and Porto's Spurtellu ravine are canyoning favourites.

Fishing

It's only recently that Corsica has discovered the joys of fishing; even in the 19th century the natives preferred the mountains and left the coasts (and the malaria) to the 'invaders'. You can fish in the sea (outside of the reserves,

Outdoor Sports Specialists, Outfitters and Guides

Altore, in Calvi and St-Florent, *www.altore.com*. Hiking, climbing, canyoning, cross-country skiing, hydrospeed , helicopter tours, hang-gliding, jet ski and other water sports.

A Montagnola, 20122 Quenza, t 04 95 78 65 19, *www.a-montagnola.com*. Organizes mountain walks (and baggage transport) and canyoning in southern Corsica.

Association d'Animations Sportives et Culturelles du Niolo, 20224 Calacuccia, t 04 95 48 05 22. Hiking, rock-climbing, canyoning, canoe-kayaking and cross-country skiing.

Compagnie Régionale des Guides et Accompagnateurs de Montagne de Corse, 20024 Calacuccia, t 04 95 48 10 43, *http:// asniolu.club.fr*. High-altitude walks, GR20 and mountain-climbing.

Corsica Forest, 20290 Borgo, t 04 95 38 27 98, *www.corsica-forest.com*. Canyoning, trekking, and *via ferrata*.

Corsica Trek, Le Moulin, 20215 Venzolasca, t 04 95 36 79 44, *http://corsicatrek.free.fr*. Made-to-order walks and treks with an experienced guide.

Couleur Corse, 13 Bd François Salini, 20000 Ajaccio, t 04 9510 52 83, *www.couleur-corse.com*. High-altitude walks, GR20, sea kayaks and zodiacs, canyoning, mountain biking and riding excursions.

In Terra Cosca, Gare SNCF BP39, 20218 Ponte Leccia, t 04 95 47 69 48, *www.interracorsa.fr*. Hiking, mountain-biking, rock-climbing, canyoning, kayaking-canoeing, hydrospeed.

Jean-Paul Quilici, 20122 Quenza, t 04 95 78 64 33, *www.jpquilicimontagne.com*.

Corsica's most famous mountain guide and climber, specialist in climbing the Aiguilles de Bavella and author of practical climbing guides: offers treks, *via ferrata* and canyoning.

Médimonti, 20214 Moncale, t 06 81 09 49 82. Mountain guide Claude Castellani will pick you up in Calvi for treks, canyoning or even snowshoeing.

Muntagne Corse in Liberta, 2 Av de la Grande-Armée, 20000 Ajaccio, t 04 95 20 53 14, *www.montagne-corse.com*. One of the oldest firms: GR20 and other treks with or without luggage, sea canoes, sailing, canyoning, etc.

Objectif Nature, 3 Rue Notre-Dame de Lourdes, 20200 Bastia, t 04 95 32 54 34, *www.objectif-nature-corse.com*. Hiking, excursions on horse or donkey, mountain bikes, rock-climbing, kayaking, hydrospeed, white-water rafting, hang-gliding and four-wheel-drive.

Tour Aventure, 1 Rue du Général Fiorella, 20000 Ajaccio, t 04 95 50 72 75, *www.tour-aventure.com*. Wide choice of excursions, year-round mountain bikes, lots of walks, treks, family trips with shepherds, sea kayaks.

UCPA, at Triu Funtanella and Prunète, t 04 95 25 91 19, *http://holidays.ucpa.com*. Outdoor activities specialists, offering accommodation and full board with weeks dedicated to hiking, mountain bikes, climbing, riding, sea kayaking, canoeing, diving, white-water rafting, tubing and hydrospeed and more.

Xtrem Sud, L'Ospedale, Porto-Vecchio, t 04 95 72 12 31, *www.xtremsud.com*. Canyoning, rock-climbing, trekking and more.

that is) without a permit as long as your catch is for your own consumption. Freshwater fishing requires an easily obtained permit from a local club; tourist offices can tell you where to find them.

Golf

Corsica's terrain isn't very golf-friendly, but there's one spectacular 18-hole course designed by Robert Trent Jones, **Golf de Sperone**, near Bonifacio, t 04 95 73 17 13,

www.sperone.net, rated the 6th best in France, and two 9-hole courses: **Bastia Golf Club**, Borgo, Rte de l'Aéroport, t 04 95 38 33 99, and **Golf de Spano**, Cocody Village in Lumio, near Calvi, t 04 95 60 75 52.

There are also three 6-hole practice courses: at **Porticcio**, Giga, t 04 95 25 95 05; **Golf du Reginu**, Speluncato (6km from L'Ile-Rousse), t 04 95 61 51 41; and **Golf de Lezza**, Rte de Bonifacio, t 04 95 70 32 90.

Hang-gliding/Paragliding

Corsica has no lack of cliffs to float off, either hang-gliding (delta) or paragliding (parapent), but there are very few safe places to land: Cap Corse is one of the most popular places. *See* listings in the box, left, or contact:

L'Altagna, Ajaccio, **t** 04 95 10 33 07.

Lucif'Air, Ajaccio, **t** 04 95 23 42 85, *http://perso.wanadoo.fr/lucif-air.*

Corsi Kite, Bastelicaccia, *www.corsikite.com.*

Piu Altù, Bastia, *www.piualtu.com.*

Cap Corse Parapent, Canari, **t** 04 95 37 84 81.

Hang Gliding Club Alpana, at Farinole, **t** 04 95 37 14 39.

ALE Niulinche, in Calacuccia, **t** 04 95 48 04 43.

Residence Arco Plage, Olmeto Plage, **t** 04 95 74 06 47.

Cime Ale, Cervione, **t** 04 95 38 83 99.

Aguladdia, Ile-Rousse, **t** 04 95 60 37 30, *http://parapente-balagne.ifrance.com.*

Les Ailes Insulaires, Mezza Via (near Ajaccio) **t** 06 07 13 36 86, *http://ailes.insulaires.free.fr.* Also *see* addresses in the box, left.

Horses and Donkeys

Corsica has its own race of small riding horses, handsome, refined and robust, with a touch of the Arab in them introduced by the Saracens in 8th century; the Corsicans call them *paganacce*, 'the pagans', for their proud attitudes. Used regularly for transport up until the 1950s, they are undergoing a revival as equestrian tours in the mountains become increasingly popular. Many riding stables are listed in the text, some involving riding treks over several days. For a dose of real Corsican atmosphere, attend one of the summer races up in Zonza.

Some addresses for equestrian holidays:

A Cheval en Corse, Rte de Baracci, 20110 Propriano, **t** 04 95 76 08 02, *www. horseback-riding-adventure.com.*

Domaine de Croccano, Sartene, **t** 04 95 77 11 37, *www.corsenature.com.*

Equinature, Sisco (Cap Corse), **t** 06 81 52 62 85, *http://equinature.free.fr.*

Club Hippique de Biguglia, San Damiano, 20620 Biguglia (just south of Bastia), **t** 04 95 30 68 62, *www.c-h-b.com.*

Balagn'ane, Olmi-Capella, **t** 04 95 61 80 88, *www.rando-ane-corse.com.* Donkey excursions in the Balagne.

Hunting

For many men in Corsica, the *chasse* is a social ritual, and most are inaugurated by members of their family as pre-adolescents.

The season runs from the last Sunday in August to the end of February, and the prime prey is boar, which is beaten out of the steep, rough wooded terrain by men and dogs of the village hunt club, who then divvy up. What the hunt clubs adamantly dislike are strangers (anyone not from the village) and every year tyres are slashed and fights break out.

Mountain-biking

Corsica, with its trails, old mule tracks, forestry roads and generally poorly maintained dirt roads in the mountains, is heaven for mountain-bikers of all abilities. In the text we've listed places that hire out *les VTTs* (*vélos tous terrains*); among the classic rides is the Désert des Agriates' coastal track, and the forests and paths of the Alta Rocca and Bavella. Local tourist offices have maps and suggestions.

Mountain-climbing

Most of Corsica's highest peaks are readily accessible to fit experienced walkers, but there are challenges for real climbers in Corsica, whether grappling up the sea cliffs near Porto or the island's ultimate ascent up the Aiguilles de Bavella. Contact one of the mountain organizations (*see* box, left).

Sailing

Yacht, motorboat and sailing-boat charters are big business in Corsica. Companies and individual owners hire them out by the hour or day, or in the case of yachts by the week or fortnight. The average cost per week for a 16m yacht that sleeps six, including food, drink and all expenses is – about what six people would pay for a week in a luxury hotel. Contact individual tourist offices for lists of firms or the **Fédération Française de Voile Ligue Corse**, Base Nautique, 20260 Calvi, **t** 04 95 60 49 43, *www. liguecorsedevoile.org.*

Skiing

The truly daring ski the GR20 (get the Parc Régional's *topo-guide* to *La Haute Route à Ski* if you're tempted).

Corsica has three **downhill ski stations** that open if enough snow falls (do ring ahead):
Station du Val d'Ese, 20119 Bastelica (1,600m), t 04 95 10 11 20.
Station du Renoso, 20227 Ghisoni (1,450–1,580m), t 04 95 57 07 67.
Station de Vergio, at Albertacce, west of Corte (1,400–1,600m), t 04 95 48 00 01.
For cross-country skiing contact:
Zicavo (1,600m): **Centre de Ski de Fond**, t 04 95 24 44 50.
Evisa (835m): **Foyer de Ski de Fond**, t 04 95 26 20 39.
Calacuccia (812m): **Association d'Animations Sportives et Culturelles du Niolo**, t 04 95 48 05 22.

Trekking – and the GR20

Trekking, or *la randonnée*, is the best way to experience Corsica's forests, mountains and wild coast, with its 1,500km of waymarked trails maintained by the **Parc Naturel Régional Corse** (*www.parc-naturel-corse.com*) and local municipalities. Some trails only take an hour, while others take several days; these have basic shelters – *refuges* or *gîtes d'étape* – along the way (*see* below). Whatever you do, never set out unprepared, and don't leave the marked trails. Severe and even fatal accidents happen every year, mainly to hikers who have strayed or got caught out unprepared in a sudden change of weather.

The main **walking season** is from mid-May to early October, when you'll need to book the *gîtes d'étape* well in advance (all are listed at *www.parc-naturel-corse.fr/randos/heberg.html*). Among the advantages of going with a guide, especially on the GR20 (*see* above, and the outdoor specialists on p.68), is that they'll make all the transport and *gîte* arrangements for you. Some will even carry your bags on ahead to the next stop.

The relevant **IGN (Institut Géographique National) contour maps** for the trails are widely available on Corsica, but also come included in the *topo-guides* or trail guides, full of essential information, in French, although there is an English translation of the *topo-guide* for the GR20, called *The Great Hike*, published by Albiana and the PNRC. Maps are available in the bigger island bookshops or from the Parc Régional offices:

Head Office: 2 Rue Sergent Casalonga, 20184 **Ajaccio**, Cedex 1, t 04 95 51 79 00/t 04 95 50 59 04. *Open all year.*
La Citadelle, 20250 **Corte**, t 04 95 46 27 44. *Open all year.*
Maison d'Infos, *Gîte d'étape* 20214 **Calenzana**, t 04 95 62 87 78. *Open April–Oct.*
Maison d'Infos du Paesolu d'Aïtone, 20126 **Evisa**, t 04 95 26 23 62. *Open June–Sept.*

The GR20

One of the most challenging long-distance footpaths in Europe, the 200km GR20, established in 1972, follows the watershed dividing Corsica's mountain spine, stretching from Calenzana, 12km inland from Calvi, to Conca, 22km north of Porto-Vecchio, taking in the most spectacular scenery on the island. Practical from June to October, once the snows have all melted, waymarked in red and white, it takes on average **two weeks** to walk in its entirety and requires a very high level of fitness (you'll walk for an average of seven hours a day, sometimes at altitudes over 6,600ft/2,000m) as well as some trekking experience, especially in the more dramatic but more difficult northern half, where ropes and *via ferrata* (iron ladders) come into play. Only one in three walkers manages to do it all, and you can easily do just half of it thanks to the train station mid-trail at Vizzavona.

The *refuges* and *gîtes d'étape* along the way (*open June–October*), are €12 per night and provide, at the minimum, dormitory beds with mattresses (but no blankets; bring a sleeping bag, because even in August temperatures at night can drop to near freezing), a wood stove, water, a gas cooker with pots and pans, etc. Many but not all sell food, and there are villages on, or a short detour off, the path, where you can stock up as well. If you haven't booked a place in the *refuges*, bring a tent and be prepared to bivouak in the shelters outside for a small fee (budget €400 for two weeks if you stay in a refuge, €200 if you camp out). You'll need a waterproof poncho or similar big enough to go over your pack (against sudden storms that seem to arrive every afternoon), excellent thick-soled boots and a few days' food and several litres of water (be wary of wild pigs and foxes, who are known to have their way with unguarded rucksacks). The

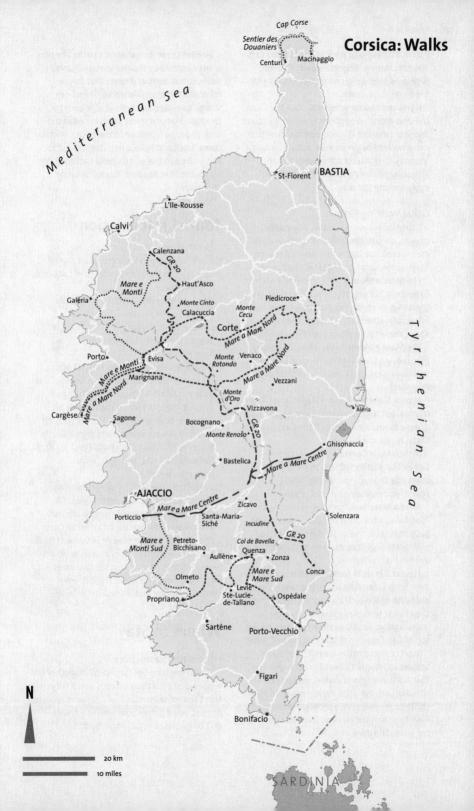

Corsica: Walks

Cap Corse

Sentier des
Douaniers

Centuri • Macinaggio

Mediterranean Sea

St-Florent • BASTIA

L'Ile-Rousse

Calvi

Calenzana

GR 20

Mare e
Monti

Haut'Asco

Galéria •

Monte Cinto
Calacuccia

Monte
Cecu

Piedicroce

Corte

Mare a Mare Nord

Porto •

Mare e Monti

Evisa

Monte
Rotondo

Venaco

Mare a Mare Nord

Marignana

Vezzani

Mare a Mare Nord

Monte
d'Oro

Cargèse •

Sagone

Bocognano

Monte Renoso

Vizzavona

GR 20

Aléria •

Ghisonaccia

Bastelica

Mare a Mare Centre

Tyrrhenian Sea

AJACCIO

Mare a Mare Centre

Zicavo

Porticcio •

Santa-Maria-
Siché

Incudine

Solenzara

Mare e
Monti Sud

Petreto-
Bicchisano

Col de Bavella

GR 20

Aullène

Quenza
Zonza

Olmeto

Mare e
Mare Sud

Conca

Levie
Ste-Lucie-
de-Tallano

Propriano •

Ospédale

Sartène

Porto-Vecchio

N

Figari

20 km

10 miles

Bonifacio

SARDINIA

essential thing is to pack as light as you can. The Parc Naturel Régional advises 70-litre rucksacks that weigh no more than 18kg for men, 14kg for women.

If you can choose when you walk the GR20, the best month is September, when it's cooler and less crowded. It's also worth noting that most walkers begin on a Saturday, Sunday or Monday, so if you set off Wednesday or Thursday you'll find fewer people in the *refuges* along the way.

Other Walking Paths

Other long-distance paths, waymarked in orange, are considerably less strenuous and are covered in a separate *topo-guide* called *Topo-Guide: Corse entre Mer et Montagne:*

The **Mare e Monti** trail is a 10-day walk from Calenzana to Cargèse; the scenery is stunning (part of it has been designated a site of world interest by UNESCO), although the lack of shade makes it hard work in the summer.

The **Mare e Monti Sud** is a five- or six-day hike though the wild empty coast between two busy west coast resorts, Porticcio and Propriano.

Mare a Mare Nord, eight stages, goes from Moriani to Cargèse, which takes in splendidly diverse landscapes, through the Castagniccia, Corte, Niolo and Porto.

Mare a Mare Centre, seven days from Ghisonaccia to Porticcio, is more difficult and takes you through the deeply forested, sparsely populated heart of Corsica.

Mare a Mare Sud, from Porto-Vecchio to Propriano, is the most popular, a year-round path that takes five or six days and passes mainly through forests, making it pleasant even in high summer.

The **Sentier de la Transhumance** goes in six days from Calenzana to Corscia, retracing the old paths taken by the shepherds escorting their flocks to higher ground in summer.

The **Sentier des Douaniers** runs around the top of Cap Corse from Macinaggio to Centuri.

Most of these paths are practical out of season, although it's best to check with the Parc Naturel Régional before setting out, and to make sure the *gîtes d'étape* are open. While the heat poses less of a problem then, you'll have to watch the clock so you don't get caught in the dark.

Besides these long-distance paths, the park is criss-crossed by shorter orange-marked paths called *sentiers de pays* that follow rehabilitated old mule tracks, often from village to village and are suitable even for children. Many of these are outlined in the text, and take from one to five hours; in many cases it helps to have a friend with a car to pick you up at the end to avoid backtracking. Again, the Parc Régional has information and maps.

Tourist Information

French government tourist offices:

UK: 178 Piccadilly, London W1J 9AL, **t** 09068 244123, *http://uk.franceguide.com*. Calls cost 60p per min.

Ireland: 30 Merrion St, Dublin 2, **t** (01) 662 9345, *http://ie.franceguide.com*.

Australia: Level 13, 25 Bligh St, Sydney, NSW 2000, **t** (02) 9231 5244, *http://au. franceguide.com*.

USA: 444 Madison Ave, New York, NY 10022, **t** (410) 838 7800; John Hancock Center, Suite 3214, 875 North Michigan Ave, Chicago, IL 60611, **t** (312) 751 7800; 9454 Wilshire Bd, Suite 715, Beverly Hills, CA 90212, **t** (310) 271 6665; 1 Biscayne Tower, Suite 1750, 2 South Biscayne Bd, Miami, FL 33131, **t** (305) 373 8177. Nationwide **t** (514) 288 1904, *www. francetourism.com*.

Canada: 1981 Ave McGill College, Suite 490, Montreal, Quebec H3A 2W9, **t** (514) 288 4264/2026, *http://ca-uk.franceguide.com*.

The central information office for all Corsica is the **Agence du Tourisme de la Corse**, 17 Bd du Roi-Jérôme, 20000 Ajaccio, **t** 04 95 51 00 00, *www.visit-corsica.com*. Also see two excellent websites about Corsica, in English, *www. corsica-isula.com* and *www.terracorsa.info*.

Where to Stay

Hotels and *Résidences*

The whole island of Corsica put together has fewer hotel beds than Lourdes, and a very short tourist season, so if you come in July and August, you'd better book well in advance – and be prepared to pay top whack.

Hotel Prices

Note: all prices listed here and elsewhere in this book are for two in a double room.

luxury	over €230
very expensive	€160–230
expensive	€100–160
moderate	€60–100
inexpensive	under €60

Not so long ago, Corsican hotels and *résidences* (apartment hotels, but also holiday home estates) were rudimentary, unpretentious, dingy and austere, even minimalist in their offerings. Now you have to look hard to find one that hasn't been renovated and swanked up; the new ones (especially around Porto-Vecchio) are austere and minimalist, too, but according to the latest design canons, with a touch of feng shui and zen.

Single rooms are relatively rare, usually two-thirds the price of a double, and rarely, at least in season, will a hotelier give you a discount if only doubles are available. On the other hand, families or groups of friends will find **triples or quads** or adding extra beds to a double room is cheaper than staying in two rooms. Breakfast (usually coffee, a croissant, bread and jam) tends to be rather overpriced on Corsica but is nearly always optional: you'll do as well for less in a bar. In summer, many hotels with restaurants will require that you stay on **half-board** terms (*demi-pension* – breakfast and a set lunch or dinner). Many of the hotel restaurants are superb and described in the text, and non-residents are welcome. At worst, it can be monotonous eating in the same place every night. In the off-season, board requirements vanish into thin air. Many hotels, especially in resorts, close down altogether in October or November and don't reopen until Easter.

In Corsica, it's essential to **book ahead** if you're coming between June and early September, or want to stay in a quiet mountain village with only one hotel. At any time of year, phoning a day or two ahead is always a good policy, and many hotels will only confirm a room with a credit card number.

Chambres d'Hôtes and Fermes-auberges

In recent years Corsica has been blessed with some stylish new *chambres d'hôtes* (bed and breakfast), generally a few rooms in the annexe of a private home – some have pools, riding stables and other amenities; they also offer an excellent means to meet the Corsicans themselves. Sometimes the hosts provide a fixed price dinner (*table d'hôte*) on request. Often in rural areas the *chambres d'hôtes* are linked to *fermes-auberges* or farm inns, which specialize in meals made from home-grown produce.

To get listings, contact **Bienvenue à la Ferme**, Chambre d'Agriculture de la Corse, BP 913, 20700 Ajaccio, **t** 04 95 29 26 00, *www.bienvenuealaferme-corse.com*.

Gîtes d'Etape and Refuges

Gîtes d'étape are set up along long-distance trails, but you'll often find them in villages, too, if a trail passes through. Although geared to hikers, they are open to all and are as a rule very well kept. The have bunk beds, usually four to six in a room, a shower, and a kitchen for self-catering, and cost around €12 a night, €11 or so for a full dinner (if available) and €4.50 for breakfast. Some will prepare a picnic for the next day on request. You can also usually camp next door for a small fee and use the facilities (showers, etc. inside).

It's important to book during the walking season. The site *www.gites-refuges.com*, partly in English, can help.

Camping

Corsica is well equipped with campsites, which are graded with stars like hotels. At the top of the line you can expect lots of trees and grass, hot showers, a pool, sports facilities, and a grocer's, bar and/or restaurant, at prices rather similar to one-star hotels, and usually filled up with giant Italian, German and Dutch land yachts. Many offer chalets and bungalows if you haven't brought a tent. Other campsites are little hideaways tucked under the cork oaks and olive groves, some on farms (*camping à la ferme*).

As they are the only reasonably priced accommodation available in July and August, it's wise to book ahead. Because of the danger of forest fires, *camping sauvage* is strictly forbidden anywhere on the island.

Gîtes de France and Other Self-catering Accommodation

Rural Corsica is especially well-equipped with *gîtes*, many of them old farmhouses, often full of character in remote locations, and if you're travelling with family and friends it can be your cheapest option. Lists are available in French and English from **Gîtes de France Corse**, BP10, 20181 Ajaccio CEDEX 1, **t** 04 95 10 54 30, *www.gites-corsica.com*.

Other websites offering self-catering accommodation on Corsica include:

Abritel, *www.abritel.fr.*

Comme Chez Vous,
www.comme-chez-vous.com.

Holiday in Corsica, *www.family-holiday.org.*

Holiday Rentals, *www.holiday-rentals.com.*

Homelidays, *www.homelidays.com.*

Locations-France, *www.locations-france.com.*

Louer en Corse, t 06 14 32 93 45,
www.louezencorse.com.

Pour les Vacances,
www.pour-les-vacances.com.

VisitCorse, *www.visitcorse.com.*

Other options are to write to the local tourist offices for lists of holiday rentals, or look around on arrival (a good option out of season), or to contact one of the holiday/special interest firms listed on p.58, which tend to offer special deals on charter flights and car hire as well.

Ajaccio and Around

07

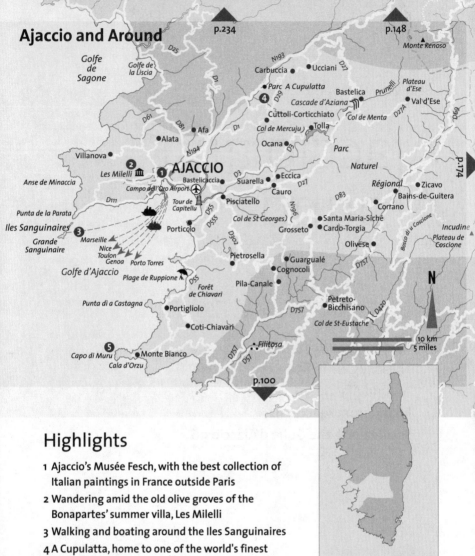

Ajaccio and Around

p.234
p.148

Golfe de Sagone

Golfe de la Liscia

Monte Renoso

Carbuccia
Ucciani
N193
Parc A Cupulatta
Bastelica
Prunelli
Plateau d'Ese
Cascade d'Aziana
Val d'Ese
Cuttoli-Corticchiato
Col de Menta
Col de Mercuju
Tolla
Ocana
Parc

Afa
Alata
Naturel
Villanova
Régional
Zicavo
Les Milelli
AJACCIO
Bains-de-Guitera
Bastelicaccia
Suarella
Eccica
Anse de Minaccia
Campo dell'Oro Airport
Cauro
Corrano
Pisciatello
D83
Punta de la Parata
Tour de Capitellu
Santa Maria-Siché
Iles Sanguinaires
Grande Sanguinaire
Porticcio
Col de St Georges
Grosseto
Cardo-Torgia
Olivese
Incudine
Plateau de Coscione
Marseille
Nice
Toulon
Genoa
Porto Torres
Pietrosella
Guargualé
Cognocoli
Golfe d'Ajaccio
Plage de Ruppione
Pila-Canale
N
Forêt de Chiavari
Punta dì a Castagna
Petreto-Bicchisano
Portigliolo
Col de St-Eustache
Coti-Chiavari
Filitosa
10 km
5 miles
Capo di Muru
Monte Bianco
Cala d'Orzu

p.100

Highlights

1 Ajaccio's Musée Fesch, with the best collection of Italian paintings in France outside Paris
2 Wandering amid the old olive groves of the Bonapartes' summer villa, Les Milelli
3 Walking and boating around the Iles Sanguinaires
4 A Cupulatta, home to one of the world's finest collections of turtles
5 Sandy beaches around Capo di Muru

Ajaccio, capital and metropolis (pop. 55,000) of Corsica, basks under palms and orange trees at the bottom of the island's biggest beach-skirted bay, trickling out towards the wild and beautiful Iles Sanguinaires. It is a hustling, bustling little Mediterranean city, white and pastel, parasolled and poodle-friendly, even if somewhat lacking the sober granite otherness that characterizes the rest of Corsica. But this is never far away: this chapter also penetrates inland to places easiest reached from Ajaccio and its sunny shore – Zicavo, one of the most remote villages on the island, and Bastelica, home of Sampiero Corso, the most Corsican of Corsicans.

Ajaccio/Aiacciu

It was at Ajaccio that I became entranced with the South.

Henri Matisse

It was when Matisse was visiting his sister, a schoolteacher in Ajaccio, that he had the head-on collision with the light and colour that would revolutionize his art. Sitting on a modest version of the Bay of Naples, Corsica's capital city was the first resort on the island and, with the excellent art in its Musée Fesch and the Iles Sanguinaires, the city is still worth a day or two's visit. Other aspects of Ajaccio are less straightforward, beginning with the town's most famous son. Ajaccio, while not particularly liking Napoleon while he was alive, is proud of him as proof of just what a Corsican, given half a chance, can do. Plus he has always been good for souvenirs.

History

Corsica's 'Cité Impériale' started off humbly enough as a 'rest stop' (*adjacium*) for sheep, although legend would have it that there was a Homeric hero in the woodpile, Ajax, who stuck around long enough to leave his name. Roman Adjacium became a bishopric, mentioned in a letter of 601 by Pope Gregory the Great, only to be wiped off the map by the Saracens in the 10th century. The area northwest of the train station has long been known to be the location of Adjacium, and in 2005 archaeologists dug on the site of a future car park on Rue François-del-Pellegrino, known as the *site Alban* (after a 1930s tobacco factory, of which only the 'Moorish' facade still stands). The archaeologists hit pay dirt, uncovering a 5th-century baptistry and African-style font, part of Adjacium's cathedral of Sts John and Eufrase, dedicated to the martyrs whose relics were brought here in the 5th century by bishops from North Africa. The baptistry was abandoned in the 8th century and a cemetery was laid out on top, where 81 well-preserved tombs were uncovered, in a surprising variety of burials – in amphorae, in the ground, in cist tombs, etc.

In the Middle Ages the site was claimed by the lords of Cinarca, the Genoese and the kings of Aragon, before a town was actually refounded in 1492 as a Genoese colony by the Bank of St George. Sampiero Corso captured it for France in 1553 and began building the citadel; when the Genoese returned, they finished the fort, and in 1592 relaxed the hitherto strict laws that had prevented the Corsicans from living in Ajaccio with the Genoese. Many made a living from coral – in 1770 there were some 600 coral-divers in the city. Without a fertile hinterland, however, growth remained slow until Napoleon came along and made his home town the capital of Corsica.

Napoleon, in fact, changed everything. The Bonapartes, minor nobility who came to Corsica from Tuscany in the 16th century, were among the élite of Ajaccio, and Carlo, Napoleon's father, was at Pasquale Paoli's side in 1768. After the battle of Ponte Nuovo in 1769, however, Carlo soon became 'Charles', and like many ambitious Corsicans collaborated with the new regime. In 1771 he received his *acte de reconnaissance de noblesse*, enabling him to petition Corsica's governor, the Comte de Marbeuf, to grant scholarships to his two eldest sons. Although as a student Napoleon had written

'Never recognize the French as our masters!' (a statement often quoted by the Corsican nationalists), as a young artillery officer he saw things differently, and gave enthusiastic speeches at Ajaccio's Jacobin club. In 1792 he managed, by pulling out all the stops, to get himself appointed Second Colonel of the Ajaccio-Tallano battalion of Paoli's National Guard. When Paoli fell out with the Convention after the Sardinian fiasco (see p.123), Napoleon abandoned him and plotted to capture the citadel of Ajaccio from the Corsicans for France. When several Ajacciens were shot dead in a reprisal, Napoleon was blamed; Paoli put a curse on the Bonapartes, and the future *enfant prodige de la gloire* picked up his mother and siblings and sailed for France, less to meet his destiny than to avoid the revenge.

There were hard feelings on both sides. Rather than bestow any imperial bounty on his home town, Napoleon's 'normalization' of Corsica was so severe and repressive that, when he abdicated, the Ajacciens hurled his bust into the sea. But as time passed, and disillusionment with the Restoration and Louis-Philippe grew, it occurred to the city that Napoleon, after all, had put Ajaccio on the map, so they returned the favour, renaming streets after the Bonapartes. Unlike his warrior uncle, Napoléon III took an interest in Corsica and visited Ajaccio in 1860 and 1869, just as the town's mild climate made it a popular English watering hole. In the Second World War, the Résistance was especially active here, and on 9 September 1943 Ajaccio became the first city in France to be liberated; the first landing in France of the Free French took

Perfume, Song and Dance

Napoleon wasn't the only bright star in Ajaccio's firmament. The founder of the modern perfume industry, **François Coty** (1874–1934), was from Ajaccio; he went to Grasse as a young man to learn his trade, and in 1904 founded in Paris what has become, through various metamorphoses, Coty Inc. of New York, the world's largest perfumer. In 1907, realizing that the bottle should be just as alluring as its contents, he hired René Lalique to design his legendary flask for Ambre Antique; in 1917, he invented the mythic perfume Chypre. With the money rolling in, Coty expanded into newspapers, buying *Le Figaro* and *L'Ami du Peuple*, making them into organs of his increasingly right-wing politics. In 1923 he ran for senator of Corsica, dining with a Corsican bandit to win votes, and narrowly lost after a murky scandal. By 1929, he was worth $350 million, but lost much of it in the Wall Street Crash and in an acrimonious divorce. He was elected mayor of Ajaccio in 1931, and increasingly supported Mussolini, advocating a similar kind of fascism for France, but died three years later. The home stadium of First Division AC Ajaccio is named after him, but otherwise the locals tend to keep him in their skeleton-closet.

Ajaccio is, however, inordinately proud of another native. The inimitable **Tino Rossi** (1907–83) was one of France's most popular singers from the late 1930s to the '60s, an operetta crooner whose *Petit Papa Noël* comes around every December in France with the inevitability of *White Christmas*. Yet another local to make good is the ballerina **Marie-Claude Pietragalla**, *première danseuse* at the Paris Opera before she became director of the Ballet National de Marseille and of her own company. One of her creations is a ballet called *Corsica*, with polyphonic music by Petru Guelfucci.

place by way of the submarine *Casabianca* on the night of 13 September, when 109 of the finest troops were landed to harry the Italians off the island.

Since 1991, the presence of the Assemblée Territoriale and regional government has added a bit of meat to Ajaccio's sauce, although differences haven't been confined to parliamentary debate. The Palais de Justice and other public buildings show the bullet holes of drive-by strafings in the wee hours, and there have been incidents that have made national headlines, most notably in February 1998, with the murder of the *préfet* of Corsica, Claude Erignac, shot in the street after leaving the theatre.

To this day Ajaccio is the last place in France with a strong Bonapartist party, the right-wing Comité Central Bonapartiste. In a not entirely welcome blast from the past, the Comité Central was challenged in the March 2001 municipal elections by a genuine Bonaparte – Prince Charles Napoléon, a descendant of Jérôme; to everyone's surprise, the leftist candidate Simone Renucci beat both Bonaparte teams, for the first time in decades.

Getting There

By Air

Ajaccio's airport, Campo dell'Oro, t 04 95 23 56 56, *www.ajaccio.aeroport.fr*, is 8km from the city and linked by bus no.8 roughly once an hour (t 04 95 23 29 41), leaving from the *gare routière* on Quai l'Herminier.

Airline Addresses

Air France/Corse Méditerranée, 3 Bd Roi Jérôme, t 0802 802 802.
Nouvelles Frontières (for charters), 12 Place Foch, t 04 95 21 55 55.
Ollandini Charter, 1 Rte d'Alata, t 04 95 21 10 12.

Car Hire at the Airport

Ada, t 04 95 23 56 57.
Avis, t 04 95 23 56 90.
Budget, t 04 95 23 57 21.
Europcar, t 04 95 23 57 03.
Hertz, t 04 95 23 57 04.
National Citer, t 04 95 23 57 15.
Rent a Car, t 04 95 23 56 36.

By Sea

Ajaccio is the second busiest ferry port on Corsica. **Port information**, Quai l'Herminier, t 04 95 51 21 80.
SNCM Ferries, t 08 91 70 18 01, go to Marseille and Nice (with fast ferries to Nice in 4hrs).
Corsica Ferries, t 08 03 09 50 95, go to Toulon and Nice night and day, year-round.
CMN, t 08 10 20 13 20, go to Marseille and Porto Torres (Sardinia).

By Train

There are three trains a day from and to Corte, Bastia and Calvi. The **station** is at the top of Bd Sampiero, t 04 95 23 11 03.

By Bus

The *gare routière* is next to the port, on the Quai l'Herminier, t 04 95 51 55 45.
Eurocorse, t 04 95 21 06 30, *www.eurocorse. com*, has 2–4 buses a day for Propriano, Sartène, Porto-Vecchio and Bonifacio, and four a day for Corte, Ponte Leccia and Bastia.
Ceccaldi, t 04 95 21 38 06, has two buses a day (exc. Sun) for Tiuccia, Sagone, Vico and Evisa.

SAIB, t 04 95 22 41 99, has two buses a day in summer (exc. Sun) for Tiuccia, Sagone, Cargèse, Piana, Porto and Ota.
Marignana Ricci, t 04 95 51 08 19, has one bus a day to Porto Pollo and Olmeto-Plage, another to Propriano, and two a day for Sartène, Levie, Zonza and Bavella.
Santoni, t 04 95 22 64 44, has one bus a day for Zicavo (exc. Sun).
Bernardi, t 04 95 28 70 47, goes to Bastelica once a day in summer, and three times a week othertimes.
Balesi, t 04 95 51 25 56, runs from Ajaccio to Porto-Vecchio by way of Aullène, Quenza, Zonza, Bavella and L'Ospedale, daily in July and August, twice weekly otherwise.
Casanova, t 04 95 25 40 37, goes several times daily to Porticcio and its beaches.

Getting Around

By Mini-Train

Like most cities in France, Ajaccio has a *petit train* that does the rounds for the footsore, at least from April to October. There are two routes, one around the main sites in town, and another one out to the Punta de la Parata, overlooking the Iles Sanguinaires; departures run hourly from 9am from Place Foch, t 04 95 51 13 69.

By Bus

City bus TCA information: 75 Cours Napoléon, t 04 95 23 29 41.
Also **Ajaccio Vison**, Quai Napoléon, t 04 95 17 50 33, which offers tours of the Imperial city on an Imperial bus.

By Boat

Nave Va boats, t 04 95 51 31 31, *www.naveva. com*, cross the bay to Porticcio in season from Ajaccio's Port Tino Rossi; they also make excursions out to the Iles Sanguinaires, the Réserve Naturelle de Scandola, and Bonifacio.

By Car

The traffic in Ajaccio is barbaric; take advantage of one of the several large car parks by the port or under Place Général de Gaulle, but get there by 10am because they fill up fast.

Car Hire in Town

Avis, 1 Rue Paul Colonna d'Istria, **t** 04 95 23 92 50.

Budget, 1 Bd Lantivy, **t** 04 95 21 17 18.

Europcar, 16 Cours Grandval, **t** 04 95 21 05 49.

Hertz, 8 Cours Grandval, **t** 04 95 21 70 94.

Citer, 16 Bd Lantivy, **t** 04 95 51 21 21.

Rent a Car, 51 Cours Napoléon, **t** 04 95 51 34 45.

By Taxi

Cabbies queue in Place Général de Gaulle, **t** 04 95 21 00 87, and at the corner of Cours Napoléon and Av Pascal Paoli, **t** 04 95 23 25 70, or try **t** 04 95 25 06 18.

By Bike

Corsica Moto Rent, 51 Cours Napoléon, **t** 04 95 51 34 45. For the hire of scooters and motorcycles.

Rout'Evasion, 8 Av Noël Franchini, **t** 04 95 22 72 87. Specializes in bicycles of all kinds.

Tourist Information

Office Municipal du Tourisme d'Ajaccio: 3 Bd de Roi Jérôme, **t** 04 95 51 53 03, *www. ajaccio-tourisme.com. Open Mon–Fri 8–6, Sat 8–12 and 2–5; July and Aug Mon–Sat 8–8.30, Sun 9–1 and 4–7.* Ask them about their €10 museum pass, valid for a week for all six museums in town.

Agence du Tourisme de la Corse, 17 Bd de Roi Jérôme, **t** 04 95 51 00 00, *www.visit-corsica. com.* For the whole island. *Open Mon–Thurs 8–12.30 and 1.30–6, Fri till 5.*

Bureau d'Information du Parc Naturel Régional de Corse, 2 Rue du Sergent Casalonga, **t** 04 95 51 79 00, *www.parc-naturel-corse.com.* For all the information you need on the park, *gîtes* and transport; they also sell all the Corsican *topo-guides. Open June–Sept Mon–Sat 8–6, other times Mon–Fri 8–12 and 2–6.*

Festivals and Events

January Dance festival.

2 June *Procession St Erasme,* yacht regatta and ball. See *www.regates-imperiales.com.*

June *Les Voix du Lazaret,* a singing festival in the Lazaret Ollandini.

Summer Thursdays Changing of the Imperial Guard at 7pm, in Place Foch.

July *Au Son des Mandolines,* a massive mandolin festival, *www.ausondes mandolines.com.*

July and August *Festival de Musique* and *Polyphonies de l'Eté,* concerts.

Mid August *Fêtes Napoléoniennes,* a popular city-wide birthday party for Boney.

September *Journées Napoléoniennes,* a festival for enthusiasts.

Shopping

Square César-Campinchi. The best **market** in Corsica, especially for local cheeses and *charcuterie,* takes place every morning till noon. It's at its biggest at weekends.

Villages Corses, 44 Rue Fesch, **t** 04 95 51 08 05. Boutique specializing in Corsican sausages, cheeses and sweets.

Galéani, 3 Rue Fesch, **t** 04 95 21 47 88. A bakery with the best *canestrelli au citron* and a full range of typical Corsican pies.

U Stazzu, 1 Rue Bonaparte, **t** 04 95 51 10 80. Just behind Napoleon's birthplace, and one of the best shops on the island for top-quality, authentic Corsican specialities, especially their own *charcuterie* .

GIE Art'Isula, 57 Rue Fesch, **t** 04 95 50 54 67. Shop selling crafts by local artisans.

Chrysolithe, 27 Rue Bonaparte, **t** 04 95 21 62 50. Jeweller Anne-Marie Odier combines precious metals with red coral, eyes of the sea, and native Corsican minerals, including the rare *diorite orbiculaire.*

U Tilaghju, 12 Rue Forcioli Conti, **t** 04 95 51 21 40. Mohairs and ceramics.

Atelier du Couteau, Port Charles Ornano, **t** 04 95 10 16 52, A plethora of hand-made Corsican knives, including handles made of petrified mammoth ivory.

Sports and Activities

Nave Va, 15 Bd Sampiero, **t** 04 95 51 31 31, *www.naveva.com.* Excursion boats to the

Iles Sanguinaires daily at 3pm, and from April to October to the Réserve Naturelle de Scandola, Calanches de Piana and the cliffs of Bonifacio, departing at 8.30am and returning at 7.30pm.

E Ragnole, 12 Cours Lucien Bonaparte, **t** 04 95 21 53 55, *www.eragnole.com*. A **diving** club; the Gulf of Ajaccio has some splendid diving spots, especially around the Iles Sanguinaires.

Couleur Corse, 13 Bd François Salini, **t** 04 95 10 52 83, *www.couleur-corse.com*. Offers a cocktail of outdoor activites, from walking along the GR20 to a zodiac circuit around the island.

Tour Aventure, 1 Rue du Général Fiorella, **t** 04 95 50 72 75, *www.tour-aventure.com*. Hiking, mountain-biking and much more.

A Muntagne Corse in Liberta, 7 Rue Mediterranée, **t** 04 95 20 53 14, *www. montagne-corse.com*. Hiking specialists, especially on the GR20.

Les Ecuries du Prunelli, 10km from Ajaccio at the Campo dell'Oro, **t** 04 95 23 03 10. The nearest riding stable, with afternoon gallops along the beach.

Starry Nights at the Observatory, Route des Sanguinaires, **t** 04 95 21 22 01. *Summers at 9.30pm.*

Where to Stay

Ajaccio ✉ 20000

Ajaccio keeps its nicest hotels along the beach-lined road to the Iles Sanguinaires.

Luxury

****Eden Roc, Rte des Sanguinaires, **t** 04 95 51 56 00, *www.edenroc-corsica.fr*. This is the most chichi, with spacious rooms with a Louis XVI touch, and such amenities as a thalassotherapy centre (one of two on Corsica), steam bath, waterskiing and small private beach; there are lovely views over the islets, and a good restaurant.

***Dolce Vita, Rte des Sanguinaires, **t** 04 95 52 42 42, *www.hotel-dolcevita.com*. Modern hotel with a lovely seaside terrace, flowery garden, beach and palmy pool, with fine views across the gulf to the Iles

Sanguinaires; rooms are plush and colourful. *Closed Nov–15 Mar.*

Very Expensive

****Les Mouettes, 9 Bd Lucien Bonaparte, **t** 04 95 50 40 40, *www.hotellesmouettes.fr*. On the road leading to the Iles Sanguinaires, a charming, classy hotel-restaurant with 20 rooms and gardens directly on the beach, plus a pool that is very easy to loaf around. *Closed mid-Oct–mid-April.*

Stella di Mare, Rte des Sanguinaires, **t 04 95 52 01 07, *www.hotel-stelladimare.com*. Although the buildings themselves are basic concrete, many give directly on to the sea, and there's a pool and aqua-sub centre. Half-board only. *Closed Nov–Mar.*

Expensive

***Albion, 15 Av Général Leclerc, **t** 04 95 21 66 70, *www.albion-hotel.com*. Pleasant modern hotel with air-conditioned rooms and free parking in a residential area near the centre; rooms facing the garden are quieter. *Closed Nov–Mar.*

***Hôtel du Golfe, 5 Bd du Roi Jérôme, **t** 04 95 21 47 64, *www.hoteldugolfe.com*. By the port, a short walk from both the ferries and buses; pleasant soundproofed and air-conditioned rooms with TVs, and most with balconies.

***La Pinède, Rte des Sanguinaires, **t** 04 95 52 00 44, *www.la-pinede.com*. Not by the sea, but overlooking it, 300m up a sign-posted lane 4km from Ajaccio centre. Very comfortable, under the pines, and set away from the seaside hurly-burly; big pool and tennis, too.

***San Carlu, 8 Bd Danielle Casanova, **t** 04 95 21 13 84, *www.hotel-sancarlu.com*. By the citadel, attractive and soundproofed, 100m from the beach. Equipped with fans; one of the few hotels in Ajaccio with disabled access and parking. Prices near the bottom of this category. *Closed 20 Dec–20 Jan.*

Moderate

***Fesch, 7 Rue Cardinal Fesch, **t** 04 95 51 62 62, *www.hotel-fesch.com*. Handsome hotel in the centre of old Ajaccio, with austere hand-crafted furnishings in the air-conditioned rooms, mini-bars and TV, although parking can be a problem. *Closed 20 Dec–6 Jan.*

★★★Impérial, 6 Bd Albert 1er, t 04 95 21 50 62, On the southwest side of town by the sea, with tidy, slightly old-fashioned rooms; the room price includes a parasol on the small private beach. Half-board obligatory in July and Aug. *Closed Nov–Mar.*

★★Kalliste, 51 Cours Napoléon, t 04 95 51 34 45, *www.hotel-kalliste-ajaccio.com*. In a 19th-century granite palace, absolutely central, recently renovated and air-conditioned, with parking in a nearby garage. They also have studios sleeping up to four.

★★Marengo, 2 Rue Marengo, t 04 95 21 43 66, *www.hotel-marengo.com*. Nothing fancy, but small, quiet, fairly central (near the casino), well kept and air-conditioned. Not all rooms are en suite, though. *Closed mid-Dec–mid-Mar.*

★★Hôtel du Palais, 5 Av Beverini (off Cours Napoléon) t 04 95 22 73 68, *www.hoteldu palaisajaccio.com*. Recently redecorated hotel, centrally located, with double glazing, air-conditioning and sparkling en suite rooms.

★★Alata, in Alata, 10km north of Ajaccio, t 04 95 25 35 74. Modern hotel with recently renovated air-conditioned rooms in a quiet mountain village with big views over the Golfe d'Ajaccio. The hotel's bar/restaurant is a favourite local hangout.

Inexpensive
Camping de Barbicaja, Rte des Sanguinaires, t 04 95 52 01 17. By the beach, 3km from Ajaccio and 100m from the nearest bus, with shade. Closest to town, so often crowded. *Closed Oct–Mar.*

Eating Out

Expensive
Le Bilboq, Rue des Glacis (on Place Foch), t 04 95 21 35 40. The best-known seafood restaurant in town, run by an ex-boxer; feast on the famous spaghetti with lobster while being serenaded by Tino Rossi for the ultimate Ajaccio experience; around €50. *Closed Sun.*

U Pampasgiolu, 15 Rue de La Porta, t 04 95 50 71 52. One of the most popular in Ajaccio for its delicious cuisine, with an excellent and filling seafood platter for €24, but lots of other choices as well. *Booking essential.*

Grand Café Napoléon, 10 Cours Napoléon, t 04 95 21 42 54, *www.grandcafenapoleon. com*. Built in 1821, Corsica's oldest and grandest café and meeting place was given a Second Empire dance hall in the early 1900s. Try the delicious risotto with mussels, cuttlefish and parmesan (*menus from €28–44, weekday €16 menu*). Even if you don't eat here, join the crowd for a coffee or a drink on the terrace and watch *le tout Ajaccio* pass by. *Closed Sat eve, Sun.*

A la Funtana, 9 Rue Notre-Dame, t 04 95 21 78 04. Around the corner from the cathedral, a cosy little restaurant with a fine touch in the kitchen and a mix of Corsican and southwest French cuisine, accompanied by fine wines. Best to reserve. *Menus at €38 and €58. Closed Sun, Mon.*

Moderate
Le 20123, 2 Rue du Roi de Rome, t 04 95 21 50 05. Near the cathedral, the décor of this restaurant reproduces the owners' village of Pila Canale. One menu only for €26: a meaty and very authentic feast of *charcuterie*, soup or *tarte au brocciu*, choice of pork, boar or veal prepared in a variety of ways, Corsican cheese and a delicious *fiadone*, all with wine from Pila Canale and traditional music; book. *Eves only, closed Mon and mid-Jan–mid-Feb.*

Le Piano, 13 Bd du Roi Jérôme, t 04 95 51 23 81. Classic French cuisine near Place Foch, with a terrace overlooking the market. A pianist tickles the keys on weekend evenings. *Lunch menu €13, others up to €32. Closed Sun lunch, and open later than most, serving till 11pm.*

Les Champs de Blé, 11 Bd du Roi Jérôme, t 04 95 51 39 26. Wide choice of Italian dishes, salads, pastas, pizzas, meat and seafood and various gratin dishes as well. *Menus from €16.*

A Casa, 21 Av Noël Franchini, t 04 95 22 34 78. A bit out of the way, on the north end of town, off Bd Charles Bonaparte. The food is good and filling, but the main draw here are the Friday and Saturday night magic shows put on by the owner, a magician – do book for these. *Single €30 menu on show nights, other wise €13 upwards. Closed Sun, and 10 Dec–10 Jan.*

L'Ariadne Plage, Rte des Sanguinaires, t 04 95 52 09 63. Ajaccio's oldest beach shack, where global recipes and fresh seafood go with Fred the patron's love of world music; if you like to dance reggae or salsa, this is one of the best places to be in Ajaccio on a Saturday night. *Closed Nov–Easter.*

Don Quichotte, Rue des Halles, t 04 95 21 27 30. An old favourite on a street of many restaurants, with a touch of Marseille on the menu (*aïoli*, etc.) and good daily specials from €14. Don't miss the Italian Renaissance statue of the Madonna discovered during renovation work on the building. *Closed Sun and Nov.*

Inexpensive

De France, 59 Rue Fesch, t 04 95 21 11 00. Top off a visit to the Musée Fesch with tasty Corsican *charcuterie* and French classics. *Closed Sun and in Nov.*

Chez Paulo, 7 Rue de Roi de Rome, t 04 95 51 16 47. Pasta and pizza at kind prices, with full menus at €20; don't miss the home-made chocolate mousse. *Closed Sat and Sun lunch.*

Da Mamma, Passage Guinghetta, t 04 95 21 39 44. With a pleasant terrace opposite the post office, off Cours Napoléon; the best option in town for authentic Corsican cuisine. *Menus from €11. Closed Sun and Mon lunch, and Jan, Feb.*

Pizzeria U Papacionu, 16 Rue St-Charles, t 04 95 21 27 86. Good pizzas and good salads served outside. *Closed lunch, Sun eve, and Oct, Nov.*

Globo, Espace Diamant II on top of the Casino, t 04 95 51 03 90. Young and trendy place with salads at lunch; in the evening it turns into a lively cocktail bar.

Around Ajaccio

Auberge d'Afa, 8km north in Afa, t 04 95 22 92 27. Nice shady terrace where you can tuck into tasty Mediterranean Corsican cuisine with a constantly changing choice of dishes, from courgette flowers filled with a mousse of scorpion fish to fresh figs

roasted with chestnut honey. *Menu Corse €20, otherwise around €40. Closed Mon except in Aug.*

A Vigna, Piscia Rossa, above Afa, t 04 95 23 08 62. New and popular for its succulent and copious servings of roast lamb and beef on a skewer, cooked over a wood fire. *Around €38.*

Entertainment and Nightlife

A L'Aghja, 6 Chemin de Biancarello, t 04 95 20 41 15. The city's most important arts centre, with concerts (especially traditional Corsican music and singing), dance and theatre. In the suburb of Brasilia.

Ajaccio Casino, Bd Pascal Rossinio, t 04 95 50 40 60, *www.casino-ajaccio.com*. A lively place, especially on Saturdays. Slot machines, poker, roulette, piano bar, etc., as well as a disco next door and a trendy wine bar, **La Part des Anges**. Over-18s only. *Open daily 3pm to 3am.*

La Bahia, Plage du Ricanto , t 04 95 10 31 33. Café-restaurant, leisure centre, nightclub.

Café Volupté, 2 Av de Paris. Popular little bar and centre of a local cultural association, serving teas and coffees and chocolates from around the world.

Cinema Laetitia, 24 Cours Napoléon, t 04 95 21 07 24. Your best chance in town for a good movie, sometimes even subtitled instead of dubbed.

Fashion Coffee, 2 Av du Premier Consul, t 04 95 50 73 55. Colourful Art Deco coffee and fashion shop, plus art gallery – popular with the bright young things of Ajaccio.

Lazaret Ollandini, Rte de Lazaret, Quartier Aspretto (on the road to the airport), t 04 95 23 92 00. Contemporary art centre in a former quarantine station.

Santa Lina, Rte des Sanguinaires, t 04 95 52 09 77. Disco popular on weekends, till 6am.

Au Son des Guitares, Rue de Roi de Rome, t 04 95 51 16 47. 'The Temple of Corsican Voices for over half a century'. Hear Tino Rossi's classics from 10.30pm on, weekends in June, July and September, and nightly in August.

The City Centre

Place Général de Gaulle

Modern Ajaccio's centrepiece, Place Général de Gaulle, a big open square filled with palms overlooking the sea, was created when Ajaccio's walls were torn down in 1801. Its old name was the 'Diamant' (after a prominent family) and in the 1980s it was re-cut with bland new shops and office buildings, although some of the old cafés, such as **L'Empereur**, have kept their turn-of-the-20th-century decor. Viollet-le-Duc, that busy 19th-century restorer-desecrator of France's medieval buildings, is behind the square's bronze **memorial to Napoleon and his brothers** (on foot), all looking very serious in their silly Roman togas. The Ajacciens call the ensemble the *grand encrier de bureau*, 'the big inkstand'. All of these brothers – Lucien, Prince of Canino (1775–1840), Joseph, king of Spain (1768–1844), Louis, king of Holland (1778–1846) and Jérôme, king of Westphalia (1784–1860) – proved so useless (with the exception of the earnest Louis, father of Napoléon III) that Stendhal was moved to remark, regarding Napoleon, 'that it would have been better for him had he no family at all'.

Old Ajaccio and Napoleon's Début

An emperor will be born near Italy...
Nostradamus

Just below and east of Place de Gaulle lies the once exclusive 15th-century Genoese town, now the core of Old Ajaccio, the part of town that feels the most 'Corsican'. On Rue St-Charles is Napoleon's birthplace, now the **Musée National de la Maison Bonaparte** (*t 04 95 21 43 89, www.musee-maisonbonaparte.fr; open April–Sept Tues– Sun 9–12 and 2–6; Oct–Mar Tues–Sun 9–12 and 2–4.45; adm*). The first Bonapartes moved into the house in the late 17th century and eventually purchased it. The original furnishings are nearly all gone – when the Bonapartes hightailed it to France in 1793, the Paolistas ransacked the house and made it a barracks. Napoleon's career is famous for its bizarre coincidences, and the first (and last) was that Hudson Lowe, who would be his jailer on St Helena in 1816, was quartered here in 1794. In 1802, Letizia had the old place embellished with the 97,500 French francs sent as reparations for English war damage, but she never lived there again, and Napoléon III added his touches as well. But expect to be disappointed: the only authentic piece of furniture is the sedan chair that carried Madame Mère, in labour, home from Mass to give birth to 'N', as he would become known on bridges, his own furniture and souvenir teacups across France. At home his nickname was Nabulio, Corsican for 'little meddler'. The main feature of his simple bedroom is the trap door that enabled him to escape the Paolistas in 1793. An early portrait shows him in the uniform now displayed in the Musée Fesch, while his death mask is said to be *the* original of at least two dozen floating around Europe, made by his doctor on St Helena. Strangest of all is the picture of the Bonaparte family tree, made out of the hair of an admirer.

N was two years old when he was baptized along with a baby sister, who later died (Letizia gave birth to 13 children; eight survived), in the relatively plain **Cathédrale**

Notre-Dame de Miséricorde (*open 8.30–11.30 and 2.30–6, Sun am only*). Begun in 1554, the original plans of the Venetian architect Giacomo della Porta were much more grandiose, but the then bishop of Ajaccio reduced its dimensions and severely simplified the façade. His successor, Bishop Giuseppe Giustiniani, much regretted his cheapskate economies, and when he laid the last stone in 1593 he added the inscription on the door: 'What he wouldn't have given to have laid the first.' It may also be a rueful reference to the portal itself: he bought and paid for it three times. When Bishop Giustiniani sent a sea captain named Acquaviva to collect it from Carrera, Acquaviva, a drunkard and gambler, lost both his ship and its marble cargo in a card game. Returning, he lied about a terrible storm that had sent his ship to the bottom; the bishop gave him another chance, and commissioned another portal. This time an angry God delivered Acquaviva's ship into the hands of Moorish pirates. The captain made it back to Ajaccio many years later to tell the story, by which time the bishop had already ordered a third portal (c.o.d. this time). The second one, complete with Giustiniani's coat of arms, now decorates a mosque in Tunis.

Besides the famous baptismal font where Napoleon was christened, the cathedral houses, on the left, an atypically gloomy *Vierge du Sacré-Cœur* by Delacroix in a chapel decorated with stuccoes. The big Baroque main altar was lifted from a church in Lucca by Napoleon's sister Elisa Bacciochi, when she was the Grand Duchess of Tuscany. Inscribed on the pilaster by the entrance is Napoleon's last wish before he died in 1821: 'If they exile my body [from Paris] as they've exiled me while alive, I would like to be buried by my ancestors in the Cathedral of Ajaccio, in Corsica.'

The church of **St-Erasme**, further down Rue Forcioli Conti, was begun in 1602 as the chapel of the Jesuit college and dedicated to Our Lady of Mercy, the *Madonnuccia*, during a plague in 1656. After the Revolution, it was re-dedicated to Erasmus, patron saint of sailors: his statue makes the rounds on 2 June, and there's a good collection of ex-voto ships' models, attesting to his prowess.

Closer to the port and citadel, the little **Musée du Capitellu**, 18 Bd Danielle Casanova (t *04 95 21 50 57; open April–Oct Mon–Sat 10–12 and 2–6, Sun 10–12; adm*), is run by a descendant of Napoleon's Bacciochi in-laws. The focus is on the history of Ajaccio and antiques that once belonged to its great families, including dinnerware Napoleon used on his campaigns, watercolours (one, of the Col de Bavella, is by Turner's nephew), busts of Corsican heroes, a copy of Paoli's constitution of 1755 and another of the French *Code Corse* that replaced it. The house next door, with a plaque, was the home of Danielle Casanova, a young heroine of the Résistance who died in Auschwitz.

The army still uses the honey-walled **Citadel** built by the Genoese, so it's off limits except in September during the *Jours du Patrimoine*. Here Corsican paratrooper captain Fred Scamaroni was imprisoned by the Italians. Sent in 1943 by De Gaulle to set up radio units in Ajaccio to relay information on enemy activities, Scamaroni was betrayed by a tortured comrade; after undergoing torture himself, he unravelled a wire from his cell and strangled himself, rather than risk giving anyone else away. On his cell wall, he left a note written in his own blood: *'Je n'ai pas parlé, vive la France.'* Little **Plage St-François**, under the Citadelle, is the town beach, while the **jetty** by the Citadelle is the ideal place for a stroll as the lights of Ajaccio twinkle at dusk.

Place Maréchal Foch and Into the Borgo

Rising up from the Citadel, Rue Bonaparte was the Genoese main street, the *carrughju drittu*, lined with *palazzi*, among them the Pozzo di Borgo family home at No.15, whose son Carlo-Andrea was Napoleon's childhood friend before becoming his bitterest enemy (*see* pp.90–91). Rue Bonaparte originally led up to the single town gate and parade ground, now occupied by **Place Maréchal Foch**, a favourite place to dawdle, with its stately palm trees, cafés, and of course another statue of old Boney in a toga, guarded by four earnest if silly lions spewing water. Ajaccio's heavenly patroness, the *Madonnuccia*, watches over the city from a niche over a souvenir shop. After beating back the plague in 1656 and miraculously chasing away a bombarding Anglo-Sardinian fleet in 1747, she was deemed more effective on the city gate than cooped up inside a church. When the gate was destroyed she was moved here, with her inscription: 'They have placed me here as guardian.'

The biggest building on the square, the **Hôtel de Ville**, has a reception hall known as the **Salon Napoléonien** (*t 04 95 51 52 53; open summer Tues–Fri 9–11.45 and 2–5.45, Mon 2–5.45; winter Tues–Fri 9–11.45 and 2–4.45, Mon 2–4.45; adm*) with medals and coins, a copy of N's birth certificate in Genoese dialect, another death mask, and family portraits, including the Emperor of the French displaying the proper marble features for the job, and another of him riding over the St Bernard Pass on a mule – rather unlike the more famous one by David, of Bonaparte pointing the way on a rearing white stallion. The bust of his son, the sad wan Napoléon II, King of Rome, is the one that his father kept on St Helena (the child would be abandoned in Austria by his mother Marie-Louise and die of consumption at the age of 21). Other portraits are of Napoléon III, his empress Eugénie, and their son, who fought with the British Army and was killed in 1879 by the Zulus.

The Genoese town was wrapped in walls until 1801. Beyond lies the first 'suburb' or Borgo, home to shopkeepers and coral fishermen, who were often at odds with the nobles in the walled *ville*. On the Borgo's long, straight **Rue Cardinal Fesch**, the curious building at No.27 with two floors of galleries was the Maison des Corailleurs, or coral workers. No.41 was the birthplace of Tino Rossi, and No.44 was the Jacobin Club, where the young Napoleon tried to rally his fellow citizens to the cause.

Musée Fesch

50 Rue Cardinal Fesch, t 04 95 21 48 17, www.musee-fesch.com. Open July–Aug Mon 1.30–6, Tues–Fri 9–6.30, Fri also 9pm–midnight, Sat and Sun 10.30–6; April–June and Sept Mon 1–5.15, Tues–Sun 9.15–12.15 and 2.15–5.15; Oct–Mar Tues–Sat 9.15–12.15 and 2.15–5.15; adm.

Napoleon's mother, Letizia, was a famous miser, and her half-brother, **Joseph Fesch** (1763–1839; only six years older than Napoleon), was no piker in accumulating the spoils of his nephew's success, either. Yet of all the family he was the only one to leave anything of significance to Ajaccio: the finest collection of Italian paintings in France outside Paris. Fesch was an archdeacon in Ajaccio in 1789, but when the Revolution made it sticky for priests, he duly left the Church. It was when he accompanied

Napoleon as his Commissioner of Supplies to Italy that he fell in love with Italian art. When he found himself in the position of being the only ecclesiastic in a family that was about to take over Europe, he rediscovered his calling and in 1802 Napoleon made him bishop of Lyon, cardinal, and minister plenipotentiary to the Holy See, a position Fesch used to convince the pope to crown Napoleon emperor. Before uncle and nephew fell out – when Napoleon imprisoned the pope in an attempt to bend him to his will – Fesch accumulated a major art collection, works 'liberated' by the Grande Armée, and others floating around on the market after being sold or confiscated during the Revolution – 18,000 paintings, according to Fesch's own estimate.

Living in exile in Rome, the cardinal decided to found an art academy in his home town and to leave it 1,000 paintings to edify the students. When he died in 1839, however, the building wasn't completed, and Napoleon's brother Joseph, the trustee, pounced on the collection, forcing Ajaccio to go to court to get its share of the paintings. It won, eventually, but only after Joseph had had his pick and sold off much of the rest, mostly the fashionable 16th- and 17th-century painters of the time, and sent the so-called 'primitives' to Corsica, leaving Ajaccio to have the last laugh.

Behind Fesch's statue in the courtyard, some 200 paintings are on display. The oldest work (c. 1330) is a very Byzantine golden triptych by the Master of Rimini. Other early paintings include a *Bishop by* Bernardo Daddi, a *Virgin* by Bartolomeo Veneto, and another golden *Virgin* by Giovanni Boccati (1450; a fine work from this somewhat obscure painter from the Marche), Lorenzo di Credi's *St Francis receiving the Stigmata*, and a very early *Madonna* by Giovanni Bellini. Botticelli's tender *Virgin and Child, supported by an Angel* (1470), the museum's best-known work, was painted when the artist was only 20, and just finding his own style after leaving Filippo Lippi's studio. Yet another lovely *Madonna* is attributed to Raphael's circle. The lumpy, contorted *Virgin and Child with a Holy Martyr and St Jerome*, could only be by Cosmé Turá of Ferrera. From the 16th century comes the striking *Four Ages of Woman*, by Santi di Tito, a variation on a usually masculine theme. There's a surprisingly austere *Deposition* by Mannerist Rosso Fiorentino, a strange *sfumato Holy Family* from the early 1500s by Domenico Bartolomeo Puglio di Ubaldini, Titian's powerful *Portrait of a Man with a Glove*, and a *Leda and the Swan* (with a raunchy beak kiss) by Veronese's workshop.

Fesch had a weak spot for Pier Francesco Cittadini, whose precise visions of fruit and Oriental rugs fill in the gaps both here and upstairs, where the museum hangs the Baroque art that slipped through Joseph Bonaparte's fingers: Andrea Pozzo's *Architecture with Presentation of Jesus in the Temple*; sweet anonymous paintings of *Orpheus Enchanting the Animals* and *Noah's Ark*; and a *St Sebastian* and *The Martyrdom of St Peter* by Luca Giordano (here in his Caravaggio mode). Then there's a room full of Corrado Giancinto, whose vision of heaven considerably features La-Z-Boy armchair clouds. There's an impressive dead turtle by Giuseppe Recco; battle scenes by Micco Spadara of Naples, and by the school of Salvatore Rosa; a view of Rome by Vanvitelli; landscapes by Gaspar Dughet; a little *King Midas* by his brother-in-law Poussin; and the original Flying Nun, in *St Teresa Saving a Sinking Ship*, attributed to Ludovico Gimignani. A 19th-century *Vue de la Marine d'Ajaccio* shows a steam ship puffing away where the ferries now dock.

The basement is full of Napoleana, with Horace Vernet's *Battle of Alma*, and portraits of Cardinal Fesch, the young Letizia, Jérôme Bonaparte and his mistress – the famous beauty Countess of Castiglione, who, when her looks faded, broke all the mirrors, locked the shutters and doors and died – and Félix Bacchiochi, married to Napoleon's sister Elisa (who, as the museum guard sniffed, was the 'only true Ajaccien' in the whole adventure, the Bonapartes being Italian parvenus). Besides a panoply of piffle inspired by the Little Corporal's career, there is a startling evidence of how little he really was, thanks to the slightly moth-eaten uniform he wore as a Colonel of the Chasseurs de la Garde, a gift to Ajaccio from former president Giscard d'Estaing.

It will set you back another €1.50 to see the **Imperial Chapel**, flanking the courtyard. This was built by Napoléon III in 1859 according to the terms of the will of Cardinal Fesch, who wanted the Bonapartes buried together in one place. It is built in a cold neo-Renaissance style, and everything in it is fake from the marbles to the stuccoes and casement ceiling, with the exception of the Coptic cross on the altar, which Napoleon pinched in Egypt and gave to his mother. The ten tombs are real enough, too – of the cardinal, and Madame Mère (Letizia Ramonlino, d. 1836) and Monsieur Père (Carlo Bonaparte, d. 1785) and other assorted Bonapartes, including Prince Louis-Napoléon (d. 1997), a descendant of Jérôme and father of the current pretender, Charles-Napoléon, a political businessman who serves on Ajaccio city council.

Another wing of the Palais Fesch houses the **Bibliothèque d'Ajaccio** (*t 04 95 51 13 00; open Mon–Fri 10–6*), founded, according to the new calendar introduced by the French Revolution, on the 26 Floreale in the year IX (16 April 1801) by Lucien Bonaparte, with a collection of documents and rare books augmented by the Cardinal's donation; it's also a research library on Napoleon, housing just about every book ever written about him, and some he annotated on St Helena. The walnut shelves are themselves classed as historical monuments, as is the 59ft/18m wooden table.

North and West of Place Général de Gaulle

Just north of Place de Gaulle, off Cours Napoléon is the **Préfecture**, where Paris' representatives in Corsica perform their often thankless tasks. In the entrance hall you can see the handsome 'Bon Pasteur' sarcophagus, discovered in 1938; dated to the 3rd century AD, this shows beliefs at the dawn of Christianity: the dead man and the Four Seasons are accompanied by the Good Shepherd – and Dionysos.

Behind the Préfecture, the **Musée A Bandera**, Rue du Général Lévie (*t 04 95 51 07 34; open daily July–15 Sept Mon–Sat 9–7, Sun 9–12; 16 Sept–June Mon–Sat 9–12 and 2–6, closed Sun; adm*), is the creation of an association of history buffs and, provided that you read French, offers a good introduction to Corsican history, with displays ranging from the island's megalithic past to the Second World War, including paintings of corsairs and photos of bandits charming the 19th-century gentry, and a special look at the battle of Ponte Nuovo of 1769, the Anglo-Corsican kingdom, and the Corsican Rangers.

On the western edge of town, between long, straight Cours Grandval and the sea rises the **Quartier des Etrangers**, Ajaccio's former British ghetto, still a genteel haven, although many villas where the likes of Joseph Conrad and Empress Sissi once sojourned are now offices or clinics, or have been replaced by apartment blocks. The pioneer resident here was a wealthy, flower-loving Scotswoman, Thomasina Campbell, whose *Southward Ho!* (1868) brought the Victorians flocking to Corsica the way Peter Mayle brought their descendants to Provence. They settled above Ajaccio, where it was 'healthier', painted watercolours and played bridge; the Corsicans found them of interest mainly for their top hats. Many stayed in the Belle Epoque Grand Hôtel Continental (now the offices of the Collectivité Territoriale de Corse or CTC) with its still beautiful exotic gardens, and attended services in an Anglican church (now a school of music and dance), built by Campbell at 2 Rue du Général Leclerc. Rue Miss Campbell leads down to the Casino, built in 1934.

At the top of the street in the **Place d'Austerlitz**, another statue of Napoleon holds forth – a large copy of the famous one in his old frock coat and bicorn hat that now stands in the Invalides after a 20-year sojourn on top of the column in Place Vendôme in Paris. A stele lists his 33 famous (and obscure) victories and his pedestal is engraved with his contributions to France, most of which are still going strong. Nearby, the artifical **Grotte de Casone** is where Napoleon played before his father sent him to boarding school at nine (his masters there described him in a report as 'Corsican, heart and soul, a Corsican from head to toe').

Just up from Place d'Austerlitz, the **Bois des Anglais** is a last remnant of the British colony, a wooded walk laid out in 1880. Here too you'll find the beginning of an easy and well-marked 9km footpath, the scenic **Route des Crêtes**, which follows the rim of Ajaccio's hills towards the solar power station at Vignola, near the beach, where you can catch city bus (no.5) back to the centre of town. The views over the Ajaccio and its gulf are grand, but avoid going up on very windy days.

Around Ajaccio

Rival Country Houses

Five km northwest of Ajaccio, off the D61 to Alata, stands the austere but very Corsican country house of the Bonapartes, **Les Milelli** (*gardens open daily; house may one day reopen to the public; ask at the Ajaccio tourist office*). Napoleon, while reminiscing on St Helena, liked to say with pride that the Bonapartes never had to buy bread, oil (they were the first to plant an olive grove in Ajaccio, which is still there) or wine, since so much of it came from this farm. The house also came in handy as a refuge for Letizia and her daughters when the Ajacciens were after Napoleon's head in 1793, and he came up here for a last visit with his future marshal Joachim Murat in 1796, on their way to Egypt. On his deathbed, his thoughts strayed here; he thought of his old nurse, and willed her the family vineyard. Although you can no longer visit the house, you can wander through the beautiful grounds; one section has been planted with a variety of Mediterranean flora.

The **Château de la Punta** (*http://perso.wanadoo.fr/lapunta*) 5km further up the D61/D461 towards Alata, was the country house of the Pozzo di Borgo. When Pasquale Paoli returned to Corsica in 1790, he made Charles-André (Carlo-Andrea) Pozzo di

Borgo (1764–1842) his right-hand man, snubbing the ambitious Bonaparte brothers because their father had changed sides so quickly in 1769. Pozzo's smouldering personal hatred for Napoleon – which Paoli never shared – began with the Sardinian débâcle (see p.123). When the Anglo-Corsican kingdom bit the dust, Pozzo went into exile with Paoli, and from there to Russia, where he served the Tsar and reportedly advised him to burn Moscow rather than let Napoleon winter there; he later fought at Waterloo with the Duke of Wellington and became a fixture of the English court. In honoured Corsican fashion, hatred for the Bonapartes continued in the blood; Charles-André's nephew, after the overthrow of Napoléon III and the burning of the Palais des Tuileries in Paris in 1870, bought the stones and brought them here and built a reproduction of the pavilion where Napoleon the Emperor had resided, for the sheer pleasure of irking the Bonapartes. When, like the Tuileries, it burned in 1978, it was the Bonapartists' turn to gloat. Unlike the Tuileries, it has been rebuilt; the views are superb, and even better if you continue walking another 45 minutes up to the top of **Punta Pozzo di Borgo** (2,555ft/799m) for the views over the bays of Ajaccio and Sagone, and Corsica's highest mountains.

To the Iles Sanguinaires

The north shore of the Golfe d'Ajaccio is a 12km tentacle of the city, lined with beaches and hotels; in summer you can avoid the nightmare of trying to park here by taking bus no.5 from Place de Gaulle, which goes out to Punta de la Parata every half-hour. On the way, the Route des Sanguinaires passes a little Baroque **Greek chapel**, where the Greeks of Cargèse worshipped when they took refuge in Ajaccio in 1731 (see p.269). The chapel was actually founded a century earlier by the Pozzo di Borgo family; a plaque has a quote from the *Mémoires* of Joseph Bonaparte:

> Our daily walks with Napoleon continued down to the sea, on beyond the Chapel of the Greeks, skirting a gulf as beautiful as Naples', in a land embalmed by the exhalations of myrtle and orange blossoms. We often didn't return home until dark.

Beyond, the sandy beaches have adopted the names of their concessions: Le Scudo, Ariadne, Vignola, Marinella (of Tino Rossi fame), Week-End and Macumba. Fans, or the merely curious, can now visit the **Villa Tino Rossi** at Le Scudo (*t 04 95 52 11 70; guided tours Fri–Mon 10.30–12 and 2.30–6.30; adm exp*), with his furnishings, photos, pool shaped like a guitar, and correspondence with Marcel Pagnol.

The road ends at the **Punta de la Parata**, 12km from Ajaccio, where a footpath leads up to the Genoese tower that guards the entrance to the Golfe d'Ajaccio, looking out to the four dramatic **Iles Sanguinaires**, a sanctuary for sea birds, covered with rare flowers, reached by Nave Va excursion boats (see p.80). The Genoese tower is a classic place to watch the sun set, when the light ignites the black blood colour of their name (although spoilsports say the name really comes from Sagone, the bay to the north). The biggest island, the **Grande Sanguinaire** or **Mezzumare**, was once a quarantine station for coral-fishers returning from the coasts of Africa, and its lighthouse was kept in 1863 by writer Alphonse Daudet, who described it in one of his *Lettres de Mon Moulin*, back when it was populated with goats and miniature horses.

North of the Punta de la Parata towards Capo di Feno are a series of quiet sandy coves and Ajaccio's best beach, the **Anse de Minaccia**, an easy 1½hr walk or so along the **Corniche du Couchant** path, beginning at the tennis courts about 500m east of the Punta de la Parata car park, or by the D111B (turn off near the First World War memorial, the Terre Sacré). The bustle of Ajaccio seems far away here, where the dunes and sands are fine and the sea turquoise, and only a few beach huts dot the landscape. People also come here looking for pretty little spiral shells called the 'eye of the sea' or the *œil de Ste-Lucie*, which bring good luck.

Inland from Ajaccio

A Cupulatta Turtle Sanctuary

A Cupulatta means 'turtle' in Corsican, and that's what you'll find here – 120 species in a wooded sanctuary, 21km up the N193 from Ajaccio (*t 04 95 52 82 34, www. acupulatta.com; guided tours June–Aug daily 9–7; April, May and Sept–mid-Nov daily 10–5.30; adm*). Philippe Magnan was a mild-mannered accountant until his dog brought him a wounded turtle one day in 1985, and ignited a *grande passion* for the little armoured beasts. Recently opened to the public, his collection is the largest in Europe, with turtles and tortoises from around the world (including the largest, from the Seychelles, which live up to 200 years, and the horror movie co-star, the Amazonian matamata). He'll also tell you some of their secrets: how the alligator turtle attracts fish by dangling a worm-like thing in the back of its throat, or how a turtle's sex is determined by the temperature of the eggs. They run a special breeding programme as well as a hospital, taking in victims of fires and lawnmowers. If it's hot, come early in the morning, when the turtles are more likely to be pottering about.

The Gorges of the Prunelli to Bastelica

Before streaming into the Golfe d'Ajaccio from its source at Monte Renoso, the river Prunelli cuts a gorge diagonally down the midriff of Corsica. Roads ascend on either side of the gorge, making for a popular round trip to Bastelica. While the narrow D3 up the north side takes in the better scenery, it requires a bit of nerve near the top.

The D3 begins 13km from Ajaccio, in **Bastelicaccia**, a residential district set back from the coastal hubbub but also the city's market garden, lush with citrus. Ten km up, a side road to the left crosses a bridge to **Eccica-Suarella**, a tiny wine village with a stele marking the spot where Sampiero Corso died on 17 January 1567. The chronicles say he wasn't the first Corsican hero to fall here; while crossing a wooden bridge here in the year 1000, the count of Corsica, Arrigo Bel Messere, was slain by a javelin thrown by a Sardinian mercenary of the lords of Tralaveto, who then drowned Arrigo's seven young sons beneath the bridge in a place known as the 'well of the seven chicks'.

From the bridge, the D3 passes **Ocana**, famous for *brocciu*, then rises dramatically up the north side of the Prunelli gorge, to the **Col de Mercuju**, where a path leads to a spectacular belvedere over the gorge and the Prunelli dam, built in the 1960s to keep the lights burning in Ajaccio. Just beyond is **Tolla**, a pleasant village set in orchards

Getting There

Transports Bernardini run **buses** from Ajaccio (opposite the train station) to Bastelica, **t** 04 95 20 06 00.

Where to Stay and Eat

Bastelicaccia ✉ 20129
Motel L'Orangeraie, D3 at Funanaccia, **t** 04 95 20 00 09, *www.inforcorse.com/oranrivoli* (*moderate*). Studios by the day or week sleeping 1–5, with kitchenettes and barbecues in a lush, fragrant Garden of Eden setting. There's a small pool, too. Be sure to book well in advance in the summer; no credit cards.

La Village, **t** 04 95 20 09 84. In the centre, a little restaurant with a good reputation for its dishes made from local ingredients, some with an exotic touch – Corsican veal, for instance, prepared *à la Valdostana. Menus from €16.*

Pisciatello ✉ 20117
Auberge du Prunelli, at Pisciatello, on the N196, **t** 04 95 20 02 75. Once a coach house with a beautiful shady terrace, made into an outstanding Corsican restaurant by the aunt of the current owner, René Orlandazzi, who is serious about keeping up traditions. You'll find all the classics, but also some more unusual dishes such as stuffed onions, *beignets de milobi* (sea anemones), *escargots à la corse*, and *tarte à la romicia* (wild sorrel). *Menus €18 lunch, or €30, with wine. Closed Tues and Jan.*

Cuttoli ✉ 20167
Auberge U Licettu, on the D303 at Plaine de Cuttoli, north of Bastelicaccia, **t** 04 95 25 61 57, *www.u-licettu.com*. High up in the hinterland; Ajacciens come here to fill up on portions of *soupe corse*, terrine, *charcuterie*, roast meats, cannelloni au *brocciu*, cheese and home-made desserts – *all for €34*. Book and come starving. They also have rooms (*moderate*) and a pool. *Closed Mon and Jan.*

Bastelica ✉ 20119
★★Le Sampiero, by the church, **t** 04 95 28 71 99 (*inexpensive*). Old-fashioned décor, and friendly owners. Good *charcuterie* and *brocciu* omelettes in the restaurant, with a €15 menu. *Closed Nov, and Fri in off season.*

Chez Paul, **t** 04 95 28 71 59. Little family-run restaurant with lovely views, where Mme Valentini prepares Corsican mountain specialities (come hungry); try the courgettes with *brocciu*. Menu €15.

Santa-Maria-Siché ✉ 20190
★★Le Santa Maria, **t** 04 95 25 70 29, *www.santa-maria-hotel.com* (*inexpensive*). A good place to stop if you're touring the area. Small, comfortable rooms on the edge of town, and food – not spectacular but OK – served under the watchful gaze of Napoleon.

Zicavo ✉ 20132
Gîte d'Etape Le Paradis, on the D69, **t** 04 95 24 41 20 (*inexpensive*). Double rooms here as well as bunks, and a fine restaurant serving home-grown vegetables, home-made bread, home-made pâté and *charcuterie* and home-made desserts. No credit cards.

overlooking the reservoir, a cool place to spend a summer afternoon while Ajaccio swelters. After Tolla the road is narrow and wild along the rocky wall of the gorge.

At the top, where the D3 meets the D27, the road passes a mixed forest of Laricio pines and chestnuts. From the **Col de Menta** the road descends past the **Cascade d'Aziana**, a 50ft/15m waterfall, to **Bastelica**, a collection of hamlets scattered in a mountain basin, surrounded by chestnut forests and famous for their *charcuterie*. At 2,650ft/808m, Bastelica remains refreshingly cool even in August, and many of its restored granite houses are the summer houses of Ajacciens. A late 19th-century bronze statue of Sampiero Corso (*see* overleaf), as flamboyant as in life, brandishes his sword in front of the church, its pedestal decorated with reliefs of his battles against Genoa. His birthplace, burned by the Genoese and lovingly reconstructed by his

Sampiero Corso, the 'Most Corsican of the Corsicans'

Born *c.* 1498, Sampiero Corso (or Corsu) was a shepherd's son, but, like many other Corsicans whose ambitions were bigger than his island, he left to seek his fortune in the one career that was always open: the military. Tall and handsome, Sampiero soon became one of the great Renaissance swashbucklers, a *condottiere* in the employ of the Medici in Florence, and then of the Medici pope, Clement VII, where he caught the eye of the French ambassador to Rome, who took the Corsican under his wing. In 1536 he joined the army of François Ier, and remained there for 30 years, fighting the armies of Emperor Charles V across Europe, 'all alone worth 10,000 men'. He saved the life of the dauphin in 1543 and, covered with fame and glory, returned to Corsica to marry Vannina d'Ornano, a beautiful noblewoman, in spite of her family's disapproval of his humble origins. Sampiero's flamboyance and fame made Corsica's Genoese governor nervous, and he imprisoned the hero in Bastia on a trumped-up charge of planning a revolt. The dauphin, now King Henri II, used his influence to have him released, but the experience rankled deep in Sampiero's heart.

In 1553, when Genoese admiral Andrea Doria famously ditched his old ally France to support Spain, Henri II decided to strike back by attacking Corsica. Sampiero opposed the idea at first, but then led 500 Corsican mercenaries to assault Bastia, while Maréchal Thermes led the French army, escorted by the fleet of the Turkish pirate admiral Dragut. They quickly took Corsica, except for the citadels of Calvi and Bonifacio, and set out to govern the island better than the now-hated Genoese, although their hands were often tied by the counter-attacks of Andrea Doria. Then, in 1557, the French administrator Orsini announced, prematurely, that the island was

admirers in the 18th century, is in the hillside hamlet of Dominacacci, up the lane to the left of the church, with a bombastic inscription to 'the most Corsican of the Corscians' by Lucien Bonaparte's Irish grandson William Bonaparte Wyse (1855). Bastelica remains a nationalist stronghold to this day. Sampiero's statue is the starting point for the 16km **Route Panoramique**, the D27A, up over the ridge dividing the Prunelli and Taravo valleys on to the **Plateau d'Ese**; here is the **Val d'Ese** ski station, with unsightly lifts and cross-country skiing when there's enough snow. A rocky, unmarked path from the plateau leads to the summit of **Monte Renoso**, the tallest mountain in these parts (7,716ft/2,352m; about seven hours there and back) for views over much of Corsica.

From Bastelica, the better road, the D27, descends to Ajaccio by way of **Cauro**, passing a pretty single-arched Genoese bridge at Zipitoli. A skull found in the wall of Cauro's church after the First World War is believed to be Sampiero's; his head was brought from Ajaccio and left here in case anyone dared to claim it.

Santa-Maria-Siché and Zicavo

It's an hour from Ajaccio to Zicavo, an excursion that offers perhaps even a greater contrast between the bright lights of the city and deepest darkest Corsica. To get there, continue south of Cauro on the N196, over the **Col de St-Georges**, under Mount Serra-Cimaggia. This is the source of Corsica's nitrate-free water, Saint-Georges,

2222

incorporated under the French crown. This was enough to disaffect many independently minded Corsicans, and the battles dragged on until 1559, when the French signed the Treaty of Cateau-Cambrésis, recognizing Genoese sovereignty of Corsica.

Abandoned by France, Sampiero travelled the courts of Europe looking for support in his now personal crusade to rid the island of the Genoese. The Genoese were active as well: in 1563, in Aix-en-Provence, Sampiero discovered that one of their agents had convinced his wife to betray him to his enemies. He strangled her, then gave her a splendid funeral. Europe was scandalized. In the French court, when Catherine de' Medici, widow of Henri II, refused to see him, Sampiero tore open his garments to expose the wounds he had received in the service of France: 'What does it matter to the king and France if Sampiero lived in harmony or not with his wife!'

His point, it seems, was taken, because Catherine secretly provided enough aid for Sampiero to make a go at liberating Corsica and, with the courage, determination and proud fatalism of his nickname, he landed near Propriano in 1564 with an army of 20 Corsicans and 50 French mercenaries. The Corsicans flocked to him, and though his insurgents captured the interior of the island, their fight was hopeless as long as the Genoese held the coast. Sampiero's bold attempt to dislodge them at Porto-Vecchio brought down the Spanish fleet and set a 2,000-ducat reward on his head.

In January 1567, Sampiero, aged 69, was ambushed and assassinated by his wife's cousin Vittolu (who in Corsican eyes, sits next to Judas in hell), whom the Genoese had discreetly employed, hoping the Corsicans would believe it was a simple case of vendetta. Sampiero's head was impaled in front of the gate at Ajaccio, and it would be 170 years before the Corsicans would challenge Genoa again.

bottled since 1998 in its classy Philippe Starck bottles at **Grosseto**. Turn left on the D83 for **Santa-Maria-Siché**, a largish village originally named Ornano – the home town of Sampiero's ill-fated wife, Vannina d'Ornano. When they married, she was 15 and he was 50, and the union elevated Sampiero into the noblity. He built a fortified palace in a spot called Vico in 1554, after the Genoese burned his house in Batelica (it's up the lane to the left of the church, ruined, and marked with a plaque). The 15th-century tower-house where Vannina was born still stands, in good nick, towards the bottom of the village, as does Santa Maria's small Romanesque church, although like an ectoderm it's only held together by a skeleton of scaffolding.

Another 20km from Santa-Maria-Siché are the **Bains-de-Guitera**, a sulphurous little spa on the banks of the Taravo, good for rheumatism. Another 7km will bring you to peaceful **Zicavo/Zicavu**, an important node for roads and trails, with an old reputation for sorcery, where on foggy nights vampires or *gramantes* were so busy that every woman on her own slept with a sickle by her bed, to defend herself.

The most spectacular local excursion, of moderate difficulty, is to the summit of Incudine, the highest peaks in the south (get the GR20 *topo-guide* in Ajaccio before setting out). By car, you can continue south on the D69, and pick up the D428 in a lovely beech wood, the **Bosco di u Coscione**, and drive on to the forest road as far as the state of your car and the state of the road permit (usually you can reach the Bergerie de Cavallara, beyond the Chapelle San Petru). From the Bergerie, a branch path leads to the GR20 and the Auberge de la Passerelle in two hours or so, before tackling the steep bit up to the **Monte Incudine**, 'the Anvil' (7,007ft/2,136m). The views take in all of southern Corsica; start as early as possible to see them at their best.

South along the Golfe d'Ajaccio

The Golfe d'Ajaccio is the biggest and deepest bay on the island, but, as the chief playground of the capital, much of the beachy coast to the south has the personality of a peanut with its smart hotels and villas, wide suburban streets, strip malls and car parks. If you want to be alone(ish), follow the string of Genoese watchtowers out to the furthest beaches, which are just as sandy, and where the city seems far away.

East of Ajaccio, where the Gravone and Prunelli rivers flow into the gulf, is a big flat space occupied by Ajaccio's Campo dell'Oro airport (named for the golden fields of wheat that once grew here). Once across the bridge, a track leads to the **Tour de Capitellu**, one of the more massive Genoese towers, but not one that Napoleon remembered fondly; this was the tower where he and 50 other men were based in April 1793, during their attack on the citadel of Ajaccio, while the French fleet was to bombard Paoli and the English. Only bad weather held up the fleet, and Napoleon and

Getting There

In July–mid-Sept, Autocars Casanova, t 04 95 21 05 17, run five **buses** a day from Ajaccio to Porticcio.

Tourist Information

Porticcio: Les Marines, t 04 95 25 01 09, www.porticcio.org. Open Mon–Fri 8.30–12.30 and 2–6.

Sports and Activities

Diving: **Corse Plongée**, La Ratajola, t 04 95 25 50 08, www.corseplongee.fr.st. Well-equipped but often very busy club. Also try **Agosta Plongée**, t 04 95 25 58 22.
Boat hire: **Centre Nautique de Porticcio**, Plage de la Viva, t 04 95 25 01 06. Windsurfs, kayaks, sailboats to rent from May to Sept.
Swimming: **Acqua Cyrne Gliss** water park, at the entrance to Porticcio, t 04 95 25 17 48; gaudy water slides. Open daily in summer 10.30–7; adm, but free on your birthday.
Walking: Two long-distance trails start or end at Porticcio. The relatively easy five-stage **Mare e Monti Sud** trail begins near Agosta

beach and crosses over the maquis-covered hills to Propriano. The low altitude and lack of shade make it hot going in the summer, though. The more difficult **Mare a Mare Centre** departs from Ghisonaccia and reaches Porticcio in seven days; pick up the topo-guide at the park office in Ajaccio.

Where to Stay and Eat

Porticcio ✉ 20166
✯✯✯✯✯**Le Maquis**, t 04 95 25 05 55, www.lemaquis.com (luxury). Sybaritic hotel on the water's edge, set in a wonderfully fragrant garden, with views across to Ajaccio and the Iles Sanguinaires. Unlike most luxury hotels, however, it began with a garden and tool-shed, which the owner, Ketty Salini, inherited from her grandfather. The shed has been replaced by pavilions around indoor and outdoor pools; the indoor one, the former greenhouse, is still filled with a lush jungle of subtropical flora. All 20 lovely rooms and five large suites are different, paved with terracotta tiles, furnished with rustic antiques and heirlooms, in a delightful laid-back and informal atmosphere to go with the private sandy beach, floodlit tennis

company and their one cannon had to hole up here, eating their horses, besieged by the furious Ajacciens. After three days they managed to escape and join the French fleet, and a few months later Napoleon returned here on the sly to meet his mother, sisters and Abbé Fesch, to whisk them off to Calvi and then by ship to Toulon. By then he had developed such a hatred for the tower that he tried to blow it up, but didn't succeed even there, although he did put a big crack in it.

Porticcio to Capo di Muru

Sprawling, charmless **Porticcio/Purtichju**, or 'Portitch' as the Ajacciens call their resort suburb, has in its favour fine beaches and a pair of superb hotels. There are two main beaches in town, **Viva** (packed with all kinds of water sports) and **Agosta**, both looking across to the Iles Sanguinaires, surrounded by holiday villas on the hills or hidden in the *maquis*. The sprawl begins to thin out south of the rocky pink granite peninsula of Isolella, where you'll find more beaches, lovely Ruppione and Mare e Sole, with silver sand overlooking a tiny islet, followed by Verghia, one of the prettiest with its parasol pines, and the charming crescent cove of **Portigliolo**. When Agatha Christie pulled up here while on holiday in Ajaccio, she thought she had reached the end of the world – and later set a story here, 'The World's End', in *The Mysterious Mr Quin*.

courts, mountain bikes, and water sports. The hotel also has one of the island's top restaurants, **L'Arbousier**, where you can feast on delicate cannelloni filled with *brocciu* and herbs, beautifully prepared seafood, tender pork cooked in arbutus honey, heavenly desserts, and a great wine list.

****Sofitel Thalasso Porticcio, t 04 95 29 40 40, *www.sofitel.com* (*luxury–expensive*). Ultra-modern hotel on the tip of a little peninsula, with a magnificent view over the gulf and large Mediterranean garden, pines and eucalyptus groves, seawater pool, thalassotherapy centre, beach, gym, water sports. The restaurant, **Le Caroubier**, with a lovely seaside terrace, serves excellent seafood and truffles, and vegetarian dishes, too. *Closed Jan and early Feb.*

**Kallisté, Rte de Vieux Molini, 800m from Agosta beach, t 04 95 25 54 19 (*moderate*). On a rutted road in the *maquis*, overlooking the sea, with airy rooms. *Closed Oct–April.*

Le Rivoli, Plage d'Agosta, t 04 95 25 06 02, (*moderate*). Modern, comfortable studios and apartments with little gardens, right on the beach, for 2–4. *Closed mid-Sept–April.*

Camping Benista near the entrance to Porticcio, t 04 95 25 19 30, *www.benista.com* (*inexpensive*). Large campsite with a pool and bungalows, 2km from the beaches.

Coti-Chiavari/Portigliolo ✉ 20138

***A Storia, Coti-Chiavari, t 04 95 27 13 14 (*from €280 a week for four*). Built of granite, the former penitentiary administration building in the village has been converted into handsome apartments furnished with character, as well as washing machines and dishwashers. Lovely views and a snack bar, too. *Closed 15 Nov–15 Dec, and Jan.*

**Céline, Portigliolo, t 04 95 25 41 05 (*moderate; half-pension obligatory in season*). Modern little hotel with a wonderful pool 300m above the beach, most rooms with sea views. *Closed Oct–Easter.*

Le Belvédère, outside Coti-Chiavari on the road to Acqua Doria, t 04 95 27 10 32 (*inexpensive; half-pension obligatory in season*). True to its name, this modern little hotel-restaurant high above the sea and surrounded by *maquis* has one of the best views in Corsica. Rooms are simple but pretty with painted furniture; the restaurant serves good Corsican dishes such as guinea fowl stuffed with chestnuts. Be sure to book. No credit cards. *Closed Nov–mid-Feb.*

The beaches are part of **Coti-Chiavari**, the centre of which enjoys lovely views. In 1714, when the site was abandoned, some 500 impoverished folk from a village outside Genoa came here in search of a better life, unaware that the area was infamous for malaria; two years later only a few disheartened survivors remained to return to Liguria. In 1852, under Napoléon III, eucalyptus groves were planted to dry up the swampy land and a **penitentiary** was built, where the prisoners herded goats and tended vines. It might not have been healthy, but the owners resented it when the state took it over by force; when they protested, the *gendarmes* burned down their houses and forcibly escorted them to Ajaccio. Conditions were little better for the prisoners: in one year, 1857, 100 out of 500 died. Closed in 1906, it remains an impressive if slightly spooky site, with its melancholy **cemetery** overrun by *maquis* (take the D55 towards Coti-Chiavari, turn right towards Campestra, and walk up the steps).

If you want an even more isolated beach, take the rough road to the **Cala d'Orzu**, a stunning sweep of sand tucked south of **Capo di Muru**. This beach was the scene of the infamous *affaire de la paillote* (*see* p.22); the beach restaurant, Chez Francis, has since been rebuilt and is back in business. Badly burned by a fire in 2003, the cape is topped with one of the best preserved Genoese towers and an unexcavated prehistoric site. The main road continues through the wild and lonely *maquis* around to Porto-Pollo and Filitosa (*see* pp.104–107).

Southern Corsica

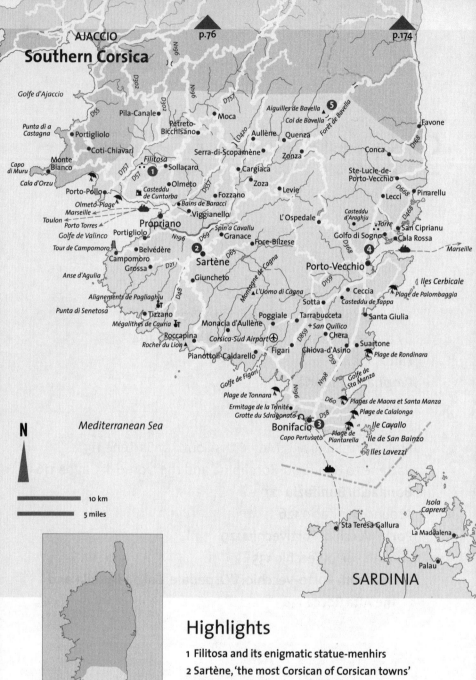

Highlights

1 Filitosa and its enigmatic statue-menhirs

2 Sartène, 'the most Corsican of Corsican towns'

3 Clifftop Bonifacio, teetering over its fjord

4 Pink and white sandy beaches around Porto-Vecchio

5 Col de Bavella, with its storm-struck Laricio pines and granite 'needles'

For many people this is the Corsica of the imagination, of hot perfumed *maquis*, frenzied granite and crescents of soft sand lapped by a sea of melted turquoise, of Bonifacio sprouting like a bouquet from a white vase of cliffs, of the boulder-whipped Iles Lavezzi, of the superb beaches of Porto-Vecchio, of the needles of the Col de Bavella. Stunningly beautiful on the outside, southern Corsica is also famous for being stunningly archaic within – the poorer and tougher region, where mountain villages, especially around Sartène, kept alive the last embers of ancient Mediterranean civilization. Here the Genoese failed to tame the clans of warlords and shepherds into farmers, leaving intact a Homeric code of honour, pride, and implacable spirits demanding the blood of vendetta. An even older layer of civiliza-tion occasionally surfaces as well, in the music and spellbinding tales of dream hunters that go straight back to the Neolithic and Bronze Ages. These ancient Corsicans left their finest monuments in the south – at holy Filitosa, Sartène, Levie and Porto-Vecchio.

With a convenient airport at Figari, and ferries from Marseille and Italy to Propriano and Porto-Vecchio, the south is the fastest-developing holiday area of Corsica. In 1999, just in the nick of time, the whole extreme southern tip of the island – from Roccapina to the Gulf of Porto-Vecchio – was set aside as the Réserve Naturelle des Bouches de Bonifacio, part of the International Corsica-Sardinia Marine Park.

From Ajaccio to Propriano

There are three ways of travelling from Ajaccio to Propriano: the direct N196 over hill and dale, or the slower more scenic coastal route, starting at Capo di Muru (*see* p.104) and following the meandering beachy north shore of the Golfe de Valinco. Or you could even cut through the dramatic (and dramatically empty) country on the D302 by way of Pila-Canale, where two excellent **statue-menhirs** stand by the road in front of the fire station. Whichever way you go, don't neglect at some point to follow the signs to Filitosa, one of the most fascinating prehistoric sites in the Mediterranean.

The Inland Route

On the N196 between Ajaccio and Propriano, **Petreto-Bicchisano/Pitretu Bicchisgia** is a typical granite hill village (or rather two, now combined into a single *commune*) with a pretty 16th-century Franciscan convent in the lower village of Bicchisano. This is now privately owned, but the convent's Renaissance art has been divided between the two parish churches: Bicchisano's has a handsome wooden Christ and pulpit; Petreto's church, higher up, got the main altar in coloured marbles, and four lovely polychrome statues.

If you aren't intimidated by narrow, vertiginous cliff-hugging roads and battered guard rails, consider taking the D420 from here to Aullène (*see* pp.142–3), over a porphyry chaos of rocks and pinnacles, at its most dramatic between the **Col de Tana** and **Col de St-Eustache**.

Getting Around

Bus connections are fairly frequent along the N196 route from Ajaccio to Propriano: contact **Eurocorse, t** 04 95 21 06 30, or **Ricci, t** 04 95 51 08 19 (who also serve Porto-Pollo).

Tourist Information

Olmeto: on the N196, **t** 04 95 74 65 87, *www. olmeto.net. Open June–Sept only, 9–3 and 4–7.*

Where to Stay and Eat

Sollacaro ✉ 20140
Le Moulin Farellacci, at Calvese on the D57 to Filatosa, **t** 04 95 74 62 28. An old olive oil press used in summer as a *table d'hôte*, serving excellent traditional Corsican dishes; *eight courses in the evening for €25, fewer for lunch for €18. Open July and Aug only.*

Olmeto/Olmeto Plage ✉ 20113
★★U Santa Maria, Place de l'Eglise, **t** 04 95 74 65 59, *www.hotel-restaurant-santa-maria. com (expensive; inexpensive out of season).* Little hotel in a traditional stone building up in Olmeto, with air-conditioned rooms and a restaurant, **Chez Mimi**, serving Corsican soup, lamb and veal, and vegetables filled with *brocciu. Menus €16–23. Closed Dec.*
Abbartello, Olmeto Plage, **t** 04 95 74 04 73, *www.hotelabbartello.com (inexpensive).* Hotel, studio flats and mini-villas right on the sea, amid the sand and boulders, with a good restaurant serving plenty of fish. *Menus €15–26.*

Porto-Pollo ✉ 20140
★★Kallisté, t 04 95 74 02 38 (*moderate– inexpensive).* The plushest place in the village, with modern rooms; half-board terms in season. *Closed Nov–Mar.*
★★Les Eucalyptus, t 04 95 74 01 52, *www. hotel eucalyptus.com (inexpensive).* Airy, simple rooms in the village centre; unpretentious seafood restaurant up on the terraces. *Closed mid-Oct–mid-April.*
L'Escale, t 04 95 74 01 54, *hotelskle@wanadoo. fr (inexpensive).* A no-frills but well-kept, laid-back place to stay right on the beach – although only one room actually enjoys a sea view. Friendly owners and good home cooking in the restaurant/pizzeria (with a big seaside terrace) are an added bonus (*menus from €18). Closed Oct–Mar.*

Around Filitosa
Chambres d'Hôtes Claude et Anita Tardif, La Cigala (signposted from Filitosa, a couple of minutes' drive away), **t** 04 95 74 29 48 (*moderate).* Three delightful rooms in an old house, with kitchen facilities and a terrace enjoying a fabulous view over Porto-Pollo. Exceptional breakfast, with old-fashioned home-made bread and jam. *Open all year.*
Auberge U Mulinu di Calzola, on the D302 on the banks of the Tavaro (near the crossroads of the D757 from Porto-Pollo to Petreto-Bicchisano), **t** 04 95 24 32 14 (*inexpensive).* Old mill restored as a small inn and restaurant, overlooking the pretty Calzola bridge.
Domaine Kiesale, 10km east of Porto-Pollo at Casalabriva, up the Taravo valley, near the Calzola crossroads and bridge, **t** 04 95 24 36 30 or **t** 04 95 74 04 55. In a huge olive grove, idyllic campsite and *gîtes* open all year (*€350 per week in season, sleeping 4–5),* plus the good **Ferme-auberge Comte Abbatucci**, serving Corsican dishes and grills, and using garden produce (*menu €25, also à la carte); closed Nov–Easter; best to book.*

Sollacaro and Olmeto

Ten km south on the N196, at the Col de Celaccia, you can make a short detour west to **Sollacaro/Suddacarò**, a handsome old *village perché* of granite houses that almost seem to have sprouted organically from the terraced mountainside, enjoying breathtaking views down the Tavaro valley to the Valinco bay. In the Middle Ages this was the fief of the d'Istria lords. The most famous was Vincentello d'Istria, who had a huge wart dangling alarmingly from his face, but came the closest to the old Cinarchesi dream of ruling all Corsica, until he was beheaded by the Genoese in 1434.

'Corsica Boswell'

It was at Sollacaro, at Vincentello's castle, that the young James Boswell arrived in October 1766 to meet Pasquale Paoli, carrying a letter of introduction from Jean-Jacques Rousseau, whom he had met the year before; a plaque near the post office commemorates their first meeting. At first Boswell was taken aback: 'I had stood in the presence of many a prince, but I never had such a trial as in the presence of Paoli.' After a long, uncomfortable silence, during which Paoli studied him keenly, apparently trying to decide if he was a spy, he then ventured to address a compliment to the Corsicans: 'Sir, I am upon my travels, and have lately visited Rome. I am come from seeing the ruins of one brave and free people: I now see the rise of another.'

This convinced Paoli that Boswell was harmless, if nothing else, and the two spent a week together and became firm friends. Paoli's parting advice to Boswell was to get married, and to 'undeceive your court. Tell them what you have seen here.' Boswell did just that, thumping the tub for Corsica, raising money to send Paoli arms, and writing his acclaimed *An Account of Corsica* (1768), which he dedicated to Paoli and which did much to make his cause well known in Britain and the American colonies. It made his reputation. 'I had got upon a rock in Corsica and jumped into the middle of life,' he declared gleefully, and, never one to shy from publicity, he made a splash at the Shakespeare Jubilee the next year, dressed up like a Corsican chieftain with a placard in his hat, reading 'Corsica Boswell'.

In 1841, Alexandre Dumas sojourned in the same castle and used it as the setting for another bestseller, *The Corsican Brothers*, this one exploring the darker, vendetta side of Corsica already made popular by Prosper Mérimée's *Colomba* (1840), complete with Siamese twins.

The N196 passes through **Olmeto**, an old granite village teetering on a mountain flank high above Propriano – until the 19th century, this was as close as anyone cared to live to the coast, but even then pirates occasionally crept up the hill to snatch villagers as slaves. Even into the early 20th century Olmeto was notorious for its many vendettas; Colomba Bartoli, the eponymous heroine of Merimée's novel, died here in 1861, aged 96 and a celebrity, in her element – her house, however, is on the verge of collapse. Olmeto's other monuments are ruins too: the 18th-century Franciscan **convent**, and to the west, the **Castello della Rocca**, home in the mid-13th century to Sinucello della Rocca, the Giudice di Cinarca (*see* p.14). In those days nearby Sollacaro's Castello d'Istria was ruled by a young widow, Sibilia of Genoa. Her beauty and political expediency led Sinucello to think she might be interested in marriage; he made enquiries and was invited by the *châtelaine* to visit. But as soon as he stepped through the gate of the castle, Sibilia had him wrapped in chains and thrown into the dungeon, where she would parade in front of him, naked, mocking him for daring to think he was worthy of her beauty. Sinucello eventually bribed a servant to help him escape and captured the castle, and got revenge on Sibilia by placing her in a hut on the Col de Celaccia, where she was offered to every passer-by. He later gave the Castello d'Istria to one of his many bastard sons, who repaid him by betraying him to the Genoese. The great-grandson of the Giudice, Arrigo della Rocca, also made the castle his stronghold during his 20-year campaign against the Genoese, with the backing of Aragon, and by 1397 he had it all except for Calvi and Bonifacio. Like his great-grandfather, Arigo ruled wisely, until 1401 when he suddenly died of a stomach ache, more likely than not caused by poison.

By the Sea: North of the Golfe de Valinco

The wooded Gulf of Valinco is the southernmost of the four bays that gouge into Corsica's east coast, its shores dotted with beaches and campsites – peaceful, for the most part these days, although in the 1980s it was nicknamed the 'Bermuda Triangle', owing to the many murders that happened here between gangs fighting to control the local nightclubs and a vendetta involving the murder of an FLNC member. Much of the north coast of the bay, at the mouth of the river Tavaro, is rather flat and marshy, but off on the end of a cul-de-sac you'll find **Porto-Pollo**, a sheltered, laid-back little seaside village in spite of being named 'troubled port' (*porti poddu*) from the bad old days when pirates sheltered here. Recently, however, another outlaw was captured in the nearby *maquis*, making headlines across France (*see* p.36).

Porto-Pollo has a beach, but there's a much better one, the huge white sand **Plage de Cupabia**, to the west (close as the crow flies, but the roads take a long loop to get there; turn left on the D155, where you'll find a sign). To the east lies the long but busier **Plage de Olmeto**; from here to Propriano the coast is dotted with holiday flats.

Over the bridge and halfway to Propriano is an important Torréen site, the **Casteddu de Cuntorba** (*c.* 1200 BC), although it's not easy to find: about 3.5km from Olmeto Plage off the D157, turn up to the left on the unmarked road for about 1.5km, until you see a track on the left; take this up to the gate, where you should leave the car (it's privately owned – just be sure to close the gate behind you). Typically, the *casteddu* stands on a height, in the midst of olive and cork oaks, with commanding views over the Golfe de Valinco. Archaeologists have carefully restored it within its circular walls of granite blocks, and it has everything a *casteddu* should have – a central monument, and areas for dwelling and for milling, storing and cooking food.

Filitosa: Faces from the Night of Time

t 04 95 74 00 91; open Easter–Oct daily 8–sunset; adm; well signposted.

Just inland up the Tavaro, Filitosa ('where the ferns grow') is an evocative, magical place: a narrow 425ft/130m spur between two streams, over a fertile plain, surrounded by oaks and olives and strewn with wild flowers in the spring and cyclamen in the autumn. It is a beautiful setting, and one that looks as if it were made to order for the Corsicans who first came here in the 6th millennium BC: on the spur is a large rocky outcrop, hollow at the bottom, that not only provided perfect shelter but may have had a religious focus as well. In *c.* 3000 BC new arrivals, or new ideas, brought the residents here into the orbit of the late Neolithic megalithic revolution.

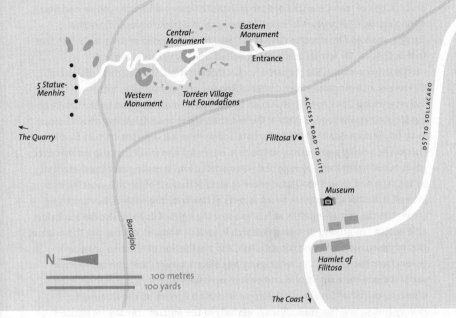

Over the centuries they would become the Michelangelos of the period, perfecting their statue-menhirs until they achieved something close to individual portraiture.

But who were the subjects of these Neolithic sculptors? According to Corsican archaeologist Roger Grosjean, who excavated the site, the Filitosans used their talent to depict their enemies, Bronze Age invaders he called the Torréens, who arrived in Corsica some time around 1700 BC: armless iconic figures, with an emphasis on their new metal weapons, which made such a powerful impression. Yet the fact that they went to such great lengths to portray their enemies – half of all Corsica's armed statue-menhirs are in Filitosa – seems odd. Did the Filitosans hope, by committing them to stone, to somehow *petrify* their enemies, or capture the dead energy of their chiefs? Or were they trophies for dead warriors? Grosjean found what seemed to be a clue in Aristotle, who wrote in his *Politics* that 'the Iberians, a warlike people, raised around their tombs as many obelisks as the deceased had killed during his life'. Other prehistorians believe they represent gods, or the dead Filitosan warriors. Only the Filitosans, as far as we know, never had bronze daggers.

What happened next is equally mysterious, and as far as anyone knows occurred only at Filitosa. When the Torréens finally conquered, they broke up some of Filitosa's statue-menhirs, buried them, or reused them whole to build their own buildings on the spur. Again, there are more questions than answers: were they furious at being depicted as battle trophies, or at being used in artistic juju? Or did the megalithic folk

The First Lady of Corsica: Dorothy Carrington

In 1948, when she first came to Corsica, Dorothy Carrington (Lady Rose) was 38 and accompanied by her third husband, the painter Sir Francis Rose, lured there by the descriptions of Jean Cesari, a Corsican resistance fighter whom the couple had met during the war. Forty years later, while working on a travel documentary about Corsica, she told film director Clive Myer, 'My life really ended and started when I set foot in Corsica. My former role-playing ended, and my vocation began.'

Little in her previous life prepared her for this vocation. The daughter of General Sir Frederick Carrington, a friend of Cecil Rhodes, and of a society mother who loved the arts, young Dorothy was orphaned by the age of ten and raised by the family of her stepfather. She read English at Oxford, then spent years travelling about Europe in an upper class Bohemian set of artists and writers. Yet once she had set foot in Corsica, its beauty and mystery so touched her heart and mind that she would never get it out of her system; by 1949 she was divorced and spending months there, and by 1952 she had moved to Ajaccio, more or less for the rest of her life, working as a journalist, writer and lecturer on all aspects of her favourite subject. Besides being present as the statue-menhirs at Filatosa saw the light of day, she also did a considerable amount of ground-breaking research in various libraries, discovering the original text of Pasquale Paoli's first constitution, and a collection of hitherto unknown letters from Paoli, as well as writings by Napoleon's father Carlo. Her best-known works include the magnificent and evocative Heinemann Award-winning *Granite Island: A Portrait of Corsica* (1971); *Napoleon and his Parents on the Threshold of History* (1988); and the groundbreaking study of the *mazzeri*, *The Dream Hunters of Corsica* (1995).

In 1986, she was made a Chevalier de l'Ordre des Arts et des Lettres; in 1991 she was awarded an MBE and became the first to receive an honorary doctorate from the University of Corsica. When she died in 2002, aged 91, she had just completed a life of Napoleon's father, *Portrait de Charles Bonaparte d'après ses écrits de jeunesse et ses mémoires*, which was published posthumously; she was laid to rest according to her wishes, in the Cimetière Marin of the Iles Sanguinaires, looking towards the sea.

themselves adopt the Bronze Age cult of the Torréens and use the stones to incorporate elements of their older religion into the new? Two *torres* were built, the Central and Western Monuments, in a *casteddu* of stone huts, a Cyclopean wall and a lookout platform to the east. At some point, a shepherd built his hut out of the Torréen stones and menhirs. Then, in the 1940s, Charles-Antoine Cesari, who owned the land, began to remove the stones to build a wall on his farm. He found some nice long pieces of granite, ready-cut – which to his surprise had faces.

In her book *Granite Island*, Dorothy Carrington describes how she met Cesari's nephew in London and came to stay with the family in 1948, prompted by his description of the mysterious statues, and wrote on seeing the first one: 'It was still monstrously impressive, this hero-image lying on its back in the *maquis* worn by uncounted centuries of wind and rain. The head recalled nothing I had seen so much as one of Picasso's more brutal drawings.' In 1954, Roger Grosjean began the systematic excavation of the site with Cesari, whose sons, both archaeologists, now own and administer the site. In all, they found some 70 statue-menhirs, numbering them as they went along. Unfortunately they have also seen fit to install pushbutton multilingual audio stations on the site, which boom out explanations that shatter the once mystical atmosphere (to avoid them, try to arrive early or late).

Along the path to the site, as if guarding it, stands **Filitosa V**, the biggest and best-armed statue-menhir. The entrance to the fortified *casteddu* is by way of the **Eastern Monument**, a Torréen tumulus, with a lookout platform. Beyond the platform are the ruins of a **Torréen village**, where the oldest pottery shards were found, from 5850 BC. The great statue-menhirs, **Filitosa VI**, **Filitosa IX** and **Filitosa XIII**, with the most lifelike features, stand by the **Central Monument**, while other standing stones and statue-menhirs have been stood upright near the spots where they were discovered, buried by the Torréens. The Central and the even more impressive **Western Monument** by the rocky outcrop were originally vaulted *torres* standing some 20ft/6m high; you can still make out the two little rooms. These show evidence of fires, which has led to speculation that these two may have had a religious as well as a defensive purpose. The ruins of Bronze Age huts are here as well.

From the Western Monument, rough steps descend north to a bridge over the Barcajolo stream, where five statue-menhirs have been erected around a magnificent 1,200-year-old olive tree, the oldest one in France, with a trunk wide enough to hide the little donkeys who often graze here. The granite quarry of the menhirs was located just to the right of the olive tree. As you leave, visit the small **museum**, which shelters other statue-menhirs: **Filitosa XII**, unique for its arms, hand and foot, the eerie face of **Trappa II**, and the statue-menhir **Scalsa-Murta** (1400 BC) with its finely drawn backbone and ribs, a sword and shoulder belt, and helmet with holes in it which may originally have held horns, and which led to Grosjean's theory that the Torréens may have been the Shardana (*see* p.10). There are photos of the excavations, and other finds from Filitosa: axe heads, a torque, loomweights and pots.

Propriano/Pruprià

Sheltered at the back of the Gulf of Valinco, Propriano is the age-old port of the Sartenais. Sampiero Corso and his handful of men landed here in 1564 on his doomed mission to liberate Corsica from the Genoese, but over the next few centuries it was attacked so often by pirates that hardly a house was standing when the French took over, and for long after. Slowly rebuilt in the 19th century, Propriano has grown into one of the largest towns on the island (in Corsican terms this means over 3,000 year-round residents), in large part thanks to the wheelings and dealings of a nationalist and criminal triumvirate comprising former mayor, Emile Mocchi, son of an Italian immigrant (convicted in 2000 and 2005 on counts of extortion); his nephew, leader of one of the nationalist groups; and Jean-Jérôme ('Jean-Jé') Colonna, former link in the 'French Connection' and one of the island's most notorious 'godfathers'.

Getting Around

By Boat

CMN sails year-round between Propriano to Marseille, and Porte Torres, Sardinia; **SNCM** also links Propriano to Marseille, and in summer to Toulon.

For both, contact **Agence Sorba**, Quai l'Herminier, t 04 95 76 04 36.

By Bus

Eurocorse, 22 Rue Général de Gaulle, t 04 95 76 13 50, *www.eurocorse.com*, runs 4 buses a day in summer, 2 in winter and on Sun, to Ajaccio, Bonifacio and Porto-Vecchio.

Ricci buses, 8 Rue Général de Gaulle, t 04 95 76 25 59, go to Ajaccio, Sartène, Levie and Bavella twice a day, once on Sun.

By Car, Taxi and Bike

Car hire: Avis, 34 Rue du Général de Gaulle, t 04 95 76 39 00; **Budget**, Rue Jean Pandolfi, t 04 95 76 00 02; **Europcar**, Route de la Corniche, t 04 95 76 00 91; **Hertz**, Agence Sorba, Quai L'Herminier, t 04 95 76 04 36; **Citer**, 25 Av Napoléon, t 04 95 76 11 84.

Motorbike hire: JLV, 25 Av Napoléon, t 04 95 76 11 84.

Mountain bike or scooter hire: Tout Terrain Corse, 25 Rue Général de Gaulle, t 04 95 76 15 32.

Taxis: t 04 95 76 11 03, or **t** 06 14 40 38 84.

Tourist Information

Propriano: Port de Plaisance, t 04 95 76 01 49, *www.propriano.net*. Open summer Mon–Sat 8–8, Sun 9–1 and 4–8; winter Mon–Fri 8.30–12 and 2–7.

Sports and Activities

Boating and Boat Excursions

Paesi di U Valincu, t 04 95 76 16 78, *www. corsica.net/promenades*. Excursions in glass-bottomed boats of the Golfe de Valinco, Roccapina, Senetosa, Bonifacio, the Réserve Naturelle de Scandola, Calanches de Piana, Girolata and Iles Sanguinaires. They are popular, so be sure to book.

Promenades en Mer Valinco, t 04 95 76 04 26. Tours of the gulf in a boat or catamaran, to Campomoro, Porto-Pollo and the lighthouse at Senetosa. Another excursion features an underwater concert.

Centre Nautic Valinco, t 04 95 76 33 27, *www. propriano.net/nautic*. Boat and windsurf hire.

Locanautic, t 04 95 76 31 31, *www.locanautic. com*. Hires out motorboats by the day or half-day.

Diving

The real wonders of Propriano are under the sea. **Valinco Plongée**, in the Port de Plaisance, t 04 95 76 31 01, **Club U Levante**,

---

As a resort, Propriano seems a bit brash beside Corsica's age old seaside towns, but it has all the necessaries: sandy beaches (the **Lido**, 1km away, is the closest and best, and has life guards in the summer; **Baracci beach** to the north is scrappier and subject to strong winds and undercurrents) and around the gulf, a busy marina, boat and diving excursions, and a row of seafood restaurants.

An old/new attraction 4km inland on the D257, the **Bains de Baracci** (**t** *04 95 76 30 40; open April–Oct daily 9–12 and 3–8; Nov–Mar daily 9–12 and 2–7; adm*), makes use of a sulphurous spring that comes out of the ground at 52°C, used since ancient Roman times (according to an inscription, Hadrian himself came for a soak). It was rebuilt by Russian emigrés in the early 1900s with a Grand Hotel; the spa bit was fixed up and reopened in 1992, and is recommended for arthritis, rheumatism and psoriasis. There's also a Jacuzzi, and tennis courts.

South of Propriano along the gulf, the road crosses the river Rizzanèse on the Ponte de Rena Bianca. On the right of the road stand a pair of **menhirs**, named *U Frate e a Suora*, who legend says were a monk and a nun who fell in love and made a dash for

and **Campomoro Plongée**, at Campomoro,
t 04 95 74 23 29, know all the best spots.

Air Tours

Aéroclub du Valinco, at the Tavaria aerodrome,
t 04 95 76 09 82. For a remarkable bird's-eye
view of south Corsica, tours lasting 20 or
55mins, and parachute jumps.

Riding

Centre Equestre de Baracci, just northeast of
Propriano on the Rte de Baracci, t 04 95 76
08 02, *www.horseback-riding-adventure.
com*. Rides into the hinterland by the hour or
half-day, or for a real adventure they do a
two-week across Corsica tour. They also have
some dorm rooms and a good restaurant.

Walking

Propriano lies near two long-distance trail-
heads, the **Mare e Monti Sud** to Porticcio (*see*
p.97) and the very popular 5-stage, 4–5-day
Mare a Mare Sud to Porto-Vecchio, through
the best parts of the Alta Rocca, including the
archaeological site at Levie. No snow in the
winter and lots of shade in the summer from
the beautiful forests make it walkable year-
round, and the way is well equipped with
village *gîtes d'étape*. The trail begins by the
gîte d'étape at Burgo up the D557, 7km from
Propriano; for information contact the Parc
Naturel Régional Corse, t 04 95 50 59 04.

Where to Stay and Eat

Propriano ✉ 20110

★★★★**Grand Hôtel Miramar**, Rte de la Corniche,
t 04 95 76 06 13, *www.miramarcorse.com*
(*luxury*). One of the 'Small Luxury Hotels of
the World', modern and smartly styled with
terracotta floors, set in a flower-filled garden
over a beach. All 28 spacious rooms and
suites have balconies (some have Jacuzzis),
with views across the gulf. Pool and sauna in
the grounds; riding, boats, water sports and
mountain bikes on offer. The restaurant, with
a huge bay window, serves lovely Mediterranean cuisine. *Closed mid-Oct–mid-April.*
★★★**Le Lido**, Av Napoléon, t 04 95 76 06 37,
le.lido@wanadoo.fr (*very expensive–moderate*). Built over the beach in 1932, with
small but individually decorated rooms,
most with sea views and air-conditioning
(reflected in the price). Magnificent terrace
and restaurant specializing in fish, with
swish dishes such as *St-Pierre et son cappuccino crème de violet*, and chocolate *petites
folies* for dessert (*menu €27*). Half-pension
mandatory in July and Aug. *Closed Oct–April.*
★★**Motel Bartaccia**, Rte de la Corniche, t 04 95
76 01 99, *http://perso.wanadoo.fr/bartaccia*
(*€500 a week for two in high season*). Studio
rooms, by the Miramar, a short walk from
the beach and just under 1km from the
centre. It has a pool and garden, and big off-
season discounts. *Closed Dec–Mar.*

it, only to be petrified by divine wrath. Just across the bridge, the D121 follows the
south coast of the Golfe de Valinco on a corniche, passing the beautiful beach at
Portigliolo, a 4km arc of fine sand in a wild setting – although it can be dangerous
when windy. It then continues to **Belvédère**, with the promised view over the gulf, and
Campomoro, a serene fishing village once inhabited by the Saracens (hence the
name) and one of the most idyllic spots on Corsica, with a handful of houses, a shop, a
restaurant, boats, a gorgeous duney sandy beach and a fragrant eucalyptus grove;
however, protected as a nature reserve, it's no secret, and in July and August, parking
can be a nightmare. At the end of the point, a 20-minute walk takes you to the
Genoese **Tour de Campomoro** (1568), recently restored and open for visits in summer,
when it holds exhibitions by the Conservatoire du Littoral. There's another beach here
and the little *criques* full of crystal water and little fish make it a favourite for
snorkellers. The village belonged for centuries to the Durazzo family of Fozzano (*see*
below), who were also in charge of the tower. The coast south of here has no roads
or trees for miles, but there's a lovely path through the *maquis* and bizarre rock

★★L'Ibiscus, Rte de la Corniche, t 04 95 76 01 56 (*moderate*). Built in the 1990s on the heights above town, apart from the summer chaos; not much to look at but a good quiet base; many rooms have views of the sea.

Bellevue, Av Napoléon, t 04 95 76 01 86, *www.hotels-propriano.com* (*moderate*). Salmon and blue and right in the centre, overlooking the marina. Colourful rooms, recently refurbished, some looking on to the sea, some on to the quieter courtyard.

★★Loft Hotel, 3 Rue Jean-Paul Pandolfi, t 04 95 76 17 48 (*inexpensive*). In the centre, in a former wine warehouse, with large sparkling rooms. *Closed Oct–Mar.*

Camping Lecci e Murta, Portigliolo, t 04 95 76 02 67, *www.camping-lecciemurta.com* (*by the week*). Well-equipped, beautiful site 300m from the beach, with bungalows, a pool, tennis, shop and a bar-restaurant.

Terra Cotta, 29 Av Napoléon, t 04 95 74 23 80. The plushest restaurant in Propriano, with Moroccan-inspired décor and creative cooking for a nice change of pace; save room for the lovely *fondant au chocolat guanaja*. *Around €30. Open daily June–Oct, other times closed Sun eve, Mon and Jan–mid-Mar.*

Le Cabanon, Av Napoléon, t 04 95 76 07 76. Sit on the terrace facing the gulf, and tuck into *bouillabaisse*, well-prepared grilled fish, lobster and other freshly caught denizens of the deep. *Good-value menus from €20, cheaper* formules *at lunch. Closed Nov–April.*

L'Hippocampe, Rue Pandolfi, t 04 95 76 11 01. A local favourite; the owner is a fishermen and in the evening serves what he's caught (the lobster is delicious if you feel like splurging). Wines from Sartène. *Menus from €13–30. Closed Sun out of season, and Dec–Mar.*

Auberge San Ghjuvani, 4km east of Propriano on the D257, just beyond the Baracci baths, t 04 95 76 03 31. Although it doesn't look like much, this is a very popular farm restaurant, serving gargantuan helpings. The *escargots*, made according to the local recipe, are famous. *Menus €17–35.* On Friday night there is traditional polyphonic singing; be sure to book. *Closed Nov, and Mon out of season.*

Campomoro ✉ 20110

Le Ressac, t 04 95 74 22 25, *www.hotel-ressac.fr* (*inexpensive*). Modern building, a great place to stay, but filled by the same clients year after year. Views are over the sea or olive grove; another plus is the best restaurant in the village (*menus €19–28*). *Half-board only in season (€110 for two). Closed mid-Oct–Mar.*

Campomoro, t 04 95 74 20 89 (*inexpensive*). Campomoro's other hotel, linked to the Restaurant des Amis seafood restaurant, with 10 simple rooms on the sandy beach. *Half-board €110 for two. Closed Oct–May.*

Camping Peretto Les Roseaux, t 04 95 74 20 52. Terraced, tranquil campsite on the hillside amid the palms, eucalyptus and oranges; showers operate by tokens. *Closed Nov–Mar.*

formations as far as the **Anse d'Agulia**, a lovely sheltered cove with a beach, where the granite boulders look like petrified penguins and a giant turtle.

Inland from Propriano

From Propriano, the D19 heads inland to the rather gloomy wine-making *village perché* of **Arbellara** before delving north for **Fozzano/Fuzzà**, 12km from Propriano, an atmospheric place of fortified granite tower houses on a rocky spur. It was here in 1839 that Prosper Mérimée found the inspiration for his novel *Colomba*, a romantic tale of Corsica framed around a gruesome vendetta between the Carabelli and Durazzo families, whose 17th-century tower-houses still stand.

The feud was spurred on by his heroine, or anti-heroine, the implacable Colomba Bartoli, née Carabelli, born in 1775 and who was 65 when Mérimée met her and who, as he put it, 'excelled in the making of rifle cartridges and who knows all about sending them to people who have the misfortune of displeasing her'. For his character, however, Mérimée borrowed the beauty of her 20-year-old daughter Catherine, since, when the famous events happened, Colomba was already 58. The trouble began in 1830, when a Paoli, an ally of the Durazzo family, compromised the honour of a Carabelli girl and refused to marry her. Soon after, three men were killed, two of them Carabellis. Colomba demanded vengeance and plotted an ambush in 1833, but it backfired: four men were killed, two Durazzi and two Carabelli, including her own son, Francescu. Things reached such a pitch that a peace treaty was signed 'in the name of God, the country, and the King of France' in Sartène's cathedral the same year. Colomba lived until 1861, wryly amused at the fame Mérimée's novel brought her, but still refusing to forgive the Durazzi even on her deathbed. She was buried here at her son's side. In the spring the surroundings are full of wild orchids. Her house, with a certain irony, has been converted into Fozzano's cultural centre.

The road continues north a few kilometres to **Santa-Maria-Figaniella**, once a seat of the della Rocca warlords. Its 12th-century **church**, set apart on a crag, is one of the best Pisan Romanesque churches of the south, made of beautifully dressed granite, decorated with charming little *modillions* – animals, serpents and little human heads.

On your way back to Propriano, backtrack a few kilometres from Arbellara to the bridge over the Rizzanèse and the D69; after a few kilometres it passes the most striking bridge in Corsica, the **Spin'a Cavallu**, 'horse croup', built by the Pisans (not the Genoese, as the sign says), a steep, almost triangular span that has withstood the Rizzanèse's floods better than many newer bridges, at least until 1993, when it was damaged by an exceptionally violent surge, and had to be restored. In the dog days of summer, the river below makes a popular swimming hole. From here you can continue to Ste-Lucie-de-Tallano in the Alta Rocca (*see* pp.143–4).

Sartène/Sartè

Its very appearance breathes war and vengeance.
A. C. Pasquin Valéry, 1837

When Prosper Mérimée called Sartène 'the most Corsican Corsican town', he was referring to its seemingly endless vendettas and the brooding tension that gripped it for decades. On grey days in particular, this atmosphere lingers in the narrow streets, under the shadows of tall grey granite houses; from a distance the town looks as if it grew inch by inch out of its mountain amphitheatre. But Sartène, if stern and sombre, is also beautiful, with one of the best-preserved historic centres on Corsica. And Mérimée's comment remains as true as ever, as the town fervently keeps alive old traditions, in its holy days, polyphonies and, notably in past decades, in the local wines.

Sartène developed in the early Middle Ages, when 11 parishes, harried by pirates, united for safety. It became an aristocratic city, the unofficial capital of the feudal barons who controlled the *Dila dei Monti*. The first della Rocca built a castle here in the 13th century, but it wasn't an auspicious beginning: he was assassinated by his own nephews, and his wife and retainers died when the castle well was tainted with toad poison – according to the chronicles of Giovanni della Grossa, who was born near Sartène in 1388 and wrote the first history of Corsica. After the last lord died in 1511. the Genoese enclosed Sartène with a wall, but it failed to keep out Sampiero, who besieged the town for 35 days in 1565 and razed it. In 1583, it was easy prey for Hassan Pasha, the king of Algiers, who sailed off with 400 residents for the slave markets.

Sartène later remained so faithful to Genoa that Paoli had to come in person in 1763 to rally its powerful barons to his cause. With the coming of the French, Sartène channelled its energy into murderous clan warfare. As in Chicago in the 1920s, Sartène's North Side (the Sant'Anninchi, supporters of the Bourbons) fought the poorer South Side (the anti-monarchist Borghegiani) with incessant gun battles from 1830 until the island governor, with great difficulty, got them to sign a peace treaty in 1834. Afterwards the town settled down to a more normal level of vendettas, including a famous one that led to the complete destruction of the Roccaserra and Pietri families in a feud that began over a dog. Until the 20th century many Sartenais went about armed, and windows were walled up. In the 1940s, the last (official) bandit of Corsica, Muzarettu, came to die in Sartène's San Damiano convent.

Good Friday and *U Catenacciu*

You may have may gleaned from their history that the Sartenais often had consciences as troubled as anyone, but where they are unique is in the method, at once very private and very public, they have found of expiating their sins. Any man who feels a powerful burden of guilt can apply to the parish priest to be the *Grand Pénitent* or *U Catenacciu*, 'the chained one'; the waiting list is so long that the next available slot is in 2040. The priest is the only one who knows his identity, though this naturally doesn't stop everyone from trying to guess who he is or steal a peek.

The *Grand Pénitent* comes secretly at night to the presbytery a few days before Good Friday, where he remains hidden. On Good Friday he and the lesser penitents fast for 24 hours. At 9.30pm the church door is solemnly opened, and everyone waits for the *Grand Pénitent*, who emerges in red robes and a hood covering his face, with a heavy cross on his shoulder and the chains clanking after his bare feet. Then the procession begins. The clergy lead the way, and the black penitents follow, carrying a bier bearing a statue of the Dead Christ; in former times they were known as the 'Jews', whose task was to beat the *Grand Pénitent* with rods. One hooded man in white plays 'Simon the Cyrenaean', who helps the Christ-like figure when he falters from exhaustion, or falls from the press of people around him.

The route of the Stations of the Cross through Sartène is long and steep, its granite streets lined with locals and tourists. It takes three hours for the *Catenacciu* to stumble through it, making his way to the church of St-Sébastien on the far edge of the Borgu, then back to the Hôtel de Ville (symbolizing the palace of Pontius Pilate), then down through the arch into the Quartier Santa Anna. As he clanks his mournful way through the shadowy streets, the crowd takes up the dolorous ancient chant '*Perdonu miu Diu!*' with medieval fervour. In the end, the *Pénitent* returns to Place Porta, now symbolic of Golgotha. As a relief after all the tension, on Easter Monday everyone heads into the countryside for the first picnic of the year.

Getting Around

Eurocorse buses, t 04 95 77 18 41, link Sartène with Ajaccio, Bonifacio and Porto-Vecchio 4 times a day and twice on Sun. Also, **Ricci**, t 04 95 51 08 19, provides at least one service linking the town to Propriano, Ajaccio, Levie, Zonza, Ste-Lucie-de-Tallano and Bavella.

Tourist Information

Sartène: 6 Rue Borgo, t 04 95 77 15 40. Open Mon–Fri 9–12, May–Sept also 3–7.

Sports and Activities

Santa Pultru Ranch, Tizzano, t 04 95 77 23 15. For horseback rides to the beaches, menhirs and creeks.

Altra Manera Diving Centre, Tizzano, t 06 60 74 87 19. Dives exploring the local underwater fauna and flora.

Where to Stay and Eat

Sartène ✉ 20100

***La Villa Piana, Rte de Propriano, t 04 95 77 07 04, www.lavillapiana.com (moderate). Cosy modern hotel in a beautiful setting under old oaks, with lovely views from the pool back towards Sartène, only 1km away; it also has tennis and a pool, but no restaurant. Wheelchair access. Closed Nov–Easter.

**Les Roches, Av Jean Jaurès, t 04 95 77 07 61 (moderate). The only hotel in Sartène town, with views from most rooms. It can get hot and noisy in high summer.

**Rossi Hôtel Fior di Ribba, Rte de Propriano, t 04 95 77 01 80, www.hotelflordiribba.com (moderate). 1km from Sartène, a cosy hotel or accommodation in much nicer little ochre maisonettes in the Fior di Riba, a garden of oranges, lemons, pomegranates and figs. There's also a pool. Closed Nov–mid-Mar.

Auberge Santa Barbara, Rte de Propriano, 2km south of Sartène, t 04 95 77 09 06. Sunny Corsican dishes with a big emphasis on local vegetables, served on a terrace surrounded by flowers; the soupe de paysan is thick and good, or there's aubergines au gratin, lamb stuffed with herbs, a lovely flan for goat's cheese lovers and pain perdu with pears. Traditional menu €27. Closed 15 Oct–15 Mar; 15 Mar–end May closed Mon.

Mariulinu, Av Gabriel Peri, t 04 95 77 22 83. A specialist in pasta dishes, but they also have a good selection of main courses. Around €20. Closed Sun.

Auberge de Pero Longo, Lieu-dit Navara, on the N196 just south of Sartène, t 04 95 77 07 11. Simple but exquisite dishes and fine wines to taste on a wine estate – one of the area's recent success stories. Menus start at €15. Closed 15 Sept–15 June.

Roy Théodore, Roi de Corse, in the old town at 13 Rue des Frères Bartoli, t 04 95 77 17 77. Little restaurant with tables in the pedestrian lane or in a cool vaulted room, good for traditional Corsican rib-sticking dishes such as ragoût de mouton with beans. Menus from €11.

Around Sartène

Les Maisons de Murtoli, Ortolo Valley, t 04 95 71 69 24, www.murtoli.com (luxury). The ultimate in Corsican eco-chic, owned by the Grand Hotel Cala Rossa in Porto-Vecchio: a 3,000-acre private estate with dunes, coves, and the 4km white sand Plage d'Argent dotted with 7 beautifully restored stone bergeries sleeping 2–12 by the week (or by the night in April and May), scattered in the maquis or by the sea – austere but with high-tech kitchens and all necessities. Nearly all have private pools, while others have hammams and saunas; there's a daily

On his visit to Corsica, Napoléon III granted the barons not only patents of nobility, but the tax concessions that encouraged them to plant the empty lands around town with vineyards, today the mainstay of the local economy. These days Sartène, by area the second-largest commune in France after Arles, is held up as one of the best-governed towns on the island; if the 33km of coast south from Campomoro is now a natural reserve, thank Sartène city council. Music-lovers will recognize the town as maid service, breakfast and shopping delivered to your door, a *potager* to pick vegetables and more. They'll also help you hire a 4x4 to get around. *Closed Oct–Mar.*

Domaine de Croccano, Rte de Granace (D148), t 04 95 77 11 37, *www.corsenature.com* (*moderate*). Three B&B rooms and a fine restaurant in a big granite house of character, looking down towards the sea. Christian Perrier also offers excellent walking and riding excursions in Corsica, including a 7-day riding or walking 'In the Trail of the Romantics' package. *Closed Dec; book months in advance.*

Ferme-auberge A Tinedda, on the N196 at Rizzanèse, 5km north of Sartène, t 04 95 77 09 31 (*moderate*). Attractive rooms in quiet countryside and a family farm-based restaurant with a filling €25 menu. *Closed Dec–Feb.*

Auberge Coralli, Rte de Bonifacio, Roccapina, t 04 95 77 05 94 (*inexpensive*). Simple – and the only – hotel at Roccapina, with views over the lion and beach, with a decent restaurant; *half-pension in summer, by the week only in June–Sept. Closed Nov–Mar.*

Fromagerie d'Acciola, 8km south of Sartène on N196, t 04 95 77 14 00. A goat farm which sells *brocciu* (*except in Aug and Oct*) and other farm products; also runs a little *table d'hôte* from June to Sept, serving dishes starring the local produce while the goats scamper to and fro. *Around €15.*

Tizzano ✉ 20100

★★★Le Golfe, t 04 95 77 14 76 (*expensive*). Small and welcoming hotel on the beach with sea views, and a good restaurant – try the octopus salad. *Closed Nov–Mar.*

★★★Lilium Maris, t 04 95 77 12 20, *www.lilium-maris.com* (*expensive*). The 'Sea Lily' is a new, well-equipped hotel with rooms with all mod cons, teak furniture and balconies, right on the beach. *Closed Nov–mid-April.*

Camping d'Avena, t 04 95 77 02 18 (*inexpensive*). Near the sea, with a shop and a restaurant with theme nights. Bring your own tent. *Closed Oct–April.*

Chez Antoine, t 04 95 77 08 63. Near the port, and a favourite for passing yachties; there is good seafood on a €25 menu, but also cheaper lunch specials. *Closed Oct–April.*

Pianottoli-Caldarello ✉ 20131

★★★U Libecciu, down at La Marine, t 04 95 71 87 93, *www.hotellibecciu.com* (*very expensive*). Opened in 1995, this has 80 rooms right on the sea, a tranquil place surrounded by *maquis*. Bedrooms are arranged on three levels, and there's a pool, and plenty of sports on offer, windsurfing and tennis, a kids' club, etc., and a good restaurant, too. *Closed mid-Oct–mid-April.*

Figari ✉ 20114

Les Bergeries de Piscia, t 04 95 71 06 71, *http://perso.wanadoo.fr/ferme.auberge.piscia* (*moderate; half-board €83 per person*). Up a winding mountain road above Figari, with views all the way to Sardinia, six attractive rooms full of personality in a stone building (the owner used as many local building materials as possible) set in a garden. There's a pool, and a restaurant featuring dishes made with the owners' own *brocciu*; his flocks roam the surrounding 250 acres of *maquis* (*menu €35, including drinks and all you can eat*).

Ferme-auberge Pozzo di Mastri, on the D859 towards Sotta, t 04 95 71 02 65. Proper country atmosphere in a big stone house with an arbour to get you in the mood, and platters of *charcuterie* and *crudités*, leg of lamb or roast boar and tasty vegetables and cheeses, nearly all produced on the farm, right down to the olive oil. 'Menu unique' €38. Open daily, winter by reservation only.

the seat of the Scola di Cantu di Sartè, a school dedicated to the revival of Corsican choral music, under Ghjuvan-Paulu Poletti, singer and leader in the Corsican *riacquistu*; his group, *Le Chœur d'Hommes de Sartène*, has performed all around Europe.

The heart of Sartène is surprisingly cheerful: the leafy and atmospheric **Place Porta** (or de la Libération), is surrounded by cafés and the 16th-century **Hôtel de Ville**, the former fortress-palace of the Genoese governors, with the town coat of arms over the door. In the 19th century it was also the place where the guillotine finally resolved the Roccaserra–Pietri vendetta. The granite church of **Ste-Marie** is here too, rebuilt in the late 18th century and furnished with a 17th-century Baroque altar made in Tuscany, where treaties ending vendettas were solemnized. Against the back wall are the cross (70lbs) and chain (30lbs) borne by the *Catenacciu* on Good Friday.

The arched passage in the Hôtel de Ville descends into Sartène's old centre, the Manighedda or **Santa Anna** quarter, where a claustrophobic web of narrow alleys – living granite mingled with the dead, houses piled together, steep steps (replacing the original ladders to the first floor that could be quickly withdrawn to turn a home into a mini-castle), evoke medieval Corsica perhaps better than any other place on the island. Santa Anna's rival, the airier and more open Borgu, extends south of Place Porta, with most of the town's shops and more vaulted streets higher up, especially the Rue des Voûtes.

Sartène is especially proud of its brand new **Musée de la Préhistoire** (*t 04 95 77 01 09; open May–Sept Mon–Sat 10–12 and 2–6; Oct–April Mon–Fri 10–12 and 2–5; adm*). The Sartenais is exceptionally rich in prehistoric sites (*see* section below), and while this extensive collection of artefacts doesn't climb any great artistic heights, you can see what the Corsicans got up to in prehistoric times: from the early Neolithic era (6000 BC) there are flint tools and incised pot shards; from the megalithic period (3000–1500 BC), two statue-menhirs, one red (apparently they were all once painted in sacred ochre), photographs of sites and more pot shards; from the Iron Age (700 BC–AD 100), ceramics out of asbestos fibres and necklaces with 'porcelain' pearls. There are also some Roman-era coins, and a few painted medieval plates.

To see, or taste, what all the fuss is about the local wine, stop at the **Domaine Saparale** at 5 Cours Bonaparte (*ring ahead, t 04 95 77 15 52*) and pick up a bottle of red casteddu or white vermentino. The *domaine* is a wine estate in the upper Ortolo valley, so vast that it once had its own village of 100 workers, with shops and even a police station; completely abandoned, it was recently taken in hand by young oenologist Philippe Farinelli, whose family had owned it for generations.

Prehistoric Sites and Megaliths South of Sartène

The Sartenais was a busy place 4,000 years ago, back when there were probably more trees; today it has a savage beauty and bakes in the summer sun, so be sure to bring a hat and water. The closest prehistoric site to Sartène, **Alo Bisugè**, lies south on the N196 to Bonifacio; turn right on the D48 towards Tizzano, and then branch first right, taking the unmarked D21 in the direction of Grossa. After 4km you'll see the *casteddu* on the left. It's one of the oldest – Neolithic, carbon-dated to *c.* 2000 BC, and later occupied by the Torréens. It's small but complex, with a double Cyclopean wall, huts, and round and oblong buildings, both with cut-stone rectangular hearths. The view takes in a 12th-century church in a field, transformed into a barn.

Returning to the D48, continue south and take a left fork in the road to Cauria, winding past vineyards and *maquis* to a plateau, with beautiful views over the Gulf of Murtoli, where a sandy track leads to the **Mégalithes de Cauria**, which consist of three sites dating back to the same period as Alo Bisugè. Near the car park, in a low walled enclosure, you'll find the **Alignement de Stantari**, 25 statue-menhirs, two with heads, rough features, faint shoulders and swords, older than the ones at Filitosa. Some 400 yards away, in a copse of trees under a granite outcrop, the **Alignement de Rinaju** consists of 45 menhirs in rows orientated north–south – abnormal in the context of megalithic Europe, where the alignments are believed to have had some kind of astronomical function. On a low rise above the *maquis*, a sign from the car park points the way to the 15-minute walk to the **Dolmen de Funtanaccia**, the biggest and most beautiful on Corsica, 'discovered' by Mérimée in 1840. Its impressive granite chamber, 8½ft/2.6m long and 6ft/1.8m high, resembles a little house; the locals called it the *Stazzona di u Diavuli*, the Devil's Forge. Its depths are illuminated on the day of the winter solstice.

Backtrack to the D48 and head towards Tizzano. A few hundred metres past the Domaine Mosconi, you'll see on the right a sign for the menhirs – it's another 1.2 km on a rough road to the biggest alignment of menhirs in the entire Mediterranean, the **Alignements de Pagliaghju** (or Palaggiu). Dating from 1800 BC, these are seven groups of 258 stones – six are over 10ft/3m high, lined up on a north–south axis, some still upright, others tilting at various angles, some flat on the ground. Some are carved, mostly rudimentarily, into what Roger Grosjean, who studied them in the 1960s, labelled *menhirs protoanthropomorphes*, although there are also three proper statue-steles engraved with swords. Grosjean saw them as a magical army, lined up to thwart invaders by sea, and at twilight they take on the rosy glow of the setting sun.

Tizzano/Tizza, however, offers a chance to cool off with its sheltered little marina and wonderful white sandy beach, formerly Corsica's prime nudist playground. A ruined 15th-century Genoese fort once did what it could to keep pirates at bay; a dirt track leads up to it, and beyond to lovely little coves. During the Second World War, they were so remote they were a training ground for the Maquis under Special Operations Europe leader Andrew Croft.

Sartène to Bonifacio: Roccapina and the Uomo di Cagna

Back on the main N196 towards Bonifacio, snack bar L'Oasis de Lion is a good place to stop and have a look down at the **Rocher du Lion**, where the wind has chiselled a pinkish granite lion (with a 'crown' in the form of a ruined tower) on a promontory, looking over the magnificent two-mile-long, soft, sandy **Plage de Roccapina**; another chunk of granite nearby resembles an elephant's head. Sheltered and safe, Roccapina is the best and busiest beach in these parts (the road down is signposted 'Camping de Roccapina'), although the surrounding dunes and wetlands are fenced off as a nesting area for a variety of birds. A rocky path leads up to the Genoese watchtower on the ridge, with views over an even longer sandy beach, but you need a boat to get there. Note that although paths lead up to the lion, climbing it is dangerous, if not deadly – expert rock-climbers disdain it, however, for the Camel, Elephant, Moby-Dick or Horse, all in rough red granite. The most challenging and spectacular, however, is the 'Edge of Lace', 100m behind the Lion.

There may even be a box of diamonds buried somewhere nearby. A bandit, Barrittonu, had his lair in the natural shelters or *taffoni* around the lion, and he was there on the night of 17 April 1887, when the luxury steamer *Tasmania* rammed into the Ilots des Moines and sank. It was on its way from Bombay to Marseille, and carried on board a trunk of dazzling jewels from the rajahs of India for Queen Victoria's Jubilee, valued at eight times the price of the ship. As another ship, the *Stella*, hastened to salvage the gems, rumours of it spread in Sartène. The *Stella* managed to rescue the trunk, but a box of diamonds was never recovered. The story goes that Barrittonu got hold of it and buried it in the *maquis*, just before he was arrested and taken off to a penal colony, never to return.

The strangest of the many strange rock formations of the Sartenais, however, is inland: the **Uomo di Cagna** (3,992ft/1,220m) standing like an inverted exclamation mark at the end of Corsica's mountain spine. The 'man of Cagna' is made of a giant spherical boulder balanced on a sheer granite pinnacle, in the midst of a wilderness of granite and limestone that provided safe refuge for the Resistance during the war. From the wine village **Monacia d'Aullène/Monaccia d'Audde**, drive as far as the hamlet of **Gianuccio**, where you can pick up the well-marked path. It's a 5hr walk there and back, passing by way of other weird, rocky shapes rising out of the *maquis*. Where the path splits, note that the left-hand fork is easier but longer, and takes in the view of another remarkable formation to the north, the Uomo di Ovace. Once you've spotted the Uomo di Cagna in the distance it's another 45 minutes to the base. The top of the pinnacle is so sheer that dauntless climbers using a complex system of ropes only managed to reach it in 1970.

There are good beaches below Monacia, including the village beach, the **Plage de Conijonu**, 4km away down a narrow track; a lovely path at the end of the beach leads around in 20 minutes to another Genoese tower. The N196 next passes **Pianottoli-Calderello**, in a chaos of granite, with a quiet beach, before the narrow **Golfe di Figari**, a sure haven for sailors.

Bonifacio/Bunifaziu

Isolated on a limestone pedestal by the southern tip of Corsica, Bonifacio is one of the most remarkable towns in the Mediterranean and one of the most visited on the island. It is ideally approached by sea at twilight, when the colours are rich and glowing; before your ship are pale cliffs, so clawed by the wind and eaten by the waves that in places they bulge out like giant white mushrooms. And on the rim, teetering vertiginously on a thin promontory, rise the tall, narrow houses of Bonifacio. Where, you wonder, is the port? But then all at once the cliffs part to create a sinuous fjord, and in you sail. It has all the high drama of myth, and Homer seems to describe it perfectly in Book X of the *Odyssey*:

Bonifacio

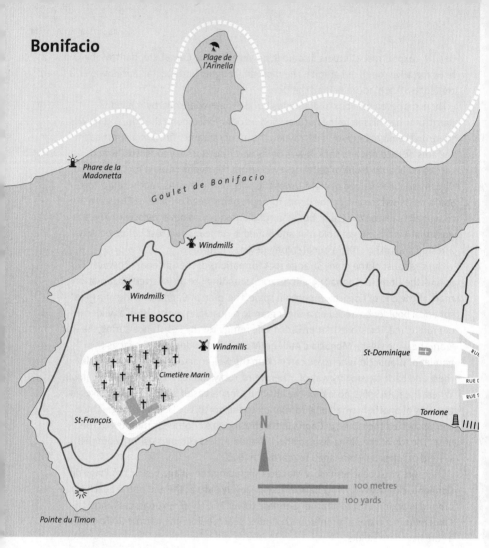

Here, then, we found
a curious bay with mountain walls of stone
to left and right, and reach far inland, –
a narrow entrance opening from the sea
where cliffs converged as though to touch and close.

In sail the Greeks, except for Odysseus, who moors his ship outside the entrance. Which is wise of him, because his companions soon discover that the locals, the Laestrygonians, have no manners at all: they rip the Greeks apart, and when they make a run for their ships the Laestrygonians bombard them with boulders from the cliffs, smashing ships and men 'to bits – poor gobbets the wildmen speared like fish and bore away'. Only Odysseus and the crew of his ship manage to escape becoming kebabs. The incident may even have been a dim historical memory; the Mycenaean

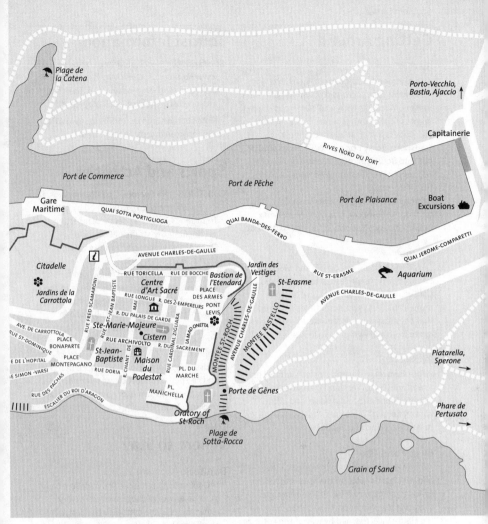

Greeks did have trade counters on Sardinia, and perhaps met with a memorably nasty reception when they tried to expand into Corsica.

These days visitors to Bonifacio tend to be fleeced rather than stoned, especially if they come in July or August. If you have to come then, at least try to walk around it at night after the tour groups are gone – like Sartène, Bonifacio is chock-full of atmosphere, although in this case it's as Ligurian as any town on the Riviera; Bonifaciens still speak a Genoese dialect that their fellow Corsicans find nearly incomprehensible.

History

People have been in Bonifacio long enough for its legends to ring true. One cave here yielded an 8,000-year-old skeleton known as the Dame de Bonifacio, the oldest ever found on Corsica. An ancient Greek coin from Rhegium in Calabria was found

Getting Around

By Air

The **Aéroport Sud-Corse**, in Figari, **t** 04 95 71 10 10, www.figari.aeroport.fr, with regular links to Paris, Marseille, Nice, and numerous charter flights in the summer, serves half a million passengers a year. In July and August, **Transports Rossi, t** 04 9571 00 11, run a **shuttle bus** into Bonifacio roughly every 90mins for €8; **taxis** make the same half-hour journey from €40–50.

Car hire: Avis, t 04 95 71 00 01; **Budget, t** 04 95 71 04 18; **Europcar, t** 04 95 71 01 41; **Hertz, t** 04 95 71 04 16; **National Citer, t** 04 95 71 02 00.

By Boat

SAREMAR, t 04 95 73 00 96, and **Moby Lines, t** 04 95 73 00 29, run ferries to Santa-Teresa-di-Gallura in Sardinia. Sailings take an hour – or more if the wind's up; sometimes it's so up that the crossings are cancelled. Frequencies range from 4 in winter to 10 in August.

By Bus

Four **Eurocorse** buses a day (2 in winter) go to Sartène, Porto-Vecchio, Figari, Roccapina, Olmeto, Propriano and Ajaccio; and 4 (2 in winter) **Corsica Tour** buses, **t** 04 95 70 10 36, go to Porto-Vecchio and Bastia.

By Car and Taxi

In the summer, arrive early to avoid the frequent traffic jams on the road into town. **Parking** can be very difficult, even though there are big pay car parks by the port and in the Haute Ville, reached by way of the Porte de France, a road tunnelled under the walls in 1854. Access to the latter is strictly limited in summer. A **tourist train** makes the steep trip up into the Haute Ville from the port for €5. You can **hire a car** from **Hertz**, Quai Portigliolo, **t** 04 95 73 06 41, or **Europcar, t** 04 95 73 10 99. For a **taxi**, call **t** 04 95 73 19 08.

Tourist Information

Bonifacio: Rue Fred Scamaroni, **t** 04 95 73 11 88, www.bonifacio.fr. Open May–Sept daily 9–8; Oct–April Mon–Fri 9–12 and 2–6. There's also an annexe by the port, open May–Sept.

Note that in summer Bonifacio's two ATMs frequently run dry: come preprared.

Sports and Activities

Golf: The 18-hole **Sperone Golf Club, t** 04 95 73 17 13, www.sperone.net, designed by Robert Trent Jones, boasts a spectacular setting overlooking the straits of Bonifacio. Open all year except for 2 weeks in Feb; closed Thurs.

Diving: The Iles Lavezzi are renowned for underwater beauty, deep red coral and the variety of fish, especially the enormous brown groupers. Contact **Atoll Plongée**, Quai Banda del Ferro, **t** 04 95 73 02 83, www.atoll-diving.com, or **Barakouda**, Av Sylvère Bohn, **t** 04 95 73 13 02.

Windsurfing: **Bonifacio Windsurf**, Piantarella, on the Sperone road, **t** 04 95 73 52 04, www.bonifacio-windsurf.com. Also **TamTam**, on Santa Manza beach, **t** 04 95 73 11 59.

Where to Stay

Bonifacio ✉ 20169

★★★Genovese, Quartier de la Citadelle, **t** 04 95 73 12 34, www.hotel-genovese.com (very expensive). On the cliffs over the port, 14 lovely rooms in a pale rosy villa; all light, airy, modern and comfortable, some with spectacular views, plus a new decked pool excavated in the town walls, with vertiginous views. There are also three luxury suites by the port. Breakfast served on the garden terrace. Closed Dec–Feb.

here, and the Romans were here, too, although they preferred the Etang de Sperone to the east. Yet in spite of its strategic location and port, there was no permanent town on the cliffs until 828, when Bonifacio, Marquis of Tuscany, on his way home from fighting the Saracens in Sicily, saw its potential and sent over the first colonists. In 1092, the Pisans took it over. Their rivals, the Genoese, captured it in 1181; they slyly attacked just after a wedding, when the Pisans were drunk.

★★★**La Caravelle**, 37 Quai Comparetti, t 04 95 73 00 03, *www.hotel-caravelle-corse.com* (*very expensive–expensive*). Handsome 19th-century house under the *citadelle*, overlooking the port; inside there's a pretty garden courtyard. The bar occupies a 13th-century chapel; the fine restaurant has a terrace under the palms and specializes in seafood (try the stuffed oysters or lobster-filled ravioli, with a touch of anise) (*menus from €29–64*).*Closed mid-Oct–Easter.*

★★★**Centre Nautique**, on the Quai Nord, t 04 95 73 02 11, *www.centre-nautique.com* (*expensive*). A trendy, comfortable, seaworthy place to stay by the port with 10 large stylish rooms, each on two levels; the restaurant with its Milanese chef serves up exquisite and filling pasta and seafood (*around €40; closed Tues out of season*).

★★★**Santa Teresa**, Quartier Santa Teresa, t 04 95 73 11 32 (*expensive*). On the edge of the Haute Ville, a peaceful 48-room hotel with a car park, contemplating the views towards Sardinia. *Open Mar–Oct.*

★★★**Roy d'Aragon**, 13 Quai Comparetti, t 04 95 73 03 99, *www.royaragon.com* (*expensive–moderate*). On the marina, with comfortable, recently remodelled rooms; the ones on the top cost more but have a terrace with an exquisite view.

Le Royal, 8 Rue Fred Scamaroni, t 04 95 73 00 51, *www.hotel-le-royal.com* (*expensive–moderate*). Plain but comfortable air-conditioned rooms in the Haute Ville, just off Place Bonaparte, with a view down to the port.

★**Hôtel des Etrangers**, Av. Sylvère Bohn, t 04 95 73 01 09 (*moderate, breakfast incl.*). On the Ajaccio road, a short walk from the port, friendly old place built into a cliff, with parking. *Closed Nov–Feb.*

Domaine de Licetto, Rte du Phare de Pertusato, t 04 95 73 03 59, *denisefavy@aol. com* (*inexpensive*). In a quiet setting, 2km

from the port with a fine view back over Bonifacio. The excellent restaurant, open evenings in season only to those who book, serves a single, delicious, all-inclusive *€31 menu*. No credit cards.

Near Bonifacio

★★★★**Hôtel et Spa des Pecheurs**, Cavallo, t 04 95 70 36 39 (*luxury*). Your chance to stay on one of the most exclusive islands in the Med, in a sprawling granite bungalow complex by a white sand beach, with a thalassotherapy spa and international restaurant. *Closed Oct–April.*

Marina di Cavu, Calalonga, t 04 95 73 14 13, *www.marinadicavu.com* (*luxury*). Beautifully set in the granite and olives 200m from the beach, around a magnificent pool with a spa and cascades. Air-conditioned, well-equipped villa bungalows, apartments and rooms, with views over the islets of Cavallo and Lavezzi. *Open all year.* Plus an excellent restaurant (*closed Nov–Mar*), serving fresh Mediterranean cuisine (*menu €46*).

★★★★**U Capu Biancu**, Domaine de Pozzoniello, Rte de Canetto, t 04 95 73 05 58, *www. ucapubiancu.com* (*luxury–expensive*). Isolated at the end of a long drive outside Bonifacio, a stylish, enchanting retreat on a private beach; each room and suite is lovelier than the next. The hotel has its own boat for outings or waterskiing, diving gear, mountain bikes and canoes, and a restaurant specializing in creative Mediterranean cuisine. *Closed Nov–April.*

★★★**A Trama**, Rte de Santa Manza, 2km from Bonifacio, t 04 95 73 17 17, *www.a-trama.com* (*expensive*). Sweet modern rooms with all mod cons and very comfortable beds in several bungalows, each with a terrace, spread out in a lush garden of olives and palms, with a beautiful pool in the centre and fine restaurant (*menu €29*). The rooms are a great bargain out of season.

The Genoese massacred the Pisans and replaced them with 250 Ligurian families, who were given enough tax exemptions and privileges (including the right to mint their own coins and engage in piracy) to govern themselves as a pint-sized republic, all to defend Genoa's 'eye in the midst of the waters'. In return, Bonifacio remained ever faithful to Genoa, holding tight in 1420 for five months during a siege and blockade led by the king of Aragon, Alfonso V (*see* box, p.125).

***A Cheda**, Cavallo Morto (2mins from Bonifacio off the Porto-Vecchio road), t 04 95 73 03 82, *www.acheda-hotel.com (expensive; half-board only in season)*. Charming villa-style hotel with rooms of character in a fragrant garden in an old olive grove, with a pool, hot tub and sauna; works with the Atoll diving centre. Family rooms sleeping four available. The pretty garden restaurant, under young chef Sébastian Mortet, offers a wide choice of Mediterranean dishes and seafood, flavoured with herbs from the *maquis*. Big brasserie menu at lunch and a *menu gastronomique* at night (*set price €26*).

A Loghia di Cavallu Mortu, Rte de Porto-Vecchio, t 04 95 73 05 41, *www.cavallumortu.com (expensive)*. Three rustic/elegant B&B rooms in the countryside, in an old stone house, and a *soignée* breakfast with home-made jams. She (Fabienne) writes books about Corsican cuisine; he (Alain) makes a delicious olive oil.

****Hôtel du Golfe**, 6km east of Bonifacio at Santa Manza, t 04 95 73 05 91, *http://golfe.hotel@ wanadoo.fr (moderate)*. Nice welcoming little hotel 50m from the beach, with a good restaurant. *Half-pension only. Closed mid-Oct–mid-Mar.*

Camping Rodinara, at Rodinara bay, 18km northeast of Bonifacio, t 04 95 70 43 15, *www.rodinara.fr (inexpensive)*. Some 400m from one of Corsica's most beautiful beaches, an impeccable campsite with a lovely pool. *Closed Oct–15 May.*

Eating Out

Bonifacio is famous for its aubergines (*mirizani*) *à la bonifacienne*, stuffed with *brocciu*, but most of the restaurants that line the port specialize in fish. Note that some of the best (A Cheda, La Caravelle, Domaine de Licetto) are in the hotels (*see* 'Where to Stay').

Les Terrasses d'Aragon Rue Castille Vecchio, t 05 95 73 51 07. Lovely sunset views from the terrace at the top of the king of Aragon's stair and *soignée* gourmet cuisine, featuring spaghetti with sea urchins and lobster *bouillabaisse*. *Menus €26–62.*

Le Voiler, 81 Quai Comparetti, t 04 95 73 07 06. Elegant, long time favourite by the port – try the courgette flowers stuffed with clams and chocolate desserts. *Lunch menu €25, evenings à la carte c.€50. Closed Jan, Feb, and Wed and Sun eves in low season.*

Stella d'Oru (Chez Jules), 7 Rue Doria, t 04 95 73 03 63. Another good choice up here, with famous aubergines *à la bonifacienne*, good ravioli and other pasta dishes, pizza, fish and lamb, served with an excellent Patrimonio. *Menu €23. Closed Oct–Mar.*

Les Quatre Vents, 23 Quai di Banda del Ferro, t 04 95 73 07 50. By the ferry port for Sardinia, an Alsatian change of pace, with *choucroute* and the works, as well as Corsican dishes. *€20 menu. Closed Mon eve and Tues.*

Kissing Pigs, 15 Quai di Banda del Ferro, t 04 95 73 56 09. Reasonably priced bistrot-wine bar run by Mary-Maud and Natale Ferrico, specializing in *charcuterie*, grilled meats and plates of cheeses – all the things that go nicely with a bottle of wine, carefully chosen among the island's famous and lesser known labels – such as the Blanc du Clos de Sarcone. *Menus €10–20.*

Cantina Doria, Rue Doria, t 04 95 73 50 49. Delightful family-run restaurant in the Haute Ville, offering *€12 and €15 menus* that are so popular (the Corsican lasagne is especially good) that you had better book. *Closed Wed eve, and Nov–mid-Mar.*

Lollapalooza, 25 Quai Comparetti, t 04 95 73 04 54. Reasonable restaurant (*menus at €14 and €15*) but also a popular cocktail bar, often with live music in summer. *Open till 3am.*

In 1528, plague decimated the town, leaving only 700 survivors from a population of 5,000. The next trial came in 1553 in the form of Sampiero Corso with the French army, and the terrible Dragut and his Turkish corsairs. For 18 days and nights they pulverized Bonifacio from the sea and nearby plateau of Capettu; the entire population, including women and children, rallied once more to the walls when the Turks and French attempted to take the battered city. Their courage was such that Dragut was on the point of giving up, when by luck he captured Dominique Cattaciolo, returning from Genoa with 15,000 *écus* as aid for Bonifacio. Cattaciolo was persuaded to deliver instead a forged letter from Genoa saying that it was impossible to come to the rescue and the town should surrender. Negotiations were then made with Dragut, who guaranteed the Bonifaciens their lives and belongings; only, once the gate was opened, the Turks massacred the garrison and were starting on the civilians when Sampiero stopped Dragut by offering to pay for their lives. A few years later, with the Treaty of Cateau-Cambrésis, Bonifacio was returned to Genoa with the rest of Corsica.

Once Corsica became French, Bonifacio lost its privileges and its merchants drifted away. Relations with Sardinia just over the strait were occasionally strained as well, notably in 1793, when the Revolutionary Convention decided to send an expeditionary force against it, to niggle the king of Sardinia and his English allies. Paris sent word to Pasquale Paoli, as General of the Corsican National Guard, to muster 6,000 men for the task. He only managed to find a third of that number, including one Napoleon Bonaparte, and placed them under the command of his kinsman Colonna-Cesari. It was Napoleon's first action, but far from his very first conquest; in fact it was a scene out of an *opéra bouffe*. The French sailed from Bonifacio to the Maddalena islands, where a local fisherman bamboozled them by sailing to and fro among the ships for three days, firing off his cannon, until the French turned tail. The repercussions, however, were serious: the Convention, influenced by Lucien Bonaparte, demanded that Paoli come to Paris to explain himself; Paoli responded by declaring himself *generalissimo* of an independent Corsica; Napoleon sided with France and started a civil war.

The Port and the Porte de Gênes

In the mid-19th century, when the coast was clear, Bonifacio spread down to the port, where today restaurants and cafés look out over the yachts bobbing in the marina. Amid them, along the Quai Comparetti, there's the **Aquarium de Bonifacio** (*t 04 95 73 03 69; open Easter–Oct 10am–midnight; Nov–Easter 10–8; adm*), hollowed out of the cliff; the tanks contain all kinds of local marine life, and weird surprises like flying crab. Older than the other buildings, the 13th-century **St-Erasme** was the church for fishermen, who were not allowed into the Haute Ville. Besides the usual procession for the saint on 2 June, another takes place on 20 June in honour of St Silverius, patron saint of lobster fishermen. Bonifacio also has five coral divers, whose catch is strictly regulated. The local coral (as you can see in the town shops) is a deep red colour: the stronger the current, the redder it becomes, and the current in the strait of Bonifacio is one of the strongest in the Mediterranean.

From St-Erasme, a stepped lane ascends to the walled Haute Ville; where it meets the road there's the **Oratory of St Roch**, marking the spot where the last plague victim died in 1528; the adjacent **belvedere** offers views of the old city rising from the cliffs, and chunks of limestone that have broken away and fallen into the sea, reminiscent of the boulders tossed by the cannibal Laestrygonians on Odysseus' hapless Greeks – the largest, philosophically called the **Grain of Sand**, broke off 800 years ago. Occasionally, houses fall off too (one slid into the sea in 1966) and no one is quite sure how to reinforce them and the cliff. A stepped path designed for horses leads from here around to Capo Pertusato (*see* below) and another down to a tiny beach. Above is the original and only gate into town, the **Porte de Gênes**, a Z-shaped passage once closed by eight heavy doors and a drawbridge; the mechanism is still in place.

Just within the gate, the **Place des Armes** still contains four of its seven underground silos, capable of holding an estimated 25 tonnes of grain, which enabled the Bonifaciens to survive their various sieges. Next to this, the 15th-century **Bastion de l'Etendard** guarded the gate and now houses the **Mémorial** (*open April, May, June and Sept Mon–Sat 11–5.30; July and Aug daily 8–7; adm*), a real hotchpotch, including morose tableaux depicting Bonifacio's past: Charles V's visit (he was returning from his disastrous crusade in Algeria in 1541, and ran into a storm) and the beautiful horse that his host Filippo Cattaccuilo loaned him and then killed, so that no one would ever sit where the imperial buttocks had rested; Napoleon's doings in Bonifacio; the sinking of the *Sémillante*; as well as a copy of the skeleton of the Dame de Bonifacio (the original is in Levie, *see* p.144), a real one of a Turkish soldier, and the town's first film projector. Admission includes a stroll along the bastion and the tiny **Jardin des Vestiges**, where ruins of the Pisan walls are now planted with flowers. At the end of Rue du Portone, **Place du Marché** (where the locals play *boules* in the evening) gives on to the **Belvédère de la Manichella**, with views over the cliffs, strait and Sardinia.

The Haute Ville

Although much rebuilt after its various sieges, the picturesque Haute Ville still looks much as it did in the 14th century when it was populated by thousands instead of hundreds. The houses resemble tenements, some as high as seven storeys, and often only wide enough to have one room per floor. As in Sartène, extremely steep and narrow stairs replace the original ladders that were drawn up each evening. The ground floors would contain an olive press or a donkey stable, or were used by the merchants to store their goods. The little arches between the houses are buttresses, but also act as canals to carry water off the roofs into underground cisterns; water was always at a premium here. Battered coats of arms hang over the doors.

The biggest cistern of all was under the **Loggia** in front of the 13th-century Romanesque-Gothic church of **Ste-Marie-Majeure,** next to a landmark 14th-century white stone campanile with four tiers. The loggia sheltered meetings of the town notables, the *anciens*; here, too, the *podestà* (a mayor appointed by Genoa) rendered judgement twice a week. Bonifacio's children now use it to play football, while their elders meet in the ex-cistern below, now used as a conference room. Although Ste-Marie was given a major facelift in the 18th century, older bits survive inside: a 3rd-century Roman sarcophagus used as a font, and the fine white marble tabernacle of the dead Christ and eight mournful cherubs, made in Genoa in 1465. The church also contains a piece of the True Cross, a gift, they say, from St Helen, the mother of the Emperor Constantine, after her ship was miraculously spared in a storm. It is kept in the sacristy in a niche, and in the old days when the weather was especially bad the *curé* and mayor and a posse of Bonifaciens would take the relic out to the Manichella Belvedere where they prayed for relief.

Opposite, the **Maison du Podestat** was the residence of the Genoese *podestà*, and still bears the arms of Genoa la Superba. The Palazzu Publicu is now the **Centre d'Art Sacré** (*open April–Oct 10.30–1.30 and 5–7.30; adm*), housing items from the churches, 17th-century Italian paintings, and exhibitions on Bonifacio's five Confraternities who take part in the elaborate Maundy Thursday and Good Friday processions. When the processions pass one another in the street they silently acknowledge the other's presence by touching banners, the way files of ants touch antennae.

Rue des Deux Empereurs earned its name, as the plaques attest, by hosting two emperors, Charles V and Napoleon, who stayed here in 1793 with relatives before the Sardinian fiasco. Towards Place Bonaparte, the charming little 18th-century church of

The Famous Defence of Corsica's Gibraltar

In 1420, Barcelona was reaching the apogee of its power in the Mediterranean when its dashing 24-year-old king, Alfonso of Aragon, turned up in Bonifacio with his fleet and blockaded the narrow entrance to the port with his ships, determined to take the city by siege or starvation. Sardinia was already his after a long war, and Corsica was almost his, too, thanks to his ally Vincentello d'Istria; Calvi had surrendered at the mere sight of his fleet. Only Bonifacio remained in the way of his taking the kingdom of Corsica and Sardinia that the pope had bestowed on his ancestors. No one in their right mind would have put an *écu* on Bonifacio's chances.

The whole town mobilized, men, women and children, hurtling down rocks, beams, boiling water, and powdered lime into the faces of the attackers, stabbing them with harpoons tied to poles, the women rebuilding the walls as the men were killed. The name Marguerite Bobbia pops up over and over again as the brain behind the defence. In the third month, when the Bonifaciens were starving, they made a truce, giving the Aragonese 32 children as hostage and agreeing to surrender if no help came from Genoa within 40 days. They then built a boat in the town, and lowered it into the sea; word reached Genoa, which, fearful of losing her 'eye in the sea', sent seven galleons full of provisions to the rescue. Only the winds prevented them from arriving, and on the 40th day Alfonso demanded the keys to the city. The famished survivors begged another day, and the Aragonese graciously agreed.

In the middle of the night the Aragonese were wakened by church bells and waving banners, and the sight of what looked like an army on the walls. It was all a desperate bluff; the women had donned the armour of the dead soldiers and with the surviving men put on such a bold display that the Aragonese were convinced that the Genoese had somehow succoured the town, and the battle began again. Finally on Christmas Day the Genoese appeared and, after a fierce battle, rammed their way in past the blockading ships and delivered the supplies; five days later they rammed their way back out again. This wasn't in the script, and Alfonso, as he duly re-formed his blockade, was feeling rather discouraged. Then a message reached him from the queen of Naples, offering him her throne in exchange for his protection. On 5 January he sailed away in relief, glad to get away from Corsica. The Genoese had only to bide their time in Bonifacio and Calvi (which they soon recovered), wait for a false move from Aragon's viceroy Vincentello, and Corsica was theirs again.

St-Jean-Baptiste houses a remarkable 16th-century sculptural group in wood, representing the beheading of the Baptist.

Part of Bonifacio's original Pisan defences was a mighty tower, the **Torrione**, which was demolished in 1901 but rebuilt in the 1980s; from here (Rue des Pachas) the 187-step **Escalier du Roi d'Aragon** (*open April–Oct daily 9–8; adm*), cut in the rock, descends precipitously to sea level. According to legend, it was built by the troops of the king of Aragon during a single night in 1420 in an attempt to break the stalemate in their five-month siege, but they were thwarted by the vigilance of the heroine Marguerite Bobbia (*see* box, p.125). In reality the stair, which descends to a natural spring, is much older; some people even say the first steps were carved in Neolithic times, and it has been constantly improved since. You can walk down, stroll along the sea and hike back up again, although not if the wind is up.

The Bosco

The Genoese **Citadelle** was built over the Pisan quarter, and its walls now shelter the Jardins de la Carrottola and the car park in Place Bir-Hakeim, with a **Monument to the Foreign Legion**. This was rescued from Saïda in Algeria in 1963 and brought here by the Foreign Legion, which took up residence in Bonifacio until 1989; the presence of the kepi-ed ones caused the authorities to close up the city's old wells, which are said to descend 800ft/245m – because legionaries were using them to escape. The tourist office is just below, while just above is **St-Dominique** (*open July–15 Sept daily 2.30–8; adm*), Corsica's most important Gothic church, reputedly built by the Templars in 1270 before it passed on to the Dominicans in 1309. The interior is richly furnished, with 18th-century Italian paintings on the mystery of the Rosary and a pair of sculptural groups that go on procession: one, weighing 1,765lbs, shows a wildly operatic *Flaying of St Bartholomew* (with a note of black humour in the peckish little dog). The church's acoustics make it a favourite for recording polyphonies.

This quarter beyond was named **Bosco** by the Pisans for its woods, although the trees were cut down in the 18th century, leaving a moody, flat, barren plateau. Bonifaciens ground their grain in the 13th-century **windmills** here, one of which has been restored. At the far west end of the plateau, beyond the empty Foreign Legion barracks, awaits one of the most evocative corners of Bonifacio: the **Cimetière Marin**, where the family mausoleums, with poppies sprouting between the cracks, resemble little white houses or churches looking out towards the setting sun – it's one of the most romantic places in town to watch the sun go down. At the end of the cemetery stands another Gothic church, the late 14th-century **St-François**, part of a convent founded after a visit by the eponymous saint.

Around Bonifacio

Cliffs and Islands, by Sea

From the sea, Bonifacio and its cliffs resemble a giant's messy office gone mad – piles and piles of white paper rising at all angles with the town perched on top like a

paperweight. Boats bobbing in Bonifacio's port will take you along them, to a secret lagoon and (if the sea is calm) into the **Grotte du Sdragonato**, the Dragon's Cave, illuminated by a cleft in the ceiling that resembles a map of Corsica. The surrounding cliffs above were used in the film *The Guns of Navarone*. Excursions also pass along the southern tip of the island, known as the **Gouvernail de la Corse**, the 'rudder of Corsica', with its Second World War gun turret, reached by a long tunnel. There's also a great view of the King of Aragon's Stair slicing diagonally up the cliff.

The longer excursion visits the low, wind-sculpted granite **Iles Lavezzi**, surrounded by a crystal sea. Most companies go to and fro, so if you bring your own supplies (food, water, snorkel) you can have a day out at the fine beach or creek – follow the coastal path past the first beach, which tends to be packed. In spring, botanists come to seek out its tiny endemic plants, some of which have relatives only in South America. (How did they get here? No one knows.) Uninhabited except for a donkey and some goats, the islands' only structures are shepherds' huts, a funerary chapel, cemetery and a pyramid memorial that commemorates the wreck of the French naval frigate *La Sémillante* in 1855, which took all 773 men down with her en route to the Crimean War, in one of the worst ever shipwrecks in the Mediterranean.

The excursions also offer a glance at the larger **Ile Cavallo**, dignified by a flotilla of yachts. Cavallo is owned by a shady Italian consortium, which has made it into an exclusive retreat for millionaires (Princess Stephanie of Monaco, etc.), who maintain a private militia to keep the uninvited away, in spite of the French law that allows public access to the coasts. Some excursions will take you past the granite quarries here and on the neighbouring islet of **San Bainzo**; worked by slaves, the quarries were abandoned at the end of the Roman Empire – you can make out the crude bust of Hercules Saxanus, the god of hard labour, another of an unidentified emperor, and half-dressed columns lying about, waiting for a galley that never came.

In the early 19th century, so many bandits, both Corsican and Sard, escaped justice by fleeing over the strait that it was patrolled by warships. Now you don't even need a passport. A good way to spend a day is a trip to **Sardinia**: drive east of the ferry port of Santa-Teresa-di-Gallura to Palau, and make the short ferry hop to La Maddalena island, a granite fantasy island with beaches in a crystal sea and a bridge to Caprera, the island once owned by Garibaldi. Sardinia is famous for its *nuraghi*, Bronze Age towers that resemble miniature castles. There are two good ones in Azarchena, 15km south of Palau, two 'giant's tombs', and a dozen other prehistoric curiosities (the Azarchena tourist office has a good map) – as well as the glamorous Costa Smeralda.

Just West of Bonifacio

At the mouth of the Ventilegne river, a road leads down to the big sandy beach of **Tonnara**, facing a pair of tiny islets. On the way, about 7km from Bonifacio (signposted on the left on the N198 towards Sartène), a narrow road leads the granite **Ermitage de la Trinité**, splendidly set among a tangle of granite boulders and olives. It stands near a Neolithic holy site – a *taffoni* of boulders (now serving as a grotto for a statue of the Virgin), where the island's first Christian hermits lived. Their original chapel was rebuilt in the 13th century, and heavily restored in 1880 with an Eye of God and the *In Domino Libertas* motto of Bonifacio over the door. On the hill above, the metal cross seems to be held in place by a giant granite fist.

To the Lighthouse and Beaches

Bonifacio's beaches aren't as good as Porto-Vecchio's, but they may be less crowded.

A 5km path along the cliffs beginning near St-Roch (*see* above) or a rather terrifying road off the D58 both lead to the **Capo Pertusato lighthouse**, standing 290ft/90m over the sea at the southernmost tip of Corsica (*open after 3pm*). Even if you don't climb the lighthouse, the wild headland, carpeted with wild flowers in spring, offers breathtaking views back to Bonifacio and across to Sardinia, only 12km away across the strait. Long ago, a granite isthmus linked the two islands together. Survivors of this land bridge – a smattering of little islets at the ends of both islands – make the passage much narrower than it appears and, in spite of fifteen semaphores and lighthouses, every now and then one of the 10,000 ships a year that pass through the strait comes to grief, most recently the cargo ship *Monte-Stello* on New Year's Day 1994. In the worst tempests, waves reach the lantern of the Madonetta at the entrance to Bonifacio's fjord, around 90ft/30m above the sea.

Just beyond the lighthouse is the immaculate 18-hole **Spérone Golf Club**, one of the most beautiful courses in Europe and a magnet for all the jet-set spillover from Sardinia's Costa Smeralda, who haunt this corner of Corsica. The course is owned by a Paris businessman, who in 1997 broke the *loi de silence* when the Cuncolta tried to extort protection money from him (*see* p.22). Bonifacio's nearest beach (and best windsurfing) is just east at **Piantarella** (beware that in summer the parked cars can be stretched for over a mile along the road). For a quieter beach, the white protected cove of **Le Petit Spérone** is a 15-minute walk south along the edge of the golf course (keep an eye out for errant balls); the ruins of the port of a luxurious Roman villa from the 1st century AD in the vicinity suggest that this was the realm of wealth and privilege even 2,000 years ago. Another road, the rutted D258, leads to a quiet beach at **Calalonga** to the north of Piantarella, where the sea floor is sandy and shallow for a long way out, although if the wind blows the wrong way junk and litter move in.

Further north, in a sheltered gulf ideal for windsurfing, are beautiful beaches set in pink granite: **Santa Manza** and **Maora**, where funboard championships are held in May. The road to both of these passes the abandoned **Couvent St-Julien**, built by the Knights of St John and dedicated to helping wayfarers, and where St Francis stayed in 1215 on his return from Spain to Italy. Further north again, off the N198, a little road signposted 'Hotel Capu Bianco' (turn left at the fork) leads to the **Plage de Canetto**, a pretty little sandy cove under the cliffs, which tends to be fairly quiet.

Halfway to Porto-Vecchio is the most beautiful of Bonifacio's beaches, **Rondinara**, a broken circle of sand resembling a green Polynesian lagoon. However, now that the road is paved, you have to come in the winter or at dawn to see it as it looks on the postcards – and pay to park. A fire in 2003 charred some of the surroundings.

Porto-Vecchio/Portivechju

Là, sulla collina, la cità di Portivechju
Incù li monti par curona e lu mare par specchju

(There on the hill, the city of Porto-Vecchio,
with mountains for a crown and the sea for a mirror).

In the last 20 years, little Porto-Vecchio has grown every which way to become Corsica's third city, with over 11,000 year-round inhabitants, as well as the island's top tourist destination – so many Italians visit that the coffee served in the local cafés is as good as you get in Italy. Besides the bonus of a proper espresso, however, it's not hard to see the allure: the old town is charming, the nearby beaches and hotels are among the finest on the island, and the nightlife sizzles. And just above Porto-Vecchio stands the magnificent L'Ospedale forest, and roads lead high into the Alta Rocca, to some of Corsica's most celebrated beauty spots, including the five-star Col de Bavella.

History

Porto-Vecchio's name, 'old port', is no lie. The area is rich in prehistoric sites: the city was the *Portus Syracusanus* mentioned by Ptolemy, founded in the 5th century BC by

Getting Around

By Air

In July and August, **Transports Rossi**, t 04 95 71 00 11, run a **shuttle bus** roughly every 90mins linking Porto-Vecchio to Corsica-Sud airport in Figari (*see* p.120), departing from the Café La Marine by the port.

By Boat

Port information, t 04 95 70 06 03. **SNCM** ferries link Porto-Vecchio to Marseille several times a week. In summer, **Med Mar**, t 04 95 70 06 03, sail to Naples.

By Bus

Eurocorse, Rue Pasteur, t 04 95 70 13 83, go to Bonifacio, Figari, Sartène, Propriano and Ajaccio 3 times daily in summer, and once or twice daily at other times; **Balesi Evasion**, t 05 94 70 15 55, also go to Ajaccio. Two daily **Rapides Bleus** buses, 7 Rue Jean Jaurès, t 04 95 70 96 52, travel up the east coast to Bastia. **Ile de Beauté** buses, 13 Rue Général de Gaulle, t 04 95 70 12 31, go to Ajaccio by way of Bavella and the villages of the Alta Rocca once a day.

In summer, regular **shuttle buses** (t 04 95 70 13 83 or t 04 95 71 40 09) run several times daily from Porto-Vecchio to its beaches, as far north as Pinarellu and south to Palombaggia.

By Car, Bike and Taxi

Beware that Porto-Vecchio, especially the Haute Ville, rivals Bonifacio for summer traffic snarl-ups, and in July and August cars are banned altogether.

Car hire: **Europcar**, Rte de Bastia, t 04 95 70 14 50; **Hertz**, Quai Pascal Paoli, t 04 95 70 32 05; **National Citer**, Port de Plaisance, t 04 95 70 16 96.

Scooter, bike or **mountain bike hire**: **Les Années Jeunes**, Av Georges Pompidou, t 04 95 70 36 50; or **Corsica Moto Rent**, Rte de Bonifacio, t 04 95 70 03 40.

Taxis: t 04 95 70 08 49; a trip to the airport at Figari will be around €60.

Tourist Information

Porto-Vecchio: Rue Camille de Rocca Serra, t 04 95 70 09 58, *www.destination-sudcorse.com*.

Open Oct–April Mon–Fri 9–12.30 and 2–6.30, Sat 9–12.30; May–Sept daily 9–8.

Sports and Activities

Boat Excursions

Trips to the Iles Lavezzi (*see* p.127) and Sardinia are operated by **Societé Djinn**, t 04 95 70 56 61 or t 06 77 15 73 79, *http://ledjinn. free.fr*, sailing out of the Baie de Santa Giulia. **Croisières San Antonio**, t 04 95 72 04 95, offers day tours to Bonifacio and the Iles Lavezzi, with lunch and swimming included. **Croisières Ruscana**, t 04 95 71 41 50, *www.croisieres-ruscana.com*, sails from the Porto-Vecchio Marina and Pinarellu to the islands and the cliffs of Bonifacio.

Diving

The main attractions are the Iles Cerbicale and the sunken *Pecorella*. Contact: **La Palanquée**, Les Marines, t 04 95 70 16 53. **Kallisté Plongée**, Plage de la Palombaggia, t 04 95 70 44 59, *www.corsicadiving.com*.

Walking

Porto-Vecchio is the best place to start the **Mare a Mare Sud** path to Propriano (*see* p.109). For information, call t 04 95 70 50 78 in summer, other times t 04 95 51 79 10. If you mean to tackle the **GR20**, the path ends or begins at Conca, to the north. A shuttle bus links Porto-Vecchio with the *gîte d'étape* at the beginning; for schedules, call t 04 95 71 46 55. **Balade avec un Nez**, t 04 95 70 34 64 or t 06 19 89 65 36. Twice-weekly botanical tours in French of the *maquis*, with an emphasis on its perfumes. **Corsica Forest**, t 06 16 18 00 58, *www.corsica-forest.com*. Canyoning, *via ferrata*, trekking, jeeps, jet skis – you name it, all with guides and equipment.

Where to Stay

Porto-Vecchio (near centre) ✉ 20137

Hotels are spread out everywhere, and will be full up and expensive in July and August. **★★★Alcyon**, 9 Rte de Bastia, t 04 95 70 50 50, *www.hotel-alcyon.com* (*very expensive*).

A modern, stylish little hotel with friendly owners near the centre of Porto-Vecchio, with a good buffet breakfast. *Open Mar–Dec.*

★★Le Goéland, La Marine, t 04 95 70 14 15, *www.hotelgoeland.com (very expensive– moderate, depending on view)*. One of the best – big rooms in the best location in town, on a small private beach, within walking distance of the Borgo. *Closed end Oct–Easter.*

★★★★Roi Théodore, Rte de Bastia, t 04 95 70 14 94, *www.roitheodore.com (expensive)*. Less than 1km north of town, a swish, tranquil hotel recently given a complete Mediterranean-style facelift plus a pretty garden, spa, sauna, tennis and infinity pool with a waterfall and an excellent restaurant. They also have a motor boat you can hire. *Half-board mandatory mid-June–Aug, €305 for two. Closed Jan–Feb.*

★★Holzer, 12 Rue Jean Jaurès, t 04 95 70 05 93, *www.corse-eternelle.com (expensive)*. In the centre, an immaculate Logis de France hotel with 30 air-conditioned rooms and a garage.

★★Mistral, corner of Rue Jean Nicoli and 5 Rue Toussaint Culioli, t 04 95 70 08 53 *(moderate)*. Within walking distance of the centre, simple rooms with air-conditioning and a bit of a garden. They also have apartments in the building opposite. *Closed early Nov–Feb.*

La Cuve, Quai Syracuse, t 04 95 25 10 21, *www. lacuve.com (moderate: high season €1,100 per week for up to four people)*. Old wine warehouse, vintage 1960, set near the port and salt marshes, converted into stylish apartments.

Panorama, 12 Rue Jean-Nicoli, t 04 95 70 07 96 *(moderate)*. Tidy little place next to the Citadelle, some rooms with a view. *Closed Oct–May.*

Camping L'Arutoli, 2km from Porto-Vecchio on the D368 to L'Ospedale, t 04 95 70 12 73, *www.arutoli.com (inexpensive)*. In an oak forest, with a big pool and pretty terrace; bungalows to rent for the tentless. Book in advance in summer. *Closed Nov–Mar.*

Around Porto-Vecchio

★★★★★Grand Hôtel Cala Rossa, at Cala Rossa, in Lecci-di-Porto-Vecchio, t 04 95 71 61 51, *www.hotel-calarossa.com (luxury)*. On its own peninsula, on the fine golden sands of a private beach, this Relais & Châteaux hotel is one of the most luxurious places to stay in Corsica, with 55 Mediterranean-style rooms with flat-screen TVs in stone buildings, surrounded by a 150-acre park of giant pines and tamarisks. The hotel has its own excursion boat, windsurfers, sailboats and waterskiing, sauna, hammam, gym, tennis and a superb, sophisticated Michelin-starred restaurant in a lovely setting, the domain of one of Corsica's top chefs, Georges Billon *(menus €75–98). Closed Jan–Mar.*

★★★★Casa del Mar, Rte de Palombaggia, t 04 95 72 34 34, *www.casadelmar.fr (luxury)*. New Relais & Châteaux boutique hotel overlooking the sea with 8 rooms and 12 suites designed with plenty of natural lighting, zen and feng shui (and ADSL and WiFi), each with a terrace with a view. Other amenities include a helipad, state-of-the-art high-tech spa, fitness centre, hammam, temperature-controlled outdoor pool in a garden and 'Quiet Room' for meditation, private little beach and beach bar, and an excellent restaurant specializing in Mediterranean cuisine. *Closed mid-Nov–mid-Mar.*

★★★★Le Pinarello, Ste-Lucie-de-Porto-Vecchio t 04 95 71 44 39, *www.lepinarello.com (luxury)*. Directly on the sands, a new, exclusive, minimalist little hotel popular among paparazzi targets. The rooms, decorated in teak and white linen, have views over the sea; if the beach outside is too busy, a boat waits to take you to more remote strands. The hotel is linked to the restaurant **Le Rouf** (see 'Eating Out'). *Closed Nov–May.*

★★★Le Belvédère, Rte de Palombaggia, t 04 95 70 54 13, *www.hbcorsica.com (luxury)*. A dream beachside hotel, in a lush garden under the parasol pines, with 16 luminous air-conditioned rooms and three suites, an enormous pool, and a lovely restaurant terrace with fossils embedded in the walls and sunny fresh cuisine that fits Corsican ingredients into the great Mediterranean traditions, with an Italian touch here, a French one there. They even bake their own bread. Great desserts (try *fruits rouges en gelée de muscat au sorbet brocciu vanillé*) and Corsica's finest wines. *Menus start at €65. Closed 15 Jan–Feb.*

★★★**E Casette**, Rte de Palombaggia, t 04 95 70 13 66, *www.ecasette.com* (*luxury*). New, peaceful hotel and family villas '*tendance chic et zen*' amid the *maquis* and overlooking the Golfe, midway between the beach and Porto-Vecchio.

★★★**Hôtel-Résidence U Benedettu**, north of Cala Rossa on the Presqu'île du Benedettu, t 04 95 71 62 81, *www.ubenedettu.com* (*luxury–expensive*). A Relais du Silence hotel in a lovely isolated setting on its own little peninsula, with 10 spacious rooms right on the beach as well as pavilions equipped with kitchenettes, etc. that go for €880 a week for three people. Good Corsican restaurant, **A Perla**, with a lovely terrace. *Half-board obligatory late June–early Sept.*

★★★**Le Moby Dick**, at Santa Giulia, t 04 95 70 70 00, *www.sud-corse.com* (*very expensive*). A touch of the Caribbean here, isolated between the sea and a lagoon, with 44 big air-conditioned rooms and balconies set on a private beach of pure white sand. There are also pavilions, perfect for families, with a fine restaurant. *Half-board in season. Closed Nov–April.*

★★★**Caranella Village**, Rte de Cala Rossa, Lecci-de-Porto-Vecchio, t 04 95 71 60 94, *www.caranella.com* (*expensive*). Well-equipped hotel in a garden setting, with rooms, studios, apartments and villas sleeping up to six, 300yds from Cala Rossa beach. Heated pool, two tennis courts, and bikes to hire, baby-sitting, room service and house-keeping on offer. *Closed Nov–Mar.*

★★★**Hôtel du Golfe**, Pinarellu, t 04 95 71 40 70, *www.corsica-hotel-legolfe.com* (*expensive*). Studios on the beach that sleep up to five, rented by the day or week (€1,200 a week in Aug). Open all year.

Littariccia, Rte de Palombaggia, t 04 95 70 41 33, *www.littariccia.com* (*expensive*). Turn up the old dirt road through the olive groves to a genuinely peaceful B&B enclave, all stone and wood, with huge rooms, wide shady terraces overlooking the trees and Palombaggia beach, and a pool.

Residence Les Oliviers, Rte de Palombaggia, t 04 95 70 36 42, *www.residencelesoliviers.com* (*expensive*). Little stone cottages, prettily furnished and located in a peaceful setting in the trees and *maquis* 2km from

the famous strand, although there's a pool on site as well. *Prices in high season start at €1,000 for two per week. Closed Nov–April.*

★★**Lauriers de Palombaggia**, Rte de la Plage, t 04 95 70 03 65, *www.palombaggia.fr* (*expensive*). Six airy double rooms around the pool, in a garden setting, a short walk from the famous beach. *Closed Nov–Mar.*

★★**San Giovanni**, Rte d'Arca, 5km from Porto-Vecchio, t 04 95 70 22 25, *www.hotel-san-giovanni.com* (*moderate*). Quite a bit back from the beaches but offers a haven of peace and quiet in the trees and garden. Big contemporary rooms, an attractive heated pool, tennis and bike hire. Charming management, good family cooking. *Half-board mandatory in July and Aug; €140 for two. Closed Nov–Mar.*

Camping California, at Pinarellu, t 04 95 71 49 24 (*inexpensive*). 50m from the beach, under the pines; restaurant, tennis and playground. No credit cards. *Closed 15 Oct–15 May.*

Camping Santa-Lucia, N198, Ste-Lucie-de-Porto-Vecchio, t 04 95 71 45 28, *www.campingsantalucia.com* (*inexpensive*). Well-run campsite under the cork oaks, with a pool and plenty of games for the kids, and bungalows. *Closed Nov–Mar.*

Conca ✉ 20135

Gîte d'Etape La Tonnelle, t 04 95 71 46 55, *latonnelleconca@hotmail.com* (*inexpensive*) Doubles, triples and dormitory beds near the beginning (or end) of the GR20. The owner operates a shuttle bus from Porto-Vecchio, connecting with the buses from Bastia.

Eating Out

Porto-Vecchio has a few dishes you may not see elsewhere in Corsica, including smoked ricotta and *tarte aux herbes* made with spinach and chard, and Italian favourites like *bruschetta*. Sea urchins are a popular *hors-d'œuvre*. Two of the finest restaurants in Corsica are at the hotels Belvédère and Cala Rossa; otherwise, there are many restaurants (summer only), that change chefs annually.

Le Rouf, Pinarellu, t 04 95 71 50 48. Fashionable seafood restaurant/music bar on the beach. *Evening menu €60. Closed Oct–April.*

Le Cabanon Bleu, north of Porto-Vecchio on the Plage de St-Cyprien, **t** 06 11 69 00 56. Trendy, cool, laid-back, very expensive celebrity-ridden beach restaurant, hard to find at the end of a non-signposted dirt track; most of the clients arrive by yacht (the address is by GPS co-ordinates, Lat. 41°38'44" north; Long. 9°21'38").

Le Lucullus, 17 Rue du Général de Gaulle, **t** 05 65 70 02 17. Stylish gourmet bastion serving a mix of traditional (oven-baked kid with *pommes de terre confits*), the day's catch and creative dishes. *Around €30 without wine.*

Le Passe-Temps, on the road to Cala Rossa beach, **t** 04 95 71 63 76. Join the crowd on the shady patio for succulent grilled meats (*around €25*) and pizzas as good as you get in Napoli.

Chez Mimi, 5 Rue du Général Abbatucci, **t** 04 95 70 21 40. An old favourite, in business for the past three decades making customers feel right at home with their traditional Corsican land and sea dishes. *Menu €25.*

Le Troubadour, Rue du Général Leclerc, **t** 04 95 70 08 62. Trendy atmosphere and delicious food from the mountains – *ravioli al brocciu* with mushrooms – as well as the sea – try the *suprême de rascasse* with wild herbs; good choice of wines. Every night from May to Sept, gather after dinner in the piano bar to hear Corsican songs and French boulevard classics. *Menu traditionnel €23. In summer open eves only, till 2am.*

Sous la Tonnelle, Rue Abbatucci, **t** 04 95 70 02 17. An intimate place in the city walls, with excellent specialities such as chicken breast coated in ground hazelnuts. *Menu €22. Open every eve in July and Aug, lunch and eve in June and Sept; other times closed Sun eve and Mon lunch.*

L'Antigu, 51 Rue Borgo, **t** 04 95 70 39 33. Pretty view from the terrace over the port and wonderful Mediterranean cuisine with a slightly exotic touch – such as sea bream *royale* with Corsican dried ham and sun-dried tomatoes in a lobster sauce. *Menu €21, lunch €17. Closed Sun lunch.*

Le Tourisme, 12 Cours Napoléon, **t** 04 95 70 06 45. In the heart of the old town, delicious mussels, pasta dishes and salads prepared with a light touch and a knowing hand. *Formules a bit dear but menus from €20–36. Open all year, but closed Sun lunch.*

37.2, Cala Rossa beach, **t** 04 95 71 70 24. Laid-back bar-restaurant on the sea, where you can choose your own lobster or the likes of lasagne with aubergines and avocado mousse, grilled meats or pizza. *Under €20 except for lobster. Closed mid-Sept–April.*

Le Figuier, Rte de Cala Rossa, 6km from Porto-Vecchio, **t** 04 95 72 08 78. Very popular and lively summer restaurant serving pizzas (made by genuine Neapolitans), salads and grilled meats served on big wooden tables in a delightful garden setting. *Under €15. Closed Oct–April.*

Entertainment and Nightlife

Cinémathèque de Corse, in the Espace Jean-Paul de Rocca Serra (the Centre Culturel), 7 Rue de Bastia, **t** 04 95 70 35 02, *www.casadilume.com*. Founded in 1983, this has some 3,000 films and a fascinating collection of film posters, all involving Corsica in some way. Most naturally feature the big N (Napoleon), but there are also a number of rare films shot in the 1920s.

Les Plaisirs du Vin, Rue Général de Gaulle. Atmospheric wine bar with snacks.

La Taverne du Roi, 43 Rue Borgo, by the Porte-Génoise, **t** 04 95 70 41 31. An atmospheric place for a drink, with guitarists and singers performing old Corsican songs and others. Fills up early so try to arrive by 10pm. *Closed winter.*

Shankabar, Place de l'Eglise, **t** 04 95 70 06 53. Trendy bar in the Haute Ville with a cool Moroccan décor, cocktails, *tapas* and snacks, and DJs on summer nights. *Closed Oct–May.*

Via Notte, Rte de Porra on the south edge of town, **t** 04 95 72 02 12, *www.vianotte.com*. In short, *the* club on Corsica – palms and waterfalls, a huge outdoor dance floor with room for 3,000, famous DJs, furniture by Philippe Starck plus a pool, cocktail bar, sushi bar, five other bars, restaurant. *Admission €10, €7 with a flyer, which includes three free non-alcoholic drinks for the designated driver. Open till 5am, closed Sept–June.*

Mosquitoes and Salt

For centuries, standing waters were the curse of Porto-Vecchio; *'a frebba li tumba e l'acqua l'ingrisgia'* ('the fever fells them and the water ages them') is what Corsicans used to say of its inhabitants. Under the Genoese, the city was abandoned many times, often as not because all the inhabitants were stricken with malaria. Today Porto-Vecchio likes to call itself the 'pearl of the south', but you'll also see its older nickname, the Ville de Sel, or 'salt city'; the annual 900 tonnes it produces supply much of Corsica's needs (mostly for preserving meat). Under the Genoese, salt was panned in the Golfe de Santa Manza, but, fearing that the Corsicans were smuggling it out and selling it on the sly, they destroyed the pans, preferring that the island import its salt from Ibiza so they could tax it at the port (the old Genoese, it must be said, really were terrible money-grubbers). The setting up of the industry in Porto-Vecchio was the one lasting thing accomplished on the island during its short rule by George III, king of England, Scotland and Corsica, when in 1795 he authorized Gio Paolo Roccaserra to establish pans in the old mosquito-breeding grounds.

the Greek city of Syracuse. In 1992 a fire in the *maquis* at the mouth of the river Oso revealed another ancient settlement that may have been Ptolemy's *Rhoubra*. Then, for long centuries, nothing, thanks or no thanks to pirates, in particular the dreaded Dragut who made the islet of Ziglione one of his lairs.

In spite of the threat, the Bank of St George founded Porto-Vecchio in 1540. With its sheltered bay, porphyry rock to build on, shallow lagoons (quickly converted into salt pans) and easy access to timber, it seemed the perfect spot. Instead, malaria and fate saw it destroyed and abandoned in 1546, 1564, 1579 and 1589. The Genoese, if nothing else, were tenacious, and after each set-back sent down more colonists. In 1769, Pasquale Paoli and his allies made Porto-Vecchio their last stand, before surrendering the city to the French troops and sailing off to exile with an English escort.

In 1872, the city found a new trade making bottle-stoppers, when a Catalan company founded a factory to take advantage of Porto-Vecchio's huge cork oak forest, the largest on Corsica. In 1935 a new railway line was built to Bastia, just in time for it to be bombed and abandoned in the war. But what really changed the prospects of Porto-Vecchio was DDT, and, when the cork factory closed in 1975, tourism was ready to hop in and take its place. Purists complain that by Corsican standards it is 'built up', and while it's true that many of the newer holiday homes and *villages de vacances* draped over the coastal hills are straight off a Mediterranean holiday assembly line, compared to, say, the Côte d'Azur, it's still low-key.

Old Porto Vecchio: the Borgo (Haute Ville)

Still enclosed in its Genoese walls high over the port, the nugget that is old Porto-Vecchio is laid out like a barbecue grill – a pleasant Corsican town with rather more boutiques and bars than average; on summer nights it really comes into its own. Massive plane trees and cafés line the main **Cours Napoléon**, while **Place de la République** is distinguished by a Bel Ombre or *bella sombra* (Phytolacca dioica), an enormous twisted tree from South America planted in 1901, giving shade to the cafés and to the 19th-century granite church of **St-Jean Baptiste**, left unfinished when the funds ran out. Atmospheric **Rue Borgo** runs under the seaward walls, where the **Porte Génoise** was once the sole entrance to town. At the north end of this, the **Bastion de France** resembles a steam iron and now contains a gallery that hosts special exhibitions; on the south side, the **Bastion di A Funtana Vechju** has a hole in it, left by Sampiero Corso's cannonballs when he captured the town in July 1564. The area was crawling with pirates as usual; when Sampiero tried to make an alliance with them, the Genoese sounded the alarm, and their ally, Philip II of Spain, sent his fleet to the rescue in November to chase Sampiero out. The port and salt pans shimmer below.

Around Porto-Vecchio

Beaches

Porto-Vecchio owes its popularity to a series of lovely beaches within a short drive of town, all equipped with bars and restaurants. Those to the **south** are part of the greater Bonifacio Marine Reserve, including the stunning **Plage de Palombaggia** with sands and dunes of powdered sugar and parasol pines fringing an emerald sea, lapping pink boulders sculpted by the elements. There's a huge shady car park, but even this often fills up. On the horizon are a group of islets, the **Iles Cerbicale**, a nature reserve where crested cormorants nest.

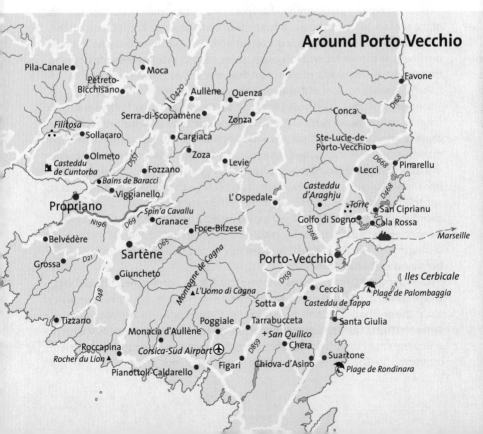

If Palombaggia beach is too busy, try the **Plage d'Asciaghju** just south. The very popular **Santa Giulia**, 12km from Porto-Vecchio, surrounded by luxurious summer houses, is a superb crescent of pale sand rimming a little gulf of pure turquoise, and offers every conceivable sport.

North of Porto-Vecchio, a cluster of villas and *villages de vacances* surrounds the mouth of the river Oso. The first beach in the **Golfo di Sogno** (7km) is a favourite for windsurfing, followed by the lovelier **Cala Rossa** (11km), in a pretty pine- and villa-fringed bay of pink sand and turquoise water. Further north, **San Ciprianu** is an enormous white beach with a lagoon just behind, and views over the needle peaks of Bavella. Twenty kilometres north of Porto-Vecchio, the holiday honeypot begins to dribble to an end around **Ste-Lucie-de-Porto-Vecchio** and its seaside hamlet **Pinarellu**, sitting on a handsome bay of white sands under the tall pines, overlooking a Genoese tower on a small islet. This is the last big bite out of the coast; to the north, it runs straight as a die (by Corsican standards, at any rate) to Bastia.

Things weren't always so sweet in these parts: **Lecci** to the south and **Conca** to the north of Ste-Lucie were, according to an old Corsican proverb, two of the three 'last villages built by God' ('*Zoza, Conca, e Lecce/Sô l'ultima paesi chi Diu fece*'), presumably when He was too tired out to do any better. Now Conca is a shimmering goal, at least in the minds of the hiking fraternity with their blisters – it's at the end of the GR20.

Prehistoric and Other Sites South of Porto-Vecchio

Porto-Vecchio was also a very popular spot in the 2nd millennium BC, although most of the sites require something of a scramble to visit. Five km south, in **Ceccia** (off the D859 to Figari), the **Site de Ceccia** is a 20min walk along a hard-to-find path from the last house on the left. Up on a rocky spur, it's an isolated, circular *torre* from *c.* 1350 BC that may have either had a religious significance or served primarily as a lookout tower; unusually, no signs of a nearby village were discovered.

Continuing another 1.5km from Ceccia on the D859, a sign marks the 300m easy (for once) path through the fields to the more typical **Casteddu de Tappa**. Set among a chaos of granite boulders, Tappa was inhabited from the 4th millenium BC on – making it one of the 'first' villages on Corsica; Cyclopean walls surround the remains of a *torre* that was originally much taller, reached by way of a very narrow stair built into the walls. Transhumance has been a way of life on Corsica since at least 2000 BC, and this may have been a winter settlement on the plain – goats still come to skip over the rocks to the extent that you should expect a fine coating of *kaka*. Archaeologists found evidence of centuries of habitation, of inhabitants grinding and storing grain (or acorns in hard times). The cool underground passages may also have been used as cheese cellars.

From Tappa, the D859 continues southwest to **Sotta**, a rather dishevelled-looking village spread out along the road. From here the D59 twists its way up to Levie (*see* p.144), the destination in September 1943 of the Sturmbrigade SS Reichsführer. As tanks and trucks carrying 200 men lumbered up the road, they were ambushed 21 times, and finally thwarted altogether when the Résistance blew up a bridge – events commemorated by a modern statue-stele before the tunnel.

South of Sotta are three curiosities to seek out. Lost in vineyards 7km south of the D859 to Figari, **San Quilico** (1150) is Corsica's tiniest Pisan chapel (24ft by 10ft/7.3m by 3m), still in perfect condition, topped by its original *teghie* roof tiles. Driving around southern Corsica, you may have already noticed some of the larger granite boulders with natural overhangs bricked in to form a shelter; these are called *orri* (singular *orriu*). Chera, south of Sotta on the D959, has the most famous one, the **Orriu de Chera**. Neolithic shepherds sheltered here, and it was commonly believed that the *orriu* was haunted by an ancestral spirit linked to the Culioli family, one who was antagonistic to Christianity and imprisoned in a goat with iron hooves. Although the Culioli put a cross on top, the infernal goat twisted it in a rampage. The *orriu* once began to groan when a Culioli child fell ill, warning that enemies of the family were plotting to destroy them in an ancient vendetta; thanks to the timely warning of the spirit, they were able to survive. The even more fantastical **Orriu de Cani** is 4km north (look for the hand-painted sign), up a trail from the hamlet. It resembles a fairy-tale witch's house, and was locally believed to be precisely that.

North of Porto Vecchio: The Casteddu d'Araghju and Torre

Built on a 820ft/250m rocky spur, the **Castello d'Arraggiu/Casteddu d'Araghju** (*c.* 2000 BC) is the most impressive of Porto-Vecchio's prehistoric sites – a veritable Bronze Age fortress, with grandiose views stretching across the Gulf of Porto-Vecchio that would detect any unfriendly visitors. Follow the signs along the D759 to the car park, from where it's a steep 20-minute walk up a rocky path (wear sturdy shoes – or take it easy and hire a horse to do the work from the riding stable just outside the hamlet of Araghju, *t 06 14 58 66 25*). Granite walls up to 7ft/2m thick and standing between 10ft/3m and 16ft/5m high enclose a 390ft/120m perimeter, here and there incorporating natural rocks. A monumental entrance from the east gives on to a corridor which still has its paving stones. At the end of the corridor, at the highest point, is a courtyard where people and animals could take refuge in times of danger, surrounded by chambers and niches built into the thick walls. The circular central monument is a simple one, with two chambers with separate entrances; opposite the main entrance is a room believed to have been a guard room, like the ones often found in the *nuraghi* of Sardinia. A well supplied the *casteddu* in case of siege. The huts of a Torréen village are a 15-minute walk away.

Nearby **Torre** is another important site, just off the N198 above the hamlet of the same name (turn right on the little lane after the garage and park by the sign that says *Propriété Privé* – it's a 20-minute walk up the path to the right). Archaeologist Roger Grosjean believed that the isolated, semi-circular tower built against a big granite rock was one of the first erected by Corsica's Bronze Age invaders, hence the name he gave them, the Torréens (*see* **History**, p.10). There is a corridor inside that forks, but not a *cella*, and the speculation is that it was for cremations, as it does have a chimney inside. Some archaeologists, however, think that both Torre and Tappa are older than Grosjean thought, and date from the late Neolithic period.

Inland from Porto-Vecchio: L'Ospedale, Col de Bavella and the Alta Rocca

The great *massif* of L'Ospedale behind Porto-Vecchio, and the Alta Rocca region just above it, make up the southern quarter of the Parc Naturel Régional, and offer some of the most stunning forest and mountain scenery in Corsica, crisscrossed by hoary transhumance trails and the Mare a Mare Sud path from Porto-Vecchio to Propriano. In the Middle Ages the handsome villages here were the fief of the della Rocca family, and much of the area is still covered by two huge forests, L'Ospedale and Zonza, of beech, cork, chestnut and pine. The rivers are perfect for cooling off in the summer.

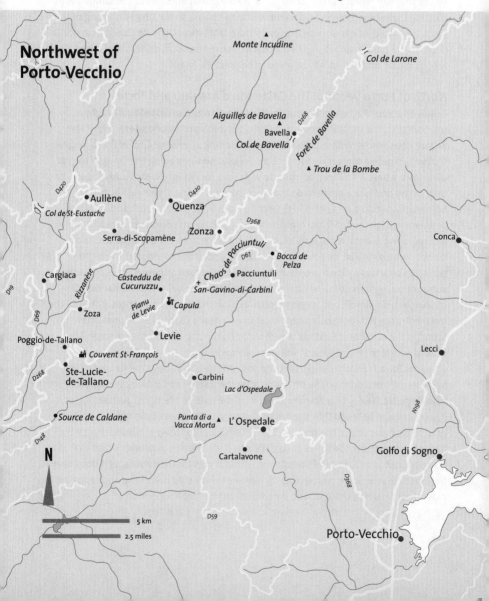

Northwest of Porto-Vecchio

Monte Incudine

Col de Larone

Aiguilles de Bavella

D268

Bavella

Col de Bavella

Forêt de Bavella

Trou de la Bombe

D420

Aullène

Col de St-Eustache

D420

Quenza

D368

Zonza

Serra-di-Scopamène

Chaos de Pacciuntuli

D61

Bocca de Pelza

Conca

Cargiaca

Rizzanèse

Casteddu de Cucuruzzu

Pacciuntuli

San-Gavino-di-Carbini

D9

Pianu de Levie

Capula

D69

Zoza

Poggio-de-Tallano

Levie

Couvent St-François

Lecci

Ste-Lucie-de-Tallano

D268

Carbini

Lac d'Ospedale

N198

Source de Caldane

D148

Punta di a Vacca Morta

L'Ospedale

Cartalavone

Golfo di Sogno

N

Porto-Vecchio

D368

D59

5 km

2.5 miles

L'Ospedale/U Spidale

From Porto-Vecchio the newly widened D368 rises 19km to the already noticeably cooler village of **L'Ospedale**. Its name derives from a hospital or *hospitium* set up in 1762 for Porto-Vecchio's malaria victims, who took refuge here in the hot summer months. From here the Golfe de Porto-Vecchio resembles a green fjord. Prosper Mérimée used L'Ospedale as the setting for *Mateo Falcone* (1829), a tragic tale of family honour, published a decade before he even set foot in Corsica. After his trip, he made a few corrections, but retained the advice: 'If you've killed a man, go into the *maquis* of Porto-Vecchio, and live there in all security, with a good rifle, balls, and powder; don't forget a brown cape with a hood, to serve as your cover and mattress. The shepherds will give you milk, cheese and chestnuts, and you'll have nothing to fear from the law or the relatives of the dead man, except when you have to descend into town to replenish your ammunition.'

Above the village the road runs under the deep, shady, cool **Forêt de l'Ospedale** of pines, cork oak and ilex, up to the pretty **Lac de l'Ospedale** enclosed by a dam (it may look tempting, but bathing is forbidden). From the car park, 1km after the dam, you can make the walk (if you're fit, it's supposedly 30 minutes down, 40 minutes up, but most people take twice that long; wear good walking shoes) through a striking landscape of pines and granite boulders to the *marmites de géant* – big potholes filled with water, sculpted by the river Oso – ending up, after a short, steep decline, at the beautiful 230ft/70m waterfall known as **Piscia-di-Gallu** ('Cock's Piss'). Another, quieter walk is from the nearby hamlet of **Cartalavone** up to a 4,311ft/1,314m belvedere with an equally pungent name, **Punta di a Vacca Morta** (Dead Cow Point), overlooking both the Golfe de Porto-Vecchio and Golfe de Valinco on the west coast, as well as the Aiguilles de Bavella (*see* below) and much of the Alta Rocca. The landscape here is a granite chaos under a few tortured pines, blasted by the wind and lightning.

Zonza, the Col de Bavella and the Chaos of Pacciontoli

The pretty granite village of **Zonza**, 40km from L'Ospedale, is wrapped in chestnut and ilex forests at a major crossroads. It has the most places to stay in the Alta Rocca, and can claim to have hosted two royal guests, King Theodor of Corsica in 1736 and Mohammed V, Sultan of Morocco. The latter was escorted here by the French Ministry of the Interior after he was deposed in a *coup d'état* in 1952; he and his family lasted for five months in Zonza before the cold and snow chased them down to Ile-Rousse.

A summer tourist office has maps for local walks, including an orange waymarked *sentier de pays* which will take you in six hours to San Gavinu and back; another path, taking just over four hours, circles around to Quenza. Another of Zonza's claims to fame is the highest racetrack in Europe, the **Hippodrome de Zonza** (or **de Viseo**), where the horses run on summer holidays, generally 14 July and 15 August.

The main excursion from Zonza, the one that causes traffic jams in the summer, is along the extraordinary **Route de Bavella** (D268) to the northeast, where the marvellous views around each bend reach their epiphany in one of the island's five-star attractions, the **Col de Bavella** (3,996ft/1,218m), with unforgettable views over the 'Corsican Dolomites' – the spiky porphyry needles of the **Aiguilles de Bavella**

Getting Around

See Porto-Vecchio (p.130). Also, **Autocars Ricci**, t 04 95 51 08 19, have at least one bus a day except Sun, and 3 in the summer linking Ajaccio, Sartène and Propriano to Ste-Lucie-de-Tallano, Levie, Zonza and the Col de Bavella. **Balesi Evasion**, t 04 95 70 15 55, run a service Mon–Sat linking Bavella and Ajaccio by way of Aullène, and go to Bavella and Zonza from Porto-Vecchio. **Ile de Beauté Voyages**, t 04 95 70 12 31, also provide a daily link between Zonza and Porto-Vecchio and Ajaccio.

Tourist Information

Zonza: t 04 95 78 56 33. *Open May–mid-Oct, Mon–Sat 9–1 and 2–6.30, Sun 9–12.*
Note that the only **ATM** machine in the Alta Rocca is in San-Gavino-di-Carbini.

Sports and Activities

Xtrem Sud, 500m above L'Ospedale, t 04 95 70 34 68 or t 04 95 72 12 31, *www.xtremsud.com*. Organizes treks, rock-climbing and canyoning excursions in the area.
Corsica Madness, Bavella, t 04 95 78 61 76 or t 06 13 22 95 06. Canyoning, guided treks, mountain bike hire, from Easter to Oct.

Hippodrome de Viseo: Horse-racing in July and Aug.
A Montagnola, Quenza, t 04 95 78 65 19, *www.a-montagnola.com*. Organizes mountain walks (and baggage transport) and canyoning.
Jean-Paul Quilicci, Quenza, t 04 95 78 64 33 or t 06 16 41 18 53, *www.jpquiliccimontagne. com*. The most famous mountain guide in Corsica, who organizes mountain walks and climbs, canyoning, *via ferrata* and more.

Where to Stay and Eat

L'Ospedale ✉ 20137

Le Refuge, t 04 95 70 00 39. Popular family-run restaurant next to the dam, where *maman* in the kitchen prepared tasty home cooking for *around €20*.
U Funtanonu, t 04 95 70 47 11. A summer *auberge* up on the pass, serving plates of *charcuterie* and cheeses with Corsican wines. *€15–20. Closed Oct–May.*

Zonza ✉ 20124

L'Aiglon, t 04 95 78 67 79, *www.aiglonhotel. com (moderate)*. The 'Eagle' is a charming little hotel in the village centre, with old-fashioned rooms and a restaurant serving some seldom-seen dishes – roast pork with

(7,000ft/2,134m) or 'Horns of Asinao', with Monte Incudine looming behind. The top of the pass is marked by a statue of Our Lady of the Snows, standing atop a mound of boulders covered with votive plaques; the best views are just beyond, especially if you come at dawn or sunset. The **Forêt de Bavella** that extends on either side of the pass was damaged in a massive forest fire in 1960, but has since been luxuriantly replanted with maritime and Laricio pines, although stark traces of the old fire somehow add to the austere beauty. At the hamlet of **Bavella**, the stone shelters with corrugated iron roofs are summer houses and sheepfolds; during his visit to Corsica, Napoléon III was so struck by the misery of Conca (*see* p.136) that he granted each inhabitant born there a 99-year lease on a bit of Bavella, to escape the summer heat and malaria.

From the car park there are a couple of easy but beautiful paths. One 2-hour walk, waymarked red, leads through the Laricio pines, with trees over 150ft/46m high (the Genoese would come up here to harvest timber for masts) to the remarkable **Trou de la Bombe** or **U Cumpeleddu**, a curious 26ft/8m-diameter hole eroded in the rock wall over the forest, that really does look as if someone had dropped a bomb in it; if you fig cream or veal with orange; try the *maquis* honey ice cream.

★★Le Tourisme, t 04 95 78 67 72, *www.hoteldu tourisme.fr* (*moderate*). Rooms are handsome and rustic in this old stone building, many overlooking the valley; breakfast is €10 but includes far more than the usual bread, jam and coffee. The restaurant has big views over the forest and serves heaped portions of Corsican specialities (*menus from €18 to €34*). *Closed mid Nov–mid-Mar.*

Résidence Le Mouflon d'Or, on the Rte de Levie, **t** 04 95 78 72 72, *www.lemouflondor.com* (*moderate*). A good comfortable bet for a week's stay in the mountains – villas in a wooded park sleeping four, with a big pool. *€840 in high season. Closed early Oct–Mar.*

★★L'Incudine, t 04 95 78 67 71 (*inexpensive*). Small cosy Logis de France in an old granite building, with recently refurbished rooms and a good restaurant specializing in *charcuterie* and lamb dishes (*menu du jour €16, closed Mon lunch*). *Half-board in August €120 for two. Closed mid-Oct–Mar.*

La Terrasse, t 04 95 78 67 69 (*inexpensive*). Family-run restaurant-hotel with freshly decorated rooms and the best views in town, plus good home-cooked Corsican meals (*menus €17–27*). *Closed Nov–Mar.*

Auberge du Sanglier, t 04 95 78 67 18. In the centre of Zonza since 1924, this is where Astérix and Obélix would eat *sanglier* (boar). either served in a *civet* with chestnut gnocchi or prepared in a terrine with myrtle. *Menu du berger €20. Closed Jan and Feb.*

Col de Bavella ✉ 20124

Auberge de Bavella *www.auberge-bavella.com,* **t** 04 95 72 09 87. Right at the top of the pass. Good filling food to go with the mountain air: drink in a view of the pinnacles from the terrace over home-made *charcuterie* and grilled trout. *Menus €16–22.* They also serve breakfast, and have a few cheap dormitory **rooms** that serve as a *gîte d'étape* for the GR20. *Closed Nov–Mar.*

Quenza ✉ 20122

★★Sole e Monti, t 04 95 78 62 53, *www.sole monti.com* (*expensive–moderate; half-board terms*), Simple Logis de France rooms in a very friendly family-run inn made of granite, with a charming garden to soak up the sun. The restaurant is excellent, featuring Corsican specialities given a modern light touch, with all the perfumes of the *maquis*; the fixed price menu (*€28*) changes daily, and follows the seasons, or you can order *à la carte* – try the local *charcuterie* and cheeses, the wild pig or the succulent lamb grilled with herbs from the *maquis. Closed Oct–April.*

have a head for heights, you can even walk up to edge for the dizzying views. Keep an eye out for the enormous lammergeiers who nest near here. The other walk is the one-hour **Promenade de la Pianona**, leading to a natural platform set in the tortured pines, offering another sublime view over the Aiguilles, from a different angle.

Beyond the Col de Bavella, the 21km road to **Solenzara** is very narrow and can be scary in the summer when you may well run into lots of oncoming traffic. On the other hand, it takes in more breathtaking scenery, especially around the **Col de Larone**, with its soaring rock walls. Some 3km before the pass, at a place called **Araggiava**, you can park by the road and follow the Polischellu stream up to little waterfalls where you can bathe.

Another attraction near Zonza is the circuit through the **Chaos de Pacciuntuli**. Off the road to Levie, stop first at **San-Gavino-di-Carbini**, a curious church with a crowned head over the door and monolithic columns, dedicated to the obscure Roman soldier martyr St Gavin of Porto Torres, Sardinia. From here, take the D67 towards the hamlet of **Pacciuntuli**. The road passes by strange granite clumps rising out of the *maquis*. Along the way, keep your eyes peeled for a **dolmen** (1.8km after

Gîte d'Etape Chez Pierrot Milanini, 5km north of Quenza towards Coscione, at Ghjallicu, **t** 04 95 78 63 21 (*inexpensive*). Dormitory beds, *table d'hôte*, and a horse to explore the wild Plateau du Coscione. *Be sure to reserve. Open all year.*

Gîte d'Etape Corse Odyssée, Quartier Pentaniella, **t** 04 95 78 64 05, *corseodyssee@aol.com* (*inexpensive*). Simple dormitory rooms and a campsite with local walking and canyoning experts, who hire out all the equipment you need to descend the rushing waters, even if it's your first try. *Closed mid-Oct–late Mar.*

Aullène ✉ 20116

*****Hôtel de la Poste**, **t** 04 95 78 61 21 (*inexpensive*). An old-fashioned hotel built as a postal relay station in 1880. Has 20 simple rooms with a WC on each floor, and a restaurant serving good home-cooked meals, specializing in home-made *charcuterie*. The owner is the author of a detailed little guide to walking paths in the area, and loans copies out to interested guests. *Half-board is obligatory in August. Closed Oct–April.*

Camping de Serra de Scopamene, 8km south of Aullène, **t** 04 95 78 63 21 (*inexpensive*). Very pleasant, peaceful campsite. *Open all year, but ring first.*

Ste-Lucie-de-Tallano ✉ 20112

Chambre d'Hôtes Palazzo, Rte de Zonza, **t** 04 95 78 82 40 (*moderate*). Three rooms with plenty of character and a *gîte* in an old stone building, with delicious home-made jams, etc. for breakfast. Book early. *Closed Dec–Feb.*

Santa Lucia, in the main square, **t** 04 95 78 81 28. A pretty restaurant with *menus at €17 and €23. Closed Sun, Jan and Feb.*

Levie ✉ 20170

Ferme-auberge A Pignata, 5km from village on the Rte du Pianu towards Cucuruzzu, **t** 04 95 78 41 90, *www.apignata.com* (*€69 half-board only*). Nothing fancy but all you need: five simple rooms and a famous restaurant serving some of the best traditional Corsican cuisine based on products from the family farm, with the likes of *daube farcie*, soufflés of *brocciu* with mint and excellent *vin de pays* (*enormous €33 menu with wine*), and sturdy little Corsican horses to ride on the paths of the Alta Rocca. *Always open, but always book (and get precise directions).*

La Pergola, Rue Sorba, **t** 04 95 78 41 62. Sweet little restaurant with a terrace serving hearty family cooking (*€17 menu*). No credit cards. *Closed Nov–Mar.*

U Tascaronu, at the entrance to the village, **t** 04 95 78 47 07. Good *salades composées*, pizzas and barbecued meats. *Around €15.*

St-Gavino), a prehistoric shelter, and remains of menhirs (some 15 were discovered in two alignments, all facing east; many have since been felled, or used in the dry stone walls that line the road). The D67 ends at the panoramic **Bocca de Pelza** in the Forêt de Zonza; a left turn will bring you back to Zonza.

Quenza and Aullène

Dramatically set below the Aiguilles de Bavella, **Quenza**, 7.5km northwest of Zonza, is a handsome village and important base for exploring the Parc Naturel Régional. After the native Corsican deer was hunted to extinction in the late 1960s, a careful breeding programme of deer of the same breed from Sardinia was reintroduced here in 1985. Quenza's impressive granite Romanesque church of St-Georges (*Mme Balesi, who lives in the house with the pinkish shutters, has the keys*) has frescoes, a fine tapestry on the *Passion of Christ* and an old pulpit in dark wood, supported by dragons and a Moor's head (perhaps representing the Barbary pirates who plagued the coast at the time – it's due to disappear soon, for restoration) and a wooden statue of St Steven, gripping his martyr's palm as if it were a sword. Predating even the village, just off the road to Aullène, is the Pisan chapel of **Santa Maria Assunta** from the year 1000. The apse retains its roof of granite *teghie*, while inside fine but damaged late 15th-century frescoes of *Christ in Majesty* have been discovered under the plaster.

Quenza is the main sports centre of the Alta Rocca, with canyoning, riding and cross-country skiing up on its atmospheric **Plateau du Coscione** (U Pianu), Corsica's little Scotland just over 9km to the north, towards Zicavo. Two rivers, the Taravo and Rizzanèse, have their sources here, and its lush grasses and marshy bogs made it prime summer grazing ground, a tradition still followed by a handful of shepherds, although in not-so-traditional jeeps. Herds of wild pigs wander about; the GR20 passes through. The one road for regular cars leads to a sheepfold, where you should leave the car. The *mairie* of Quenza has a map of walking itineraries, many following the old transhumance paths; in the summer the plateau looks its best in late afternoon, although try not to get caught in one of the violent thunderstorms that often erupt here. Deer and eagles are often sighted; bring binoculars.

Aullène/Auddè translates as 'crossroads', and it lies on a once-important one between the Alta Rocca, Sartène and Corte. Today a handsome scattered village rather off the beaten track, it has impressive granite houses from the 16th century and deep chestnut groves planted under the Genoese. The granite church of San Nicolao (*the keyholder lives opposite, in the house with a stair*) has a curious 17th-century pulpit, better preserved than the one in Quenza, with four dragons and a Moor's head underneath. For the heartstopping road over the **Col de St-Eustache** to Petreto-Bicchisano, *see* p.101. Alternatively, an even more seldom travelled *corniche* road, the D69, goes south towards Sartène; at the Pont d'Acoravo you can backtrack to Ste-Lucie if you want to make a loop of the Alta Rocca.

Ste-Lucie-de-Tallano/Santa-Lucia-di-Tallà

Set above the green Rizzanèse valley, **Ste-Lucie-de-Tallano** is the loveliest village of the Alta Rocca, piled compact on a hill, with skirts wrapped in olives and grand circle views towards the Gulf of Valinco. It was the favourite stronghold of the pious, art-loving Count Rinuccio della Rocca, the very last of the Cinarchesi lords. In the 1490s, at the height of his power, when he was allied with Genoa and controlled much of southern Corsica, Rinuccio founded the pretty **Couvent St-François** (1492) on the edge of town and lavished gifts on the village, now all housed in the 17th-century church of **Ste-Lucie** (*key at café Ortoli, opposite*): there's a lovely marble Italian Renaissance relief of the *Virgin and Child* and a retable of the *Virgin and Child and Crucifixion*, with a delightful rustic background behind the sorrowing mourners, attributed to the 16th-century Master of Castelsardo, a Sardinian painter in the Spanish-Flemish tradition. Rinuccio's career as Corsica's first art patron came to an end when he decided to chase the old Cinarchesi dream of becoming lord of all Corsica; after three futile wars against the Genoese, he was assassinated in 1511 by his own peasants, fed up with all the strife. Then the Genoese came and bashed the town for good measure, but it was soon rebuilt as the tall old houses on the hill testify. In times of danger the villagers took refuge in the powerful, four-square 16th-century **Casa Turra**, hurtling beehives and boiling olive oil down on attackers.

Ste-Lucie is famous for an extremely rare grey stone called diorite orbiculaire, or corsite, or, briefly, 'Napoleonite', the only rock in France once protected by the military, when in 1809 General Morand sent in troops to protect the quarry. Now exhausted – much of what Napoleon failed to extract was removed by German contracters a few years back – Corsica's diorite is especially prized for its crystallizations in concentric orbs that resemble leopardskin. It features in the Medici chapel in Florence, on Napoleon's tomb in Les Invalides in Paris, and in the base of Ste-Lucie's **Monument aux Morts** in **Piazza di l'Ulmu** – a square that was once the *curé's* garden and which also has an impressive fountain of 1875. For a long time the stone was believed to be exclusive to Corsica, although another vein (but not as pretty) was recently found in Finland. There are other examples in the Café Ortoli.

There may be no more diorite, but there is still olive oil. Ste-Lucie's groves make some of the best, and it is celebrated every March with a harvest festival. At other times you can learn all about it in a guided tour of a restored press, **U Franghjonu** of 1848, signposted from the centre (*guided tours summer only, Mon–Sat 9–12 and 3–6; adm*); and buy some at **Chez Jacques Léandri,** next to the church (*t 04 95 78 81 94; open May–Sept afternoons*) or at the **Cave à Huile Santa Lucia** by the tower (*t 04 95 78 81 03; open Mar–Sept*).

The nearby hamlet of **Poggio-de-Tallano/Poghhju-di-Tallà** has an excellent early 12th-century Pisan chapel of sun-gilded granite blocks, **San Giovanni**, modelled after the church of the same name in Carbini (*see* below) and now used as a cow barn; isolated in the olives and woods, it's a half-hour walk along a mule path. The delightful *modillions* are scupted into boars' heads and funny human faces.

Ste-Lucie is relatively far from the sea, but the environs have fine swimming holes. At **Zoza** to the north, the river Rizzanèse has hollowed out a bucolic series of cool, clear **Piscines Naturelles**, reached by an easy path from the bridge; one pool is deep enough most of the year to dive into; in summer there's even a snack bar. Even more popular is the stress-soothing **Source de Caldane**, a sulphurous bubbly hot spring (37°C) that flows into a pool surrounded by bathing cabins south of Ste-Lucie, signposted on the Sartène road. For medical reasons you're only allowed 20 minutes in the water; there's also a nearby restaurant. Come early or late to avoid the rush (*t 04 95 77 00 34, open May–mid-Oct 9am to 9.30pm; adm*).

Levie and the Casteddu de Cucuruzzu

Southwest of Zonza, **Levie/Livia**, the capital of the Alta Rocca, is a big village and an essential stop for anyone interested in ancient Corsica. Start off with the **Musée de l'Alta Rocca**, now in a brand new building just under town on the Cabini road (*t 04 95 78 46 34; due to open in 2006*). Here is the skeleton of the oldest Corsican, the **Dame de Bonifacio** (6570 BC), discovered in a tomb at the entrance of Bonifacio's port, buried with a layer of red clay brought from a few miles inland. Like many pre-Neolithic people, she was tiny – 4ft 9 inches – and her life couldn't have been easy: her right hand was atrophied and paralyzed, her upper left arm had been broken, and she suffered from severe articular inflamation in her feet, which would have made walking painful. Yet, obviously with a little help from her friends, she lived to be 35 and was laid in her sepulchre with a good deal of trouble. Recently, like the mummies in Egypt, she had to be saved a second time – from modern bacteria. Another skeleton is a rare complete one: the *Prolagus sardus*, the extinct 'rabbit cat', that lived on both Corsica and Sardinia. There are pots, tools and relics from Capula and Cucuruzzu and other prehistoric sites in the area going back to the 7th millennium BC, coins and pottery from the Middle Ages, and a superb ivory *Christ* from *c.* 1516, sculpted by a student of Donatello and donated to Levie, so they say, by Pope Sixtus V, whose Peretti ancestors were said to have migrated from Corsica to Savona, once part of the Republic of Genoa.

Up on the 2,400ft/730m plateau, the **Pianu de Levie/di Livia**, high over the valleys of the Rizzanèse and Fiumicicoli, has Corsica's most important and beautiful archaeological site after Filitosa, the **Casteddu de Cucuruzzu et Site Archéologique de Capula** (**t** *04 95 78 48 21; open July and Aug 9.30–8; April–June and Sept–Oct 9.30–6; wear good walking shoes, especially if it has rained. Visits take 2–3hrs, so allow yourself enough time; adm includes a headset with a guided tour in English*), recently classified by UNESCO as a World Heritage Site. To get there by car follow the road to Ste-Lucie for 3.5km and turn right up a narrow track; on foot, take the orange-marked path from the fountain, which cuts out most of the road. From the Maison d'Accueil, a 15min walk under a canopy of trees acts as a kind of time tunnel, taking you into the primordial past of oak and granite before you reach **Cucuruzzu**. This is one of the most elaborate of all Torréen *casteddi*, a summer settlement founded on a spur in *c.* 1500 BC and used until the Iron Age, *c.* 700 BC. It consists of a walled *enceinte* made of huge boulders and a upper *torre* orientated towards the east, and a village of stone huts. Access was limited to a steep narrow stair, designed to foil intruders. The walls are fortified with casements and have gaps in them for archers. The tower has two doorways under massive lintels that lead into a single room, which retains its original vault. A necropolis was discovered under a rock shelter, with signs of hearths; nearby was an ossuary, where it appears bones were deposited to make room for new burials. Climb to the top for a wonderful view across to the Aiguilles de Bavella.

The visit continues to **Capula**, 20 minutes away, set on a hill covered with giant oaks, in another magnificent landscape, where a passing druid wouldn't look out of place. Originally a Bronze Age *casteddu* like Cucuruzzu, it was inhabited from 1800 BC. In the 10th century, one Count Biancolacco converted it into a feudal castle, and it remained inhabited until 1259, when the Giudice di Cinarca ordered it to be dismantled to punish its headstrong owners. A ramp suitable for horses leads into its high circular walls, a picturesque mix of prehistoric stone and medieval brick. At the foot of the wall stands a headless statue-menhir; menhirs from the ancient site were reused to make the lintel, and there are signs of prehistoric metalworking in the area. There are ruins of a 13th-century chapel of **St-Laurent**, and nearby stands a new one, built of the old stones after the First World War, and the site, on 9 August, of a yearly pilgrimage, picnic and traditional songs.

Carbini and its Heretics

South of Levie, the tiny, isolated village of **Carbini** is visible for miles around on its hill. It was an important town in the Middle Ages (its territory once stretched all the way to Porto-Vecchio) until it became the centre of the Giovannali heresy. This started in 1350 as a confraternity founded by two della Rocca brothers, Polo and Arrigo, grandsons of the Giudice; the name they chose, Giovannali (or Ghjuvannali), is thought to derive from their adherence to the gospel of St John to the exclusion of the other three gospels, or perhaps from Carbini's church of San Giovanni. It was a period of great disorder following the Black Death, when many felt that Europe had been punished by God for not obeying the scripture. The della Roccas questioned the hierarchy and luxury of the Church, and promoted communal ownership of land, goods, and money and equality between men and women; they refused to pay taxes and they refused to marry, so rumours accused them of holding nightly orgies in their churches once they blew out the candles. They soon attracted thousands of adherents across Corsica, enough to alarm the local nobility, who weren't getting their taxes, and certainly enough to alarm their ally Pope Urban V, who in 1355 excommunicated and preached a crusade against them, setting off a war of Corsicans against Corsicans: an estimated 20,000–30,000 men, women and children were killed in Carbini, Zevaco, Ghisoni, Valle d'Alesani and other villages, their homes pillaged, and their chapel of San Quilico in Carbini razed. Carbini, repopulated by folk from Sartène, was rendered safe once more for orthodoxy and taxation.

Near the ruined walls of San Quilico stands the late 11th-century Romanesque church of **San Giovanni Battista**, which has preserved the old granite *teghie* on the roof and some fine *modillions*, with human heads, animals and geometric designs. Next to the church is the tall and elegant **campanile**, much admired by public monument inspector Mérimée during his tour, which was restored according to his recommendations in the 19th century, when the crenellations on top were replaced with a pyramidal stone roof. The campanile was built by a certain Master Maternato, who also designed at least two bridges in Corsica. There is a legend that the bell tower so impressed the people of Carbini that they meant to murder the architect when he completed his task, to prevent him from making any others, but he got wind of their plans and stalled the work, saying he needed some very special tools to complete the task. He sent five villagers to his home at Forciolo to fetch them, but his family, suspecting trouble from the oddness of their request, kept the villagers hostage until Master Maternato finished the campanile and returned home safe, sound and paid.

From Carbini you can re-descend to the coast by way of the D59 – but be warned this is a road even the Corsicans say is impossible – via Sotta (*see* p.136), or take the longer, easier way looping back around to Zonza.

Corte and the Interior

09

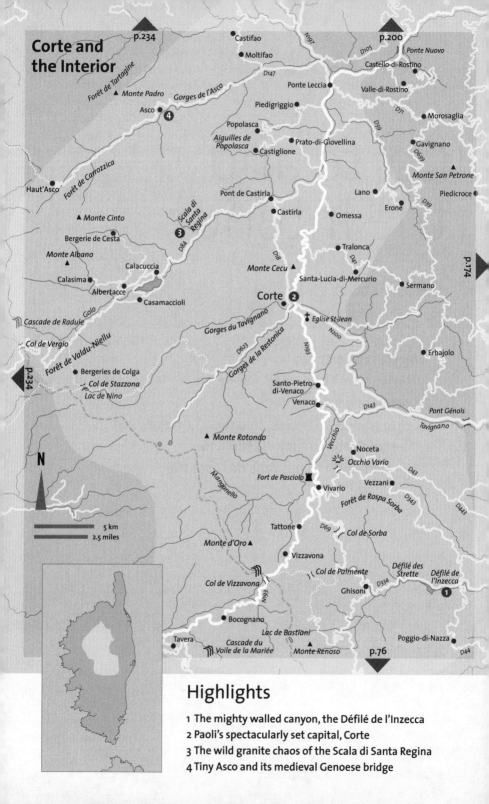

Corte and the Interior

p.234
p.200
p.174
p.234
p.76

Castifao
Moltifao
Ponte Nuovo
Castello-di-Rostino
Valle-di-Rostino
Ponte Leccia
Piedigriggio
Morosaglia
Popolasca
Prato-di-Giovellina
Gavignano
Aiguilles de Popolasca
Castiglione
Monte San Petrone
Forêt de Tartagine
Monte Padro
Gorges de l'Asco
Asco **4**
Lano
Piedicroce
Pont de Castirla
Castirla
Omessa
Erone
Haut'Asco
Forêt de Carrozzica
Monte Cinto
Scala di Santa Regina **3**
Tralonca
Bergerie de Cesta
Santa-Lucia-di-Mercurio
Monte Albano
Monte Cecu
Calacuccia
Sermano
Calasima
Albertacce
Casamaccioli
Corte **2**
† Eglise St-Jean
Cascade de Radule
Golo
Gorges du Tavignano
Erbajolo
Col de Vergio
Forêt de Valdu-Niellu
Gorges de la Restonica
Bergeries de Colga
Col de Stazzona
Lac de Nino
Santo-Pietro-di-Venaco
Venaco
Pont Génois
Tavignano
Monte Rotondo
Vecchio
Noceta
Occhio Vario
Fort de Pasciolo
Vivario
Vezzani
Manganello
Forêt de Rospa Sorba
Tattone
Col de Sorba
Monte d'Oro
Vizzavona
Défilé des Strette
Défilé de l'Inzecca **1**
Col de Palmente
Col de Vizzavona
Ghisoni
Bocognano
Lac de Bastiani
Tavera
Cascade du Voile de la Mariée
Monte Renoso
Poggio-di-Nazza

N

5 km
2.5 miles

Highlights

1 The mighty walled canyon, the Défilé de l'Inzecca
2 Paoli's spectacularly set capital, Corte
3 The wild granite chaos of the Scala di Santa Regina
4 Tiny Asco and its medieval Genoese bridge

Like their island neighbours the Sards, Corsicans historically have been landlubbers, most of them taking to the sea only when they needed to escape; perhaps it was the Corsican in him that made water (and Waterloo, and islands, for that matter) the curse of Napoleon's career. In short, if you are in search of authentic *corsitude*, it's to the heart of the island you must go, into its tallest mountains and villages where the sea is only a distant rumour, seen only from the highest heights. It is also, incidentally, breathtakingly, heartstoppingly beautiful. There are taller mountains in Europe, but few are so *intense*, all jammed together in such a small space (although they make it seem like a very *large* space), their savage granite lushly cloaked in towering Laricio pines and chestnuts or *maquis*, sliced by dramatic gorges, rushing rivers and splashing waterfalls. Of course the best way to see it is on foot, and there are scores of trails, even some easy ones for a few hours' walk in the woods, besides the fantastical but gruelling GR20.

The one proper town of the interior, Corte was the laboratory of Paoli's precocious democracy and to this day it remains Corsica's spiritual capital. Ajaccio belongs to Napoleon and France, Bastia is still half Genoese, but granite Corte in the granite heart of Corsica remains the alternative. Historically, the wilds of central Corsica were bandit country, especially the south, while northwest of Corte, under the impregnable ramparts of the island's highest peaks, the Niolo and the Valle de l'Asco were almost completely cut off before the 20th century.

Ajaccio to Corte

The Corsican Alps – the sweeping spine of Punta Migliarello, Monte Rotondo, Monte d'Oro and Monte Renoso, all well over 6,000ft/1,830m – form the southern half of the Parc Naturel Régional, and it's remarkable just how quickly the landscapes change from Mediterranean to the kinds of vistas you expect to see around Grenoble, minus any trace of scrubbed Swiss cuteness. Even banks are scarce on the ground here. The N193 from Ajaccio is one of the few roads from the west to penetrate the fastness.

Besides bandits, these mountains are haunted by ogres; one supposedly destroyed the medieval village of **Tavera** (34km from Ajaccio, just south of the N193), although others say it was a landslide. You can still see the ruins to the east, near the Voile de la Mariée waterfalls (*see* below). Tavera was the birthplace in 1518 of one of several Corsicans who made it big after they were captured by pirates, this one Pietro Paolo Tavera, who converted to Islam (the one way to escape from slavery) and became Hassan Corso, a captain of the Janissaries and *kaïd* of Algiers. However, when he was elected *dey* in 1559, the sultan, afraid of his influence, had him gruesomely executed. Another Corsican, the *kaïd* Youssef of Tlemcen, avenged his death by killing the sultan's candidate. In 1961, a striking statue-menhir was found here, the *Homme de Tavera*, with deep-set eyes and what looks like a Bronze Age hairnet.

Bocognano/Bucughanu

Further up the N193, **Bocognano** and its deep green sea of chestnuts are squeezed between Punta Migliarello and Monte Renoso, with a grandstand view of jagged

Monte d'Oro. A stalwartly traditional town, it has a fountain made of a wall of stones the size of bowling balls (1883) as its chief monument. In early December, however, Bocognano really comes to life, holding the biggest and most important fair on the Corsican calendar, *A Fiera di a Castagna* (*www.fieradiacastagna.com*), dedicated to chestnuts, but also to everything Corsican, with plenty of crafts.

Bocognano's Bandits: One Little Leg and Two Beautiful Thighs

Bocognano is best remembered in local lore as the home town of Corsica's most flamboyant bandits, two pairs of brothers, all surnamed Bonelli. The first pair were among Paoli's most avid supporters, who after the Corsican defeat at Ponte Nuovo took to the *maquis*. One was executed in 1808 after a revolt in the Fiumorbo; the other, Ange Mathieu, better known as Zampaglinu, 'Little Leg', was captured and dragged off to prison in Toulon, where many die-hard supporters of Paoli died in appalling conditions. Zampaglinu, however, escaped, and managed to make it to Sardinia, where he got together a band of 50 supporters to return to Ajaccio. As 500 French troops closed in to capture them, Zampaglinu and company climbed up a rocky pinnacle and dispersed the French with an avalanche of boulders. He then made good his escape by stealing a sheep, approaching a fisherman as if to sell it, and then pulling out his stiletto and ordering him to take his band to Sardinia. After a 16-year exile in London, he returned to Corsica with Paoli, but stayed on after Paoli's second exile in 1795, fighting the English, whom he blamed; they, more efficient than the French, cornered him near Vizzavona and shot him.

The second pair of Bonelli brothers, Antoine (b. 1817) and Jacques (b. 1832), were nicknamed Bellacoscia, after their father, a shepherd, who fathered 18 children on his harem of three sisters, earning himself the name 'Beautiful Thigh'. His two sons' Robin Hood-style exploits entertained all Europe in the middle of the 19th century. Antoine became a bandit after murdering the mayor of Bocognano in 1848 when he tried to sell the communal grazing land the family used in the wilds of the Pentica Gorge. He was soon joined by his brother Jacques, and they made their house in the ravine into a fortress, where they waged a guerrilla war on the French authorities with the aid of the local sympathizers; whenever the *gendarmes* planned to attack, they were warned and always escaped. A price of 50,000 francs was put on their heads; no one was interested.

In 1870, the two brothers appeared in Ajaccio with a band of sharpshooters and volunteered to fight the Prussians, and their crimes were forgiven; but after the war they were no sooner back in Corsica than they went back to their old bandit ways, while stylishly entertaining important guests in their hideaway, including Baron Haussmann, a princess of Saxe-Weimar, Prince Roland Bonaparte, and several writers. Having survived an expedition ordered against them by the Minister of War in 1888, Antoine, aged 75, gave himself up at the Vizzavona train station. He was tried in Bastia, acquitted to general acclaim, but exiled to Marseille (he soon sneaked back to Corsica). Jacques never surrendered, and before he died of pneumonia in 1897 his last request was that no man should ever tread on his grave, so his friends dammed a stream and buried him in its bed.

Getting Around

The towns beween Ajaccio and Corte are linked by the little *micheline* **train**, which stops at Bocognano, Vizzavona (**t** 04 95 47 21 02), Vivario (**t** 04 95 47 20 13) and Venaco (**t** 04 95 47 01 32) 4 times a day en route to Corte.

Where to Stay and Eat

Bocognano ✉ 20136

There's an old Corsican saying, '*Per u biu e u maghia, ci vole anda in Bucugna*' ('For good food and drink, you have to go to Bocognano').

*Le Beau Séjour, t 04 95 27 40 26 (*inexpensive*). Simple rooms in the bosom of the mountains, and a restaurant featuring home-made *charcuterie* and omelettes *au brocciu* (€14 *and 20 menus*). *Closed Nov–mid-April*.

L'Ustaria, t 04 95 27 41 10. Napoleon, as he was fleeing Ajaccio, was ambushed here by Paolistas, but was able to escape thanks to the great-great-great-grandfather of the owner of this restaurant. Today people come for the imaginative cuisine: sea anemone fritters with myrtle, ragoût with morrels, roast kid with polenta and bilberries, and much more. *Menus* €16–40. *Open lunch and dinner June–Oct, otherwise lunch only*.

Ferme-auberge A Tanedda, t 04 95 27 42 44. Lovely views over the Monte d'Oro, a friendly welcome and good seasonal country cooking, including a delicious *tourte aux légumes*, grilled kid and boar in various fashions. *Menus from* €16. *Book ahead. Closed Nov–Mar*.

Pizzeria Copacabana, t 04 95 27 42 21. Pizzas, grilled meats and salads under the trees,

Vizzavona ✉ 20219

Monte d'Oro, La Foce (just under the pass), **t** 04 95 47 21 06, *www.monte-oro.com* (*inexpensive*). Handsome old inn up at the pass, surrounded by trees just off the main road, built in 1880 to house road engineers and preserved in aspic since. Cosy old-fashioned rooms, and a nice restaurant. If you're at the station, 3km away, they'll collect you. They also have an inexpensive refuge, for those with sleeping bags.

I Laricci, Gare de Vizzavona, **t** 04 95 47 21 12, *www.ilaricci.com* (*inexpensive*). Laid-back hotel by the station in a 19th-century mansion, with big rooms. Book if you don't want to end up in one of the cheap dorm beds in an annexe; the food is average but they do prepare sandwiches, etc. for hikers. *Closed Nov–mid-April*.

Usteria A Muntagnera, Col de Vizzavona, **t** 04 95 46 31 02 (*inexpensive*). Restaurant and Corsican specialities shop near the Cascade des Anglais with tasty shepherds' plates at €14. *Closed Nov–April*.

Vivario ✉ 20219

Macchje e Monti, t 04 95 47 22 00 (*moderate–inexpensive*). By the train station, a little family-run hotel-restaurant with 6 rooms popular with hikers; *half-board mandatory*

A tributary of the Gravona comes thundering down 492ft/150m in a lovely series of falls, the **Cascade du Voile de la Mariée** ('Bridal Veil Falls'), 3km south of Bocognano on the D27, and half an hour's walk from the road, although, after the snow has all thawed, the cascade has a definite morning-after look. Another path, this one taking two hours, begins at the recently restored chestnut mill, follows and crosses the Gravona, then winds north into the old stomping ground of the Bellacoscia brothers, the Pentica Gorge, to the **Clue de la Richisua**, a unique spot where the sheer granite walls rise nearly 200ft/60m over a tumbling stream that dallies here and there in natural emerald pools, perfect for a dip. For something bolder, A Muntagne Corse in Liberta (*see* 'Ajaccio' listings, p.82) organizes canyoning descents from walls to falls. Another trail beginning from the same chestnut mill will take you for a view over the Glacier de Busso, said to be the only spot on Corsica where the snows are so impacted that they withstand the summer heat; even in August the spot may bring out the goosebumps.

in summer. Be sure to try the leek *beignets* on the pretty restaurant terrace (*menus from €13*). *Closed Nov–Feb.*

Vezzani ✉ 20242
La Station, Grande-Rue, **t** 04 95 44 00 54 (*inexpensive*). Five pleasant rooms and family-run organic restaurant in a former petrol station.

U Sambuccu, 3km south of the village, **t** 04 95 44 03 38 (*inexpensive*). Friendly hotel in the pine woods, with a pool. Also an excellent place to tuck into mountain cuisine, with kid and boar holding pride of place on the menu (*menus start at €15*). *Closed Dec–Feb..*

Ghisoni ✉ 20227
***Le Kyrie**, Castarella, **t** 04 95 57 60 33 (*inexpensive*). The one place to stay, no frills but no chills either, with an OK restaurant-bar.

Ferme-auberge de l'Inzecca, on the D344 at the Défilé de l'Inzecca, **t** 04 95 56 62 62. Wild pigs are raised here and served up in the *charcuterie*, along with trout or veal, tripe, boar stew or lasagne; they also make their own liqueurs. *Menus at €24 and €28. Open daily April–Sept, weekends only Oct–Mar.*

Ferme-auberge U Sampolu, at Sampolo, **t** 04 95 57 60 18. In between the ravines, above the artificial lake, a handsome old stone farmhouse that specializes in *charcuterie*, veal and beef, along with aubergines *façon corse*, delicious sheep's cheese and big portions of *fiadone*, accompanied with *vin*

de Fiumorbo; by reservation only. *Menus at €15–18. Closed Oct–mid-May.*

Venaco and Around ✉ 20231
****Paestotel e Caselle**, Le Vallon, **t** 04 95 47 39 00, www.e-caselle.com (*moderate*). A comfortable base in a panoramic position by a river, 5km east of Venaco on the D143: bungalows and big rooms (some with disabled access), a pool, sauna, mountain bikes and a good restaurant. Also self-catering cottages. *Closed mid-Oct–mid-April.*

****Auberge du Bosquet**, 2km north at Santo-Pietro-di-Venaco, **t** 04 95 47 00 11, www.auberge-du-bosquet.com (*inexpensive*). Simple rooms with flowery wallpaper and a respectable restaurant with a €15 Corsican menu. *Closed Oct–Mar.*

La Ferme de Peridundellu, 4km from Venaco, **t** 04 95 47 09 89. Get there by taking the D43 for 4km towards the Vallée du Tavignano. Excellent little campsite by a torrent (*open April–mid-Oct*) and good cooking: homemade *charcuterie*, goat's cheese *feuilleté*, rabbit cooked in herbs, and *fiadone* (*menu €14 changes every day; by reservation only*).

Restaurant de la Place, Place du Pont, **t** 04 95 47 01 30. In the centre of Venaco, one of the best restaurants in the area, where the Corsican dishes are given a little extra *je ne sais quoi*. Delicious *tianu d'agneau* and famous *rougets* (red mullet) *au brocciu*, and walnut *tarte* for dessert. *Menu €13. Open daily May–Sept; Oct–April closed Mon.*

The Heart of the Alpes de Corse: The Venachese

The N193 continues up from Bocognano into the Venachese, one of the most sparsely populated micro-regions on Corsica, although it wasn't always so – the abandoned threshing floors, old barns, ruined mills and *bergeries* suggest that it supported far more people in the past. The road passes through the beautiful beeches and Laricio pines of the **Forêt de Vizzavona**, the single most popular place in Corsica for casual walks. The **Col de Vizzavona** (3,815ft/1,163m) is the watershed between the *Dila dei Monti* and the *Diqua*, and marks the midway mark of the GR20; hikers often start or finish at the little train station at **Vizzavona**, a blip on the map (pop. 50). The village as such isn't visible from the road, but lies to the side, hidden in the pines. The station doubles as the local grocer.

The parked cars at **La Foce**, 1km below the Col de Vizzavona, belong to families who take the easy 45-minute path that links up with the GR20 for picnics and dips in the pools of the Agnone, after it shoots down in the austere **Cascades des Anglais** ('the English Falls', although no one remembers where it got the name). Another walk beginning just south of the Col de Vizzavona leads to the ruins of a **Genoese fort**, with a remarkable view over the mountains. Here too is a 45-minute path to **La Madonuccia** (signposted 'Bergeries des Pozzi'); the 'little Madonna' turns out to be a pile of boulders that rather fancifully resembles a statue of the Virgin, but the mountain views beyond her are superb. To see the finest parts of the forest, pick up the GR20 Sud (an easy stretch) from the Maison Forestière de Vizzavona to the **Bocca Palmente** (two hours), with gorgeous views over Monte Renoso.

Corsica's fifth highest peak, **Monte d'Oro** (7,838ft/2,389m), offers views as far as Italy from its summit and tempts many amateurs, often to their dismay (you really need to be very fit, have a good head for heights, and all the proper gear, and beware that there are often dangerous patches of snow near the top into July). Although it sounds like 'Golden Mountain', the name comes from the same *dore* ('many waters') root as the Dordogne; even so, there's no water along the way, so you'll have to carry lots. The

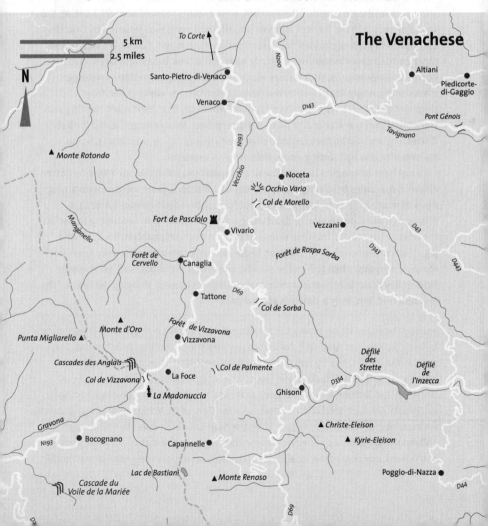

Battling for Souls

In the past, midnight on 31 July was a time of dread across Corsica, when fires were lit around houses and churches, and sharp iron instruments such as scissors or knives would be left around doors and windows to keep Death away. For this was the night when the usually solitary *mazzeri* or shamans or 'dream hunters' (*see* **Aspects of Corsitude**, p.33) would join into militias and go into the mountain passes to fight *mazzeri* militias from other villages in ghostly dream battles (*mandrache*). Their weapons were knives, human bones, and stalks of asphodel, a plant known in the Mediterranean as a link between life and death ever since Homeric times. The biggest battle took place under Monte d'Oro above the Col de Vizzavona, between *mazzeri* gathered from the *Dila dei Monti* and the *Diqua dei Monti*, and decided how many people would die on their half of the island over the coming year. Death and four devils presided over the clash; afterwards, the winners handed Death over to the losers. A *mazzeru* or *mazzera* killed in the dream combat was doomed to die within the year. Sometimes they would be found dead in bed the next morning.

The parallel dream world of the *mazzeri*, whose spirits roamed at night hunting the spirits of people in the form of animals (usually wild boar), was believed by Dorothy Carrington to go straight back to Palaeolithic hunting magic. Certainly Lascaux and other painted caves in southwest France have, amid their beautifully drawn bison, horses and mammoths, stick figures identified as shamans, sometimes wearing masks. Intriguingly, Corsican *mazzeri* (who came from any walks of life, from shepherd to farmer's wife to village notable) would say that their spirit-hunting was something they were 'called' to do by a higher power. Many *mazzeri* found it all very distressing, and did all they could to save their victims during their hunts. Some managed to give up hunting altogether, after an exorcism.

It's not hard to imagine isolated Corsica wrapped in a collective spell long forgotten elsewhere. Besides becoming the spirit prey of a *mazzeru*, there were other warning signs of death a Corsican had to watch out for: the dreaded Squadra d'Arozza, a phantom funeral procession of dead villagers which would stop before the house of the next person to die; invisible drums beating in a house; phantom herds of wild pigs that crossed one's path. Corsican historian Pierre Lamotte personally knew one *mazzeru* who described to him the parallel world that pre-ordains all great events before they occur in human material reality. 'There is no such thing as the future,' the *mazzeru* told him, 'only a timeless eternal past.'

map by the train station marks the two ascents: the longer, eight-hour one beginning by the Cascades des Anglais is easier, but requires some climbing near the end. The steeper five-hour climb by way of the Bergeries de Puzzatelli ends near the precipitous zigzagging 'Scala' cut into the stone, which can be slippery.

Just beyond **Tattone**, a dirt road goes as far as **Canaglia**, starting point of another lovely path through the Forêt de Cervello to the **Gorges du Manganellu**, one of easiest walks, with plenty of places to cool off in the Magnanellu's pools along the way.

Vivario/Vivariu, next on the N198, has in its main square a statue of Diana, goddess of the hunt, emblem of the local obsession. Vivario overlooks the gorge of the Vecchio, crossed here by the little Trinichellu train on a **viaduct** constructed by Gustave Eiffel in 1888, whose engineering art has been equalled, if not surpassed, by the spanking new road bridge running parallel to it. You can hire the Trinichellu for a private party, as John Carotti, creator of *The Avengers*, once did for a birthday party with some friends. As it passed through the Venaco, Carotti arranged for the train to be held up by costumed Corsican 'bandits', only the special birthday train was delayed, and the 'bandits', to the great surprise of the passengers, ambushed the regular train...

In 1820, the good folk of Vivario found that some small-scale bandit was raiding their gardens, and a *battue*, a hunt with beaters, was organized to flush out the thief – a hairy wild man, who it turned out was a local boy who had quarrelled with his family as a 10-year-old and run away from home 20 years previously. His family tried to civilize him, but he wilted and died within a few months. From the romantic ruins of the **Fort de Pasciolo**, built by the French in 1770 (the 20-minute path begins by an unpaved car park along the N198, 1km north of the village), you can make out the **Saut du Sauvage**, a place where the gorge of the Vecchio narrows to a mere 10ft. The wild man of Vivario leapt right over it, or so they say.

From Vivario: A Loop around Ghisoni and Monte Renoso

From Vivario you can make a scenic circuit by car to the east around the **Forêt de Rospa Sorba**, by way of **Vezzani** and the D343. Along the way there is a famous viewpoint, the **Col de Morello**, and an even better one just a short walk up the goat path, at a spot known as **L'Occhio-Vario**, 'the varying eye', for the changing colours of its white granite marker. From here follow the D343 south, keeping to the right after 14km for the narrow D344 and the breathtaking **Défilé de l'Inzecca**, where the tumultuous Fium'Orbo has notched 1,000ft/300m walls in the green grey granite on its way down to Ghisonaccia and the sea. Above the ravine, the artificial **Lac de Sampolo**, surrounded by groves of olives and chestnuts affords a peaceful interlude before you plunge into a second dramatic ravine, the **Défilé des Strette**. Overhead tower the clustered peaks of **Christe-Eleison** and **Kyrie-Eleison**, whose curious names go back to 1362: when the very last of the Giovannali (*see* 'Carbini', p.146) were rounded up in this remote spot and consigned to the stake, the crowd who came to watch included an elderly priest, who took pity as the smoke poured out of the pyre and defied the bishop by chanting the office of the dead for the heretics. When the people joined in the response, their voices echoed into the mountains, and a white dove appeared and flew in a circle over the billowing smoke, then disappeared towards the peaks.

Ghisoni, a shepherds' village, is peaceful and sweet, and has for its chief monument the frescoed Chapelle de Ste-Croix. Most visitors come to climb **Monte Renoso** (7,716ft/2,352m), the least rugged of Corsica's giants, a rigorous if not difficult hike. The classic approach is from the Bergeries de Capannelle, 18km south of Ghisoni at the end of the D69, which is also a favourite cross-country ski spot when there's enough snow. From here it's three hours to the top (as always, get an early start) along a path marked with cairns, over a stream, past the verdant *source de Pizzolo* and the large grey Lac de Bastiani, where snow drifts, and then along the ridge to the summit; the entire southern half of Corsica stretches out below, as far as the coast of

Sardinia. To make the traditional nine-hour round trip, continue along the ridge to the Col de Pruno, and then to the Bergeries des Pozzi, and cross over the plateau to join the GR20; turn left to return to Capannelle.

If you're driving, the return to Vivario is by way of the D69 and the **Col de Sorba**, on a corniche road high over the green sea of trees. Ancient chestnuts border the road; the depths of the woods echo with the grunts and snorts of wild boar.

Venaco/Venacu

North of Vivario, on the road to Corte, **Venaco** (the name comes from the pre-Indo-European *ven*, or mountain) puts on an elegant façade for a village of 600 souls, with a handsome Baroque church enjoying the best views in town and containing a remarkable *trompe l'œil* ceiling inside on Abraham and Isaac. In early May thousands come to attend Corsica's most important cheese fair, *A Fiera di u Casgiu* (see *www. fromages-corse.org*). The most popular walk from here is the **Pont de Noceta**, four hours there and back along the river Vecchio, with a chance to bathe along the way in the river's natural pools.

Corte/Corti

Just north of the geographic centre of the island and in between the two great mountain-divided halves, Corte is the safety deposit box of Corsica's soul and in many ways is the logical capital of Corsica, a role it has played on more than one occasion; quite a few Corsicans, in fact, think it should be capital again. The setting is pure opera, and the stern slate-roofed Ville Haute with a citadel teetering on an eagle's nest high over the rivers Tavignano and Restonica has kept its bristling character in its steep cobbled lanes and squares; but lower Corte was hit with an ugly stick, built on the cheap for the garrisons that long occupied the town.

Since 1981 Corte has at least resumed its former role as Corsica's university town, and thanks to some 4,000 students it's by far the liveliest place in the interior. Now that the young people no longer have to leave the island to continue their education, this has given Corsica a stronger sense of shared destiny and identity, and it has produced quite a few young entrepreneurs, who want to make a go of it on Corsica, in spite of the hard work. For visitors, Corte has a striking regional museum, and is a base for excursions into the staggeringly beautiful valleys that surround it.

History

The area around Corte was occupied in ancient times, but its early history is half lost in legend. At the end of the Roman Empire, residents of coastal Aléria fled here for safety and settled in a village then known as *Venicium*. In the 8th century, the Saracens took it after a terrible battle, at a place still known as Campu Sanguisaghu ('Field of Blood'). In the 9th century, according to medieval chronicler Giovanni della Grossa, it was seized again for the Christians by Ugo Colonna, who built his Palazzo di Venaco by the church of San Giovanni.

Getting Around

By Train
Corte's station is a 15-minute walk east of town, t 04 95 46 00 97, and has 3–5 trains a day to Ajaccio and Bastia, and 2 to Calvi, changing at Ponte Leccia.

By Bus
Autocars Cortenais, t 04 95 46 02 12, go to Ghisonaccia and Aléria on Tues, Thurs and Sat from the train station, and to Bastia Mon, Wed and Fri, from 14 Cours Paoli.

Mordiconi, t 04 95 48 00 04, links Corte to Calacuccia and Porto Mon–Sat July– mid-Sept.

Rinieri minibuses, t 04 95 46 22 89 or t 04 95 46 02 12, take walkers without cars down the Gorges de la Restonica as far as the Bergeries de Grotelle; ring to book.

Eurocorse Voyages, t 04 95 32 01 63, depart from in front of the Brasserie Le Majestic Mon–Sat for Bastia and Ajaccio.

Car Hire and Taxis
Car hire: Europcar, Place de la Gare, t 04 95 46 06 02.

Taxis: t 04 95 61 01 17 or t 04 95 46 04 88.

Tourist Information

Corte: In the Citadelle, t 04 95 46 26 70, www. corte-tourisme.com. Open July and Aug Mon– Sat 9–8, Sun 10–6; June and Sept Mon–Sat 9–6; Mar–May Mon–Sat 9–12 and 2–6; Oct–Feb Mon–Fri 9–12 and 2–6.

Parc Naturel Régional de Corse, in the same building. A mine of information on walks throughout central Corsica. Open mid-June– mid-Oct.

Festivals and Events

Ghjurnate Internaziunale: annual summer reunion of Europe's noisier minorities.
Tutti in Piazza FestiBallu: popular dance festival in late July; www.tuttiinpiazza.com.

Shopping

Corsica's regional market takes place in Corte on Fridays, in the car park along Av Xavier Luciani.

Chez Marie et Jean Luc, Place Gaffory, and Les Délices du Palais, 7 Cours Paoli, are famous for their falculelle, Corte's renowned little tarts, filled with lemon-scented brocciu and baked on a chestnut leaf.

U Granaghju, Place Paoli, t 04 95 46 20 28, and L'Andatu, 26 Cours Paoli, both have a wide choice of produits corses.

Ghjoculi Smunevuli, Place Gaffory, t 04 95 47 05 52, sell an imaginative hand-made wooden toys, and a wide array of puzzles, many with Corsican themes. A Chiostra, 4 Rue Chiostra, t 04 95 46 19 53, has ceramics and faïence.

Sports and Activities

Corsica Rando Evasion, t 06 86 46 54 50, www.corsica-rando-evasion.com. Organized mountain treks by the day or week.

In Terra Corsa, next to the train station in Ponte Leccia, t 04 95 47 69 48, www.interra corsa.fr. Specialists in adventures in the Asco Valley and via ferrata, although they offer everything from canyoning, sea and river kayaking, diving, trips in four-wheel-drives or helicopters, rafting, 'tyro-trekking', tastings of Corsican specialities, Corsican concerts and much more.

Then the curtain goes down, only to rise on a village now known as Corte, occupied by the Genoese in the 13th century. Vincentello d'Istria, the Aragonese viceroy, saw Corte's potential as the strategic capital of Corsica and built his citadel on top of the town in 1419. After its foundation by such an independent spirit, Corte smouldered when the army of the Bank of St George occupied Vincentello's citadel in 1459; for their part, the Genoese governed with such diplomacy and finesse that when Sampiero Corso and the French came along in 1553, the Cortenais opened the gates

Where to Stay

Corte's hotels are modest, and a bargain after the coasts, but there are not enough to go around in summer, when reservations are imperative. The ones along the Restonica are exceptionally nice, with the river splashing away below.

Corte ✉ 20250

★★Hôtel de la Paix, Av de Gaulle, t 04 95 46 06 72 (*inexpensive*). In the centre, on a peaceful residential street at the end of Place Padua; large rooms are cosy enough and all have TVs. No credit cards. *Closed mid-Oct–Mar.*

Ferme-auberge Osteria di l'Orta, in the north part of town at Pont d'Orta, t 04 95 61 06 41, *www.osteria-di-l-orta.com* (*moderate*). B&B and a suite in an old mansion, run by the charming Marina and Antoine Guelfucci (a descendant of the Duke of Padua), who also serve delicious, gargantuan meals made of fresh farm produce, that change according to season but usually feature the local lamb (*menus at €35 and €20*). *Be sure to book.*

Kryn Flor, 3km south of Corte on the N193 at U San Gavinu, t 04 95 61 02 88 (*moderate*). Antoine Valentini was a shepherd, who now distils essential oils and runs this beautiful B&B with his wife and son; all rooms are en suite, and there's a beautiful pool and mountain views.

★★Hôtel du Nord, 22 Cours Paoli, t 04 95 46 00 68, *www.hoteldunord-corte.com* (*moderate–inexpensive*). Corte's oldest and most characterful hotel, with high-ceilinged rooms, all recently renovated.

★★Hôtel HR, 6 Allée du 9 Septembre, t 04 95 45 11 11, *www.hotel-hr.com* (*inexpensive*). On the edge of the centre towards the train station, the HR began life as a *gendarme* barracks; it

offers a garden, work-out room, sauna, a garage, launderette, restaurant and perhaps a room when the others are full – there are 135 of them, including mini apartments sleeping four. No credit cards.

Hôtel de la Poste, 2 Place Padoue, t 04 95 46 01 37 (*inexpensive*). A bargain, quiet and central. Rooms have recently been redone and all are en suite. No credit cards.

Ferme Equestre L'Albadu, Ancienne Route d'Ajaccio, t 04 95 46 24 55 (*inexpensive*). On the heights above Corte, 1km from the station (they'll collect you with advance warning), a warm-hearted *ferme-auberge* with simple rooms, shared WCs, horses to ride, and jovial farm meals, featuring the farm's own cheese and other products. They also have *camping à la ferme*. *Book.*

Eating Out

According to legend, Corte's *azziminu cortenese* (the local *bouillabaisse*) came about because the locals used to throw all their excess wine into the rivers and inebriated the trout, making them both tasty and easy to grab. But you're more likely to find the trout *in aïolu*, stuffed with *brocciu* and fried with garlic and a bit of vinegar.

U Museu, Rampe Ribanelle, t 04 95 61 08 36. Just under the museum, the Baldacci family run a charming restaurant with lickety-split service, where each dish is packed full of flavour, from the thick *soupe paysanne* to lasagne with boar sauce, trout (their speciality) or boar *en daube* perfumed with myrtle. Paoli encouraged Corsicans to plant and eat potatoes, and here they prepare them better than most; they also do an unusual chestnut pizza. Excellent red AOC

and handed Corso the key to the city. It did little good: the Treaty of Cateau-Cambrésis brought the Genoese back a few years later.

Corte played a leading role in the War of Independence. In 1729, the first rebellion in Corsica broke out just to the east in the Boziu (*see* p.182), and the island was declared independent in Corte two years later. In 1745, as Genoa, France, Sardinia and Britain played their game of Risk over the island's future, Gian' Pietro Gaffory, a Corte physician, was chosen as 'Protector of the Nation' and in 1751, under Corsica's first constitution, he was elected general of the nation. Gallant, bold and smart, he acted house wine. *Menus around €25. Closed Sun in winter, and 20 Dec–Mar.*

Au Plat d'Or, Place Paoli, t 04 95 46 27 16. Colourful and classy little restaurant, using exclusively the finest local ingredients from local suppliers: lamb and kid are prepared *à l'istretta*; the fillet of beef and wild mushroom *brochettes* are divine, as is trout in liqueur. Top it off with Corte's local sweet, *falculelli*; good list of Corsican wines. *Plat du jour €11, menu €19. Closed Sun and Feb.*

U Paglia Orba, 1 Av Xavier Luciani, t 04 95 61 07 89. Unpretentious, reliable place, on a terrace overlooking the street, where you can feast on pizzas, pasta, some highly original salads (such as one of lettuce, toasted almonds, raisins, hot profiteroles filled with ham and crème fraîche), *cipolle piene* (stuffed onions), and vegetarian dishes as well as traditional Corsican cuisine. *Menus at €14.*

Le Gaffory, Place Gaffory, t 04 95 46 36 97. Good food in the heart of the old town, serving Corsican classics with a twist – try the boar lasagne. *Around €13. Closed Oct–Mar.*

Trattoria Casanova, 6 Cours Paoli, t 04 95 46 00 79. Popular restaurant linked to a *pâtisserie* of 1887, with good €12 and €15 menus; try the *ravioli de St-Jacques* if it's on the menu. *Closed Sun.*

Le Bip's, just off Cours Paoli, t 04 95 46 06 26. Amiable, cosy restaurant in stone and exposed beams next to a café, popular with students and the locals for its good cheap renditions of Corsican classics. *Closed Sat.*

Gorges de la Restonica ✉ 20250

★★★Dominique Colonna, Rte de la Restonica, 1.5km from Corte, t 04 95 45 25 65, *www. dominique-colonna.com* (*expensive–moderate*). Stylish building with 28 rooms and suites, all with balconies and mod cons to cosset guests by the rushing river, as well as a garden and a heated pool. Today it's run by the daughter of the founder, Dominique Colonna, a goalie for Rheims, who got the money to buy this place by winning the lottery. *Closed mid-Nov–mid-Mar.*

Auberge de la Restonica, t 04 95 45 25 25 (*moderate*). Next to the Colonna, same owners, same pool. Seven comfortable rooms, all with TV. Fine restaurant serving omelettes *au brocciu* with fresh mint, *filet Restonica* (beef with Corsican cheese, flambéed in eau-de-vie), trout *in aïolu* and other delights (*menu du terroir €20*). *Hotel open all year, restaurant closed Nov–Mar.*

★★★Le Refuge, Rte de la Restonica, 2km from Corte, t 04 95 46 09 13, *www.lerefuge.fr.fm* (*moderate; half-board only*). Right on the bank of the river, a handsome hotel-restaurant, one of the few in the area with disabled access.

★★Les Jardins de la Glacière, Rte de la Restonica, t 04 95 45 27 00, *www.lesjardins delaglaciere.com* (*moderate*). Built of local stone 200 years ago, and called into action in later years as a hydroelectric plant and later an ice house; 12 air-conditioned rooms sleeping up to five and a pool by the river.

Camping de Tuani, Vallée de la Restonica, t 04 95 46 16 85 (*inexpensive*). Beautiful site by the river in the beautiful valley, with a good pizzeria. *Closed Oct–mid-April.*

Chez Cesar, at the Tragone bridge in the Restonica Valley, 10km from Corte, t 04 95 46 14 50. A great place in a superb setting for a freshly grilled lunch while exploring one of the Corsica's most beautiful valleys; it's best to book ahead to make sure he's there. *Menus €16 and €22. Closed Oct–Mar.*

so effectively that his fate was soon decided in Genoa, which eliminated him in the age-old fashion: his family's enemies, in this case the Romei, were bribed and promised security from vendettas in Genoa. In 1753, they assassinated Gaffory just outside Corte, and the Romei made a clean getaway, but Gaffory's own brother, Anton Francesco, was accused of complicity, imprisoned in the citadel and beaten to death. The five houses belonging to the Romei were demolished, and to this day the sites are considered cursed in Corte.

Gaffory's successor, Pasquale Paoli, made Corte the capital of the nation in 1755 and the seat of the Assembly, and for a brief shining moment Corte was the one place in the world where the ideals of the Enlightenment were actually put into practice. In 1765, undaunted by the troubles facing his little nation (in spite of the admiration of individuals, no government ever formally recognized it), Paoli founded a university with funds from the Corsican church, with free tuition and local Franciscan teachers, who taught jurisprudence, mathematics, theology, natural science, ethics and modern philosophers such as Locke, Montesquieu, Hume and Rousseau, all designed to form leaders of the new nation state. Enthusiastic young Corsicans left their studies in Italy to enrol – Carlo Bonaparte attended, and made an inspiring speech in honour of freedom; his son Napoleon kept a copy of it, even on St Helena.

Documents evoke what Corte the capital was like in its brief heyday. Paoli imported fancy furniture and chandeliers from Italy to give the grim governor's palace a stately look; he played cards in the evening with Carlo and Letizia Bonaparte. Corte even had a tiger and a pair of ostriches, gifts from the *bey* of Tunisia, after Paoli refused to let the Corsicans take advantage of a distressed Tunisian ship, and instead made them repair it and restore its cargo and send it on its way – in spite of their first reflex to get revenge for all the attacks by Barbary pirates. But by 1769 it was all over. Corte had a brief reprise in April 1793, when Paoli returned after having broken with the French Revolution. Loyal Corsicans rallied to him again, until Paoli was forced again into exile in 1795, and Corte's glory days as a capital were over.

The Ville Haute

The traditional meeting place of Corte, circular **Place Paoli**, has for its central ornament a smugly gloomy bronze statue of *U Babbu di a Patria*, 'the Father of the Nation', erected by public subscription in 1854 (poor Paoli! he deserves better). Cours Paoli, the main shopping street, extends north from here through the newer part of the town, while Rue Scoliscia, lined by tall, atmospheric houses, leads up into the Ville Haute and its centrepiece, **Place Gaffory**, with a statue of Paoli's predecessor, Gian' Pietro Gaffory, whose house just behind is still pocked by bullet holes from the siege of 1750.

The brave doctor's statue points at the **church of the Annunciation**, built in 1450, with four false columns as a reference to Bishop Ambroise Colonna who paid for it. Reworked in the 1600s, it has a handsome carved pulpit and 17th-century crucifix, both from Corte's former Franciscan convent. The wax figure of St Théophile of Corte as a corpse comes courtesy of Paris's Musée Grévin; a painting, sent by the Vatican, shows Corte's saint in one of his shining hours, convincing the Prince of Württemberg, employed by the Genoese on a punitive mission, to retreat from Corsica. The **oratory** behind the church marks the place where Théophile was born (as Biagio di Signori, in 1676). Famed as a mystic and Franciscan reformer, he was canonized in 1930.

Signs point up from the square to the **Belvédère**, a platform some 330ft/100m over the confluence of the Restonica and Tavignano as they rush out of their respective gorges, facing the only surviving bit of Vincentello's original citadel, the medieval tower. The Genoese used to toss prisoners down the abyss; if the victim showed any sign of life, they would send a pack of dogs to finish him off. Understandably this side

Faustina Gaffory, 'the Spartiate'

Two bas reliefs on the pedestal of Gaffory's statue evoke the stalwart courage of his wife Faustina. When Gaffory, Faustina and the patriots, fresh from a victory in St-Florent, arrived at the gate of Corte to take their home town, they found that their 13-month-old son had been seized by the Genoese; when the Corsicans attacked, the Genoese dangled the child over the walls in the line of fire. When the men hesitated, Faustina cried: 'Shoot! Shoot! God will protect the innocent! Think not of my son, think of your country!' Gaffory took the town and, by a miracle, the child survived the ordeal safe and sound (the fact that the real little Gaffory was in Bastia may have given Faustina courage). In 1750, taking advantage of Gaffory's absence, the Genoese thought to retake Corte and began with a fierce attack on his house. They didn't reckon on Faustina; when her defenders wanted to surrender, she raised a torch over a powder keg, threatening to blow everyone to kingdom come unless they fought on. They went back to their posts, and carried on fighting until her husband came to the rescue. When Gaffory was killed, she made her 12-year-old son repeat an oath of vengeance: 'I swear, by the head of my father, never to forgive his assassins. I swear an oath of eternal hatred against the Genoese and their thugs!' The women of Corte were tough cookies: in the 1700s many vowed never to marry as long as the Genoese ruled the island, because they refused to give birth to 'slaves'.

was never very well guarded, and occasionally Corsican prisoners (including Gaffory) managed to escape by shinning down with ropes. A stair and steep path follow the same route, leaving you by a favourite swimming hole in the Tavignano.

Just west, towards Place du Poilu, the austere **Palazzu Naziunale** was built as a residence for Corte's Genoese captain and converted under Paoli into the seat of the government and Corsica's university from 1755 to 1769. As of 1981, it has resumed some of its old functions, housing the Institut d'Etudes Corses. Opposite, a plaque at No.1 marks the house where Joseph Bonaparte, the future king of Naples and Spain (where he was called 'Pepe Bottles' for his drinking habits), was born in 1768 while his father Carlo attended university and served as Paoli's right-hand man. A second plaque on the same house commemorates the birth of his cousin Arrighi di Casanova, in 1778, who fought in all Napoleon's battles, and was made Duke of Padua. After Waterloo he returned to Corsica, became a senator, and retired as governor of the Invalides in Paris, where, like Napoleon, he is buried.

The Citadelle and the Musée de la Corse (Museu di a Corsica)

t 04 95 45 25 45; open April–20 June and 21 Sept–Oct Tues–Sun 10–6; 21 June–20 Sept daily 10–8; Nov–Mar Tues–Sat 10–6; closed Jan; adm. Note that access to the Citadelle closes an hour before the museum.

The Citadelle dominating Corte has gone through many changes since its construction by Vincentello d'Istria, but after the tenure of the Italians (who used it as a prison for Maquisards in the Second World War) and the Foreign Legion (1962–83), culture has taken the place of soldiers. The barracks in the lower courtyard were replaced by a new museum designed by Torinese architect Andrea Bruno in 1997, although the building is somewhat more impressive than the contents.

Much of the collection consists of ethnographic items donated by the Abbé Louis Doazan, evoking the life of a shepherd, accompanied by videos on sheep-shearing and cheesemaking, maps of transhumance trails, conch shell horns, knives and stilettos, and curiosities such as a catskin snuff box and a sheep's shoulderblade that shepherds used to tell the future. There are photos from 1887 taken by Prince Roland Bonaparte, Napoleon's great-nephew and anthropologist, and a display on Prosper Mérimée's journey in 1839, when he wrote *Colomba* and fostered many of the romantic stereotypes that attracted Alexandre Dumas, Flaubert and Maupassant to Corsica. There's a copy of an incredible 10-volume *Grand Atlas Ethnologique de la Corse*, which was written between 1935 and 1942 by an Italian linguist to justify Mussolini's desire to take the island back into the Italian fold. And there are glimpses into how very isolated pockets of Corsica could be; into the 20th century women in Farinole, Canaja and Monaccia were still making asbestos pots without a potter's wheel in the same style as in the Iron Age. The second gallery is used for temporary exhibitions relating to Corsica – on industry, tourism, religion, and so on – and at the very end are tall plastic tubes where you can stand and listen to traditional music.

Before or after the museum, walk around the Citadelle and drink in the stunning mountain views, best from the **Nid d'Aigle** (Eagle's Nest) – the only surviving bit from Vincentello's structure of 1420, reached by way of a grand staircase made of Restonica marble.

Ste-Croix and the Cours Paoli

When leaving the citadel, head left down Rue Colonel Feracci to the slightly dilapidated **Chapelle Ste-Croix**, sitting atop a wonderful picturesque marble ramp of shallow steps. This is the church of Corte's religious confraternities (*see* p.29), which as elsewhere on Corsica are currently undergoing a revival. On Maundy Thursday and Good Friday, when Corte is illuminated by candles, the white-hooded processions leave from here; on Thursday they make a *granitula*, spiralling in and out in front of the church. Ste-Croix has a lavish interior and pavement of grey Restonica marble, and on the altar a medallion of the *Virgin of the Apocalypse* and a Baroque retable.

Down below is a pretty fountain called the **Douze Cailloux** – supposedly so cold that you can only take 12 pebbles out before your hand freezes. Here Corte's pleasant shopping street, Cours Paoli, is decorated with yet another statue of a general; this one represents the aforementioned **Arrighi di Casanova**, Duke of Padua (1778–1853), sculpted by Bartholdi, whose biggest and best-known work is the Statue of Liberty. Casanova is a bit smaller.

Just South of Corte: San Giovanni Battista

The site of Corte's Roman predecessor, Venicium, is up a barely driveable track off the N200 2km east of Corte (turn right by the Catena sign); this leads a kilometre up through the trees and past the train track to the ruined church of **San Giovanni Battista**, its apse decorated with blind arches and bands of stone, schist and re-used

Roman brick, and a clover-leaf shaped baptistry. San Giovanni was Venicium's cathedral, built in the 9th century; the stones of the baptistry were re-used from a 6th-century original that had probably been built by refugees from Aléria. In the 1960s, while exploring the site, the archaeologist Geneviève Moracchini-Mazel found, 100m to the west, the ruins of a large rectangular Romanesque building, which was known in Corte as the 'palace' or the 'tomb of the Moors' – exactly where Giovanni della Grossa said it would be, and providing the most convincing evidence so far that Ugo Colonna may really have existed.

East of Corte, at Mme Valentini's farm in **Santa-Lucia-di-Mercurio**, you can visit something even older: a beautiful statue-menhir discovered along the Tavignano in 1995: the nearly 6ft/2m-high, Dumbo-eared, long-nosed **Statue-menhir Nuvallela**.

Corte's Gorges: The Restonica and Tavignano

Corte is the base for exploring two stunning valleys, the Restonica and Tavignano, both of which are recovering nicely from a devastating six-day fire in the summer of 2000. This sparked outrage even among the dyed-in-the-wool Corsicans who had hitherto tolerated arson as a local tradition. The **Gorges de la Restonica**, listed as a *grand site national* since 1985, is named for its beautiful river, named *'resta unica'* ('she remains unique') when it was the only one that continued to flow during a severe drought. The sparkling water ('diamonds in solution', as Sir Gilbert Elliot described it) cascades into transparent green pools, and the cliffs and huge boulders, are reminiscent of the Easter Island heads. The road into it is very narrow, off limits to camping vehicles. Traffic jams are common in summer: avoid them by setting out at dawn.

The view back to Corte from the simple but elegant **Restonica bridge** is one of the best. The road into the valley begins between the Tavignano and Restonica bridges, and continues 15km into the gorge, as far as the big pay car park under the **Bergerie de Grotelle**, drystone sheepfolds on the flanks of Monte Rotondo, Corsica's second highest peak. Rotondo has the lion's share of Corsica's glacier lakes with seven, and experienced walkers can visit nearly all (pick up a map at the Parc Régional information office). Two lakes, however, are readily accessible to anyone who's fairly fit: it's an hour's steep walk from the car park to the high valley plateau and the **Lac de Melo**, the source of the Restonica, although beware that the steepest parts are fitted with chains and iron ladders and are not advisable if you have small children (you need both hands) or suffer from vertigo. Another half-hour on foot will take you to the even more stunning **Lac de Capitello**, Corsica's deepest mountain lake, surrounded by sheer walls; eight months of the year it's frozen solid.

The wilder **Tavignano Gorge**, on Corte's doorstep, is accessible only on foot; the path, which you can pick up near the car park behind the museum, is a section of the nine-day Mare a Mare Nord from Cargèse to Moriani-Plage, but a short 15-minute stroll is enough to take you to a spot with a wonderful view over the Citadelle (follow signs for the Refuge de Sega). Head in the other direction (marked Gîte d'Etape U Tavignanu) and you'll descend to a bridge and a refreshing swimming hole.

West of Corte: Le Niolo/U Niólu

It seems that one has reached the limits of nature.
Abbé Gaudin, *Voyage en Corse* (1787)

West of Corte is the 2,600ft/790m stark plateau of the Niolo, Corsica's little Tibet. Some say it means 'land of the clouds', while others say it means 'afflicted'. In the shadow of huge Monte Cinto (8,878ft/2,706m), the Niolo is ringed in by other giants with sharp profiles: the sweeping curl of Paglia Orba to the west, next to the pierced Monte Tafonato, and the jaggedy spires of the Cinque Frati. There are only two roads into the Niolo by car, both tremendous: the almost lunar ravine of the Scala di Santa Regina, the age-old approach from the east, and on the west, the Col de Vergio, the highest road pass on the island, hammered out over the old transhumance paths only in the 1950s. The Col de Vergio, in the beautiful Forêt de Valdu-Niellu, is near the source of the Golo, Corsica's longest river, which drains the Niolo on its dramatic 84km, 6,500ft/2,000m drop to Canonica. Eagles soar high overhead, wild pigs – Niolo's famous high-altitude *charcuterie* on the hoof – run riot, cows mosey along the side of the road. Even in the summer, when the granite bakes under the nearby sun, it's hard to believe this is still the Mediterranean.

The Niolo is above all a land of shepherds and goatherds, whose dry stone *bergeries* mark the mountain slopes. Or rather, the Niolo is the land of their families: in the

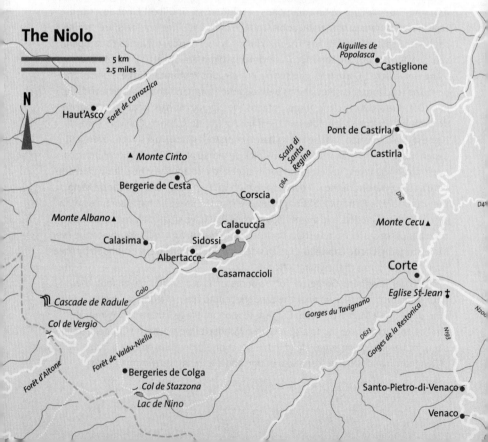

The Niolo

Getting Around

Autocars Mordiconi, **t** 04 95 48 00 04, run a daily **bus** from Corte to Calacuccia to Porto from July to mid-Sept.

Tourist Information

Calacuccia: Syndicat d'Initiative de Niolo, Avenue Valdoniello, **t** 04 95 47 12 62. *Open year-round, Mon–Fri 9–12 and 2–6.*

For guided ascents of Monte Cinto, the Cinque Frati, or more ambitious treks, contact the **Compagnie Régionale des Guides et Accompagnateurs**, Rte de Cuccia, **t** 04 95 48 10 43. The **Association d'Animations Sportives et Culturelles du Niolo, t** 04 95 48 05 22 also offers guided ascents and canyoning.

Where to Stay and Eat

Pont de Castirla ✉ 20218

Chez Jacqueline, t 04 95 47 42 04 (*moderate*). At the entrance to the Scala di Santa Regina, a good creeper-clad restaurant specializing in the famous *charcuterie* and meats from the Niolo, lasagne and more. *Book ahead; come famished for the €25 menu. Open April–Sept lunch and dinner, lunch only at other times. Closed Feb.*

Calacuccia and Around ✉ 20224

★★L'Acqua Viva, t 04 95 48 06 90 (*moderate–inexpensive*). Next to a petrol station, but comfortable en suite rooms with satellite TV in a modern building. The bar, with its big fireplace (often in use in these climes), is a popular village rendezvous. They also have a campsite, opposite.

Casa Vanella, t 04 95 48 69 33, *www.vallecime. com* (*moderate*). Four comfortable en suite B&B rooms with satellite TV.

★★Casa Balduina, Le Couvent at Albertacce, **t** 04 95 48 08 57, *www.casabalduina.com* (*moderate–inexpensive*). Pleasant small

hotel, with English-speaking owner and special deals on guided mountain hikes available. *Closed Nov.*

Hôtel des Touristes, t 04 95 48 00 04, *www. hotel-des-touristes.com* (*inexpensive*). On the other side of town, a 1928 hotel fashionable with English tourists of yesteryear with large well-kept rooms in a big, gloomy granite building and a busy restaurant. They also have bunks in a *gîte d'étape. Closed Nov–April.*

Chambres d'Hôte and Camping L'Arimone, Rte du Monte Cintu, **t** 04 95 48 00 58 (*inexpensive*). Simple bed and breakfast on the mountainside, 5km north of Calacuccia in Lozzi near the Cinto trailhead, with a good campsite next door. No credit cards. *Closed Oct–May.*

Couvent St-François-de-Niolu, 1km from Calacuccia, at Albertacce, **t** 04 95 48 00 11 (*inexpensive*). Pleasant dorm rooms and a few atmospheric if monastic doubles in a historic ex-convent, where in 1744 the French hanged 15 local rebels in the surrounding trees. Bring a towel. *No smoking, no credit cards, no ghosts.*

Gîte d'Etape, Casamacchioli (5km south of Calacuccia), **t** 04 95 48 03 47 (*inexpensive*). *Simpatico* dorm rooms and meals (€15) prepared by Mme Ingrand next to the church. *Closed Oct–Mar.*

Restaurant du Lac, right on the lake in Sidossi, 2km from Calacuccia, **t** 04 95 48 02 73. In business since 1919, a great place to tuck into generous portions of the famed *charcuterie* and cheeses of the Niolo, and dishes featuring wild mushrooms. *Menus €14 and €21; vegetarian plate €13. Closed Oct–May.*

Le Corsica, Rte du Couvent, **t** 04 95 48 01 31. Delicious *omelette au brocciu* in spring, wild trout, sturdy bean soup cooked with lamb and herbs from the *maquis* (*fasgioli incu l'agnellu*), local sheep or goat's milk cheese, *casgiu niulincu* made by two local shepherds, and baked apples or chestnut tart. *Menus €16 and €22. Closed eves in winter.*

summer the herds are up in the mountains, and in the winter they are down by the coast towards Calvi or Porto. The people make a living selling their ewes' milk to the Société Roquefort (some of it also goes into Niolo, a soft cheese made by the Santini brothers) and the chestnut trees and other old subsistence crops have all but been abandoned. Some say that the Niolins, isolated up on their plateau and generally taller and blonder than the average Corsican, are the island's aboriginal people, who in Neolithic times took refuge from the invaders on this almost inaccessible plateau; not surprisingly, as the toughest kernel of *corsitude*, the Niolins were always firmly on the side of freedom fighters and the last to hold out against the French; in 1774 their last-ditch revolt was suppressed with such model brutality, with torture, hangings and house-burnings, that they never tried again.

From Corte to the Scala di Santa Regina

The D84 is the main street of the Niolo, off the N193; from Corte, you can get there direct by way of the D18 (15km), which also offers the chance to drive up to the television receiver atop **Monte Cecu** for a splendid view down on Corte and its environs. At **Castirla**, close to the D84, signs direct you 1km below the village to the Cappella San Michele, a pre-Romanesque funerary chapel with 15th-century frescoes in the apse: a *Christ in Majesty* with a very large head, surrounded by the symbols of the Evangelists, the Apostles, the Virgin and Child and St Michael. Castirla stands at the crossroads for **Castiglione**, a seldom-visited old village hanging over the Golo and its porphyry 'needles', the **Aiguilles de Popolasca**.

'No grass, no plants; just granite, nothing but granite,' Maupassant described the Niolo in *Un Bandit Corse*, referring in particular to its Dantesque gateway, the **Scala di Santa Regina**, which begins its rise just west of Castirla. A savage *défilé* of crevices, abysses and pinnacles, where the walls tower 1,000ft/300m over the bed of the Golo, the 'Stair of the Holy Queen' recalls the parallel track used by generations of shepherds and muleteers before the opening of the road in 1889: it's so steep that much of it consists of steps sculpted out of the rock (it's waymarked in orange, from **Corscia**, 4km east of Calacuccia, if you care to walk down it). The story goes that St Martin was ploughing a field when the devil seized him and hurled him on top of the Niolo; as he fell, the mountains shattered and began to slide into the valley. Martin called upon the Virgin, and in the midst of the chaos she provided the *scala* to allow him to descend safely. On stormy days, when the granite walls reverberate with thunder, it seems as if the devil is still at it.

Calacuccia and Casamaccioli

At the top of the Scala di Santa Regina, calm and green are regained as the view opens up over **Calacuccia**, the metropolis of the Niolo with all of 350 inhabitants. Its **Lac de Calacuccia**, Corsica's largest, was created in 1968; the *base nautique* on the shore at Sidossi hires out kayaks and windsurfs for some high-altitude water fun. The pretty white parish church of **Sts Pierre-et-Paul** on the edge of the village towards Porto houses a famous wooden statue of *Christ*, one of the best and most expressive examples of Corsican folk art; if it's not open, ask at the tourist office for the key.

The end of the summer grazing season is celebrated on 7–9 September in one of Corsica's oldest and most popular fairs, held in **Casamaccioli**, a village under the chestnut trees on the south shore of the lake. The church houses the Niolo's holy of holies, the **Santa di U Niolu** or *Santa Maria della Stella*, a Baroque statue of the

Madonna and child, repainted to look like dolls, each wearing delicate golden crowns topped with stars. The story goes that in the 15th century a captain whose ship was foundering at Galéria prayed to the Virgin, who at once calmed the storm and set a star in the sky as a sign. In thanksgiving the captain donated a statue known as Santa Maria della Stella to a Franciscan monastery at Selva, in the forest of Filosorma. When this was attacked by pirates, the friars decided to move to a safer location, and put the statue on a mule, which went straight to Casamaccioli and stopped, and the statue has been there ever since. On 8 September, in honour of the Virgin's birthday, her white-clad confraternity takes her for an outing to the fairgrounds, tracing a *granitula* spiral before returning to the church. This is followed by the best traditional singing in Corsica and *chjam'è risponde* contests, which shepherds usually win, and dancing, food and drink, horse-trading, and non-stop gambling in private homes turned into casinos for the occasion.

In **Albertacce**, just west of Calacuccia, you'll find the little **Musée Archéologique Licinoi** (*t 04 95 48 05 22; open Mon–Sat 10–12.30 and 3.30–6.30; adm*). According to Ptolemy, the Licinoi (as the Greeks called the Niolins) were one of the 12 original tribes of Corsica, and the evidence here – an array of pots, grave goods and jewellery from the Niolo's 30 *castelli, taffoni*, statue-menhirs and dolmens – proves they go way back. The museum also has ethnographic items and photos of the megalithic sites. Above Albertacce, the D318 leads up to **Calasima**, the highest village on Corsica (3,592ft/ 1,095m), magnificently set on the slopes of Monte Albano; if you drive as far as you can, you'll have a grand view over the mighty shark fin of Paglia Orba and a torrent to cool off in.

Walks around Calacuccia and the Forêt de Valdu-Niellu

The Parc Régional has set up five easy orange-marked paths that circle about Calacuccia and take a few hours each; pick up the leaflet with maps at the tourist office. Others require a certain level of fitness and experience, especially the popular ascent of **Monte Cinto**, usually possible from mid-June, when the snow has melted, until mid-September. You can drive from Lozzi on a rough dirt track as far as the **Bergerie de Cesta**; from here it's about a 30-minute walk up to a simple refuge. From there it's three hours to the top, with a dawn start to avoid the midday haze and frequent afternoon lightning storms that torment Corsica's Everest. On a clear day the view takes in all of Corsica, the Tyrrhenian islands and the Alps.

To the west, the D84 continues up into the majestic **Forêt de Valdu-Niellu**, one of the largest and oldest forests on Corsica, where Laricio pines, some over 500 years old, are interspersed with white birch that turn golden in autumn. There are two classic walks through the forest, the first a rather strenuous five-hour hike there and back to uncanny Lac de Nino, the source of the Tavignano. The path marked with yellow starts along the D84 from the **Maison Forestière de Popaghja** and follows the Colga stream, dotted with weird boulders and rock formations, to the **Bergeries de Colga**; from here the path ascends steeply to the **Col de Stazzona**, where St Martin and the devil had another supernatural showdown. The grey rocks around the pass were Satan's forge, where he made a mighty plough that was pulled by huge black bulls. Martin, when he came up with his flocks in the summer, mocked him for being unable to plough a straight furrow. Angrily the devil tried to prove him wrong, but broke his ploughshare on a rock, and in a fit of pique hurled it across the mountains, piercing Monte Tafonato; while this was going on, Martin petrified his bulls, whose pointy black forms still mark the pass. From the Col de Stazzona, it's a short walk down to the striking **Lac de Nino** and the local entrance to hell, which may be why the devil was so busy in the Niolo: it's his front doorstep. Nevertheless, people have been known to bathe here and survive. The lake is famous for the extent of its *pozzines*, rich green moors amid the rocky waste that are a legacy of the last Ice Age, and which have for millennia been cropped into putting greens by the Niolins' sheep.

The second, easier walk takes two hours there and back and picks up an easy bit of the GR20, leading to the **Cascade de Radule**, made by the Golo flowing down from its source on the Paglia Orba. The path begins on the D84, 4km before the Col de Vergio, 500m above the hotel. Along the way it passes the striking, abandoned dry stone **Bergeries de Radule** and then descends to the falls, which form refreshing pools.

From the lofty **Col de Vergio** (4,845ft/1,477m), one of Corsica's great watersheds and the highest driveable pass on the island, you can easily make out the aforementioned hole in Monte Tafonato; at certain times the sun shines through it like a spotlight. Continuing west, the D84 descends through the **Forêt d'Aitone** (*see* p.267).

North of Corte to the Valle de l'Asco

On the north side of Monte Cinto, hemmed in by Corsica's tallest mountains, the Valle de l'Asco, with its deeply tinted Wild West ravine, has its share of sheer heart-thumping drama. Even more cut off than the Niolo, there's only one road into it, and it only dates from 1937, when the Asco was dammed.

Corte to Ponte Leccia

North of Corte, the main N193 passes under **Omessa**, 'the hidden', a *village perché* famed in banditry circles for its many spots suitable for ambush. Its landmark is the high Baroque belltower of the church, **St-André**, surrounded by old houses and vaulted alleys. Originally the church was a hospice called Rione, founded according to legend by the elusive Ugo Colonna; Rione, of course, recalls the seven neighbourhoods, or Rioni, of his native Rome (hence the local expression, '*Roma caput mundi/ Omessa secundi*', 'Rome, the world capital, Omessa in second place'). In 1460, the hostel was converted into a church by the Bishop of Aléria, Ambrogio (Ambroise) Colonna, who was famous for always keeping a pistol handy on the altar when he said Mass. In fact, in the 14th and 15th centuries Omessa produced three bishops named Colonna, and the church, if you're lucky enough to find it open, holds their tombs as well as a handful of 17th-century Italian paintings. In the main square, the **Chapelle de l'Annonciade** has a pretty Renaissance marble *Virgin and Child* of the Florentine school.

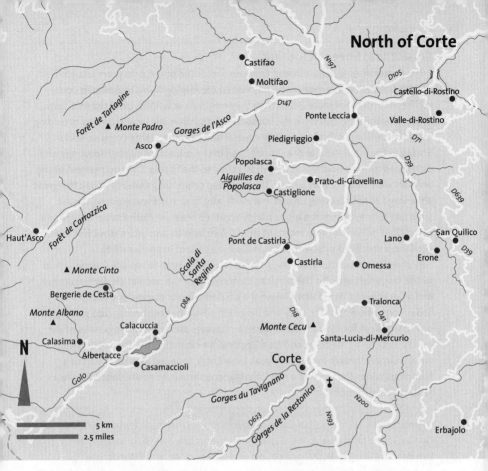

North of Omessa on the N193, 5km before Ponte Leccia, consider a leisurely 16km detour on the D39 to the right (signposted Castellu di Serravalla) into the little Casaluna valley and an obscure holy site, marked by twin Pisan chapels, San Quilico and Santa Maria. Isolated in the chestnut woods, the chapels were built, so they say, by two master masons, father and son, and by the mere sound of the son's tools on the stone the father could tell if he was doing good work, and would shout across the forest if he heard a clunk. **San Quilico**, reached by a track from the hamlet of **Tribbio**, has a curious relief of a man on the tympanum, in a long robe, standing on a snake and choking it; on the back the snake reappears with Adam and Eve. Just south on the D39, **Santa Maria** is signposted, a 500m walk up the track, guarded by a tall thin Giacometti-esque 8ft/2.4m statue-menhir, bearing a sword, and covered with centuries of graffiti (including a cross for a navel). The stories say a young girl came here and poked a stick in a tomb; Death seized the other end and, unable to move, she was literally petrified with fear. Other graffiti covers a big flat rock, the **Petra Frisgiatu**, 150m from the statue-menhir, dating back to c. 1000 BC: pentagons, diamonds, crosses, and so on – intense but unfathomable.

Corsicans in Sheep's Clothing

The pastoralism that dominated Corsican life for the past 6,000 years just ain't what it used to be, as anyone who has visited the ethnographic museum in Corte will know in perhaps more detail than they might have wished. Until the mid-19th century, however, sheep were the backbone of a sustainable local economy, providing much of the island's food (especially cheese) and clothing. Hardy Corsican flocks grazed in the mountains in the summer and in the coastal *maquis* in the winter, and developed a long smooth coat that didn't cling to the thorns. Over 90 per cent of the animals were black or dark brown, the preferred colour for garments (it had the great advantage of not showing up dirt and mud), and their wool was washed, carded, spun and woven by women into a highly weather-resistant cloth known as *U pannu corsu*. Goat hair, even more resistant than fleece, was beaten into a stout felt to make *U pilone*, a shepherd's cloak that could double as a tent in bad weather.

By the mid-19th century, however, Genoese velvet began to replace *U pannu corsu* as the favoured fabric for the Corsican costume; after the population decline during and after the First World War, the wool was used only for carpets and mattresses. Today some 100,000 black, grey and beige long-haired sheep and 45,000 goats graze on Corsica, kept for their milk and meat; as markets prefer the homogenous white wool produced by Australia and New Zealand, an estimated 100 tons of Corsican wool is simply thrown away every year. Lana Corsa, founded in 1980, is part of a European-wide effort to find a use for indigenous wools, in an attempt to make a virtue of its difference.

Ponte Leccia, 24km north of Corte, is an important crossroads for both roads and Corsica's little rail network; it's also an important market town for locals in the surrounding villages, boasting a couple of petrol stations, an ATM machine, pizzeria/restaurants, a supermarket, a hotel and other useful shops, including the workshops of **Lana Corsa** (*t 04 95 48 43 79, www.lana-corsa.com; open mid-May–Oct Mon–Sat 9–7; Nov–mid-May Mon–Sat 10–2; see box, above*), which specializes in natural, undyed garments made from the black, beige, and dark and light grey wool of Corsican sheep, in patterns derived from designs on the island's Pisan churches.

The Valle de l'Asco

Just north of Ponte Leccia, the D147 is the sole road into the Asco valley. According to Ptolemy, the original inhabitants of Asco, as in the Niolo, were known as the Licinoi or 'torch merchants', and throughout the Genoese period that's what the Aschesi did – made pitch out of their pines. Perhaps not surprisingly, pines are now rather scarce in the lower valley; what you'll see instead are hives. Asco is Corsica's most hallowed honeypot, where the busy bees produce a white ambrosia, appropriately enough from manna, or plant sap – don't pass up a chance for a taste.

Six km after Ponte Leccia, a detour to the right leads up to **Moltifao** ('many honeycombs'), a village built on terraces on a crest between the Asco and Tartagine valleys. The attractive ochre church holds some good art, including a triptych and wooden retable of the *Crowning of the Virgin* of 1545, that may have been locally made.

Another 3km on, **Castifao** is piled on steep streets and likewise surrounded by hives. Its romantically ruined Gothic convent now serves as the village cemetery.

On the D147 below Moltifao, the Parc Naturel Régional has set up a sanctuary for Hermann's tortoises, the **Village des Tortues** (*t 04 95 47 85 03; guided visits April–Sept Mon–Fri at 11 and 3.30; adm, free for under-10s*). Hermann's tortoise, France's only native land tortoise, survives on Corsica and in the Massif des Maures in Provence, but is under threat from forest fires and increased road traffic; here at least they can plod about safely under the ilex trees, and you can learn all about their little ways. Two km beyond the bridge, you can practise for the death-defying *via ferratas* in the Alps at the 850ft/260m **Via Ferrata de la Manicella**, part of a 2½hr walk organized by In Terra Corsa (*see* box, below).

Beyond Moltifao the narrow and winding road plunges into the mighty **Gorges de l'Asco**, enclosed by beetling canyon walls, rising 3,000ft/900m high, which change from orange to purple in the changing light. The road then twists up to **Asco/Ascu** where the 70 permanent inhabitants (down from 1,000 in the 1930s) live in a stupendous mountain setting. According to Corsica's medieval chroniclers, 'Asco' is derived from an 11th-century colony from Ascoli Piceno in Italy, founded by a certain Pietro

Sports and Activities

In Terra Corsa, by the train station, in Ponte Leccia, **t** 04 95 47 69 48, *www.interracorsa.fr*. Organizes kayaking, canyoning, *via ferrata* and rock climbing in the Valle de l'Asco.

La Montagne des Orgues: tours of the Baroque churches of the Valle de l'Asco (*see* p.244).

Where to Stay and Eat

Omessa ✉ 20236

Chez Sandra, in nearby Francardo (north on the N193), **t** 04 95 47 41 85. A favourite stop for good solid family cooking, with a frequently changing choice of Corsican specialities. *Menu du jour €13. Closed Fri eve and Sat lunch.*

Ponte Leccia ✉ 20218

Maison Le Stuart, by the roundabout just over the bridge, **t** 04 95 47 61 11 (*inexpensive*). Formerly the Hôtel des Touristes, the large, recently smartened-up en suite rooms are tucked behind a bar (where the owner is) and away from most of the traffic noise.

Chez Dédé, Rte de San Culombanu, **t** 04 95 47 61 88. A popular rendezvous north of Ponte Leccia, serving reasonably priced *salades*

composées, pizza, omelettes and game dishes in season.

Moltifao ✉ 20218

Camping Cabanella, Rte de l'Asco, **t** 04 95 47 82 35 (*inexpensive*). Near the Genoese bridge, where you can swim; a pleasant little family-run campsite.

Camping A Tizarella, **t** 04 95 47 83 92 (*inexpensive*). Another pleasant option, with a pool and pizzeria. *Closed Nov–April.*

Asco ✉ 20276

Ferme-auberge d'Ambroise et Nicole Vesperini, just outside Asco, **t** 04 95 47 83 53 (*inexpensive*). Charming hosts and pleasant rooms on a honey farm, with satisfying home-cooked Corsican meals in the evening. *Closed Nov–Mar.*

Le Chalet, at the end of the road in Haut'Asco, **t** 04 95 47 81 08 (*inexpensive*). En suite rooms with balconies in an ugly building in a splendid setting, ideally located for excursions into the highest mountains. There's a restaurant (*€15 menu*); also budget dorm rooms with a kitchen. *Closed Oct–mid- May.*

Camping Monte Cintu, 25km from Ponte Leccia in the forest of Haut'Asco, **t** 04 95 47 86 08 (*inexpensive*). Big campsite under the pines by the river, with a little restaurant. *Closed Nov–April.*

della Scala who found himself on the wrong side of the local Guelph and Ghibelline dispute. It is true that many of the expressions used by the Aschesi into the 19th century were incomprehensible to other Corsicans, and their wedding rites were different too; for instance, there was only one wedding ring for the whole valley, which a bride would wear on her wedding night then return to the priest the next morning with a plate of fritters. In the 18th century, Asco was best known for their *paceri*, 'peacemakers', who were locally elected to negotiate settlements between feuding families; such *paceri* existed elsewhere in Corsica, but the Aschesi were considered the best at it, and other Corsicans will still call a wise individual a '*saviu d'Ascu*' (a sage of Asco).

Below Asco, the village's handsome 15th-century hump-backed Genoese bridge was used by muleteers to reach the Niolu; until 1937, this was the main road in and out of the valley. Today people come to swim in the tinglingly cold green pool by the bridge.

West of Asco, the road rises steeply and the river changes its name to Stranciacone as you enter the **Haute Vallée de l'Asco**, where the first Laricio and maritime pines of the **Forêt de Carrozzica** appear. The trees have had a hard time of it, first from the pitch-makers, then fires, and then an avalanche, but today they look tall and prosperous; this upper valley is now a Natura 2000 site for the 20 rare species that live here, including Corsican nuthatches, golden eagles and lammergeiers. In 1968, the Foreign Legion was given some real work to do on Corsica, when they extended the road from the dam up to **Haut'Asco**, set in a *cirque* of five mountains, all well over 6,000ft/ 1,828m, including **Monte Cinto**, Corsica's highest. Government funds also went into building a wart of a ski station, the island's first.

The upper Asco valley is also one of the most likely spots to see a *mouflon*; Asco and Bavella are the only two places where they survive, unhybridized, in the wild; the 300 individuals here are believed to be the last remnants of the first flocks brought over and domesticated in Neolithic times. Ring the Asco *mairie* to visit the **Maison du Mouflon et de la Nature**, in the Forêt de Carrozzica (**t** *04 95 47 82 07, www.eco-musee-corse.com; open Mon–Sat 2–5.30*). At the time of writing the Asco herd (separate from the Bavella herd for over a century) is the subject of a EU Life Nature Scheme, intended to increase numbers and extend their stomping grounds to other parts of Corsica.

The ascent of Monte Cinto from Haut'Asco is more dramatic and demanding than from the Niolo, taking about six hours, but isn't really possible until late June because of ice. The GR20 passes through here, and you can take it, without too much difficulty, northwest up to the **Crête de la Muvrella** in about two hours, to get into *mouflon* territory and take in the ravishing views, or maybe even continue for another half-hour to the little lake. In the other direction lies one of the most challenging stretches of the path, the majestic *Cirque de la Solitude*, with its vertigo-inducing *via ferrata*. No matter where you go, start early, especially in August, to avoid the storms that blast Cinto in the afternoon.

The East Coast and the Castagniccia

10

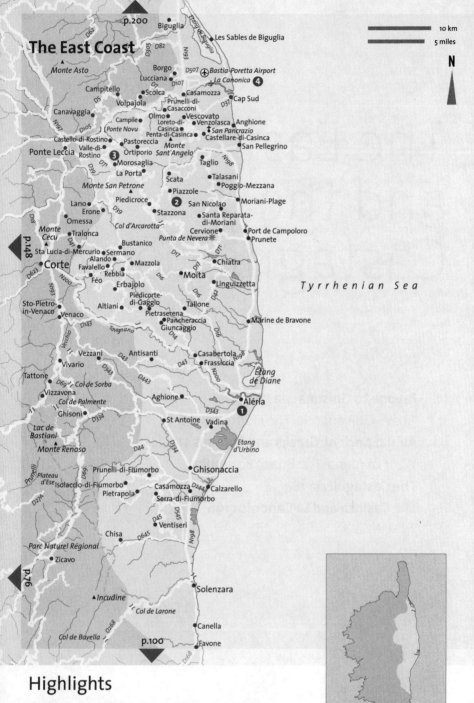

The East Coast

p.200

Biguglia
Les Sables de Biguglia

Monte Asto

Borgo
Lucciana
Bastia-Poretta Airport
La Canonica
Campitello
Scolca
Casamozza
Cap Sud
Volpajola
Prunelli-di-Casacconi
Canavaggia
Olmo
Vescovato
Campile
Loreto-di-Casinca
Venzolasca
Anghione
(Ponte Novu)
Penta-di-Casinca
San Pancrazio
Castello-di-Rostino
Pastoreccia
Castellare-di-Casinca
Valle-di-Rostino
Ortiporio
Monte
San Pellegrino
Ponte Leccia
Sant'Angelo
Morosaglia
Taglio
La Porta
Scata
Talasani
Monte San Petrone
Piazzole
Poggio-Mezzana
Lano
Piedicroce
San Nicolao
Moriani-Plage
Erone
Stazzona
Santa Reparata-di-Moriani
Omessa
Col d'Arcarotta
Cervione
Port de Campoloro
Monte
Cecu
Tralonca
Punta de Nevera
Prunete
Bustanico
Sta Lucia-di-Mercurio
Sermano
Corte
Alando
Mazzola
Chiatra
Favalello
Rebbia
Moita
Féo
Erbajolo
Linguizzetta
Piedicorte-di-Gaggio
Altiani
Tallone
Pietraserena
Marine de Bravone
Pancheraccia
Giuncaggio
Vezzani
Antisanti
Vivario
Casabertola
Frassiccia
Tattone
Col de Sorba
Etang
de Diane
Vizzavona
Col de Palmente
Aléria
Ghisoni
Aghione
St Antoine
Vadina
Lac de
Bastiani
Monte Renoso
Etang
d'Urbino
Prunelli-di-Fiumorbo
Ghisonaccia
Plateau
d'Ese
Isolaccio-di-Fiumorbo
Casamozza
Calzarello
Pietrapola
Serra-di-Fiumorbo
Parc Naturel Régional
Chisa
Ventiseri
Zicavo
Solenzara
Incudine
Col de Larone
Canella
Col de Bavella
Favone

p.148
p.76
p.100

Tyrrhenian Sea

10 km
5 miles

N

Highlights

1 Aléria, with its beautiful Greek vases and oysters
2 The Castagniccia, the world's biggest chestnut forest
3 The granite village of Morosaglia, birthplace of Paoli
4 The mosaic-floored Pisan cathedral of La Canonica

Compared to the stern drama of mountain, granite and *maquis* that prevails on Corsica, the rolling east coast with its farms, vines, citrus and olive groves and poplars seems soft and fluffy, perhaps even a bit boring. Yet it was the island's star attraction for the ancient Greeks and Romans – easily accessible to their triremes and galleys, well watered and fertile – and essential to Corsica's shepherds, who brought their flocks down here to graze in the winter. For nearly everyone else, however, it lost a good deal of its charm for about 2,000 years, thanks to barbarians and pirates and the arrival, some time in the early Middle Ages, of the anopheles mosquito. One of the few good things that came out of the Second World War, however, was DDT: the US Army, while based here in 1944, doused the coast so thoroughly that malaria is now a distant memory. Now the coast's 100km of sandy beach draws flocks of transhumants in camper vans, who know it as a convivial place for simple sun and sea. Solenzara is probably the best place for that, although Aléria has the attraction of its excellent archaeology museum and oyster lagoon. The mountains, always hovering in the background, are never far if you need a dose of altitude.

Towards Bastia, these mountains suddenly crowd the coast again to form a pair of characterful micro-regions, the Castagniccia and the Cascina. The former in particular is rich in *corsitude*, with its tiny villages and frescoed churches like islands submerged in a roiling sea of chestnut trees. This was the busiest part of Corsica a century ago, the fervent heart of the 18th-century independence movement; now it's wistful, more than half abandoned and as uniquely atmospheric as any place in Europe.

Favone to Ghisonaccia

The coast between Favone and Solenzara, which gets a disproportionate number of sea shells, was dubbed the Côte des Nacres (Mother of Pearl Coast) in the 1970s. After the Golfe de Pinarellu (*see* p.136) however, it loses much of its cachet, although it does have three accessible sandy beaches, at **Favone**, **Canella** (the prettiest – turn at the sign for La Dolce Vita restaurant), and **Solenzara**, the biggest. The name may ring a bell: it's nothing fancy, but it's the only beach on Corsica that inspired a song by Iggy Pop. Historically the area is associated with one of Napoleon's stalwarts, Commandant Poli, who was married to the daughter of his beloved nurse. He appeared in Solenzara to scout out a refuge for Napoleon in case his escape from Elba failed, but his presence didn't sit too well with the Restoration governor, the Marquis de Rivière, who tried to hire a bandit to kill him for 5,000 pieces of gold (but he was a *bandit d'honneur*, so he refused) and then tried to poison him, and failing that led an army after him. The entire Fiumorbo (*see* below), including children and old women, rose up in Poli's support, and defeated the French; the next governor wisely signed a peace treaty and general amnesty for all Corsicans. The construction of an air force base nearby brought the first visitors, and the town added a marina. Now a low-key resort, Solenzara lies at the base of the beautiful if narrow D268 to Bavella (*see* p.139).

To get to the metropolis of the coast, **Ghisonaccia** ('wretched little Ghisoni' as it was named by the wintering shepherds, who regarded it as a malaria-infested dump compared to their beloved mountain village) you have to cross the Pont de Fiumorbo,

Getting Around

Rapides Bleus Corsicatours, t 04 95 31 03 79, link Bastia to Porto-Vecchio by bus twice a day (except Sun off season), stopping off at Solenzara, Ghisonaccia and Aléria.

Solenzara Marine Service, t 04 95 57 45 50, www.smsboat.com, hires out bikes and scooters as well as boats.

Tourist Information

Solenzara: N198, t 04 95 57 43 75, www.cotedesnacres.com. Open summer daily 9–12.30 and 4–9; winter Mon–Sat 9–12.
Ghisonaccia: N198, t 04 95 56 12 38, www.corsica-costaserena.com. Open summer Mon–Sat 9–12.30 and 2–8, Sun 9–12.30; winter Mon–Fri 9–12.30 and 2–6.30, Sat 9–12.30.

Sports and Activities

Ghisonaccia lies at the end of the beautiful, if relatively seldom walked, Mare a Mare Centre path that girdles Corsica from Porticcio, divided into seven stages, much of it in the Parc Régional. The tourist office has a list of gîtes d'étape along the way, but don't set off without the Topo-guide Corse: Entre Mer et Montagne.

Boat hire: Costa Serena Nautique Club, t 06 09 06 12 90, by the Marina d'Oru, Ghisonaccia.
Diving: Club de la Côte des Nacres, Port de Solenzara, t 04 95 57 44 19, www.sccn-solenzara.org.
Riding: Ranch Bon-Annu, Favone, t 04 95 73 20 91; Ranch U Cavallu di U Fiororbu, Ghisonaccia, t 04 95 57 37 12.

Where to Stay and Eat

Favone ✉ 20145
**U Dragulinu, t 04 95 73 20 30, www.hoteludragulinu.com (expensive). Provençal-style hotel with 32 rooms right on the pretty sandy beach. Closed Nov–April.
A Mezza Rena, on the beach, t 04 95 73 20 45. Good summer-by-the-sea food: pizzas, grilled fish, chips, and salad; full meals for around €16. Closed mid-Sept–June.

Solenzara ✉ 20145
**La Solenzara, N198 (the main street), t 04 95 57 42 18, www.lasolenzara.com (moderate). A few minutes' walk from the beach and the most stylish place to stay – the 18th-century residence of the local boss, with big, high-

literally the 'bridge over troubled waters'. There is still something of a woebegone air to Ghisonaccia, a town created almost entirely in the last 50 years, with fertile fields and a massive beach, **Vignale**, chock-a-block with luxury campsites and villages de vacances. The military base is another mainstay, with the advantage of keeping the town open all year. The town's chief work of art is not something you'd expect: the church of **San Michele** decorated with gaudy neo-Byzantine frescoes by the Cretan painter Nikos Giannakakis. To the north lies a peaceful lagoon, the **Etang d'Urbino**, where oysters and mussels are cultivated, and where cons who have committed crimes of passion labour at France's last prison farm.

Above Ghisonaccia: The Fiumorbo

Ghisonaccia lies under a small circle of isolated mountain villages poking over the hills and cork oak forests, collectively known as the Fiumorbo, a name that has often meant a big headache for the government. The Fiumorbo's fearless, independent-minded shepherds and bandits rose up in 1769 against the French, only to be crushed. In 1799, Paolists, Royalists and pro-British Corsicans exiled in Tuscany fomented a ceilinged rooms, a lot of stucco and up-to-date-bathrooms; plump for one of these rather than a more ordinary room in the annexe. The garden under the palms has a lovely pool. *Closed mid-Nov–mid-Mar.*

Orsoni, N198, t 04 95 57 40 25, *www. hotelorsoni.com (moderate–inexpensive).* Charming little family-run hotel, with recently renovated rooms and a good restaurant. *Closed Nov–Mar.*

**Tourisme, t 04 95 57 40 44, *http://tourisme hotel.free.fr (inexpensive).* Renovated, air-conditioned rooms in the centre, 150m from the beach, and with a good restaurant.

A Mandria, 1km north of town at Pont de Solenzara, t 04 95 57 41 95. In a handsomely restored *bergerie* decorated with old farm implements and a delightful shady garden, dine on aubergines stuffed with *brocciu, haricots à la corse,* succulent meats including *panzetta,* grilled over a wood fire, stuffed potatoes, and more; they also do pizza. *Menu corse €20. Closed Sun eve and Mon out of season, and Jan and Feb.*

Ghisonaccia ✉ 20240

**Franceschini, Av du 9 Septembre, t 04 95 56 06 39 *(moderate).* The poshest place in town; the rooms have air-conditioning and soundproofing. *Open all year.*

Camping Serenu, at Quercetta, signposted south of Ghisonaccia, t 04 95 56 12 10 *(inexpensive).* Small, peaceful family-run campsite with a good traditional restaurant *(open eves only, all year). Campsite closed Nov–Mar.*

L'Ereur, Plage de Vignale, t 04 95 56 26 62. No, no error, but a huge menu offering everything from pizza to *civet de sanglier,* and a list of French and Corsican wines. *Menus at €28, seafood €25.*

Les Deux Magots, Plage de Vignale, t 04 95 56 15 61. The best place to tuck into a plate of seafood: shellfish in coconut milk, sea bass *brochettes,* and fruity desserts. Very popular; book in the evenings. *Menus at €17 and €23. Closed Jan–Mar.*

Le Cintra, on the south end of town, t 04 95 56 13 44. Popular for its good-value *set menus at €20* (with *foie gras*) and €13; also plenty of seafood *à la carte. Closed Sun lunch out of season.*

Pietrapola (Isolaccio-di-Fiumorbo) ✉ 20243

***Hôtel Les Thermes, t 04 95 56 70 03, *www.pietrapolalesbains.com (inexpensive).* Stay in peaceful Pietrapola and do as the Romans did, soaking away your aches and pains in the waters of Corsica's only thermal establishment. *Open all year.*

revolt here, in favour of Russia, which spread to the west coast before it too was snuffed out. Afterwards, Napoleon's hardline governor on Corsica, Général Morand, rounded up whoever he could find and executed them, or had them sent off to the infamous prison of Toulon, from which few ever returned. During the Second World War, the Fiumorbo's spirit of independence continued to smoulder, making it a hotbed of the Resistance; a fierce battle took place around Abbazia.

The houses of the main village, **Prunelli-di-Fiumorbo**, at 1,770ft/540m, shoulder one another for the grandiose view over the coast. The tall column that makes the façade of the church of **Santa Maria** so curiously assymetrical comes from a palaeochristian church, discovered in 1974 in the *maquis,* in a place called La Cursa. Today Prunelli is a one-café village where the big event of the day is the arrival of the baker's van, but it keeps a range of curios from Roman times to the Liberation in its 'memory museum', the **Musée Mnemosina** next to the post office (t *04 95 56 73 67; open Sat 3–6).* A path from the village (ask directions) leads to the ruined, startlingly archaic 6th-century church of **San Ghjuvanni Evangelista** on an isolated rock, although minus its stolen lintel, carved with the hand of God, a rose, a cross and a dove.

A narrow road from Prunelli carries on to **Isolaccio-di-Fiumorbo**, an even quieter place which bore the brunt of Général Morand's stern reprisals. In 1808, after a rebel attack on a convent in Prunelli, Morand ordered that the village's 167 inhabitants gather in the church on the pretext of checking their identity. Nine were selected for execution, and the rest were hauled off in chains to Toulon; no one ever returned.

The road back to the coast along the Abatesco leads in 7km to the clutch of granite houses that make up **Pietrapola**, prime candidate for the title of world's sleepiest spa. Its sulphurous waters were much appreciated by arthritic Romans and they still do the business today at the hotel, which has preserved its original 19th-century tubs. These waters were famed in ancient Rome for another reason as well: in 231 BC, the Corsicans attacked a booty-laden Roman army under C. Papirius Naso coming from Sardinia; the Romans gave chase, and defeated the Corsicans in a field of myrtle, *in campis murteis*, now called Morta (down by Abbazia). They then made the mistake of pursuing the Corsicans into the Fiumorbo, got lost, and nearly died of thirst before finding this spring. In gratitude for their close call, they erected a temple to the water at the gates of Rome.

Aléria: Ancient Greeks and Romans

In ancient times, these bucolic rolling hills and coastal plains watered by the sinuous Tavignano supported Corsica's two biggest cities, Aléria and Mariana. They were reduced to swampy marshes over the centuries, but Napoléon III took a first step towards the reclamation of the land by planting eucalyptus groves to suck up the excess water, but it was the DDT in 1944 that really made the difference. The French government created an organization called SOMIVAC (Société pour la Mise en Valeur Agricole de la Corse), patterned on the American Tennessee Valley Authority; SOMIVAC built dams for irrigation, did innovative agricultural research, and in the early 1960s settled thousands of *pieds-noirs* – French refugees from Algeria, not a few of them with Corsican family roots – on the newly created farms.

Originally wine, or more precisely cheap headache-inducing plonk (*gros rouge*), was their main product, and it sold by the gallon. In the 1970s it was discovered that many growers had been illegally doubling their output by using chemicals and sugar. Native Corsicans, already resentful about the favoured treatment given to the *pieds-noirs*, were outraged by the lack of action taken by Paris, as the ignominy of the cheaters threatened to taint the reputation of wine made by honest Corsican growers (a similar thing happened in Montpellier in 1907, when Languedoc's wine makers were fighting sales of cheap adulterated stuff called *la piquette*). Among the worst offenders were the powerful Depeille family; on 21 August 1975, their large *cave* in Aléria was seized by armed members of the Action Régionaliste Corse led by Dr Edmond Simeoni. The government, under Jacques Chirac, overreacted, sending in 1,250 policemen and helicopters to dislodge the militants. Two policemen were killed and one protester badly wounded in the subsequent battle; Simeoni was imprisoned, and in the next year the more radical FLNC was founded and bombings began.

The ruined Depeille estate stands (near the turn-off for the Etang de Diane) as a monument to the watershed in Franco-Corsican relations, but elsewhere the farms of

Tourist Information

Aléria: Casa Luciani, on the N198, t 04 94 57 01 51. *Open mid-June–mid-Sept Mon–Sat 9–8, mid-Sept–mid-June Mon–Sat 9–12 and 2–6.*

Sports and Activities

Domaine Mavela, U Licettu (3km south of Aléria on the D343), t 04 95 56 60 30. Fine distillery where they make fragrant *eaux-de-vie* from plums, Mediterranean citrons (*cédrats*), chestnuts, myrtle, raspberries and arbutus; try their new Corsican whisky P &M, made from chestnut flour malt produced by the Pietra brewery and aged in old cognac casks. They also have a shop selling *produits corses*: chestnut flour, wine, olive oil, honey and *charcuterie*. *Open daily 9–8, closed Sun out of season.*

Centre de Tourisme Equestre de Bravone, north of Aléria at Linguizetta, t 04 95 38 91 90, *http://perso.wanadoo.fr/gitedebravone*. Riding centre as well as inexpensive *gîtes* sleeping from 4 to 8.

Where to Stay and Eat

Aléria ✉ 20270

★★★L'Atrachjata, on the N198, t 04 95 57 03 93, *www.hotel-atrachjata.net* (*expensive*). The 'Twilight' has been spiffed up to become the class joint in Aléria; on the main road, but double glazing in the rooms keeps them quiet. They also have a restaurant serving the local oysters.

Riva Bella, t 04 95 38 81 10, *www.rivabella-corsica.com* (*moderate*). Peel off healthily at this naturist village on the beach with all the latest spa treatments, traditional hammam, special diet restaurant and – rather unexpectedly – a llama park.

★★L'Empereur, in the centre, t 04 95 57 02 13 (*moderate*). Recently renovated hotel with a pool, restaurant and air-conditioning.

★Les Orangers, by the crossroads to the beach, t 04 95 57 00 31 (*inexpensive*). Tidy little hotel, bar and pizza place by the crossroads to the beach, 3km away.

Di u Fiume, Rte de Corte t 04 95 57 02 89, *http://perso.wanadoo.fr/diufiume* (*inexpensive*). Chambres d'hôtes with big breakfasts on the river, with views up towards the fort.

La Tour, Marine de Bravone, 12km north of Aléria, t 04 95 38 81 54, *latour@tiscali.fr* (*inexpensive*). Charming bed and breakfast and *salon de thé*, 300m from the sea, immersed in greenery. Bookings a must; many rooms are reserved by repeat customers. The *salon de thé* turns into a pizzeria at night. *Closed mid-Oct–April.*

Camping Marina d'Aléria, on the N200 by the sea, t 04 95 57 01 42, *www.marina-aleria.com* (*inexpensive*). Nicest campsite on the east coast, with plenty of shade, on a long sandy beach. The bungalows on the beach sleep 4 or 5. They have tennis courts, windsurfs, kayaks, a restaurant, a pizzeria and a launderette. *Closed Nov–Easter.*

Aux Coquillages de Diane, on the Etang de Diane, t 04 95 57 04 55. The best place in town to slurp down Corsica's finest oysters, as well as other shellfish. *Around €28, booking recommended.*

L'Appiettu, next to the fort, t 04 95 38 02 51. A little place specializing in pasta with a wide choice of sauces. *Closed Mon.*

Aléria, the biggest agricultural town on the island, are thriving. Altogether the eastern plain now provides a tenth of Corsica's income, and grows a high percentage of the clementines sold in winter in France. And what goes around comes around: in Aléria itself, where the island's first olives were planted 2,500 years ago, a former agricultural chemist named Anne Amalric has won medals and recognition for some of the world's finest olive oils at the Domaine de Marquiliani.

Ancient Alalia

Even when the only building perpendicular to the ground was a pirate watchtower, old maps show that it was never forgotten that this was the site of Corsica's oldest city, Alalia. Excavations by Jean and Laurence Jehasse were begun in 1951, and while the ruins of the city of 20,000 are extensive – and unique in France, where the roots of other ancient cities such as Marseille and Nice are meagre and well buried – they would have been in much better shape had the Greeks and Romans not neglected Corsica's greatest resource, granite. The archaeologists, however, found in the necropolis hundreds of treasures that vandals and time missed, revealing in particular a Greek settlement that was far more prosperous than anyone had imagined.

History

On a low plateau, above the River Tavignano and close to the sea, Greeks from Phocaea in Asia Minor founded a trading counter they called Alalia in 565 BC. The Greeks were after copper, which had been exploited in the vicinity since c. 3500 BC, and mined up the Tavignano around Corte. When the growing Persian empire swallowed up Phocaea in 545 BC, most of the Greek population relocated here, bringing grape vines and new species of olives to plant, and made what had been a mere trading counter into a proper city. Alarmed by their new rivals, the Etruscans of Tuscany and the Carthaginians (who had bases in Sardinia and western Sicily) ganged up and attacked, and although Alalia survived, most of the inhabitants moved to the safer haven of Marseille. Nevertheless, Alalia remained a key Greek port – a landing stage for the colonies along the coasts of France, Spain, Sicily and Italy, and as ever a trading counter, sending timber, oysters and murex shells (used for purple dye) to Attica and Syracuse in exchange for ceramics and other goods. After 340 BC (the time of Alexander) imports from Attica fell off completely, and the Alalians bought Etruscan, Latin and Carthaginian goods instead. Also the tombs, until then more or less equal, begin to show a great disparity in wealth, suggesting that the feudal *latifundia* system began even before the arrival of the Romans, who would perfect it.

Occupied briefly by the Carthaginians (280–259 BC), Alalia was badly damaged in the wars of Roman conquest and in the squabbles between its leaders. To punish the inhabitants for having supported his rival Marius (*see* 'Mariana', p.198), Sulla relieved the citizens of a third of their wealth and re-founded the town with his own legionaries in 81 BC. Now known as Aleria, it would be the capital of Corsica; Caesar took a personal interest in the town plan, and Augustus made what is now the Etang de Diane an important military port, and later emperors bestowed public buildings. At its height the population reached 20,000. Christianity came early, around AD 59, and by the end of the 4th century AD Aleria was the seat of a bishopric. In 420 it was burned by the Vandals, and the population took to the hills. Some moved down later, only to be abducted en masse in 801 by the Saracens.

The Genoese attempted, without any great success, to revive Aleria, and cannibalized the ruins to build the church of **St-Marcel** (note the Greek inscription embedded in the corner) and the **Fort de Matra** (1484) that stands just opposite. To get an idea what the ancient city looked like, stop before going into the museum inside the fort to see the **model of ancient Alalia** put together by a local association (*open 9–12 and 2–6; adm free*).

Musée Jérôme Carcopino and the Excavations

*t 04 95 57 00 92. Open mid-May–Sept daily 8–12 and 2–7; Oct–mid-May
daily 8–12 and 2–5; excavations close 30mins before the museum; adm.*

The Fort de Matra now holds an **archaeological museum** named after Jérôme
Carcopino, the great Corsican historian of ancient Rome (1881–1970); the finds are
impressive, although there could be a bit more in the way of explanations. Most of
the treasures here were discovered in the immense necropolis, where many of the
Greek tombs were marked with the pentangle symbol of the Pythagorians, whose
mystical brotherhood made big inroads in Magna Graecia: the rare rock crystal
double dodecahedron in the case with the dice has a very Pythagorian look to it as
well. There are rings, lamps, pins, jewellery, Etruscan helmets and swords, but what
steals the show is an exceptional collection of 5th-century BC ceramics from Attica
and the Greek colonies in Puglia, Campania and Sicily, especially Syracuse, the New
York of its day. The subject matter of their decoration, and use (for wine), suggests
that the residents of Alalia above all liked to make merry: there are two beautiful Attic
rhytons (drinking vessels), one in the form of a mule's head, and the other a dog's
head; *askoi* painted with winged figures; a gaily erotic bowl featuring Dionysos attributed to Panaitos (480 BC); a *krater* (used for wine-mixing) with Dionysos and satyrs by
the Dinos painter; the red figure *Grape Harvest* by the Pan painter, showing Dionysos
and Silenus presiding; also note the *Dance of Drinkers* by the Leningrad painter, and
the unusual *Returning from the Banquet* by the London painter, showing two naked
and paunchy middle-aged men tipsily marching home. Roman finds include a 2nd
century AD marble bust of Jupiter Ammon with his ram's horns and a bronze military
diploma of a Corsican sailor who served in the local fleet.

The 1960–85 **excavations** of the Roman city (or more precisely, a tenth of the city)
are a short walk up from the fort, and enjoy a fine view of the river Tavignano, slowly
winding under the trees below. A plan at the entrance makes it easy to pick out the
cardo and *decumanus* – the main streets of any Roman town – as well as the trape-
zoidal forum. The forum was overlooked by an arch (now gone) and the raised
platform of the capitol, formerly crowned with the tripartate temple of Jupiter, Juno
and Minerva. Opposite are the foundations of a temple of Rome and Augustus, porti-
coes of shops and a large house called the *domus au dolium* for the large storage jar
found inside. Beyond the north portico you can make out the baths, or *Balenum*, with
the remains of their hypocaust heating and changing rooms. The original Greek
acropolis has been located to the east, and the rest of ancient Alalia probably
extended in that direction and down to the sea. The large roofed structure you can
see in a distant field to the west was the Roman amphitheatre. On the east side of
the highway lie the ruins of the *thermes*, where smelly sailors could freshen up. Now
that Paris has given Corsica more autonomy on cultural matters, excavations – stalled
for decades – may even be continued.

The Etang de Diane

The closest beach to Aléria is the sandy **Plage de Padulone**, 3km east, between the
Tavignano and the large **Etang de Diane**. This large lagoon was once the site of a

Roman naval base, dedicated to the moon goddess Diana, who had the power to calm the sea. Like the modern Corsicans, the Romans also used it for farming oysters. Their insatiable lust for the bivalves is witnessed by the lagoon's **Ile des Pêcheurs** (visible only by boat) some 400m around and made of nothing but the upper shells of oysters; the Alérians would send them to Rome in jars, salted, on the half shell, sealed with oil and wax. Napoleon, during his exile on Elba, was said to crave them and had oysters from Diane delivered twice a week (along with, perhaps more importantly, the latest news from France). Today, while there are a few wild Mediterranean ones left, most of the harvest are Portuguese oysters, sent over as newborn spat from Arcachon in mainland France). You can buy these iodine-rich delicacies (they won a gold medal at the Paris Fair in 2003), as well as mussels and clams in the shop next to the lagoon. North, there's another, smaller beach, at the **Marine de Bravone**.

West of Aléria: The Bozio/Boziu

It's 48km from Aléria to Corte along the Tavignano river, and the N200 is by far the fastest route. A triple-arched **Genoese bridge** is the main sight along the way, but if you have the inclination to dawdle there's a small circle of villages with frescoed Romanesque churches in a seldom-visited micro-region just to the north, called the **Bozio** or **Boziu**. Steep, brooding, and blanketed in chestnut forests, wedged between Corte and the Castagniccia, it's as far off the beaten track as you can get in Corsica. Only a hundred or so inhabitants remain in this time warp, in nearly impenetrable villages linked by walking paths, and narrow twisting roads that haven't changed much since the 1950s.

Although perhaps not quite as reckless and fiery as the Fiumorbo valley just to the south, the Boziu kindled two major Corsican insurrections. The first was led by **Sambucuccio d'Alando**, who was elected leader in 1358. With the war cry 'Viva popolo!' ('Long live the people!') he led a revolt against the feudal seigneurs of the Diqua dei Monti, burning the castles of all who supported Aragon; in gratitude, Genoa granted this half of Corsica its statutes as the Terre dei Comuni, making the Diqua dei Monti in effect comuni with a certain amount of autonomy, all within the greater comune of Genoa. It was in the Boziu, too, where the first sparks of the War of Independence flew in 1729, when an old man named **Cardone** in Bustanico refused to let the Genoese tax collectors seize his property after he was unable to pay his taxes following two bad harvests. His neighbours came to his aid, and, as word spread, these tiny, out-of-the-way hamlets revolted; before the Genoese knew what had hit them, the insurrection had spread like wildfire to the Castagniccia, Corte and beyond.

There are two approaches from the N200 into the Boziu. The first you'll meet from Aléria, the D14, rises above the valley to **Piedicorte-di-Gaggio** with views towards the plain and southern mountains. Its 18th-century church has kept the bell tower of its Romanesque predecessor, carved with a winged monster, a griffon and two wolves.

At **Altiani** the D14 meets up with the second road into the Boziu, the D314 from the Genoese bridge, from where it's 8.5km to **Erbajolo**, with even more stunning views across to Monte Rotondo from the belvedere by the cemetery. A path from the church

Tourist Information

Sant'Andréa-di-Boziu: Syndicat d'Initiative de Bozio, **t** 04 95 48 69 23. Tours of Romanesque churches of the Boziu. *Open summer daily 11–6.*

Events

Trail Via Romana: annual 50km race along mule paths in the Boziu and Castagniccia; contact **Boziorando**, Sant'Andrea-di-Bozio, **t** 04 95 47 11 08, *www.boziorando.com*.

Where to Stay and Eat

Piedicorte-di-Gaggio ✉ 20270

Ferme-auberge U Sortiplani, at the Pont de Piedicorti on the N200, **t** 04 95 48 81 67, *http://perso.wanadoo.fr/xavier.corazzini/ (inexpensive)*. Welcoming, tranquil place by the Tavignano, with swimming holes nearby. All rooms en suite, and there are a few camping spots and bungalows. The restaurant (*menu €25*) serves wholesome Corsican food from the farm. *Book. Restaurant closed Oct–April, rooms available year-round.*

Erbajolo ✉ 20212

L'Altu Pratu, **t** 04 95 48 80 07, *http://membres. lycos.fr/ceppu/erba (inexpensive)*. Something for everyone in this complex 20 minutes from Aléria, founded in 1995 and run by family of musicians: rooms by the night, *gîtes*, a pool, a football pitch, illuminated *boules* court and a good *ferme-auberge* serving generous portions of home-grown food (*menus change every night, €24*) and organic wine. In summer they also host concerts and other cultural events. *Open year-round; book.*

Favelello ✉ 20212

A Casa Aperta, **t** 04 95 61 09 21 or **t** 06 80 58 31 50, *http://pageperso.aol.fr/acasaaperta (inexpensive)*. Located in the countryside 9km from Corte and 3km from a riding centre, five peaceful and spacious en suite B&B rooms with a pool and *table d'hôte* dinners Mon–Sat for €17.

Alando ✉ 20212

U Fragnu, on the D339, **t** 04 95 48 68 39. A friendly *table d'hôte* lunch stop atop an old olive press, with good home cooking. *Open daily in July and Aug, but at other times book.*

Sant'Andrea-di-Boziu ✉ 20212

Casa Capellini, Poggio, **t** 04 95 48 69 33, *www.vallecime.com (moderate)*. B&B owned by Pascale and Jean-François, the latter a mountain guide who *ran* the GR20 like a marathon and won. Modern rooms in a natural setting, and delicious breakfasts featuring local honey, chestnuts and fruits; *half-board available as well.*

leads to the Pisan chapel of **San Martino**, in a wild setting where Erbajolo itself originally stood; there are some frescoes in the apse.

From here the D14 winds and winds around past **Favalello** to the Romanesque church of **Santa Maria Assunta**, covered inside with late 15th-century frescoes. These are some of the most original in Corsica, culminating with a *Christ in Majesty* in the apse, with the apostles standing below in a painted *trompe l'œil* arcade. Close to here is Sambucuccio's home town of **Alando**, under his supposed castle. Sambucuccio is an elusive character; no one knows his real name, when he was born, or how he died; in the chronicles, he vanishes off the face of the earth around 1370. The nearby village of **Alzi** is reputedly the smallest in Corsica, with a population hovering at around 10; carry on through **Mazzola** to the four hamlets of **Sant'Andréa-di-Boziu**, gazing across at each other across a deeply wooded amphitheatre; don't miss the views across the Boziu from **Rebbia**.

Between Alando and Alzi, the D15 heads north to **Bustanico**, a resolutely traditional village, famous in Corsica for kindling the War of Independence. The dozen or so houses of schist and their lauze roofs are all in admirable nick; the local restaurant-bar seems to have been preserved in formaldehyde and the church, behind its ochre façade, houses an expressive 18th-century polychrome *Christ* of local manufacture.

The best art of all in the Boziu, however, is up in the 'capital' **Sermano/Sermanu** (pop. 30), a *village perché* famous for maintaining its traditional music through thick and thin; polyphonic masses are usually sung once a month as well as during the August music festival, and on 1 November (*for information, ring the mairie, t 04 95 48 67 27*). Sermano's pride, the isolated 6th- or 7th-century **Chapelle San Niculau** is a 15-minute walk (*pick up the key from the gîte d'étape A Sulana*) and contains delightful, softly coloured frescoes, painted in the mid-15th century and in a remarkable state of preservation. They are best seen on a sunny day (even then it takes a few minutes for your eyes to adjust to the dark). Once again a *Christ in Majesty*, frowning, dominates, with the Virgin and Baptist at his sides, and eight Apostles below, while on another wall St Michael pins down the dragon.

Moïta, wedged in between the Boziu and the Castagniccia, is the capital of a little canton famous for its music as well, and in early July Moïta and surrounding villages hold a festival called the *Violoncelle de Moïta*, dedicated to the cello – in particular a curious one-off instrument made by local *luthier* Filippu Francescu Filippi in 1843 and restored in 1992 by Ugo Casalonga of Pigna. Smaller than a normal cello, it has a unique sound, and inspired the festival, which also features polyphonies by the local Confraterna di a Serra, one of the best traditional singing groups on the island.

The Castagniccia

As long as we have chestnuts, we have bread.

Pasquale Paoli

The coastal plain narrows considerably under one of Corsica's diehard unique regions, the Castagniccia (pronounced 'Castagneetch'). Gathered around the skirts of Monte San Petrone, lush, cool and often wrapped in tendrils of mist, it begs to differ from the rest of the granite island by being made of schist; on the map, it's that patch that looks like a plate of very thin tangled spaghetti strewn with meatball dots – the villages. These, on closer inspection, consist of a handful of tall, grey, schist-roofed houses clinging to the sides of steep hills, above laboriously chiselled terraces where a few vegetables, vines and olives battle on. The more prosperous villages have proud Baroque churches, extravagant and full of curlicues, yet full of moving popular touches; others make do with tiny Romanesque chapels tucked under the dappled canopy of trees. Wild pigs rule the narrow twisting roads. Going above third gear is folly; but going in third gear is delightful.

The Castagniccia takes its name from its chestnuts, the *castagne* planted in the Middle Ages. After the misery of the Black Death, the Genoese, wanting the island to have a reliable source of food, offered a bounty per tree planted, and even passed a law that allowed people to own trees on other people's land. Other chestnut forests were planted around the island, but they took to San Petrone's humid, mild schist

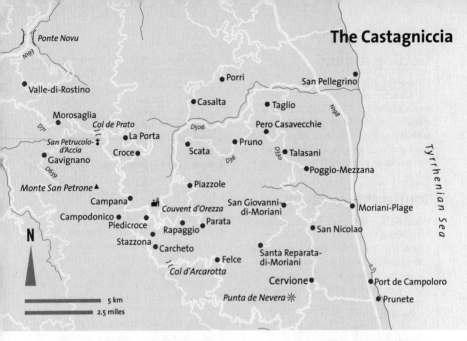

slopes like kudzu, and by the 16th century a whole chestnut civilization was in place. The locals would trade them across Corsica for cheese, wine and oil. Semi-wild pigs gorged on the forest floor and provided delicious *charcuterie*; honey was made from chestnut blossoms; furniture, baskets, shutters, wine barrels and coffins were made from the wood; even the prickly shells were used to smoke meat. By 1770, some 70 per cent of the Castagniccia was covered with chestnut trees.

Although the Castagniccia was the richest region of Corsica when the French took over, they discouraged the chestnut culture, claiming it 'promoted laziness' and a 'weak and immoral character'. Even so, in the 19th century the Castagniccia was the most densely populated rural region in Europe; according to the census, 50,000 people still lived here on the eve of the First World War, or over 100 per square kilometre. Meanwhile the great chestnut groves were going down, supplying wood for railroad ties and bark for tannin for a new tanning factory at Ponte Leccia. The Great War bled the Castagniccia of young men, as in the rest of Corsica; other inhabitants left for better opportunities in the colonies and on the continent. In drier places where the chestnuts failed to self-propagate, the *maquis* began to move in and there were fires. By the 1970s the village schools were bereft of children. The arrival of a fungus called 'ink disease' that strangles chestnut trees was another blow. Yet even today the Castagniccia is the biggest chestnut grove in Europe, although its many, once populous villages now have only around 1,000 permanent residents altogether. Some have called it the 'green desert'.

But a revival is under way in the Castagniccia, as interest grows in traditional cuisine, in creating new chestnut products, and in finding alternatives to wheat flour for people allergic to gluten. Over 7,500 acres are now in production, and Collectivité Territoriale (CTC) plans to regenerate another 2,500 over the next few years to meet the growing demand. The inner Castagniccia, part of *la Corse profonde*, has been

Getting Around

The only public transport here is along the main coastal road, the N198. **STIB buses** from Bastia, t 04 95 31 06 65, make 7 trips daily (3 at weekends) to Moriani-Plage. **Rapides Bleus buses**, t 04 95 70 96 52, travel between Bastia and Porto-Vecchio, stopping twice daily at Moriani-Plage and Prunete near Cervione.

Tourist Information

Moriani-Plage: Maison du Développement, in the centre, t 04 95 38 41 73, www.otcosta verde.com. In summer they run a shuttle up and down the coast from Prunete to the Plage de Talasani, and on Wednesday they offer a guided tour of the 'natural riches of the hinterland', with lunch stop at Cervione; book by Mon. *Open daily in summer 9–12 and 3.30–6, out of season Mon–Fri.*

Piedicroce: Syndicat d'Initiative de la Castagniccia, in the main square, t 04 95 35 82 54. *Open May–Sept Mon–Sat 9.30–12 and 3–6.*

Festivals

U Settembrinu di Tavagna: international music festival in the Castagniccia villages, sponsored by the Tavagna Club, t 04 95 36 91 94, www.tavagna.com (check out their website for other concert and events).

Activities

La Montagne des Orgues: tours of the Baroque churches of the Castagniccia (*see p.244*).

Ferme Equestre di a Conca d'Orezza: Piazzole, t 04 95 35 86 35. For exploring the by-ways of the Castagniccia.

Where to Stay and Eat

Moriani-Plage ✉ 20230

★★Costa Verde, south at San Nicolao, t 04 95 38 50 41, www.hotel-costaverde.fr

(*inexpensive*). Simple little family-run hotel/restaurant 100m from the beach. *Closed Nov–Mar.*

★★Levolle Marine, Levolle Sottana, just north at Poggio Mezzana, t 04 95 58 41 50 (*inexpensive*). Rooms, pool and a restaurant right on the sea the beach, all en suite. *Closed Oct–April.*

Camping and Bungalows Merendella, t 04 95 38 53 47, www.merendella.com (*inexpensive*). Charming flowery and shady campsite on the beach, with little wooden chalets for rent by the week. *Open June–Oct.*

L'Aria Marina, t 04 95 38 41 56. Popular and fun little restaurant on Moriani beach, with a vast choice of dishes on *three menus at €17*; they often have live music on Friday night, and *thés dansants* Sundays at 3pm – when it's best to book. *Closed Sat out of season.*

San-Giovanni-di-Moriani ✉ 20230

E Catarelle, t 04 95 38 51 64, www.corsica-catarelle.com (*inexpensive; half-board, from €65 a person*). Hotel and restaurant on a balcony high over the sea, a 15min drive to the beach. Pretty rooms sleeping up to four, including a fancy one with a Jacuzzi. Also an excellent restaurant on the terrace (*menu, €25, changes daily*). *Closed Dec–Feb.*

Santa-Reparata-di-Moriani ✉ 20230

Gîte d'Etape Luna Piena, t 04 95 38 59 48 (*inexpensive; half-board €32*). Just outside the village, first stage of the Mare a Mare Nord walk, a handsome *gîte* with beds in rooms sleeping 4–6 and excellent home-cooked food in the restaurant (*menus at €15 and €25*). *Closed mid-Oct–Mar.*

Cervione ✉ 20221

Chez M et Mme Doumens, Prunete, t 04 95 38 01 40 (*moderate*). Three beautiful rooms run by a charming couple, and home-made jams with breakfast.

Chambres d'Hôtes, at the end of the village, t 04 95 38 19 79 (*moderate*). A bright new studio room sleeping up to four.

lassoed by the Parc Naturel Régional; the Mare a Mare Nord trail wiggles through the region, and there's talk of encouraging small-scale 'green tourism'. Bed and board in the region is so sparse that it's important to ring ahead, especially out of season. The

Aux Trois Fourchettes, Carrughju Santa Croce, below the church, t 04 95 38 14 86. Delightful old-fashioned village bar-restaurant, featuring vegetables and wine from the owners' garden, and their home-made *charcuterie*; excellent cannelloni, too. A friendly place with a *good little menu at €14*.

Valle-d'Alesani ✉ 20234
San Petru, in the village, t 94 95 35 94 74. Light *nouvelle cuisine*, Corsican style: airy *beignets* of fresh goat's cheese, veal sautéed with white beans and mushrooms and stuffed artichokes. *Menus at €16 and €23. Closed Mon exc in July and Aug, and sometimes in the off season; it's best to ring ahead.*

Carcheto ✉ 20229
Torri di Tevola, t 04 95 31 29 89, *http://perso. wanadoo. fr/les-tours-de-tevola*. One of the best places to get a real feel for the area: 6 apartments sleeping 4 (*€415 a week in high season*) in a 13th-century fortified complex, owned by author Jean-Claude Rogliano, an expert on the area and on *corsitude* in general: his *Le Berger des morts* describes the area and the ancient chestnut tree, the Mal'Concilio, where the local witches meet.

Piedicroce ✉ 20229
**Le Refuge, t 04 95 35 82 65 (*inexpensive*). Hanging on the side of a mountain and a bit gruesome outside, but inside rooms are fine, and some have gorgeous views. The restaurant, one of the best in the area, specializes in *charcuterie*, game dishes and chestnut treats (*menus €17 and €26). Hotel closed mid-Oct–Mar; restaurant closed mid-Oct–Nov.*
Camping and Chambres Les Prairies, north of Piedicroce on the D506, at Scata Rumitoriu ✉ 20213, t 04 95 36 95 90 (*inexpensive*). Charming little campsite under the spreading chestnut trees, but small, so it's important to book. *Meals on request for €19. Closed Oct–May.*
Sant'Andria, at Campana, 6km from Piedicroce, t 04 95 35 82 26. Constantly changing menu featuring delicious Corsican *cuisine du*

terroir, with beautiful chestnut furnishings in the upstairs dining room. *Menu €19. Closed Sun eve and Oct–mid-April.*

La Porta ✉ 20237
L'Ampugnani (Chez Elisabeth), on the main street, t 05 95 39 22 00. Gorgeous views over La Porta and the valley, to go with traditional Castagniccia dishes, featuring *charcuterie* made of wild pigs fattened on chestnuts, and trout, veal, or boar scented with herbs from the *maquis* (*menus €16 and €24). In winter open lunch only except on Mon.*
San Pedrone, Col de Prato, t 04 95 39 20 19 (*inexpensive*). On the D71 towards Morosaglia, basic doubles with showers, basic bar-restaurant on the terrace, and a little museum of Corsican traditions, too. *Closed Oct–April.*

Pruno ✉ 20264
Auberge Chez Nénette, on the D506, t 04 95 36 92 01. Old-fashioned place founded by Nénette's grandmother and now run by her great-nephew: expect feasts of cannelloni, rabbit cooked with olives and home-grown fruit tart. *Menus at €17 and €22.* No credit cards. *Closed Nov–May.*

Morosaglia ✉ 20218
Osteria di U Cunventu, by the convent, t 04 95 47 11 79. Refined restaurant that uses local ingredients with a good deal of savvy (try the *crème de chèvre au basilic*, the Swiss chard filled with *brocciu*, and the tiramisu, Corsican style, prepared by Bernard Lepercq, refugee from a high-flying finance job in Asia. Worth the fiddly drive. *Around €35. Open weekends only in winter.*

Valle di Rustinu ✉ 20235
A Stella di Rustinu, t 04 95 38 77 09. The chef is Basque, but a convert to Corsican cuisine, famous for her home-made pâtés and *lasagne corse*, best ordered when you book. *Plat du jour €12, other menus €26–33.* The owner is a fisherman and can tell you all the best spots on the Golo river just north.

best time to come is in early October, when the chestnuts are falling and the leaves are still golden green, and the dark schist shimmers in tendrils of mist. Just don't venture in without a good map.

Chestnuts: Oldies but Goodies

In spite of what uppity 18th-century French moralists believed, chestnuts do require hands-on work. In August the ground under the trees is cleared, and beginning in October they are gathered by hand or with a rake, which helps to sort out the leaves from the nuts. Because of the steep terrain, donkeys and mules are indispensable in transporting the filled bags. Those in the know can point out 60 varieties of chestnut: *rossa*, one of the most common, are boiled and used in sweets such as *marrons glacés*; fat *carpinaghja* are the best kind to roast. Others are set aside for animal feed, for conserves, for liqueurs, etc.

The most common Corsican chestnut, however, is the *campanese* (*Castanea sativa*), which are destined to be made into flour. These are dried for three weeks on lattice work over a smouldering chestnut fire in specially built driers or *séchoirs*, requiring constant stirring and constant attention to the fire, to keep it at just the right smoky level. The chestnuts are then placed in a thresher and blower to remove every last bit of shell and bitter skin. Afterwards they are carefully sorted by hand, then baked in a slow oven until partly caramelized before being ground in a mill into a sweet flour, *farina castagnina*. The flour is used to make the age-old staple *a pulenta*, richer and earthier than cornmeal polenta, as well as in a hundred other recipes, including the hugely popular Pietra beer, which is brewed in nearby Furiani.

Seaside Castagniccia: The Costa Verde and Murianinucu

Local promoters have christened the narrow coast under the Castagniccia hills the Costa Verde. You'll find beaches at **Bravone**, **Prunete** with eucalyptus trees, and **Campoloro** with a sheltered marina. North of Campoloro, the lighthouse marks one end of the **Plage de l'Alistro**, 14km of empty sand extending up to **Moriani-Plage**, the Costa Verde's big resort, with its share of *villages de vacances*, snuggled under the hills. If you're heading that way, this is your last chance in the Castagniccia to get money out of an ATM and fill up the tank. A plaque on a beachside house marks the spot where Pasquale Paoli, aged 14, left to go into exile in Italy with his father Giacinto in 1739, vowing (well before Arnold Schwarzenegger) 'I'll be back!'

Cervione: A Saint and King, at Home

Just inland from Prunete, **Cervione** is a city by Castagniccia standards, with a web of medieval lanes that can make it a trial to find a place to park. Set in a sunny amphitheatre, it grows not only chestnuts but hazelnuts; Cervione is one of the top producers in France. Originally a coastal town called Sybrii or Serbione, it relocated to safer, higher ground in 813 after a Saracen attack. Its big Baroque church, one of the oldest on Corsica, is the **Cathédrale St-Erasme**, begun in 1578 by the bishop of Aléria, Alexander Sauli, when he moved his seat here from Vescovato (*see* below). A native of Milan, Alexander Sauli (1533–92) had been the friend and confessor of St Charles Borromeo before becoming bishop, and he spent 20 years reforming Corsica's churches, inspiring the island's 17th-century religious revival with his good works and enthusiasm; he was canonized in 1904.

His bishop's palace served as the residence of King Théodore I (*see* p.190), and, up the street to the right of the cathedral, the seminary he founded is now the seat of a remarkable **Musée Ethnographique** (*t 04 95 38 12 83; open mid-June–Sept Tues–Sat 9–12.30 and 2–7; Oct–mid-June Tues–Sat 9–12 and 2–6; closed Sun and hols; adm*), flying the single eagle flag of Corsica's one-time sovereign. Inside it has everything, including, literally, the kitchen sink – fossils, old postcards, tools, memorabilia relating to King Théodore and St Alexander Sauli, old games (the boards etched on slabs of granite), cat-skin tobacco bags, 'what one would find in a pharmacy of 1906', photos of Cervione's girls' basketball team (Corsican champions in 1952), old typewriters and mimeograph machines, and the silk and lace underwear of Elisa Bonaparte, Grand Duchess of Tuscany, which she sent to an old school chum in Cervione – being far too fancy to wear, they were converted into liturgical garments for the priest.

Below town – pick up the key at the *mairie* (*t 04 95 38 10 28*), follow the road to Prunete, and turn left at the sign to Muchjetu, then walk 15 minutes– the 12th-century **Chapelle Santa Christina** in the ruined hamlet of Furmicaccia contains sumptuous frescoes of 1473, painted when a double apse was added to the orginal nave. The *mairie* also has the key for the tiny, recently restored **Chapelle di a Scupiccia**, located an hour's walk above town. This was built to hold a beautiful 16th-century marble statue of the *Virgin*, probably made in Florence. A ship transporting it to Cordoba was wrecked here, and the *Virgin* floated ashore in her box at Prunete; the fishermen who found the statue brought it up here, where anyone attempting to reclaim their property would never find it. A path from here continues up to the **Punta de Nevera**, with views taking in much of the Castagniccia.

North of Cervione, the D330 becomes the narrow **Corniche de la Castagniccia** riding high over the coast, passing, between a rock-hewn tunnel and a pretty waterfall, the **Cascade de l'Ucelluline**, which is beautifully illuminated on summer nights. At the end of the Corniche lies citrus-growing **San Nicolao**, a typical village of the Murianinucu, as this strip of the Castagniccia is known. It has an 18th-century Baroque church, with a colourfully painted interior in *trompe l'œil*. Another, even more striking Baroque church, with a soaring bell tower, is off in the greenery around **San-Giovanni-di-Moriani**, 4km up the D34. Spread out among six hamlets, San-Giovanni's Galganera forest of yew and boxwood is one of the most important in Europe, and a nesting ground for eagles. Up near the end of the D34, the locals have blazed a series of short walks around **Santa-Reparata-di-Moriani** (pick up a map at the tourist office in San Nicolao, or at the Luna Piena *gîte*): one leads up to the **Casteddu d'Osari**, with a ruined tower over a Bronze Age site with great views as far as Italy; another goes to an iron-rich spring used by the Romans; another leads to a mysterious rock carved with crosses or, according to some, stick-figure humans.

North of San Nicolao and the Murianinucu is the **Tavagna,** another puny region, this one reached by the D330. The main village is **Talasani**, where the bar is the centre of the *Settembriu di Tavagnu* festival, which sees a wide variety of concerts from salsa to polyphonic music from late August to early September.

In another Tavagna village, tiny **Pero Casavecchie/Peru Casavechje** you can see a plaque honouring one of the most successful Corsican entrepreneurs of his time,

The Eight-month Reign of Théodore the First

When one thinks of Westphalia one thinks of ham, and Théodore von Neuhof was one of the best the region ever produced. Son of a baron, raised as a page in the French court, Théodore led a picaresque life: he had a brief career in the Bavarian army, killed his best friend in a duel, dabbled in John Law's Mississippi bubble scheme and in alchemy as well, and was captured by Barbary pirates and enslaved in Tunis in the 1730s. He managed to talk or bribe himself out of this jam, then met up with local Greek and Jewish merchants, who were looking to finance a safe refuge for themselves and their co-religionists. Hearing about the disgruntled Corsican patriots exiled in Tuscany, Théodore combined the aspirations of the two. The Corsicans were contacted, and heard wild tales of his wealth and connections. A deal was struck.

Things started off well. The Corsicans were sorely in need of good boots. When Théodore landed in Aléria in March 1736, he brought a crate of them, made of the finest Turkish leather, along with munitions and other useful things. He stepped off his ship dressed like a sultan, accompanied by a guard of honour of Corsicans, Italians and Moors. It's hard to believe that the Corsicans took him very seriously, but if his play-acting was the price to pay for the bullets, money and boots they desperately needed, they were game, and they ceremoniously escorted him up to Alesani to crown him. A constitution was drawn up by a Corsican lawyer, Sebastiano Costa, which limited the new king's powers, especially in taxation and waging war, with a council of 24 elders (one was Pasquale's dad, Giacinto Paoli). Not forgetting his Greek and Jewish backers, Théodore's one contribution to the constitution was to add an article guaranteeing freedom of religion.

The Corsicans had understood that, once Théodore was crowned, good things would flow in. Only they didn't. The king, while enjoying the perks of monarchy in his court in Cervione, lent his subjects the benefit of his military experience. But his idea of uniformed armies laying siege to cities was utterly alien to the Corsicans' far more effective guerrilla methods, so little happened – except that the Corsicans began to quarrel, and abandon or betray their king, who was running out of money. In Corte there was a rebellion against him; he had enough support to put it down, but in September he began to tiptoe away, drifting south with a last handful of supporters, before he made a dash for it in November, fleeing over the mountains from Sartène to Solenzara. He had a curtain-call off l'Ile-Rousse in 1743, when he was dangled like a piece of bait from a British warship, but there were no takers on Corsica for their old king. All washed up, he retired a pauper to London. Voltaire immortalized him rather poignantly in *Candide*, when he confessed to five genuine sovereigns in Venice, 'I am not as great a lord as you, but I really was a king just like any other. I am Théodore; they elected me King of Corsica; they called me Your Majesty, although now hardly anyone calls me Monsieur. I once minted money; now I hardly have a cent; I had two Secretaries of State, and now I hardly have a valet. I have been seen on a throne, and I spent a long time in London in prison on a straw pallet. I'm afraid I'll be treated the same here.' The five other kings listened to him with compassion. Each gave 20 sequins to King Théodore to buy suits and shirts, and Candide made him a present of a diamond worth 2,000 sequins.

Angelo Mariani (1838–1914), the grandfather, so to speak, of Coca-Cola. A pharmacist, Mariani had gone on a journey to Peru (the one in South America), where he discovered the stimulating power of the coca leaf used by the Inca; he brought some home, and invented a delicious elixir by mixing with Bordeaux wine and spices, which he launched in 1863 as Vin Mariani. It quickly became the most prescribed and popular tonic in the world – perhaps not surprisingly as each glass contained the equivalent of a line of pure cocaine. Literati such as Sir Arthur Conan Doyle, Henrik Ibsen, Emile Zola, Jules Verne, Alexandre Dumas and Robert Louis Stevenson sang its praises: Queen Victoria, American president William McKinley, the Shah of Persia, the Grand Rabbi of France and Pope Pius X all indulged; Pope Leo XIII awarded Mariani a gold medal. In 1886, a pharmacist in Atlanta, Georgia, produced a 'French Wine', but replaced the wine with extracts from the cola nut, and 'decocainized' the cocaine and replaced it with caffeine. And when the French medical academy declared Vin Mariani addictive and banned it, the new beverage Coca-Cola was ready to take its place.

The Inner Castagniccia

From Cervione the D71 hairpins for 12km to **Valle-d'Alesani/Valle-d'Alisgiani** where traditional wedding banquets achieved the epitome of chestnuttiness: a bride's family was expected to provide 24 dishes, using chestnuts in each one.

A short way up the D217 is the Franciscan **Couvent d'Alesani**, founded only ten years after the death of St Francis. It was a refuge for the Giovannali heretics in 1356 (*see* 'Carbini', p.146) before they were captured and burned at the stake. Last rebuilt in 1716, the convent hosted, in April 1736, Théodore von Neuhof's coronation as king of Corsica with a laurel wreath before a crowd of 2000 'drunk with joy'. The church has a famous painting, *The Virgin with the Cherry* (c.1450), attributed to the excellent Sienese painter Sano di Pietro.

Felce, the next hamlet, has a charming little schist-roofed church with delightful naïve frescoes (*key from the mairie, t 04 95 35 93 92*), whose painter had no qualms at all about putting himself in heaven, floating on the clouds. The tabernacle on the high altar was carved by a repentant bandit. Bandits also feature in the story of the Corsican historian Pietro Cirneo (author of *De Rebus corsicis*), who was born here in 1447, orphaned young, but sent to Italy to be educated in the humanities. Returning to Felce at the age of 20, he found himself embroiled in family feuds and, in dismay, not having learned what a Corsican should know, he got a *bandit d'honneur*, Galvano de Chiatra, to teach him the ways of the *maquis* and vendetta (although the bandit made him solemnly promise by St Pancrace, patron saint of bandits, that he wouldn't actually kill anyone during his learning period). But when the long-awaited moment came to kill his enemy, Pietro simply couldn't do it; when Galvano de Chiatra furiously confronted him, he threw down his weapons and said, 'Go ahead, kill me; but you can never make me do the infamous deed, and I henceforth dedicate my life to God.' Rather than kill Pietro, the bandit embraced and congratulated him: 'God be praised, and through you I've done a good deed. I knew all along you couldn't do it.' Pietro kept his word and became a monk and historian, and Galvano left Corsica and spent the rest of his life raising money to buy Corsican prisoners back from Barbary pirates.

Just over the panoramic **Col d'Arcarotta** (where a little market takes place on Sunday mornings in July and August), **Carcheto** (pop.19) was the base in the 19th century of a very different kind of bandit, Francesco-Maria Castelli, who lived in the ruined ivy-covered house below the village and whose stone-hearted career led directly to Carcheto's decline: having fallen out with one family, he barricaded them in their own house and forbade anyone to go near. As they slowly starved to death, a young girl took pity and went to bring them food. Castelli shot her and she spent the next 18 hours dying in the street, all alone. Even when the *gendarmes* arrived, no one lent a hand or said a word, and the police themselves had to make her a coffin and bury her. Carcheto has a church that time forgot: the endearing late 16th-century **Ste-Marguerite** (*open June–Sept, or try t 04 95 35 84 08*), with a lively coloured interior full of Baroque doodads – *trompe l'œil* and stuccoes, made by pious, self-taught Corsican artists. In the *Stations of the Cross*, painted around 1790, Corsican women sing *lamenti* around the dead Christ; the altarpiece shows Marguerite, patron of pregnant women; on the ceiling you can see her using a crucifix to repel the dragon sent to eat her by the governor of Antioch, after she refused his advances.

The Comune of Orezza: Exploded Convents and Fizzy Water

Piedicroce, the next village after Carcheto, is an important Castagniccia crossroads, and scene of an Easter fair called *Merendella in Castagniccia*, dedicated to local products – with chestnuts not surprisingly playing a starring role. It can also point with pride to its Baroque church, **St-Pierre-et-St-Paul** (1619), with a façade designed to make it look new and the oldest organ in Corsica, from the early 17th century, brought here from the cathedral in Bastia. It also has, just to the north, the evocative, ivy-covered ruins of the church of the **Couvent d'Orezza**, founded by the Franciscans in 1453 and one of the most important religious instituions in Corsica. In 1731 theologians from across the island gathered here in a *consulta* over the moral legitimacy of the revolt against Genoa; their rather Delphic verdict was that Genoa should mend her ways and that the Corsicans should unite – which the insurgents chose to interpret as approval. In January 1735 another *consulta* confirmed this by declaring Genoese laws null and the eternal separation of Corsica from Genoa. In 1790 Paoli was elected chief of the Corsican National Guard here, and met Napoleon, son of his old *aide-de-camp* who came looking for a good job, which Paoli, mistrustful of the young man's ambition, fatefully failed to give him. The Resistance were using the convent as a munitions dump; the Germans found out and blew off the roof and two of the walls in 1943. A sign warns direly of mines.

Piedicroce is part of the scattered *comune* of Orezza, which in the 19th century (hard as it is to believe today) was the single most densely populated in all France. Besides all its chestnuts, Orezza has several other feathers in its cap. One is a green stone unique to Corsica, known as *vert d'Orezza*, quarried between here and Valle-d'Alesani, and used in the Medici tombs in Florence. Below Piedicroce at **Stazzona** was a forge that made arms during the War of Independence; at **Rapaggio/Rapaghju** is Corsica's most famous mineral spring, naturally sparkling Orezza, the most iron-rich water in the world (*t 04 95 39 10 00; open April–mid-Oct Wed–Sun 8–8; mid-Oct–Mar Wed–Sun*

8–6; closed Mon and Tues). Known since Roman times, this became an important spa in the 19th century, attracting malaria sufferers and the anaemic – notably British aristocrats and French colonials from Indochina. During the Second World War it was bottled as a tonic for troops fighting in North Africa. Because it is very much an acquired taste (imagine sucking on the handle of an iron frying pan), the spas and baths closed in the 1930s, and sales of the water dropped until it closed down in 1995. But as of 2000, two locals from the Castagniccia have taken it in hand, and Orezza is available again, in new bottles designed by the British firm Claessens. New equipment oxidizes it naturally in the air, removing some of the iron and gas and making it more palatable. If you're curious, however, you can try it *au naturel* from the rust-coloured font under the trees – fill up a bottle, and in a couple of hours it turns a rich urine-yellow). And like the Castagniccia's other rising star, Pietra beer, the new Acqua Orezza has become an international darling, served in chic restaurants and water bars in Paris, Toyko and New York; multi-Michelin-starred chef Alain Ducasse is one of its greatest fans.

At the end of the Rapaggio road is **Valle-d'Orezza**, a Castagniccia Brigadoon. In the 19th century, it supplied all of Corsica with briarwood and olive-wood pipes. Now only three craftsmen still make them, and sell to visitors who knock at their doors. Another road, the slightly wider D506, forking from the bottling plant itself, has a turn-off on the right after 3km for **Piazzole**, a blip on the map but one with yet another impressive Baroque church, where in 1774 another repentant bandit (hiding in the church's attic) sculpted and painted Biblical scenes on the most colourful and charming church door in Corsica, a masterpiece of folk art.

This same D506 follows the Fium'Alto river down to the seaside hamlet of **San Pellegrino**, where legend has it the 16th-century pirate admiral Barbarossa came ashore after raiding Corsica. He made his way up the river to the foot of **Casalta**, a little village with a ruined Romanesque chapel, Santa Maria, and the house of the ex-bishop of Accia (*see* overleaf), and there he buried 'all the treasure of Corsica', although if anyone has ever found it, they haven't told.

The Holy Mountain of San Petrone

Yet another tiny road, west of Piedicroce, leads to remote **Campodonico**, 'women's camp', where they would take the children and hide out in troubled times; here, in three hours, you can take the path to the 5,797ft/1,767m summit of **Monte San Petrone**, the Castagniccia's highest peak, often snowcapped from December to March. It's not difficult but you do need proper boots and the last bit is steep; the reward is a 360-degree view, one of the best, over Corsica's central mountain chain, across to Cap Corse and over to the Tuscan coast. The mountain was sacred to the pagan Corsicans, who would light bonfires on the summit in August and December. Modern scholars debate how soon and how well Corsica took to Christianity; in his letters, Pope Gregory the Great (590–604) urged local missionaries to be more coercive towards stubborn Corsicans who insisted on worshipping idols, plants and stones.

From Piedicroce, the 'main' D71 twists around the flanks of San Petrone to **Campana**, where the church of **Sant'Andrea** houses yet another unexpected treasure, donated in the 1890s by a wealthy resident: an altarpiece of the *Adoration of the Shepherds*, complete with peasants and a basket of eggs, attributed to the 17th-century Spanish master Zurbarán, although it's more likely by one of his Andalucian followers (*the keyholder lives in the last house on the left of the church*).

A second path up San Petrone starts from the Col de Prato (up the D71 towards Morosaglia), and leads shortly to the ruined chapel of **San Petrucolo d'Accia**, which has been dated by archaeologists to Pope Gregory's time. Astonishingly, it was once a cathedral. At the end the 9th-century reconquest of Corsica, chronicler Giovanni della Grossa describes how the last king of the Moors, Abitel, son of Nugulone, took up residence in Morosaglia and made nearby Accia ('the Corsican Atlantis' that no one has ever located) his stronghold for 34 years. With his defeat, the the diocese of Accia was created out of the 'Moorish' (or more likely pagan) *pieves* of Orezza, Ampugnani and Rustino – which, perhaps not accidently, would prove to be the most agitated and rebellious throughout Corsican history. The new diocese also evened out the number of bishops to three each in the subsequent division of the island into Genoese-controlled *Diqua dei Monti* and Pisan-controlled *Dila dei Monti*. Every year on 1 August villagers from 'all the *pieves*' walk up in a procession to attend a special mass at this former cathedral of Accia; from here you can continue in three hours to the top of Monte San Petrone.

Take a right on the D515 to **Croce**, and follow it to **La Porta**, visible for miles away thanks to Corsica's finest Baroque church of **St-Jean-Baptiste** and its beautiful five-storey campanile, rising 147ft/45m high over a deep green sea of chestnuts. Built in 1707 on designs by the Milanese architect Domenico Baïna, it has a handsome ochre façade and a feeling of old wealth inside, with its colourful stuccoes, an *Annunciation* (a copy of a Guido Reni 'donated by the emperor in 1855') and a *Martyrdom of Ste Eulalie*, along with an 18th-century organ and 19th-century *trompe l'œil* paintings. La Porta was the birthplace of Horace Sebastiani (1773–1851), Napoleon's *aide-de-camp* until he was wounded at Austerlitz; afterwards, as French ambassador at Istanbul, he helped the Turks organize the city's defences and prevent the English from taking the Bosphorus. He was one of several Corsicans to prolong his political career in France after Waterloo, becoming foreign minister under Louis-Philippe.

Morosaglia and Pasquale Paoli

Beautifully austere **Morosaglia/Merusaglia**, built in an amphitheatre overlooking Corsica's highest mountains, was the birthplace in 1725 of Pasquale Paoli. He was the youngest son of the patriot Dr Giacinto Paoli, and started what would be a long life in exile at the age of 14, when he accompanied his father to Naples. When he died in London in 1807, he was buried at St Pancras, and honoured with a bust by Flaxman in Westminster Abbey. But it was his wish to lie in Corsica, and in 1889 his great-great-nephew transported his remains to a chapel attached to his home.

His birthplace is now the **Musée Paoli** (*t 04 95 61 04 97; open July and Aug Wed–Mon 9–12 and 2.30–7; Sept–Jan and Mar–June Wed–Mon 9–12 and 1–5; closed Tues and Feb; adm*). They don't get many foreign visitors here, not like Napoleon's house, but there is a video in English on Paoli's career, as well as memorabilia, his waistcoat, sword and

'A House of Crystal'

Corsicans are often accused of pride and nationalism, but they do have a case when they complain that the man they call 'the father of the country' has never been given his due, merely because of Corsica's diminutive size. Yet his Enlightenment ideals played an important role in the American Revolution that followed Corsica's by twenty years: one of the battle cries of the Americans in their own war of independence was 'Long live Paoli!'. Sons were named after him. But he gets nary a mention in history texts in the US; even in the six towns named Paoli in his honour, most people don't know his story. He was far from perfect – judging by modern terms he was more of a benevolent despot than a new Pericles – but he set standards high:

It is essential that our administration resemble a house of crystal, so everyone can see what is happening within. All secretive obscurity favours arbitrary power and breeds mistrust among the people. With the system that we follow, merit will surely develop, because it is almost impossible that intrigue can survive the cleansing action of multiple, general and frequent elections.

In his time, Paoli's ideals and personality attracted admiration from around Europe; the likes of Frederick the Great sent him a sword. He instilled a sense of responsibility and purpose even in the most feckless young men – both Carlo Bonaparte and James Boswell owed much to him. He wanted not only to govern, but to transform Corsica, which was a rather unique idea at the time. No detail was too small for his attention; the Corsicans, for instance, fondly nicknamed him 'Generale Patata' for his campaign to replace asphodel bulbs, used to make a kind of bread, with the more nourishing potato. His policies of transformation may have had little lasting effect on Corsica, but they would inspire another Corsican to do the same, on a vast scale, across France and Europe.

gun and letters, the saddle presented by the *bey* of Tunis, busts and portraits – the best ones sparkling with all the intelligence of the Enlightenment – and paintings depicting various moments in his career, including a dramatic print called *A Young Corsican convinced by General Paoli of the Necessity of his Uncle's Death*, referring to Paoli's iron law of executing any murderer and confiscating his property, in an attempt to stem the vendetta at a time when hundreds were being killed every year – Paoli even signed the death warrant of his own cousin. One exhibit is the first flag of independent Corsica, where instead of the Moor's head there is an image of the *Immaculate Conception*. Paoli was baptized in the church of **Santa Reparata**, five minutes up a steep path on top of Morosaglia, its west door decorated with a pair of serpents biting their tails. The village school was once the seat of the local assembly or *consulta*.

Just west of Morosaglia, a right on the D15B will take you to **Castello-di-Rostino**, where a dirt road leads to the path to the ruined 10th-century funerary chapel of **San Tommaso di Pastoreccia** in about ten minutes. San Tommaso has late 15th-century frescoes, and although many were damaged in a 1933 'restoration' involving dynamite, the surviving works are considered the finest in Corsica and a model for many later churches: a *Christ in Majesty* in the apse, surrounded by angel musicians and symbols of the Evangelists, the *Annunciation* and *St Michael killing the Dragon and Weighing Souls*, the *Passion* and *Last Judgement*. On the outskirts of the next town, **Valle-di-Rostino**, the ruined church of **Santa Maria** was built and rebuilt several times on the site of a Roman villa beginning in the 4th century; it still has a few of its original carvings, including one of a knife to the right of the door. On the separate baptistry – the only octagonal one on Corsica – one typanum shows Adam and Eve, another a serpent biting its own tail.

The main D115 winds down to the N193, meeting the Corte–Bastia road at **Ponte Novu**, a Genoese bridge over the river Golo (now in ruins after the Nazis blew it up). The Corsican Nation met an abrupt end here on 8 May 1769, and although what actually happened is the subject of several conflicting versions, there is common consensus that the battle was the nadir of Paoli's career – the general, who it must be said much preferred his pen to his sword, stayed two miles away, while officers of his flimsy army drifted away to the French side. Some 2,000 Corsicans impetuously attacked a French army of 13,000 and, finding (according to some) their retreat on the bridge barricaded by German mercenaries who had been ordered by Paoli to shoot anyone who ran, were slaughtered. Voltaire, who always supported liberty, wrote how the Corsicans made barricades of the bodies of their dead comrades and fought in spite of their wounds. But according to a private letter from Paoli, quoted by Dorothy Carrington, only twenty Corsicans died; the rest, terrified, shammed dead in a heap on the bridge until the French went away, while Paoli himself fled to Porto-Vecchio and sailed to Livorno, on route to London.

The Casinca and La Canonica

The pretty little region north of the Castagniccia, the **Casinca**, sits on the spurs of another mountain, **Monte Sant'Angelo**, and has more chestnut trees and olives, but now the kiwis, vines and clementines bring in most of the bacon – there's a good selection of wines and other products at the **Cave Coopérative de la Casinca** on the N198 (*t 04 95 36 99 52; open Mon–Sat*). Near the N198 and D106 crossroads stands the little 10th-century church of **San Pancrazio**, dignified with three apses. Some relics of the 4th-century Roman martyr St Pancras sent by the pope to an Anglo-Saxon king in the 7th century were behind his popularity in England; in Corsica he was the patron saint of bandits, and the rest of his relics were brought here in 1798 by the French consul in Venice. On his feast day, 12 May, a huge horse fair used to take place here, although the Genoese often tried to ban it, fearing that the crowds offered too tempting a target to passing pirates, looking for slaves. Above, the Casinca consists of a series of old schist-roofed villages set on natural balconies, most with only one street to their names, overlooking Bastia, the plain, and the Tyrrhenian sea (come in the afternoon, when the light is best). Aim for **Castellare-di-Casinca**, and lovely **Penta-di-Casinca**, a listed village wrapped around a spur, with a picture-perfect little square with a fountain. A giant rock pokes out of the centre of **Loreto-di-Casinca**, the highest

Where to Stay and Eat

Loreto-di-Casinca ✉ 20215

U Rataghju, t 04 95 36 30 66. Cheerful restaurant in a renovated chestnut *séchoir* serving platters of excellent *charcuterie*, boar pâté, lasagne, veal, boar or kid, and a classic *fiadone*. The single €24 *menu* includes the local wine; well known so book several days in advance in summer. *Open all year.*

U Campanile, by the bell tower, **t** 04 95 36 31 19. Magnificent views and big portions of the local favourites; be sure to book a table, and ask for one by the wndow. *No menu, but around €20 à la carte. Closed mid-Sept–mid-June.*

Venzolasca ✉ 20215

Ferme-auberge U Fragnu, U Campu, **t** 04 95 36 62 33. Come very hungry to this handsome dining room decorated with antique farm tools, with an olive press and a beautiful terrace. Nearly everything on the menu is grown or raised here; *soupe corse*, delicious leek and cheese *beignets*, veal with olives, or boar with beans, followed by a *digestif* (a *trou corse*) to prepare you for the cheese-filled cannelloni and home-made dessert. *Menu €33 for seven courses with pitchers of local wine. By reservation only. Open every evening in July and Aug, Dec–June Thurs, Fri Sat eve and Sun lunch.*

Vescovato ✉ 20215

L'Ortu, Route de Venzlasca, **t** 04 95 36 64 69. 100 per cent organic restaurant and snack bar in a Corsican pine cabin; don't miss the delicious juices fresh from the orchard. *Around €20. Book.*

Borgo/Casamozza ✉ 20290

★★★**Chez Walter**, Casamozza, **t** 04 95 36 00 09, www.chez-walter.com (*expensive*). Convenient if you're catching an early plane, modern and soundproofed, with air-conditioned rooms, pool and tennis, and a restaurant/pizzeria.

★★★**L'Isola**, Lido de la Marana, www.isolahotel. com, near La Canonica and the Etang de Biguglia, **t** 04 95 33 19 60 (*expensive*). Typical moderate-sized beach hotel with a pool and tennis.

village of the Casinca, with huge views and cafés under the plane trees. Next along the D237, **Venzolasca** has a striking profile of tall houses and an elegant campanile; now utterly peaceful, it was the scene of a ferocious vendetta that lasted from 1880 to 1916, which only ended when the two families ran out of men. The oldest Franciscan convent on Corsica is just above town, now partly in ruins.

Vescovato/Viscuvatu

The 'capital' of the Casinca, Vescovato means 'bishopric', and was the seat of one from 1269 to 1570 after the destruction of Mariana. Known during the Renaissance as the 'Athens of Corsica', it produced two 16th-century historians of the island, Anton Pietro Filippini and Marco Antonio Ceccaldi. A large, peaceful village of tall schist lauze-roofed houses, it rises above a large square shaded by plane trees, where the local café society resides.

Narrow lanes and a covered passage (*a loghia*) wind up to the former cathedral, **San Martino** (key at the *mairie*); it was enlarged and embellished during its heyday, most notably with a Genoese marble tabernacle of the Resurrection, dated 1441. Nearby, opposite the Bar Colonial, a plaque honours native son, sea captain Luc-Julian-Joseph de Casabianca (1762–98), Corsican deputy during the Revolution and the commander of *L'Orient* at the battle of Aboukir. He was killed when his ship was attacked by Nelson, and his 12-year-old son Giocante, who refused to be rescued, hero-ically went down with it, inspiring Felicia Hemans' poem that starts 'The boy stood on the burning deck'. In his honour, the French navy always christen an active vessel *Casabianca*, most notably the submarine that supplied the Maquis on Corsica.

Towards Bastia: La Canonica and Mariana

On the plain below, now rumbling with airport and traffic noises, the Roman consul Marius founded a colony near the mouth of the river Golo in 93 BC, for the veterans of his wars against pirates, and named it **Mariana** after himself. During the reign of Augustus, Mariana grew to become Corsica's most important port in the north, and in the 4th century it built its first Christian basilica. Razed and burned by Vandals or Lombards, it revived under the Pisans in the 9th century, after the legendary Ugo Colonna whopped the Moorish leader in one-on-one combat, and then baptized everyone. Or so say the chronicles.

However it happened, the Pisans felt secure enough in the 11th century to build one of their finest churches, the cathedral of Santa Maria Assunta, but better known as **La Canonica** (after the canons' residence that once stood here), strikingly set in the middle of the road. Consecrated by the bishop of Pisa in 1119, it owes its beauty to the purity of the proportions, the use of polychrome marble plates quarried from Cap Corse, and the Corinthian columns borrowed from the Roman town. The arch over the west door is carved with an interlaced medieval bestiary, while other decorations are so random that there are stories that they represent a secret treasure map. The interior is austere, and open for services only once a year, on Pentecost Monday.

The bishops of Mariana stayed until 1284, when malaria drove them up to Vescovato. Excavations on the surroundings began in 1959, and revealed the foundations of their palace, which was partly built over a 4th-century basilica with three naves and a square baptistry from the same period, with two stepped fonts and a mosaic floor (*protected under layers of gravel and plastic and not usually visible*). The images are straight from the early days of Christianity: there's a young deer (symbolizing eternal youth); dolphins (which save the soul from drowning, and represent the promise of eternal life); the fish symbol of Christ; and bearded figures representing the four rivers of paradise in the Garden of Eden. What has enabled archaeologists to date it with some precision is the verse from *Isaiah* on the podium, which predates St Jerome's translation of the Bible in the late 4th century.

Some 300 yards away, isolated in a field, stands the more modest Pisan church **San Parteo**, built over a pagan cemetery (note one of the gravestones stuck in the west wall). The lintel is decorated with a Middle Eastern motif: two lions guarding what is believed to be the Tree of Science in the Garden of Eden.

To get to Bastia from here, take either the busy N193 or the La Mariana beach road. In between them lies Bastia's **Poretta Airport** (Antoine de Saint-Exupéry took off from here in 1944 on a mission for the Free French, when he had his fatal crash) and the **Etang de Biguglia**, a vast lagoon full of ducks, warblers and kingfishers. The lagoon is separated from the sea by a long strip of sandy beach, lined with holiday villas and campsites – the main playground of the Bastiais. It is named after **Biguglia**, a former Roman encampment that served as the Pisan and first Genoese capital until 1479. Now it's just a quiet village off the N193.

Bastia, Cap Corse and the Nebbio

11

Bastia, Cap Corse and the Nebbio

Cap Corse

I. de la Giraglia

Tollare
Barcaggio
Tour d'Agnello
Tour Santa Maria
I. Finocchiarola

Moulin Mattei
Ersa
Cannelle
Tour
Centuri-Port
Centuri
Rogliano
Macinaggio
Morsiglia
Vignale
Tomino

Marine de Giottani
Marine de Meria
Golfe d'Aliso
Pino
Campo
Tour de Sénèque
Luri
Sta Severa
Poggio
Barrettali
Marine de Porticciolo
Cagnano
Tour dell'Osso

Pietracorbara
Marinca
Canari
Marine de Pietracorbara
Punta di Canelle

Ogliastro
Sisco
Marine de Sisco
Albo
Olcani

Monte Stello
Nonza
Castello
Brando
Erbalunga
Pozzo
Lavasina

Golfe de St-Florent
Santa Maria-di-Lota
Miomo
San Martino-di-Lota
Ville-de-Pietrabugno
Marine de Farinole
Farinole
Pietranera

Nice Marseille
La Spezia
Genova
Livorno
Toulon
Piombino
Savona

Plage de Saleccia
Plage de Lodo
Tour Mortella
Cardo
Patrimonio
Monserrato
BASTIA

Plage de Malfalco
Désert des Agriates
St-Florent
Santa Maria Assunta

Plage d'Ostriconi
Ogliastro
Casta
Col de Teghime
Monetta
Baccialu
Poggio-d'Oletta
Biguglia
Oletta

Santo-Pietro-di-Tenda
Olmeta-di-Tuda
Défilé de Lancône
Urtaca
Rapale
Piève
Sorio
Murato
Rufali
Palasca
Novella
Monte Asto
Lama

p.234   **p.148**   **p.174**

Mediterranean Sea

N

10 km

5 miles

Highlights

1 Cap Corse's coastal walk, the Sentier des Douaniers
2 Wine-tasting in the pretty village of Patrimonio
3 Corsica's best Romanesque church, San Michele de Murato
4 A truly exquisite beach: the Plage de Saleccia

For most visitors who come by sea, Bastia provides their first glimpse of the island, and for most a glimpse is enough before they trot off to the beach. Yet for anyone genuinely interested in Corsica, this bustling business end deserves a closer look. What's more, Bastia is the gateway to one of Corsica's most characterful regions – Cap Corse, that narrow finger of rugged mountains stretching 40km into the sea, a plaything of the *libeccio* wind that can blow up to 75 miles per hour. Known as the 'island within an island', Cap Corse was isolated for centuries owing to a lack of roads, leaving it to become the one part of this island of shepherds and landlubbers to make its living from the sea. Yet the Capicursini who set sail from its doll-sized ports had the same larger-than-life quality as Corsica's mountain men – one, for instance, became the model for Joseph Conrad's *Nostromo*.

Bastia's immediate hinterland, the misty Nebbio, is best known for Patrimonio wine, for Corsica's most fascinating church, San Michele de Murato, and for fashionable St-Florent, the biggest resort in the northeast, and the point of departure for the crystal seas and sublime beaches of one of Corsica's truly unspoiled corners, the Désert des Agriates.

Bastia

If Ajaccio, all in smiles and songs, is the grasshopper of Corsica,
then Bastia is the thrifty, hardworking ant.

Gustave Flaubert

Visitors to Corsica have always remarked on the striking difference between the island's two cities. Both were Genoese foundations, but Bastia, the old Genoese capital, has kept much of its old atmosphere, a bit scruffy and frayed about the edges but vibrant and active, living off the island's busiest port and small industries (among them Bastos cigarettes, Pietra beer, and distilleries) that have spread into modern suburbs south of town; one out of four Corsicans now lives in the greater Bastia area. The reigning passion is Corsica's top football squad, the Sporting Club de Bastia, which competes in the big leagues partly thanks to huge subsidies from the regional government, and which has supporters all over this part of the Mediterranean.

History

Bastia grew up as the safest and closest haven to Italy. Originally named Porto Cardo, after the collapse of the *pax romana* it shrank into a village plagued by pirates. So when the Pisans cast about for a seat for their governor, they chose safer Biguglia, just south of modern Bastia, and that remained the capital of Corsica under the Genoese until Corsican rebels burned it in 1372. The Genoese governor, Leonello Lomellino, then built a bastion (*bastiglia*, hence 'Bastia') on the promontory as a bolt hole, in case it happened again. And so Bastia sat, a lone tower over a few fishing shacks, the governor still in Biguglia, until 1479, when a certain Giovanni Bonaparte was summoned from Italy to build a citadel around the bastion that became known as the 'Terra Nova', because it was new compared to Porto Cardo below. To populate it,

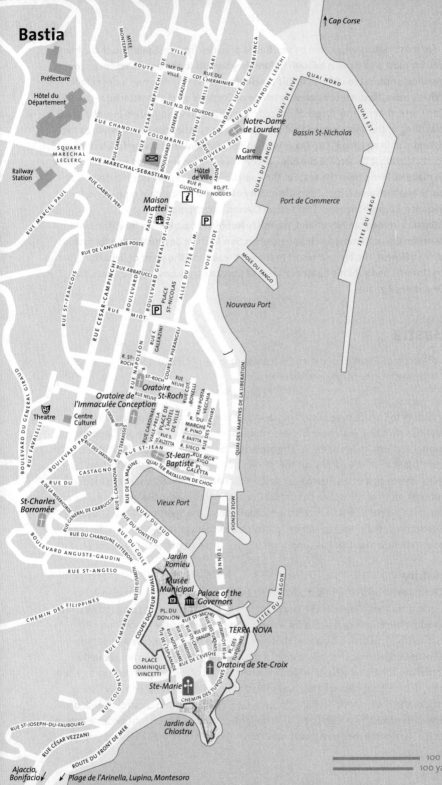

Bastia

Préfecture

Hôtel du
Département

Railway
Station

SQUARE
MARECHAL
LECLERC

↑ Cap Corse

MTEE MONTEPAGNOLE

ROUTE IMP. DE VILLE

RUE

VILLE

DE IMP. DE VILLE

RUE DU CDT L'HERMINIER

RUE SARI

RUE GRAZIANI

RUE EMILE SARI

RUE N.D. DE LOURDES

RUE DU CHANOINE LESCHI

QUAI DE RIVE

QUAI NORD

RUE CHANOINE COLOMBANI

RUE CÉSAR CAMPINCHI

BOULEVARD PAOLI

AVENUE EMILE SARI

GENERAL

RUE COMMANDANT LUCE DE CASABIANCA

Notre-Dame
de Lourdes

Bassin St-Nicholas

QUAI EST

AVE MARECHAL-SEBASTIANI

RUE CARNOT

RUE DU NOUVEAU PORT

AVENUE MARECHAL LANDRY

Gare
Maritime

QUAI DU FANGO

Port de Commerce

JETEE DU LARGE

RUE GABRIEL PERI

RUE MARCEL PAUL

RUE DE L'ANCIENNE POSTE

Maison
Mattei

RUE P.
GUIDICELLI

Hôtel
de Ville

i

RD. PT.
NOGUES

P

ALLEE DU 173e R.I.M.

VOIE RAPIDE

MOLE DU FANGO

RUE ST-FRANÇOIS

RUE CÉSAR-CAMPINCHI

RUE ABBATUCCI

BOULEVARD GENERAL-DE-GAULLE

PLACE
ST-NICOLAS

P

RUE MIOT

RUE F.
GALEAZZINI

RUE ST-
ROCH

R. ST-
ROCH

COURS H. PIERANGELI

RUE
NEUVE

RUE CDT
BONELLI

RUE CDT
VECCHIA

R. DU POSTA
VECCHIA

Nouveau Port

QUAI DES MARTYRS DE LA LIBERATION

BOULEVARD DU GENERAL GIRAUD

RUE FAVALELLI

BOULEVARD PAOLI

Theatre

Centre
Culturel

Oratoire de
l'Immaculée Conception

RUE CARDINAL
VIALE-PRELA

Oratoire
St-Roch

RUE NEUVE

R. ORSINI

RUE DES TERRASSES

PLACE DE
L'HOTEL
DE VILLE

R. DU
MARCHE

R. PINO

RUE S.
D'ALZETTA

R. BAIETTA

R. SISCO

RUE MGR
RIGO

RUE DES ZEPHIRS

MOLE GENOIS

RUE DES JARDINS

CASTAGNO

RUE DU

R. DE LA MISERICORDE

RUE GENERAL DE CARBUCCIA

RUE L. CASANOVA

RUE DE LA MARINE

RUE ST-JEAN

St-Jean-
Baptiste

RUE MGR
RIGO

PL.
GALETTA

St-Charles
Borromée

RUE DE LA MARINE

QUAI 1er BATAILLON DE CHOC

Vieux Port

BOULEVARD ANGUSTE-GAUDIN

RUE ST-ANGELO

RUE DU CHANOINE LETTERON

RUE DU COLLE

QUAI DU SUD

RUE DU PONTETTO

RUE COLONNA

RUE CAMPANARI

RUE ELISABETH

RUE HEBBERT

CHEMIN DES FILIPPINES

Jardin
Romieu

Musée
Municipal

M

PL. DU
DONJON

Palace of the
Governors

COURS DOCTEUR FAVALE

RUE NOTRE-DAME

RUE DE L'ESPLANADE

RUE ST-MICHEL

RUE DU
DRAGON

RUE STE-CROIX

PL. DES
TURQUINES

TERRA NOVA

Oratoire de Ste-Croix

TUNNEL

JETEE DU DRAGON

PLACE
DOMINIQUE
VINCETTI

RUE DE LA CITADELLE

RUE DE L'EVECHE

Ste-Marie

CHEMIN DES TURQUINES

Jardin du
Chiostru

RUE ST-JOSEPH-DU-FAUBOURG

RUE CÉSAR VEZZANI

ROUTE DU FRONT DE MER

Ajaccio,
Bonifacio↓   ↙ Plage de l'Arinella, Lupino, Montesoro

N

100 metres
100 yards

Getting Around

By Air
Bastia's Aéroport de Poretta, t 04 95 54 54 54, *www.bastia.aeroport.fr*, is 17km south of the city. Eight **STIB buses**, t 04 95 31 06 65, *www.bastiabus.com*, run between the airport and the Bastia Préfecture. Allow half an hour. Airport **taxi** (24hrs), t 04 95 36 04 65.

Airport car hire: Ada, t 04 95 54 55 44; **Avis**, t 04 95 54 55 46; **Europcar**, t 04 95 30 09 50; **Hertz**, t 04 95 30 09 50, **Budget**, t 04 95 30 05 05.

By Sea
SNCM, t 0825 888 088, has overnight ferries to Toulon and Marseille, and to Nice on the NGV boat in just 3½hrs. **Corsica Ferries**, t 04 95 32 95 95, has fast ferries to Nice, and regular ferries to Savona and Livorno. **CMN**, t 04 95 55 25 55, sails to Marseille and Porto-Torres, in Sardinia. **Moby Lines**, t 04 95 34 84 94, has ferries to Genoa, Livorno and Piombino.

By Train
The station is located 500m from the Gare Maritime, heading up Av Maréchal Sébastiani, t 04 95 32 80 60. Four *micheline* trains a day on average go to Corte, Ajaccio, and two to Calvi and L'Ile-Rousse, changing at Ponte Leccia.

By Bus
Greater Bastia, Morandi-Plage and Cap Corse are served by **STIB** buses, t 04 95 31 06 65, *www.bastiabus.com*. The *gare routière* or bus station is an empty lot by the tourist office, north of Place St-Nicolas; buses from here go to Corte and Ajaccio (**Eurocorse**, t 04 95 21 06 30), Calvi (from the train station on Beaux Voyages, t 04 95 65 15 02) and St-Florent (Santini, t 04 95 37 04 01). **Autocars Rapides Bleus**, t 04 95 70 31 03 79, go twice a day down the east coast to Porto-Vecchio, departing from 1 Av Maréchal Sébastiani opposite the post office. The nearby tourist office has timetables.

By Car
In spite of its tunnels to ease through-traffic, Bastia, like Ajaccio, often hosts continental-style traffic jams. The easiest parking is under vast Place St-Nicolas.

Car hire in town: **Ada**, 35 Rue César Campinchi, t 04 95 31 48 95; **Avis**, Bd Paoli, t 04 95 31 95 64; **Budget**, Port de Toga, t 04 95 31 77 31; **Europcar**, 1 Rue du Nouveau Port, t 04 95 30 09 50; **Hertz**, Square St Victor, t 04 95 31 14 24.

Taxis: t 04 95 34 07 00 or t 04 95 32 70 70.

Tourist Information

Bastia: Place St-Nicolas, t 04 95 54 20 40, *www.bastia-tourisme.com*. Open June–15 Sept daily 8–7; 16 Sept–May Mon–Sat 8–6.

Markets and Shopping

Every morning at 8am–1pm a little **food market** takes place in Place du Marché (aka Place de l'Hôtel de Ville), with more stands on weekends. A Sunday morning **flea market** in Place St-Nicolas sells clothes, vintage postcards, rusty tools, etc.

Maison Mattei, Place St-Nicolas, t 04 95 32 44 38. In place for over 140 years, with a façade last remodelled in the 1930s. Makers of Corsica's favourite apéritif, Cap Corse (invented in 1912 by Louis-Napoléon Mattei) they also sell nearly every other alcohol distilled on the island, and conveniently stay open till 10pm in July and August for last-minute stock-ups.

Albo, 39 Rte du Cap, t 04 95 31 93 41, *www.albo.fr*. Jewellery made of Corsican stones, coral and the eye of the sea.

free land was offered to any Genoese family who moved here. In 1570, the bishop of Mariana and Accia moved his seat to Bastia. In the 17th century, when the coast was clear (relatively) of pirates, the city expanded into a new merchant and working quarter by Porto Cardo, now known as Terra Vecchia, the 'Old Land'. Six large tanneries here provided plenty of work. A long jetty was built, and tall palaces went up.

U Paese, 4 Rue Napoléon, t 04 95 32 33 18. Famous for its Castagniccia *charcuterie*, since 1977. Also honey, cheeses and more, all made by small producers.

Cyrnarom, 29 Av Emile Sari, t 04 95 31 39 30. One of Corsica's only perfume-makers, specializing in the scents of the *maquis*, lavender and wild flowers; also runs a little museum of old distillery equipment and rare perfume bottles.

Christian Magdeleine, 2 Place Guasco (up in the Citadelle), t 04 95 31 78 99. A great place to buy a Corsican *cetera* or other special guitar, made by a professional *luthier*. *Open Thurs–Fri 9–12 and 2.30–7.*

Librairie Marzocchi, 2 Rue Conventionnel-Salicetti, t 04 95 34 02 95. Old postcards and books about Corsica.

Santa Catalina, 8 Rue des Terrasses (south extension of Rue Napoléon), t 04 95 32 30 69. For the best in Corsican *charcuterie*, wines, honeys and more, all made the old-fashioned way.

Festivals and Events

Bastia hosts a number of **film festivals** throughout the year; during each month in the winter there are festivals of Italian, British, and Spanish films as well as *U Festivale di u Filmu Arte Mare*, a Mediterranean film festival (t 04 95 58 85 50, *www.arte-mare.com*).

A number of **religious processions** take place over Holy Week, on Palm Sunday and Good Friday.

In early April, Bastia holds a *Festival de la BD*, dedicated to **comic books**.

Sports and Activities

Beaches: Closest to Bastia is the pebble **Plage de Toga** by the marine, a 10min walk north

of the Gare Maritime. For sand, head south to the long **Plage de l'Arinella**, 4km south at Montesoro, the beginning of the long stretch of beach between the sea and the Etang de Biguglia.

Objectif Nature, 3 Rue Notre Dame de Lourdes, t 06 03 58 66 09 or t 04 95 32 54 34, *http://Obj-Nature.ifrance.com*. Open year-round and dedicated to arranging every conceivable outdoor activity: guided hikes on the GR20, ascents of Monte Cinto, fishing expeditions around Cap Corse, horse or donkey excursions, hang-gliding, white-water rafting and lots more.

Club de Plongée Bastiais, Vieux Port, t 04 95 33 31 28 or mobile t 06 14 62 56 14, *www.club-plongee-bastiais.com* Open all year, for dives at all levels; reservations essential. Second World War ship- and plane-wrecks make the seas around Bastia especially interesting.

Thalassa Immersion, Ville-di-Pietrabugno, just north of Bastia by Port Toga, t 04 95 31 78 90 or t 06 11 11 54 00, *http://thalassa.immersion.free.fr*. Another excellent diving centre. *Open all year; bookings essential.*

Plaisance Location, Port Toga, t 04 95 34 14 14, *www.plaisance-location.com*. Hire a boat, jet ski, sailboat or motorbike.

Sporting Club Bastia: call t 04 95 30 00 80 or see *www.sc-bastia.com* to reserve tickets to see a match in the newly restored Stade Armand Cesari at Furiani, 4km south.

Where to Stay

Bastia ✉ 20200

People come and go, but few stay in Bastia, and accommodation is skimpy. The nicest hotels are at the north end of the city, towards Cap Corse (*see also* p.212).

***L'Alivi, Rte du Cap, Ville di Pietrabugno, t 04 95 55 00 00, 1km north of Bastia, *www.hotel-alivi.com* (*expensive*). Comfortable

---

The 1600s were a time of great prosperity for Bastia, when all Corsica's political, military, religious and financial powers were concentrated here. In 1670, when Genoa elevated Corsica to a kingdom, the Regno di Corsica, Bastia's governor took on the status of viceroy, with all the accompanying frippery. A fleet of 50 ships transported wine, olive oil, salt, wheat and iron to Genoa; Baroque churches, oratories and nearly a dozen monasteries and convents went up. Corsica's first literary academy, the

37-room hotel sitting on the rocks over-looking a small beach; all rooms have sea views; there's a pool and private car park.

***Pietracap**, 3km north of Bastia on the D131, in Pietranera, **t** 04 95 31 64 63, *www.hotel-pietracap.com* (*expensive*). Handsome modern stone building set over the sea amid the olives and gardens; rooms are big and luminous, and there's a pool and delightful bar vintage 1974. *Closed Dec–Mar.*

***Les Voyageurs**, 9 Av Maréchal Sébastiani, **t** 04 95 34 90 80, *www.hotel-lesvoyageurs.com* (*moderate*). Modern, spruced-up hotel with cheerful blue and yellow rooms and welcoming owners, close to the ferries, trains and buses.

Posta Vecchia, 8 Rue Posta-Vecchia (just behind the Quai des Martyrs de la Libération, **t 04 95 32 32 38, *www.hotel-postavecchia.com* (*moderate*). Large hotel with comfy rooms in a great location on the Vieux Port, close to a public car park. The cheaper rooms are in the older part of the building.

Cyrnéa, Pietranera, 2km north of Bastia, **t 04 95 31 41 71, *http://hotelcyrnea.monsite.wanadoo.fr* (*moderate*). Long modern hotel by the sea, with a shady garden descending to a small pebble beach, with soundproofed rooms and a garage. *Closed Jan.*

Napoléon, 43 Bd Paoli, **t 04 95 31 60 30 (*moderate*). Frescoed halls and cosy rooms with fans and mini-bars, a street back from Place St-Nicolas. Prices rise considerably in season.

Univers, 3 Av. Maréchal Sébastiani, **t 04 95 31 03 38, *www.hoteldelunivers.com* (*moderate*). Simple and central, air-conditioned and double-glazed.

Central, 3 Rue Miot, **t 04 95 31 71 12, *www.centralhotel.fr* (*inexpensive*). Exactly as the name says, with a choice of prettily refurbished rooms, priced according to their plumbing; also studios and apartments.

Le Riviera, 1 bis Rue du Nouveau Port, **t 04 995 31 07 16, *www.corsehotelriviera.com* (*inexpensive*). Adequate hotel with biggish rooms, convenient for the ferries.

Chez Mme Vignon, Montée des Philippines, **t** 04 95 32 23 70 (*inexpensive*). Up in the historic centre, a pleasant B&B with views and a little garden, a 5-minute walk from the Citadelle.

Camping San Damiano, 5km south of Bastia at Lido de la Marana, **t** 04 95 33 68 02, *www.camping.sandamiano.com* (*inexpensive*). A good campsite, right on the beach. *Closed Nov–Mar.*

Eating Out

The Italian influence in the kitchen is stronger here than anywhere else on Corsica, with good pizza and fresh pasta dishes served in most places; *aziminu* (Bastia's version of Genoa's *zimino*, or fish soup) is a speciality. Look for the classic Genoese snack, *farinata* or *socca* or *tarte aux pois chiches*, made of chickpea flour and olive oil.

La Table Périgourdine, Villa Carmen, Bd Benoîte Danesi (above Square Maréchal Leclerc), **t** 04 95 59 09 02, *www.latableperigourdine.com*. In an elegant 19th-century villa where Antoine de St-Exupéry once stayed, the *foie gras*, *cassoulet* and duck dishes of southwest France. *Around €60. Eves only, closed Sun.*

La Citadelle, 6 Rue du Dragon, **t** 04 95 31 44 70. Near the top of Bastia in the heart of the Citadelle, and a favourite for a romantic splurge, serving refined, innovative and classic gourmet dishes (*foie gras, magret de canard à la orange, langoustines au beurre d'escargot, gratin de pomme à la cannelle*) in a vaulted olive press. *Menu €28. Closed Sat lunch and Sun.*

Accademia dei Vagabondi (1660–1720), flourished; sons of prosperous Bastiais who had been educated at Padua and Bologna returned to built Corsica's first theatre. Yet the Genoese capital remained a foreign intrusion for many Corsicans, and was increasingly resented as Genoa declined and its officials grew more and more corrupt. In 1730, at the start of the War of Independence, 4,000 famished peasants and mountaineers descended on Bastia and sacked and killed most of the population

Le Ke, Port de Toga, t 04 95 30 83 60. New restaurant with a huge menu and Italian slant – fresh salads and pasta and meat dishes, and fancy chocolate desserts. *Around €30.*

Petite Marie, 2 Rue Zéphyrs, t 04 95 32 47 83. Minute place in the Terra Vecchia, popular with the locals for its big plates of fried red mullet and *langoustines* with *frites. Around €30.*

La Table du Marché, Place du Marché, t 04 95 31 64 25. Elegant restaurant with a large terrace in the atmospheric square, featuring the day's catch – seafood platters, warm oysters, *méli-mélo de poissons* flavoured with fennel. *Lunch menu €23, dinner around €40. Closed Sun.*

Le Vieux Chêne, Rte Superior de Cardo, t 04 95 34 17 06. Three minutes by car above Bastia in Cardo, enjoying big views down on the city, a restaurant with a beautiful terrace under a hundred-year oak, serving a full range of Corsican specialities (*unique five-course menu €30). Open eves only Mon-Sat, out of season Sat and Sun only.*

A Casarella, 6 Rue Sainte-Croix, t 04 95 32 02 32. On a terrace in the Citadelle overlooking the Vieux Port, dine on *storzapreti* ('priest stranglers') made of spinach and *brocciu*, and specialities such as *casgiate* (cheese baked in chestnut leaves). *Lunch menu €15, dinner €29. Closed Sun.*

Claudius, Port de Toga, t 04 95 31 73 54. Looks ordinary but this family restaurant is a favourite for its well-prepared seafood dishes; try the croquant de saumon filled with *brocciu. Plat du jour €10, full meals around €25.*

U Tianu, 4 Stretta Mgr Rigo, just off the Place du Marché, t 04 95 31 36 67. When you can't stand another fish, head up the steps to this local favourite for classic Corsican *charcuterie*, blackbird pâté, and stews. *Menus from €20.*

Le Caveau du Marin, Quai des Martyrs, t 04 95 31 62 31. Between the old and new ports, a family restaurant of renown in a cellar full of marine bric-a-brac; *aziminu* and other sea food obviously the speciality, but tasty traditional Corsican specialities, too. *Menus from €15–22. Closed Sun and Mon.*

La Voûte, 6 Rue Luce-de-Casabianca, t 04 95 32 47 11. Friendly little place under a stone vault, popular for fresh pasta – for something different try it *à la crème d'oursins* (with sea urchins). Also crispy pizzas baked in a wood fired oven. For dessert try the *mousse aux deux chocolats. Menu €21. Closed Sun.*

Serge Raugi, 2bis Rue Capanelle, on the north side of Place St-Nicolas, t 04 95 31 22 31. Top-notch ice-cream from a recipe passed down over the generations. *Closed Mon.*

Entertainment and Nightlife

After dark, the Bastiais gather in the bars in Place St-Nicolas and around the Vieux Port.

Pub Assunta, Rue Fontaine-Neuve, t 05 95 34 11 40. Former chapel converted into one of the most popular bars in Bastia, with a generous choice of beers and live music every night in summer except on Sun; they also do simple pub food. *Open till 2am.*

Le Studio, 1 Rue Miséricorde, t 04 95 31 12 94, *www.studio-cinema.com.* Art cinema showing the latest releases but also foreign subtitled films, often by special themes.

Théâtre Municipal, Rue Favalelli, t 04 95 34 98 00. In the 18th century, Bastia was firmly on the Italian *bel canto* circuit; its theatre, rebuilt in 1879 and restored in 1981, is still the venue for most concerts and plays.

L'Apocalypse, Rte de Marana 10km south of Bastia, t 04 95 33 36 83, *www.apocalypse-bastia.com.* Most popular disco in area, out by the beach in summer. *Open till dawn.*

in the unprotected Terra Vecchia. Twenty years later Paoli moved the island's capital to Corte; the French moved it back to Bastia, and during the Revolution made it the capital of one of Corsica's two *départements*. In 1794, Nelson took the city after an 11-day siege, and for two years Bastia became the capital of that never-never land, the Anglo-Corsican kingdom, with Sir Gilbert Elliot in the governor's palace and his wife presiding over such marvellous glittering fairytale *fêtes* that, when Napoleon's Army of Italy forced the British to beat a hasty retreat, the Elliots' main legacy was legends of abandoned treasure.

Bastia lost its capital status altogether in 1811, when Napoleon made Corsica one *département* and his home town of Ajaccio the only capital, beginning a rivalry for influence and rather scarce government jobs that only eased somewhat in 1975, when the island was again divided into two *départements*. In the meantime, Bastia went back to business. In 1862, after a steamship smashed into the jetty of the Vieux Port, killing 84 passengers, Napoléon III ordered a new, larger port and expanded the city to the north. When the train station opened there in 1888, it seemed a miracle – passengers landing in Bastia could be in Ajaccio in only 4hrs.

Bastia may have bustled, but it also attracted a lot of unwanted attention in 1943. The very last Germans stationed on Corsica (and Sardinia) evacuated from Bastia on 2 October, harried by the Resistance, Free French and Moroccan troops on land, British submarines by sea and Allied bombers by air. Tragically, news of its liberation failed to reach American command, who ordered a high-altitude bombing raid of the city, just as the Bastiais were out in the streets celebrating; hundreds were killed or wounded and the Vieux Port was left in ruins.

Bastia, however, has bounced back. With a population of 70,000 in the metropolitan area, it has once again overtaken Ajaccio as the biggest city in Corsica. The bad luck that bedevils Bastia, however, struck again in May 1992, when one of the stands at Furiani stadium collapsed during a European Cup match, killing 17 and wounding 2,000 supporters.

The Nouveau Port, Terra Vecchia and Vieux Port

However they arrive by road or sea, most people land in Bastia at the **Nouveau Port**, the relatively bland, 19th-century functional bit of the city's seafront façade, where only the enormous **Place St-Nicolas** with its majestic palms and plane trees can match the scale of the ferry boats berthed at the quay. The square and its cafés are the meeting place for all Bastia, while a big statue of Napoleon, here resembling an Olympic weightlifter in a toga, acts as master of ceremonies.

Long parallel streets lead south of the big square into the heart of 17th-century Bastia, the tall dilapidated houses and flapping laundry of the **Terra Vecchia**. From Place St-Nicolas, Rue Napoléon, one of the more piquant streets, passes by the **Oratoire St-Roch**, built by Ligurian masters in 1609, with a beautifully preserved Baroque interior of finely worked pews, panelling, a flamboyant organ of 1750 and an altarpiece by Giovanni Bilivert. Further along the same street, the **Oratoire de l'Immaculée Conception** (1589), built by another confraternity during the religious revival begun by St Alexander Sauli (*see* p.188), stands over a typically Ligurian black and white pebble mosaic of a pear-nosed sun. Although not much on the outside, the oratory has one of the showiest Baroque interiors in Corsica, verging on camp with its red velvet, with crystal chandeliers and a copy of Murillo's *Immaculate Conception* over the altar – palatial enough for Genoese state occasions, meetings of the Estates-General under the French monarchy, and parliamentary sessions held during the Anglo-Corsican regime, which would open with the old organ banging out *God Save* *the King*. The sacristry contains a small **museum** of holy statues (starring a *St Erasmus*, patron of fishermen) and other religious art.

Just beyond is the former city centre, **Place de l'Hôtel de Ville** (or Place du Marché), now a generally peaceful place with a chubby girl fountain, schist paving and plane trees, which shade the bustling morning market. One end of the square sees the back of Corsica's largest church, the 17th–18th-century **St-Jean-Baptiste**, Bastia's landmark, with its two towers looming over the Vieux Port; the lavish marbled and stuccoed interior shelters some of Cardinal Fesch's duller Italian paintings (*see* p.88), a fancy organ and, on the altar, something you don't see every day: a *papier-mâché* Jesus. The **Porto-Vecchio/Vieux Port**, a horseshoe packed with brightly painted fishing boats, yachts and tall ramshackle *palazzi* with cafés skirting their feet, was the port of Cardo. Although bombed in the war, it was repaired in the same old style and much of it is now populated by North African families, who add an ethnic note rare in Corsica. The south is closed off by the **citadel of Terra Nova**; for the classic early-morning view of the Vieux Port with the mountains rising behind it, follow the quay under the citadel to the **Jetée du Dragon**.

In Genoese times, the richest Terra Vecchia merchants lived just behind the Vieux Port along Rue du Général-Carbuccia. Balzac, then hugely successful but as always hugely in debt, stayed at No.23 in March 1838, when he was on his way to Sardinia, hoping to make his fortune with a silver mine that turned out to be mere antimony. Near the top of the street is the classical façade of the Jesuit church of **St-Charles-Borromée** (1635), said to be the only one in France *without* the rights of asylum because of an old Genoese law. In the same little square is Bastia's most elegant balcony, on the façade of the **Maison de Caraffa**.

Terra Nova

High on its promontory over the Vieux Port, the medieval Genoese citadel of Terra Nova is a stiff climb on foot through the terraces of the once grand 18th-century **Jardin Romieu**. When it was built, Terra Nova was Bastia's most exclusive quarter and, now that its tall old houses are being restored, it is regaining its former cachet among local trend-setters. Just inside the main gate, the large **Palace of the Governors** with its handsome façade and sundial incorporates Leonello Lomellino's round bastion of 1378. After Nelson's fleet wrecked it in 1794, the palace was rebuilt by the French and used as a prison, and it was damaged again in the fatal Second World War bombing. After undergoing a major renovation that has already taken over a decade, the palace is slated to house the **Musée Municipal** in 2006, with its exhaustive collection covering the mineralogy, history, customs, handicrafts and folklore of Corsica, with early maps, 19th-century photographs, exhibits on great men, the original flag from the War of Independence, prints and broadsides, playing cards, and trinkets and play-things of the age of Napoleon. You can learn what N really thought of his relatives in his letters, and examine one of his death masks. There are also a number of Italian paintings from the Fesch legacy, including *Christ at the Column* by Lavinia Fontana and the lively *Billiard Players* attributed to Giuseppe Bonito.

In the past, the palace's dungeons were a busy place: Sampiero Corso was unjustly held here in the 1540s by a Genoese governor jealous of his fame, igniting a lifelong enmity. Resistance fighters captured and tortured by the Nazis were imprisoned here, too. Another memory from the last war is on the terrace: the conning tower of the submarine *Casabianca*, named after the Corsican hero at Aboukir (*see* pp.197–8). In 1942, Captain L'Herminier disobeyed orders to scuttle the sub along with the rest of the French fleet in Toulon, and instead escaped to North Africa, where at great risk he made the *Casabianca* the chief link between the Maquisards in Corsica and the Free French government in Algiers, bringing arms, munitions and radios to aid the Resistance and, in 1943, the commandos who liberated the island.

Still in Terra Nova, just off Place Guasco, the grandiose **Ste-Marie de l'Assomption** was rebuilt in 1619 over an older church to fit its status of Corsica's cathedral, although it settled back again to a parish church in 1801 when the diocese moved to Ajaccio; note the bishops' hats, suspended in the vaults over the choir. Its pride, a silver *Assumption of the Virgin*, made in 1858 by a Sienese goldsmith, does a tour of the town on 15 August. Also note the big Italian-made organ and the early 17th-century *Crucifixion with Saints* in a side chapel by Ottavio Cambiaso, son of Luca Cambiaso, Genoa's greatest Renaissance painter, who lived in Bastia between 1615 and 1640. Victor Hugo, whose father was one of Napoleon's officers, spent some of his childhood in the house just opposite. Just behind the cathedral, the **Oratoire Ste-Croix** (1600) is another Baroque jewel, built on land belonging to St John Lateran, with a sumptuous Ligurian-style interior of white, gold and blue stuccoes of 1775. One chapel holds the miraculous wooden crucifix, the *Cristu Negru* or Black Christ, found floating in the sea by two anchovy fishermen in 1428. Local fishermen offer it their first catch of the year, and every 3 May, the unluckiest day of the Invention of the Cross, the crucifix is taken in a procession around Terra Nova to ward off evil.

Further down within the citadel, in the former powder store, you can visit the **Village Corse Miniature** (*t 06 10 26 82 08, www.eco-musee.com; open Easter–Oct daily 9–12 and 2–6; adm*), a labour of love made by René Mattei, recreating an old Corsican village on a 1/30 scale, built of real stone, representing all the trades of yore.

Bastia's Stairway to Heaven

One of the best views of Bastia is from the top of the town and its Corniche Supérieure. Get there by following signs (the D81) for St-Florent; as the road winds up and up, just outside the city, keep an eye peeled for the sign for **Montserrato**. This simple oratory has a rare privilege granted by Pius VII: a copy of Rome's Scala Santa, the stair trodden on by Christ at the palace of Pontius Pilate. In 1803 Napoleon made a concordat with the pope (which restored the Catholic Church to France as the religion of the majority, but naturally under his own terms), and sent into exile to Corsica from mainland France the 424 priests who refused to go along, locking them in Bastia's keep. The Bastiais, appalled at their treatment, demanded their release, which their gaoler eventually granted, on the condition that they themselves put the priests up in their homes, which the Bastiais did with such kindness that the grateful pope granted this exceptional favour; like the Lateran's Santa Scala, anyone who goes up the steps on their knees is absolved of their sins.

From here, a right on the D64 will take you to **Cardo**, the Roman ancestor of Bastia, a pleasant village with a Genoese tower and a fountain. From here you can continue north into Cap Corse along the Corniche Supérieure to Ville-de-Pietrabugno and San-Martino-di-Lota (*see* below) with remarkable views straight down into Bastia.

Cap Corse/Capi Corsu

Corsica's 'sacred promontory', Cap Corse, 40km long and 10km wide, looks for all the world like an accusing finger pointed at Genoa. Made of schist and green ophiolite, the peninsula is so high and rugged (4,343ft/1,324m at the Cima di e Folicce) that only three roads cross its width. Genoese towers guard its little coves, where the winds toss veils of spray and men have traditionally gone to sea, either as sailors or fishermen – the only part of Corsica, in fact, where the sea was always regarded as a friend (when other Corsicans used to say '*che tu vaga in mare*', 'may you go to the sea', they really meant 'go to hell').

The road that circles Cap Corse was built in the mid-19th century, a gift of Napoléon III, determined to do more for Corsica than his uncle. Until then, Cap Corse remained a place apart, accessible only by sea, as if it were Elba or one of the other Tuscan islands that float off its shore. Until the advent of the French, two families ruled and fought over it, the da Gentile in the south and the da Mare in the north; the Genoese fairly ignored it, so the two families' little fleets made a living trading with France and Italy. The one product the Cap itself produced was fine wines. When phylloxera killed the vines in 1850–60, hundreds of Capicursini were forced to emigrate,

The Wines of Cap Corse

The Carthaginians planted the first vines on Cap Corse, and in the early Middle Ages the region was the first on Corsica to grow wine commercially. The Genoese, who were quite partial to the stuff ('the wine of Cap Corse is the right eye of Corsica,' declared a 16th-century bishop), obliged each inhabitant to plant vines and to sell all of his wine to Genoa, with the muscats (now Muscat du Cap AOC) in particular demand. These days, in spite of all the difficulties (the winds, fires, a natural low yield and rampaging boars), a few vineyards still keep the tradition alive. The best known is **Le Clos Nicrosi** at Rogliano, t 04 95 35 41 17, founded in 1850 and generally recognized as the source of the finest white wines of Corsica, although there's never enough to meet the demand that extends as far as the USA. Also at Rogliano, the much smaller **Domaine de Gioelli**, t 04 95 35 42 05, once belonged to the Doria family and produces, besides the usual colours and muscats, *rapu* (a sweet red wine made from an assortment of traditional varieties, drunk before or after meals). Two other etates are open for visits, if you ring ahead. The **Domaine Pieretti** at Luri, t 04 95 35 01 03, was founded in the 18th century and passed down from father to daughter. The **Domaine de Pietri** at Morsiglia, t 04 95 35 60 93, in business since 1768, produces a delicious muscat, *rapu*, and another traditional wine, *impassitu*, made from raisins.

many going off to seek their fortune in the Americas in sugar, coffee or gold (a third of all Puerto Ricans, for instance, are of Corsican descent, and a president of Venezuela was a third-generation Capicursino; in the USA, Alabama, Virginia and Louisiana were the favourite destinations). Those *américains* who made it big often returned to build fancy Tuscan-style villas, Spanish *haciendas*, or American colonial *palazzi* in their native villages; some are now hotels, while others are still used in summer by *américains* who return, though many now speak Spanish instead of Corsican. Those who couldn't come back while alive ordered palatial tombs to receive their ashes.

The coasts of Cap Corse are stunning, but dramatically different: the mountains slope down relatively gently on the east coast. On the west coast, they plunge straight into the sea; the north coast is in between, but accessible only by foot. Beaches are tucked in here and there; they can be covered with shelves of dead posidonia leaves, which like mattresses protect the coast from erosion and shelter the fish, even if they aren't very appealing to wade through.

Up the East Coast

This is the gentle side of Cap Corse, its southernmost corner protected from the worst winds, its coves sheltering tiny fishing villages, while up on the slopes quiet villages make wine and get by through a modest amount of tourism. There are two roads north from Bastia: the scenic Corniche Supérieure (D64) begins at Cardo (*see* p.210) and skirts the green schisty hills to **Ville-de-Pietrabugno** and the eagle's nest of **San-Martino-di-Lota**, with views over Elba and the Tuscan archipelago. It has three villas – châteaux really – built by the brothers Cagniacci on their return from the Americas. Cap Corse keeps alive many old folk customs; in San-Martino, the inhabitants weave intricate Baroque altars, calvaries and churches out of palm fronds for a Good Friday procession; the best one is chosen to sit on the altar of the church.

If you take the coastal road (D80) from Bastia you'll come to **Miomo** and **Lavasina**; the first has a relatively long pebble beach and the latter an early 16th-century painting of the *Virgin and Child* attributed to Perugino, in the church of **Notre-Dame-des-Grâces**. The painting's reputation for miracles began with its acquisition by the Danesi family, who sold wine in Italy. One of their clients in Rome, unable to pay his debts, offered the painting in exchange; when the Danesi unrolled it in Lavasina, gold coins, to the amount of the debt, fell out. Its fame increased after a series of miraculous cures, and every 8 September pilgrims come from across the island to a midnight mass and torchlit procession on the beach. The church (a sorry victim of 19th-century restorers) also contains hand-made ex-votos and a striking statue of the dead Christ.

From **Pozzo**, a medieval hamlet above Lavasina, a waymarked path leads up through the *maquis* in about three hours to the summit of **Monte Stello** (4,288ft/1,307m), the second highest mountain of Cap Corse. The trail is steep but poses no great difficulty, but do check the weather before setting out, and start at dawn for the magnificent views of the Tuscan coast and peaks of Corsica; by late morning the clouds invariably move in. In summer the lack of shade makes for hot going and the views are often shrouded in haze.

Getting There and Around

Bastia's inter-urban STIB buses, t 04 95 31 06 65, from Place St-Nicolas, make frequent journeys up the east coast as far as Macinaggio throughout the year except Sundays and hols.

Tourist Information

Ville-de-Pietrabugno: Maison du Cap, t 04 95 31 02 32, www.destination-cap-corse.com

Sports and Activities

U Cavallu di Brando, Les Glacières de Brando, Erbalunga, t 04 95 33 94 02. Scenic horse-riding over the spine of the cape.

Cap Loc' Loisirs, Marine de Santa-Severa, t 04 95 35 08 20. Rent a zodiac or small boat without a permit.

Centre de Plongée de Santa Severa, Marine de Santa Severa, t 06 95 35 08 29. Diving centre.

Where to Stay and Eat

San-Martino-di-Lota ✉ 20200

**La Corniche, 12km north of Bastia, t 04 95 31 40 98, www.hotel-lacorniche.com (moderate). Up above the commotion, with fairly simple rooms and ravishing views. There's a lovely pool, and an excellent restaurant with a shady panoramic terrace, well worth a visit even if you're not staying: delicious raviolis au brocciu, lamb and perfect desserts (menus €25 and €45). Be sure to book in summer. Closed Jan; restaurant also closed Mon, and Tues eve.

Auberge U San Martinu, Place de l'Eglise, t 04 95 32 23 68 (moderate). A 19th-century 'Maison d'Américains' with four pleasant rooms, pool, and restaurant serving heaped portions of old Corsican dishes seldom seen in restaurants (menu from €13). In season be sure to book. Closed mid-Dec–mid-Feb.

Chez Céline, t 04 95 58 19 55 (inexpensive). Four traditionally decorated B&B rooms in a cool, thick-walled 19th century house with sea views and parking, 10mins from the sea.

Santa-Maria-di-Lota ✉ 20200
Maison Saint Hyacinthe, t 04 95 33 28 29, (inexpensive; breakfast incl). Something different: the Polish nuns who run a mission here offer impeccably tidy rooms and meals for groups, families or individuals, in a tranquil setting 2.5km from the sea; book.

Erbalunga ✉ 20222
★★★Castel' Brando, t 04 95 30 10 30, www. castelbrando.com (expensive). In the 19th century, a local sugar plantation owner in Santo Domingo returned to build himself a palace by the sea. The little garden has a pool and one of the oldest palm trees on Corsica; the air-conditioned rooms have many of their original furnishings. Open mid-Mar–Oct.

Le Pirate, t 04 95 33 24 20, www.restaurant lepirate.com. The best place for a romantic dinner on the Cap: in an old stone house right on the fishing port, where the seafood and everything else is fresh and charming (try the ravioli filled with fish) accompanied by fine Corsican wines. Some vegetarian offerings too. Lunch menu €32, dinner €70. Closed Mon, and Tues and Wed lunch.

L'Esquinade, t 04 95 33 22 73. A pretty terrace by the sea serving a delicious soup of rock

North at **Erbalunga** (see box, p.214), a tiny peninsula forms a port where the buildings literally have their feet in the water, as the French say, guarded by a ruined Genoese tower that gets its picture on lots of postcards. One of the chief Pisan ports, Erbalunga was the capital of the da Gentile clan; it later produced the ancestors of the poet Paul Valéry, who helped to make it the arty village of the Cap. It has a long pebble beach to the north – a rare one not bundled down in layers of seaweed.

Inland from Erbalunga the maquis covers with rocky swirling hills like green baize, softening the landscape. The da Gentile's reputedly haunted castle gave its name to **Castello**, 3km above Erbalunga, which was left in ruins in the 1550s when the family fish and duck breast with local honey. *Around €25.* No credit cards.

Sisco/Marine de Sisco ✉ 20233

U Pozzu, t 04 95 35 21 17, *www.u-pozzu.com* (*moderate*). Close to the sea (and the main road) at Sisco Marine, a comfortable enough place built on terraces, with air-conditioned rooms and a good restaurant, specializing in seafood, with a €22 menu. *Closed Nov and Dec.*

Auberge A Stalla Sischese, 300m up the road to Sisco village, **t** 04 95 35 26 34. Not much to look at from the outside, but one of the most authentic Corsican kitchens on the Cap, serving all the classics from *soupe corse* to *fiadone*. *Menus from €19.* They also have a hotel. *Closed Sun eve and Feb.*

Marine de Pietracorbara ✉ 20233

Macchia e Mare, t 04 95 35 21 36, *www. macchia-e-mare.com* (*moderate*). Set back from the road (which you cross to get to the beach), although some rooms have terraces overlooking the sea. Also a restaurant (*menus from €14*). Half-pension mandatory in July and Aug.

Hôtel des Chasseurs, t 04 95 35 21 54 (*inexpensive*). Near the beach, simple rooms with a laid-back atmosphere, in the same family for over 30 years. Also a *boules* court, and a good restaurant with lots of choices and pizza (*menus from €12*). *Closed Nov–Mar.*

Camping la Pietra, t 04 95 35 27 49, *www. la-pietra.com* (*inexpensive*) Large shady three-star campsite 300m from the beach, with tennis and a playground. *Closed Nov–mid-Mar.*

Porticciolo (Cagnano) ✉ 20228

U Patriarcu, t 04 95 35 00 01 (*inexpensive*). In a handsome old house, recently renovated rooms priced according to comfort and views. Friendly owners the Mattei family have run it for half a century. *Half-board obligatory in season. Closed late Oct– early April.*

Maison Bella Vista, t 04 95 38 46 (*inexpensive*). On the north end of the village right by the sea, the hospitable Cathy Cantoni runs a tight ship at this wonderful *chambres d'hôtes. Closed Nov–Mar.*

Torra Marina, t 04 95 35 00 80 (*inexpensive*). Four rooms by the sea and an atmospheric restaurant under the parasol pines. Fresh, perfumed cuisine; seafood receives the emphasis but there are other dishes as well; cheese-lovers should try the *fondant fromage de Calenzana. Menu €23. Closed Oct–Mar.*

Santa Severa/Luri ✉ 20228

Santa Severa, t 04 95 35 05 67, *www. marinadiluri.com* (*moderate*). Recently renovated rooms and studios sleeping up to six, all with sea views and balconies.

Chambres d'Hôtes I Fundali, Spergane, **t** 04 95 35 06 15 (*inexpensive*). In the middle of the Cap, 3km from the hamlet of Piazza, in a gorgeous isolated setting by a ruined medieval tower. Besides six pretty rooms, hosts Alain and Marie-Thé also hire out two *gîtes* by the week, one sleeping two, one four, and prepare good home-cooked meals by request. *Closed Nov.*

A Cantina, Santa Severa, **t** 04 95 35 05 67. By the little port, pizzas and excellent home-cooked Corsican dishes, including *storzapreti. Around €20. Closed Wed.*

nearly self-destructed in a feud over an adulterous wife. Just below Castello, on the route to Silgaggia, stands the 11th-century **Chapelle Notre-Dame-des-Neiges**, still in good nick and roofed with its original stone *teghie*. Inside, strikingly archaic saints, fragments of Corsica's earliest dated frescoes (1386), stare out of the gloom (*if locked, the* mairie *at Brando keeps the key,* **t** *04 95 33 90 03*).

Sisco to Luri

North of Erbalunga the coast becomes wilder towards **Marine de Sisco**, which has a small sandy, seaweedy beach and a surprising green lawn, and a tiny port that served

Easter Week in Erbalunga

Erbalunga keeps alive Easter rituals that go back hundreds of years, with roots that go deep into the pre-Christian Mediterranean, when people symbolically 'wakened' the sleeping earth in spring. At 7am on the morning of Good Friday, the hooded and robed confraternity go on a procession, beginning at the church of St-Erasme. A barefoot penitent bearing a cross weighing over 100lb leads the men, while a woman bearing a 50lb cross leads the women, all wearing a *faldetta*, or blue skirt-like kerchief. They walk through the hamlets of Pozzo and Poretto, gathering people as they go, stopping at every shrine and chapel on the way, singing the *Stabat Mater*. They return to Erbalunga before midday, and in the evening the confraternity returns at 7.30 for an impressive ceremony by candlelight, singing and walking through the lanes of Erbalunga and ending up in Place Piandifora where they form a huge spiral going in and out (the *granitula*, a symbol of the never-ending cycles of life), and then follow this by forming a Latin cross, to give it all a good Christian stamp of approval. Then the *office des ténèbres* is sung by the local confraternity at St-Erasme to words and music that have been passed on orally through the generations from father to son, while the candles are extinguished, one by one; when the church is in complete darkness, the children make a horrible clattering and banging to symbolize the thunder that shook the earth at the death of Christ.

the scattered hamlets that make up Sisco. A rare iron-working *comune* in the Middle Ages, importing ore from Elba, it was also an early centre of Christianity on Corsica. One of several caves in the area, where converts hid from Roman persecution, is near the former **Couvent Ste-Catherine** (**Santa Catalina**), 500m up the D80 from Sisco Marine, reached by a hairpinning road rising up from a large statue of Jesus. The convent is now an old people's home, but the church, unfortunately usually locked, was once famous all across the Tyrrhenian. In 1255, a captain sailing from the Near East got caught in a storm and vowed to deposit a chest of holy relics he was carrying in the first church he saw if his ship were spared. This was Ste-Catherine; the sea calmed, but when the captain tried to cheat and sail off, another storm quickly blew up and only desisted after he left the chest of relics behind.

This, after all, was an age of miracles. A few years back, crusading king Saint Louis (Louis IX) had spent a fortune on a thorn from the Crown of Thorns and had built Ste-Chapelle in Paris to house it, and all kinds of sharpsters lay in wait in the Holy Land to take advantage of the Christians' willingness to pay top money for 'relics'. The contents of the captain's chest, however, set a kind of record for credulity: there was an almond from the Garden of Eden, a bit of clay left over from the making of Adam, the rod used by Moses to divide the Red Sea, a bite of manna, Enoch's finger and sewing thread that once belonged to the Virgin. So many pilgrims came to see these wonders that the church was gracelessly enlarged in the 15th century. Over the centuries some of the relics were stolen, and in 1588, for safe keeping, the rest were locked in the altar of San Martino (*see* below). You can, however, see the crypt where they were once displayed, carved out of the rock in the form of a rotunda, with a dome on top and two curving stairs called *tomboli*. The shape, unique in Corsica, reproduces the church of the Holy Sepulchre. Also note the rather unusual fresco on the front, with stars, human heads and other motifs.

The main hamlet of **Sisco/Siscu** lies up the terraced green valley, built around the parish church of **San Martino**. Inscriptions by the high altar and a retable refer to the relics, although the only one on display, on the very rare occasion when it's open, is a striking 13th-century copper and silver mask of St John Chrysostomos, the 'golden-mouthed' patriarch of Constantinople from 398 to 407. From San Martino, a signposted track leads to the **Chapelle St-Michel** (park the car by the track leading up to the left, and walk the last 200m), the most beautiful Pisan church on Cap Corse, in a dramatic setting with views down the coast. Another road from San Martino, towards Barrigioni, passes the Villa St-Pierre, a remarkable *palazzu américain*.

North along the coast, past steep slopes of *maquis*, comes the **Marine di Pietracorbara** with a long beach at the mouth of the river and another ruined da Gentile Genoese tower. Further up the coast, the Tour Losse is the French for **Torre dell'Osso**, 'tower of bones', one of the best preserved of the Genoese watchtowers; it earned its name when a mass of human skeletons of unknown providence was found around its foundations.

Porticciolo, next on the coast, is a lovely place to break up a tour of Cap Corse, piled over a minute port and sandy beach. Just 2km north, **Santa Severa**, the port of Luri, is less bijou, but has a pebble beach, vineyards and the D180, one of the three roads that crosses over the Cap. Take this for 3.5km to **Campo**, and from its square head up a little lane, you'll find a plaque marking the modest **home of Dominique Cervoni** (1834–90), the most famous of all Capicursino mariners, thanks to Joseph Conrad. The young Conrad had just decided on a seafaring life in 1876 when he met Cervoni, first mate of the *Saint-Antoine*, and sailed with him to Venezuela. Conrad was fascinated by his 'air of a pirate and a monk' and used him as a model for the main character in *Nostromo*, as well as a host of minor characters in other books, and under his real name in *The Mirror of the Sea*. Conrad came to Campo to visit Cervoni, but only found a tomb; after all his adventures he had returned at last to his old house to die.

The D180 continues to **Luri**, midway between the coasts and encompassing 17 tiny hamlets, surrounded by lemon groves and vineyards; the latter produces an excellent rosé celebrated with all the other wines of Corsica in the main hamlet, **Piazza**, the first weekend in July. The church here has a 15th-century painting on wood of *St Peter*, with all the towers and castles of Cap Corse (as they looked back then) in the background. Another hamlet of Luri, **Cepitta**, is the base of **Cap Vert**, an association founded by botanists in 1991, dedicated to preserving the striking biodiversity of the region; besides endemics, there are plants brought over from Liguria and Tuscany, and even South America, introduced by the *Américains* (*t 04 95 35 05 07; open July and Aug Mon–Fri 9–11 and 5–7; spring and autumn 10–12 and 2–5*). The road continues over to the west coast by way of the Tour de Sénèque (*see* below). Alternatively, if you continue north along the coast you'll find little **Marine de Meria**, squeezed around its port.

Northern Cap Corse

Bustling, boaty **Macinaggio/Macinagju** with its marina has the only truly sheltered port on the Cap's coast. There are stories that St Paul, or another early evangelist, landed here; **Tomino**, just above Macinaggio, has an age-old reputation as 'Corsica's cradle of Christianity' with caves to show where the first Christians hid in the 2nd or 3rd century. The first Corsicans themselves may have landed here; a cave just north of Macinaggio yielded the oldest known human relics on the island, going back 60,000

Tourist Information

Macinaggio: Port de Plaisance, t 04 95 35 40 34, www.ot-rogliano-macinaggio.com. Open winter Mon–Fri, 9–12 and 2–7; July–Aug daily 9–12 and 4–8, Sat 9–12 and 2–7. Note that most of the monuments in the area are only open for guided visits, t 04 95 32 72 42. Macinaggio has the only **ATM** machine (at the post office) and petrol station in the area.

Sports and Activities

Capi Corsu Diving, Macinaggio, t 04 95 35 48 57. Will 'baptize' children as young as 8.
Cap Corse Location, Macinaggio, t 06 11 01 09 30. Hires out boats, mountain bikes, quads, jeeps and more.
Club Nautique, Macinaggio, t 04 95 35 46 82. Hire a sea kayak or windsurfer, or catamaran.
Compagnie U San Paulu, Macinaggio, t 04 95 35 07 09 or t 06 14 78 14 16. Visits to the wild beaches of Cap Corse, trips into the Réserve de Finocchiarola, and a Macinaggio Barcaggio shuttle for walkers along the Sentier des Douaniers who book ahead.

Where to Stay and Eat

Macinaggio ✉ 20248

★★★U Ricordu, Rte de Rogliano, t 04 95 35 40 20, www.hotel-uricordu.com (expensive; half-board terms). Won't win any beauty contests, but only a few minutes' walk from the port, with a heated pool for late-night dips, sauna, and mountain bikes to rent, plus air-conditioning. Closed Dec–Mar.
★★U Libecciu, t 04 95 35 43 22, www.u-libecciu.com (moderate; half-board obligatory in July and Aug). Functional but friendly hotel

towards the Plage de Tamarone, with 14 big quiet rooms, many with balconies. Corsican and Gascon specialities in the restaurant (menus from €15). Closed Nov–Mar.
Camping U Stazzu, 1km north of the village, t 04 95 35 43 76 (inexpensive). Unpretentious campsite by the beach, with a snack bar/pizzeria, near a riding centre. Air mattress essential. No credit cards. Closed Oct–Mar.
Osteria di U Portu, in the port, t 04 95 35 40 49. The day's catch, simply prepared, but also excellent cuisine du terroir – crêpes made with chestnut flour, charcuterie, ravioli filled with brousse in meaty tomato sauce and more. Menus €15 at lunch, otherwise €22. Closed Wed from Dec to Mar.
La Vela d'Oro, in a lane back from the port, t 04 95 35 42 46. Good little restaurant, offering a choice of fish (€16) and meat (€15) menus as well as lobster dishes. Closed Wed.

Rogliano ✉ 20247

★★★U Sant'Angellu, t 04 95 35 40 59, www.hotel-usantagnellu.com (expensive; half-board mandatory). Former town hall in the centre of the village, converted into a hotel and restaurant. Rooms are spacious, and some have sea views, but the restaurant terrace has the best views of all. Well-prepared Corsican dishes on a €14 menu, or splurge on lobster. Open mid-April–mid-Oct.

Barcaggio ✉ 20275

★★La Giraglia, t 04 95 35 60 54 (moderate, with breakfast). Corsica's northernmost hotel is on the sombre side but if you aren't overly sensitive to the décor it makes a great hideaway; 14 rooms in a stone building wrapped in creeper, with its feet almost in the sea. No restaurant, no Internet. Book well in advance in season. Closed Oct–Mar.

years. Plaques on the waterfront commemorate historic moments: the sending of four ships to fight at Lepanto in 1571, and the landing of Paoli in 1790 after his exile in England. 'O my country, I left you a slave, I rediscover you free!' he cried as he kissed the ground. Macinaggio's beach is usually half hidden under the posidonia, although 2.5km north a dirt road ends at the sandy **Plage de Tamarone**.

Tamarone also marks the beginning of the **Site Naturel de la Capandula**, which encompasses the northeastern tip of Cap Corse and the peninsula's most beautiful beaches; in spring some 21 rare flowers bloom here. It's only accessible by sea, or by foot by way of the **Sentier des Douaniers**, an easy and beautiful coastal path along cliffs and wild dunes blazed by Genoese da Mare lords, who ruled Cap Corse from the 12th to the 16th century, and punctuated it with their towers, ruined windmills and limekilns. The whole Sentier des Douaniers from Macinaggio to Centuri-Port takes about eight hours (wear good shoes, and bring plenty of water; there's no shade), but the best bit is the three-hour walk between Macinaggio and Barcaggio, taking in the pretty **Plage des Iles** and the **Chapelle Santa Maria della Chiapèlla**. This chapel started out as two churches, from the 10th and 12th centuries, which were only united in the 19th century, so that their two apses form uneven buttocks – although some say the two apses are the result of a long-running feud between two families who refused to worship at the same altar.

Just off shore, the three **Iles Finocchiarola**, named for their wild fennel, attract hundreds of migratory birds from Africa, including the extremely rare Audouin's gull with its red bill; to make it as cosy as possible for them, no humans are allowed near from March to August. Further along, the path is marked by the romantic ruin of the Genoese **Tour Santa Maria**, surrounded by water and sundered neatly in twain by Nelson's fleet in 1793, so that its three vaulted floors stand open to the elements. The path continues past the fine sandy beaches at Cala Genovese and Cala Francese to the second of three Genoese towers (*see* box, p.218), the **Tour d'Agnello**, looking out towards the lighthouse atop the steep **islet of Giraglia**, the northernmost bit of Corsica. Beyond is **Barcaggio**, a world's end with a handful of houses in a gorgeous setting and a blasé attitude towards remaining cute for tourists; its wide and windy beach of white sand is popular with the local cow population. Barcaggio can also be reached by road from Rogliano (*see* below) and Ersa, as can **Tollare**, an even dinkier collection of houses a 45-minute walk further along the Sentier des Douaniers.

In an amphitheatre above Macinaggio, **Rogliano/Ruglianu** is made up of seven hamlets, dotted with three ruined da Mare castles. In 1869, Empress Eugénie was returning from the opening ceremonies of the Suez Canal when her yacht was forced by a storm to drop anchor at Macinaggio. She was warmly welcomed, but had to struggle three kilometres up a goat path with her entourage to reach shelter at Rogliano; when she returned to Paris, she sent money for the construction of the road, still called the Chemin de l'Impératrice. **Bettolacce**, the main hamlet, has a well-preserved Genoese tower and the handsome 16th-century church of **Sant'Agnellu**, full of gifts: there's a marble altar paid for by the Roglianais community of Puerto Rico, a choir screen from Eugénie, and an altar dedicated to St Anthony of Padua, donated by a young man from Rogliano. He had fallen in love with a noble girl of Florence, whose father would allow him to marry her only if he donated an altar to the church of his baptism. After it was done, however, the young man went to the father and said he wouldn't marry his daughter after all, because Corsicans never make deals about love. On a spur above Bettolacce in **Vignale** stand the striking ruins of the 12th-century **Castello de San Colombano**, once seat of the da Mare, whose rule was so harsh that the locals called it the *Castellacciu* or 'bad castle'. One scion, Giacomo Santo da Mare, went over to Sampiero Corso in 1553; he was killed, but the Genoese paid his family back by destroying the castle. It was rebuilt, and burned down in 1947.

Life in a Genoese Tower

Cap Corse was more vulnerable to pirates than any other part of the island, and the Tour Santa Maria is a good example of the 32 towers (of the 91 on Corsica as a whole) erected in the 16th century by Andrea Doria and the Bank of St George to defend their investments from pirates and other marauders. As might be expected, all the locals in the area who benefited from the protection were made to chip in and pay for them, but for once the Corsicans considered it money well spent. Built either on cliffs or at sea level, each round tower (nearly all the square ones were built privately) was designed for its setting, to be within sight of two other towers, and to offer refuge; strengthened by interior vaulting, the walls were some 17ft/5m thick, observation platforms were 60ft/18m high, and doors to the mid-level living quarters stood 20ft/6m off the ground, reached by ladders that could be pulled up in seconds. A cistern at the lower level collected rainwater, and sufficient stores ensured a tower could endure a siege. Local taxes also paid the tower guardians, or *torregiani* – five or six per important tower, two or three in the smaller ones – and they had to follow strict rules. Only one man at a time was permitted to leave, never for more than two days and only for provisions or to collect money. They were forbidden to pay others to do their job (this at a time when a man could always pay someone else to go to war for him). They kept sailors informed about the safety of their route, and each night remained in contact with their neighbouring towers, using fire or smoke signals to say all's well. If it wasn't, the watch blew trumpets and lit a fire on the platform, igniting a chain reaction along the coast and into the mountains by way of fires lit on the *parvis*, or terraces, in front of the churches (in case of fog the mountaineers blew warnings on conch shells), and within the hour all Corsica was on the alert.

Others, besides the Genoese, found the towers handy as well. In 1761, the Tour Santa Maria was Paoli's base after he failed to capture Macinaggio, and from here his little Corsican fleet sailed to capture the island of Capraia from the Genoese, precipitating the end of Genoa's reign on Corsica. When defended by the French in 1794, the Anglo-Corsicans found the towers proved devilishly hard to capture. Nelson had his way with this tower after a day's battle, but another one, at Punta de Mortella by St-Florent, held out and severely damaged two British warships, and it took two days of furious bombardments by the British land guns before its garrison finally surrendered. It occurred to the Admiralty that similar towers could help defend *their* island from Napoleon's threatened invasion – hence the Martello towers built around the south coasts of Britain, Ireland and the Channel Islands.

Down the West Coast

Approaching from Rogliano, the road continues up to the Col de Serra, where you'll see something rare on Corsica – a windmill, the **Moulin Mattei**, restored after the First World War by the Cap Corse *apéritif*-makers, who have always been among the canniest marketing people on Corsica and who offer tastings of their products along with a magnificent view.

The next group of hamlets (at the west end of the Sentier des Douaniers, *see* p.217) belongs to **Centuri** (Roman Centurium), a bijou port with the most important fishing fleet on Cap Corse, pulling in three tons of lobster and ten tons of fish each year. It has all the ingredients to make it a favourite stop for visitors as well – delicious seafood, a bustling atmosphere, colourful houses under green serpentine roofs, lovely sunsets, a handful of artists painting fishing smacks – all, that is, except a good beach (the closest is at Barcaggio). The little islet offshore saved the bacon of the da Mare and Avogari, Genoese aristocrats who dared to challenge Corsica's overlord, the Giudice di Cinarca, in the 13th century; defeated by the Giudice's forces, they took refuge here. For the lack of a boat, the Giudice couldn't catch them, and in the middle of the night they set sail and founded the town of Calvi.

Centuri was famous for the Cipriani family, who came from Florence and were mentioned by Dante, but who were forced in the political turmoil of the 15th century to take refuge here. In the 18th century the family produced four giant brothers, all standing over 6ft 6ins, who followed colourful destinies in the Caribbean and else-where; a son of one of them, Count Leonetto Cipriani, fought in America and later for the Duke of Tuscany, and became a negotiator for Vittorio Emanuele II in the reunifi-cation of Italy and for Napoléon III, then returned to Centuri to die in the village's landmark, the neo-medieval turreted **Château de Bellavista**. Just below the road you can turn up to the charming hamlet of **Cannelle**, an ensemble of flowers, fig trees, medieval lanes and a pretty columned fountain with a view down to the sea.

South of Centuri, the scenery changes abruptly. The vertiginous *corniche* road is cut high into mountain and *maquis*, over views plunging steeply into a sea of indigo and royal blue. The little harbours tucked below are mostly invisible from the road, while certain bends offer sudden views across the Golfe de St-Florent to the north coast of Corsica and the shadowy mountains rising behind.

No fewer than nine Genoese towers (three still in good nick) guarded the first settlement, **Morsiglia**, from marauders. A road descends to the little **Golfe d'Aliso**, with a red sandy beach, and beyond is the turn-off on the D180 for Luri. This climbs into the pines to the **Col de Ste-Lucie**, marked by a church and steep path that in half an hour will take you up to the **Tour de Sénèque**, a 13th-century observation post impossibly balanced on a lofty spur of the Montagne de Ventiggiole, with tremen-dous views taking in both coasts of Cap Corse. Legend has it that it marks the spot where Seneca spent seven years (AD 41–9) when the emperor Claudius exiled him at the age of 39 for seducing his niece Julia. Fortunately for him he was a Stoic, because after his cushy life in Rome he didn't care for Corsica in the least. 'What could be as bare, what could be as craggy as this rock where I find myself? Could there be any soil

Sports and Activities

Club Bleu Marine Compagnie, Morsiglia, **t** 04 95 35 60 46. Diving club.

Cap Corse Parapente, Canari, **t** 04 95 37 84 81. If you've never tried hang-gliding before, this is a great place to start, with an instructor at your side.

Where to Stay and Eat

Centuri-Port ✉ 20238

Le Vieux Moulin, on the port, **t 04 95 60 15, www.le-vieux-moulin.net (moderate; half-pension for two €165). Famous restaurant and simple rooms in a *palazzu américain* of character, built in 1863 by a Corsican who made his pile in Santo Domingo. Owner Pierre Alessandrini will soon make you feel at home, and eating fresh seafood on the superb terrace overlooking the little port at sunset is hard to beat. *Closed Nov–mid-Feb.*

La Jetée, on the jetty, **t** 04 95 35 64 46 (moderate). Adequate rooms (surprisingly not all with sea views) in a 19th-century house, and a restaurant with good inexpensive menus (from €15). *Closed Oct–Mar.*

U Marinaru, 200m from the port, **t** 04 95 35 62 95 (inexpensive). Rooms with a view, a warm welcome and delicious seafood – reservations essential in summer. *Closed Oct–Easter.*

Camping L'Isulottu, 1km from Centuri, **t** 04 95 35 62 81 (inexpensive). The only campsite on the east coast, a short walk from a mediocre pebble beach, with shade, pretty views, a restaurant, pizzeria and games. *Closed Christmas–Feb.*

A Macciotta, on a little lane above the port, **t** 04 95 35 64 12. The owner fishes, his wife cooks, and their daughter waits tables. The freshest of fish (mixed fish platter €18, lobster menu €41 are some of the choices) served with the local white wine. They also have a daily special that's not fish, if you can't bear the sight of another fin. *Closed Nov–Mar.*

La Langoustier, at the end of the port, **t** 04 95 35 61 98. Good value lobster and other seafood in a restaurant owned by a fisherman, with menus starting at €13.

Pino ✉ 20228

La Tour Génoise, **t** 04 95 35 12 29. In a lovely setting overlooking the coast, good seafood,

so poor in resources? Any population so fierce? Any country that looks so horrid? A more wretched climate?' Besides penning crabby verses, the great philosopher bided his time, writing *Consolations* to other people and studying natural history, dreaming of the day he could return to Rome – which happened at last when Claudius' wife Agrippina intervened for him and made him the tutor of her son Nero. Other villages on Cap Corse have claims to having hosted the philosopher, but this one has the best story: the weeds growing around the tower's base are called 'Seneca's nettles' after the randy exile tried his powers of seduction on the local girls, and was beaten back by outraged Corsicans with stinging nettles. Unfortunately for the story, excavations around the tower revealed no sign of Roman occupation to go with the nettles.

Back on the west coast, the next slice of civilization is **Pino/Pinu**, a colourful and once very wealthy little hamlet dotted with towers cascading down the slopes in a lush setting. Its 18th-century Baroque church of Santa Maria has a triptych tenuously attributed to the late 15th-century Florentine master, Fra Bartolomeo. A steep road descends to a teeny port and pebble beach at the **Marine de Scalo** marked by a Genoese tower and the **Couvent St-François**, founded in 1486, with a fresco over the portal. Pino was the home of Antoine Liccioni, who as a young man sailed to America in 1819, vowing to return only when he made his fortune. Which he did, finding more gold in South America than all of Cap Corse's *américains* put together and using it to soul food (Corsican-style tripe and pigs' trotters) and pizzas, too. *Menus at €20 and €30. Open mid Mar–Oct.*

Barrettali ✉ 20228

Marinella, Marine de Giottani, t 04 95 35 12 15 (*inexpensive*). Perfect for anyone seeking peace and quiet, a basic hotel restaurant with 9 rooms by the port and a little pebble beach. The restaurant (*€23 menu, with wine*) serves a delicious *soupe de poissons. Closed mid-Oct–mid-May.*

Canari ✉ 20217

I Fioretti-Couvent St-François, t 04 95 37 80 17 (*moderate*). Six rooms, well laid out in the cells of a Baroque convent.

Au Bon Clocher, Hameau de Pieve, t 04 95 37 80 15 (*inexpensive*). A little family-run hotel-restaurant in front of the bell tower, specializing in fresh fish and vegetables from the garden. *Closed mid-Oct–Feb.*

U Scogliu, Marine de Cannelle, t 04 95 37 80 06. A steep descent from the *corniche* road but worth it for the delicious fresh seafood dishes and famous grilled lobster by the sea in a bijou setting. *Around €50 à la carte.* One of the best on Cap Corse, so

it's best to book; to be really swish arrive by boat. *Closed early Oct–April.*

Nonza ✉ 20217

Les Tamaris, just north at Marine d'Albo, t 04 95 37 81 91, *www.lestamaris.com* (*moderate*). Comfortable 32-room hotel in a renovated old building, 50m from the beach; rooms well-equipped. *Closed Dec–April.* Reasonable *half-board* arrangement possible with the nearby restaurant, **Chez Morganti, t 04 95 37 85 10, which does elaborate seafood dishes as well as good lamb (*menus from €15*).

*Auberge Patrizi, t 04 95 37 82 16 (*moderate*). On Nonza's little square, a short walk from the beach. *Half-board only*, with 12 rooms and an excellent restaurant (*moderate*) serving succulent Corsican veal with white beans. *Closed mid-Oct–Mar.*

Olmeta du Cap ✉ 20217

Relais du Cap, Marina de Negru, t 04 95 37 86 52, *www.relaisducap.com* (*moderate*). Peaceful B&B rooms and an apartment in a house with a lovely terrace right on the sea, by the Genoese tower. Communal cooking facilities available. *Closed Nov–Mar.*

buy up half of Guyana. Yet the house he built here, in the hamlet of Metino, is relatively modest.

The coastal road continues south in its most beautiful stretch to **Barrettali**, where the landmark is a mini-Pantheon, the elaborate tomb of the Altieri-Calizi family. Below lies the little **Marine de Giottani**, with its hotel and pebble beach. A tall white 16th-century **campanile** (erected in part as a landmark for sailors) signals **Canari** to the south, a collection of 11 hamlets once known as the 'village of a hundred captains'. This was (probably) the *Kanèlatè* cited by Ptolemy, and is known, geologically, for a ferrous rock that naturally crystallizes in perfect little cubes or *piedra quadrata* (they are especially dense in a place called Oreglia). Said to be sovereign against fatigue, it was common for anyone bound on a long walk to tie one to their left leg.

Canari has a intriguing late 12th-century Pisan church, **Santa Maria Assunta** (*usually closed*) in the hamlet of **Pieve**, built, perhaps, on the site of a Roman temple. Made of another local stone, green schist, and still topped with its original lauze roof, it is decorated with several curious bits and bobs – a block showing two primitive figures with upraised hands and a disc (possibly Eve tempting Adam with a very large apple), strange human and animal masks, some around an inscription added in 1455 proclaiming a miracle (wheat growing out of stone), while the lower part is scratched with enigmatic graffiti. On Maundy Thursday, the local confraternity, followed by the parishioners, make a *granitula* procession in front of the church before walking to the convent and church of **St-François**, founded in 1506. This contains the white marble tomb of Vittoria da Gentile (d. 1590), wife of the local lord, shown holding her baby daughter and a model of her husband's castle.

The next part of the coast is the brutally ugly bit, stripped and scarred by the grey rejects of an **asbestos mine**, active from 1932 to 1965 and once proud to be the biggest in Europe. Now everyone is just waiting for the hideous rusting fixtures to go away.

Albo/Albu has a large pebble beach at its marina, but the main attraction in these parts is **Nonza**, teetering on a narrow 350ft/100m cliff over the sea with a ruined castle and beyond it, towards the tip and 540ft/165m over the sea, a green schist **tower** built by Pasquale Paoli on the site of the castle. Its stunning setting deserves a good story, and it has one: in 1768 1,200 French soldiers, come to take what France had just purchased from Genoa, besieged Nonza, the last unconquered bit of Cap Corse. The Corsicans were led by a determined captain, old Jacques Casella, who walked on crutches. As the siege continued, the Corsican garrison, thinking it was a hopeless cause, all deserted, but Casella defended the tower on his own, ingeniously fixing wires that enabled him to shoot muskets in a regular line of fire, all the while shouting commands as if his men were still there. Eventually the French, frustrated, called for a truce. Casella demanded that his garrison be allowed to leave the tower, freely and with all honours, and when the French accepted they were shocked to see a single old man on crutches emerge, proud and fierce. If you visit the tower – in summer it hosts photographic exhibitions – peep down through the hole at the entrance, the **Trou du Diable**, with a vertiginous view straight down to the beach.

St Julie is one of the patron saints of Corsica, and Nonza is celebrated as the site of her martyrdom. The most common story has it that she was a beautiful Christian slave of a Carthaginian whose ship had stopped in Nonza's little harbour. Coveted by the local Roman ruler, she refused to have anything to do with him or participate in his pagan rites, and was raped and nailed to a cross, while her tormentors chopped off her breasts. The *Acts of the Saints*, however, say that her tormentors were Arian Christian Vandals; others say that she really died in Carthage in the 3rd century, and that her relics were brought to Nonza when the Vandals exiled the bishops of North Africa to Corsica. Whatever the case, Julie was always revered in Nonza, and still is today, with a pilgrimage on 22 May. A chapel was built on the site of her martyrdom, and, where her breasts were thrown on a rock, two miraculous springs began to flow. In 734 the Saracens destroyed her chapel, but not before Julie's relics were taken to safety in Italy, eventually ending up in Brescia. In the 16th century a new pink church of **Ste-Julie** was dedicated to her in Nonza and has a painting of her crucifixion (*key at the mairie*). Her never-failing spring, the **Fontaine des Mamelles**, is halfway down a path of 260 steps to Nonza's **beach**. Tinted an unnatural black by asbestos waste, it's reputedly safe, although you aren't supposed to swim here, but if you have the puff it's worth going all the way down for the view up to the tower (while there, you can add your message to the others in white stones). When you finally make it back up the hill, have a drink under the plane trees in the delightful village square, next to a fountain with a statue of Paoli.

Between Bastia and St-Florent: Patrimonio and the Col de Teghime

Six km south of Nonza, there's a sandy beach at the **Marine de Farinole**, before the D80 delves inland to the Bastia–St-Florent crossroads. Just up the Bastia road, rolling limestone hills covered with vines announce **Patrimonio/Patrimoniu**, the heart of the oldest AOC wine-growing area on Corsica (since 1968), reputed for its reds, muscats and white vermentinos – considered some of the finest in the Mediterranean, partly due (or so they say) to the wind that keeps the soil dry. Overlooking sheltered St-Florent bay, Patrimonio enjoys a sunny microclimate in an amphitheatre that Paoli dubbed the Conca d'Oro (the 'golden shell') after the fertile Conca d'Oro just east of Palermo. For the **wine estates** to visit, *see* box, p.224.

Patrimonio's photogenic church on a hill, **St-Martin**, dates from the 16th century and has little to see within, although a shelter below the church houses the striking statue-menhir **U Nativu** (*c.* 800 BC), 7ft 6 in/2.25m tall and the only one on Corsica made of limestone rather than granite. Discovered in 1964 by a farmer at a place called Nativu, it has prominent ears, eyebrows, chin and an open mouth as if it were howling; an inverted T on the chest could be a stylized breastbone.

The D81 continues 17km to Bastia, hairpinning up to the **Col de Teghime** (1,758ft/536m), a pass with commanding views over Cap Corse's mountain spine, with the

Festivals

Les Nuits de la Guitare: mid-July, in Patrimonio. For information, call t 04 95 37 12 15, or see *www.festival-guitare-patrimonio.com*. The festival has its origins thanks to the amazing talent of two self-taught brothers, Gilbert et René Dominici, who played in every style and made Patrimonio something of a Mecca for guitarists who came to jam with them. The festival, founded in 1990, continues the tradition, attracting some of the best-known guitarists from around the world.

Where to Stay and Eat

Patrimonio ✉ 20253

Casa Albina, Mulinu Suttanu (4km from St-Florent), t 04 95 37 00 57, *www.casa-albina-corsica.com* (*moderate*). Two charming B&B rooms sleeping up to 4 and three *gîtes* sleeping up to 6 in old stone farm buildings, beautifully renovated and hidden in the hills in a large with shady terraces and a large garden. No credit cards. *Open all year.*

Château Calvello, t 04 95 37 01 15 (*moderate*). Beautifully furnished, spacious B&B rooms in a 16th-century feudal castle amid the vines, with the sea only five minutes away.

U Casone, t 04 95 37 14 46 (*moderate–inexpensive*). In the village, a big grey family house with well-kept, large if fairly basic rooms, overlooking the sea or countryside. Breakfast on the terrace. *Closed Nov–Mar.*

U Lustincone, Rte du Cap, t 04 95 37 15 28, *www.u-lustincone.com* (*inexpensive*). Near the village, 9 comfortable rooms in a quiet position, with a restaurant specializing in seafood and meats grilled on vine cuttings; *menu corse* €19.

Le Bartavin, t 04 95 39 07 66. *Maquis*-scented mountain cuisine in the village centre; try the charcuterie and succulent *pavé de bœuf*. Around €18. Open non-stop, even in winter.

Osteria San Martinu, t 04 95 37 11 93. By the post office, a summer restaurant with a big barbecue, specializing in steaks grilled over vine shoots, cannelloni and bottles of Patrimonio wine. *Menu €20. Closed Oct–Mar, and Wed.*

Patrimonio

The **Domaine Oregna de Gaffory**, at Morta Majo (*t 04 95 37 45 00; open 9–12 and 2–7, weekends 9.30–12 and 3.30–6.30*), puts on summer exhibitions by local artists. Also try **Clos di Bernardi**, in Patrimonio (*t 04 95 37 12 22, open daily 9–12 and 2–7*); **Domaine Gentile**, at Olzo (*t 04 95 37 01 54; open Mon–Sat 8–11.30 and 2–6.30*), and **Domaine Pastricciola**, on the road to St-Florent (*t 04 95 37 18 31; open 9–7*); for **Domaine Antoine Arena**, in Patrimonio (*t 04 95 37 08 27*), you'll need to book. Patrimonio's **Cave des Vignerons** (*t 04 95 37 00 92*) offers tastings of wines from several vineyards.

Tyrrhenian Sea and Golfe de St-Florent on either side, although if the *libeccio* is huffing and puffing it can be hard just to stand upright. Come is at sunset to see the east side of the cape go dark while the west glows in the setting sun. A monument on the summit commemorates the Moroccan troops sent over from Algeria to reinforce the Resistance, and who in a crucial bit of fierce fighting in early October 1943 forced the last Germans to withdraw from Bastia.

St-Florent/San Fiorenzu

St-Florent, a favourite port of call for yachts from the Côte d'Azur, is a mythical place for the French, cool, casual and laid-back, the 'St-Tropez of Corsica', a St-Flo to match the continent's St-Trop. Set on a mountain-girded bay at the mouth of the river Aliso, it grew up in the 15th century around a Genoese citadel. When that became too costly to maintain in 1667, the Genoese razed the walls, malaria invaded and the town was almost deserted until the 19th century, although Nelson found it full of potential: 'Give me the Gulf of St-Florent and two frigates, and not a single ship could leave Marseilles or Toulon.' A marina was built in 1971, and ever since yachts have bobbed gently – there is mooring for 800 – while their owners fill the seaside watering holes and play *boules* under the old plane trees in Place des Ports.

For a good view over the hinterland, visit the big round Genoese tower or **Torrione**, which was restored after having taken some hard knocks from Nelson in 1794; in the Second World War the British returned to use it as a secret supply cache for the Resistance. Although the most beautiful beaches are to the west in the Désert des Agriates (*see* pp.229–31), the huge if exposed **Plage de la Roya** stretches under the citadel, or there's the more sheltered **Olzu** and **Tettola** below the Patrimonio road.

Before there was St-Florent, there was the Roman/early medieval town of Cersanum (or Nebium, as it was called after the 9th century), its centre marked by the elegant Pisan Romanesque cathedral of the Nebbio, **Santa Maria Assunta**, signposted 1km from the centre (stop at the tourist office for the key). Built around 1140, on the same model as La Canonica (*see* p.198), it is a basilica much beloved of local sparrows, made of warm limestone, with pilasters and blind arcading and capitals carved with serpents, six-pointed stars, spirals, oriental lions and other creatures in a kind of medieval Art Deco. The interior with its three naves is equally simple and harmonious, and sports more intriguing decoration on the capitals, as well as the body of St Flor.

Getting There and Around

By Bus
Cars Santini, t 04 95 37 02 98, run year-round from Bastia, and in July and August from l'Ile-Rousse and Calvi.

By Car and 4x4
Car hire: Hertz, t 04 95 37 20 52: also **St-Flo 4x4 Locations** (necessary for the Désert des Agriates), Rte de la Plage, t 04 95 37 06 42, www.stflo4x4.com.

Tourist Information

St-Florent, Route du Cap Corse, t 04 95 37 06 04. Open July and Aug daily 8.30–12.30 and 2–7; Sept–June Mon–Fri 9–12 and 2–6.

Sports and Activities

CESM, Plage de la Roya, t 04 95 37 00 61, http://cesm.free.fr. Paris-based sailing and diving club offering lessons, with an emphasis on marine biology; they can arrange accommodation.

Dominique Plaisance, t 04 95 37 07 08, www.dominiqueplaisance.com. Rent a canoe, kayak or boat without a licence to explore the secret niches of the coast by the half-day, day or week. Closed Nov–Mar.

Florentica, t 06 07 96 00 55, www.croisieres-corse-florentica.com. Book a 1-day, 3-day or 7-day cruise in a 6-cabin sailing boat around Corsica.

Altore, Plage de la Roya, t 04 95 37 19 30, www.altore.com. Year-round adventure sports centre, offering hang-gliding, canyoning, kayaking and snowshoe mountain hikes.

Sun Folies, Plage de la Roya, t 06 13 07 39 83, www.sunfolies.com. Watersports of all kinds from water-skiing to fly-fishing, jetskiing and boat hire.

Where to Stay and Eat

St-Florent ✉ 20217
La Maison Rorqual, towards the Désert des Agriates, t 04 95 37 05 37 or t 06 13 02 02 11, www.maison-rorqual.com (luxury). Set in a garden by the sea with an infinity pool and private motor boat for excursions, the five most exquisite and original rooms in the area are set in a former sheepfold; don't miss the website in English.

★★★La Roya t 4 95 37 00 40, www.hoteldelaroya.com (luxury; half-board only in season). Modern, family-run hotel on the beach with rooms arranged around a courtyard, with a pool and lawns; all rooms have balconies, and St-Florent is a 15-minute walk away. Closed Feb.

★★★Tettola, on the beach 1km east of the centre, t 04 95 37 08 53, www.hoteltettola.com (expensive). Airy and pleasant seaside hotel with a pool on the beach and spruce air-conditioned rooms. Closed Nov–Mar.

In the 5th century, the Vandals, who were die-hard Arians in the raging controversy over the true substance of Christ, took as much pleasure out of persecuting orthodox Christians as vice versa, and when the Byzantines took Corsica and sent the Vandals packing to North Africa, the Vandal king Huneric exiled every non-Arian bishop he could find to Corsica. One was Florent, who then served as bishop of Nebium. His relics were taken to Treviso in the early Middle Ages, and in 1770 the Bishop of Nebbio, regretting the lack of local relics, asked the pope if there weren't perhaps some holy bones he could spare. Clement XIV duly sent over a skeleton of a 3rd-century martyr found in Rome's catacombs (one could tell he was a martyr by the accompanying vial of blood); the bishop built up some features in wax, and dressed the body as a Roman soldier, and baptized him 'St-Flor' to fit the name of the town; he now rests in a glass casket by the door. Every three years (2006, 2009, et seq), on Pentecost Monday his relics are taken down to town in a procession. The bishopric of the Nebbio was suppressed in 1790, which put an end to a curious custom: as the bishop also held

★★Thalassa, at Strutta (2km up the Patrimonio road), t 04 95 37 17 17, *www.thalassa-hotel.com* (*expensive*). Well-equipped rooms with satellite TV, pretty pool, and big buffet breakfast. A bit far from town but a short walk (300m) from the beach. Disabled access. *Closed 15 Oct–Mar.*

★★Treperi, 1km out on the Rte de Bastia, t 04 95 37 40 20, *www.hoteltreperi.com* (*expensive–moderate, breakfast incl.*). Big bright rooms in a motel in a pretty garden setting overlooking the bay and vines, equipped with a pool and tennis courts. *Closed mid-Nov–mid-Mar.*

★★★La Dolce Notte, Rte de Bastia, t 04 95 37 06 65, *www.hotel-dolce-notte.com* (*moderate*). Pleasant little Provençal-style hotel by the beach, 500m from the centre; rooms have satellite TV. *Closed Nov–Feb.*

★★Madame Mère, Rte de Bastia, t 04 95 37 40 50, *www.hotel-madame-mere.com* (*moderate*). One of St-Florent's first and biggest hotels, in a quiet setting a few minutes from the beach. Traditional rooms, with views over the sea and mountains. Pool, restaurant, parking.

★★Maxime, Rte de la Cathédrale, t 04 95 37 05 30 (*inexpensive*). Newish family-run hotel just off the Place des Portes, near the river Poggio. Most mod cons, and places to park your car, or small boat, as the case may be.

Le Montana, Rte d'Oletta, t 04 95 37 14 85, *www.auberge-lemontana.com* (*inexpensive; half-board in July and Aug*). A calm-friendly place with a walled pool just 2.5km from St-Florent; well-kept if scantily furnished rooms. Restaurant featuring good home cooking and seasonal Corsican specialities.

Camping La Pinède, 1km from the Plage de la Roya, t 04 95 37 07 26 (*inexpensive*). Spacious and good shade, and a lot less crowded than the beachfront sites. They also have a pool and chalets. *Closed Oct–April.*

Camping Kalliste, Rte de Calvi, t 04 95 37 03 08, *www.camping-kalliste.com* (*inexpensive*). Good campsite on the sands, with large pitches and a restaurant. *Closed Nov–Mar.*

La Rascasse, on the port, t 04 95 37 06 99. Excellent seafood restaurant with a quayside terrace, serving the likes of *velouté de rascasse* and medallions of monkfish with green pepper. *Menu €30. Closed Oct–Mar, and Mon out of season.*

La Gaffe, Port de Plaisance, t 04 95 37 00 12. Great place to find the day's catch, lovingly prepared: sea bass *fricasséed* with vegetables, or lobster in a salad with tropical fruit, or flambéed, or in three sauces. *Menus from €29. Closed Tues, and mid-Nov–Jan.*

Ind'e Lucia, in the old village by the fountain, t 04 95 37 04 15. Popular for its pretty terrace and genuine Corsican *charcuterie* and other classics. Good choice of reasonably priced wines. *Menus from €20.*

La Maison des Pizzas, Places des Portes, t 04 95 37 08 52. One of the most popular places in town, offering 20 different pizzas (including the Corsican, with *figatellu*, bacon, pepper and olives), excellent salads and other simple but well-prepared dishes.

the title of count, he was allowed to wear a sword and say Mass with two pistols on the altar.

The Nebbio/U Nebbiu

St-Florent is the capital of the Nebbio, the 'land of mists'; you can see where it got its name in the winter, when foggy tendrils grip the undulating green hills and quiet *villages perchés*. The hills form a basin – Paoli's aforementioned Conca d'Oro – of pastures, olive groves and vineyards around the Aliso river, while behind them rises a nearly impenetrable wall of mountains. You can make a loop through the Nebbio from St-Florent, by way of Patrimonio and the Col de Teghime (*see* p.224), then head south to Oletta on the D82.

A colourful pile of houses, **Oletta** has always been a centre of Corsican nationalism. It was the birthplace of the Abbé Saliceti, nicknamed Peverino ('little pepper'), who quarrelled with Paoli and went to Rome, where he became doctor to Pius VI; but, when the French invaded Corsica, Paoli forgot their differences and invited him back to fight. Oletta was then held by the French, and Peverino and a band of local Paolists plotted to sneak in through a cellar and take the town, only the French got wind of the scheme and were waiting. Peverino died of his wounds in the fight, but his comrades were condemned to a gruesome death. After being brutally tortured, they were forced to carry heavy torches in flaming wax as they knelt to ask forgiveness for their conspiracy; then they were taken to the square, where their arms, legs, thighs and kidneys were broken and torn before they were stretched on a wheel raised on a post to the sky and left to die. Their bodies were exposed along the road to Bastia, and all their property was confiscated. The 18th-century church of **St-André**, witness to all this (such horrific, disproportionate punishments were not uncommon under the *ancien régime*, right up to the Revolution), is the replacement for a 12th-century Pisan church, of which a primitive relief of the *Creation* stuck in the façade is all that

Sports and Activities

Ranch Corsican Buffalo, Murato, t 06 62 32 46 00. Western-style cowboy riding lessons and treks.

Where to Stay and Eat

Oletta ✉ 20232

A Maggina, t 04 95 39 01 01. Family-run restaurant, serving the specialities of Bastia (sautéed veal, sardines stuffed with *brocciu*, shoulder of lamb rolled in mint, etc.) with a lovely terrace and view (*menus from €21*). They also have three **rooms** (*inexpensive*), with more great views and en suite facilities. *Best to book. Closed Nov–Feb.*

Murato ✉ 20239

Besides its famous church, Murato has two celebrated restaurants where you can spend three or four hours feasting on heaving platters of Corsican delights.

La Ferme de Campo di Monte, below Murato, turn left at the Bar Victor on a winding lane and over the bridge, then follow the sign, t 04 95 37 64 39. Nothing less than the finest *ferme-auberge* in Corsica, in the perfect setting: a 17th-century stone farm with its original wooden fireplace, intimate rooms filled with antiques and a terrace with

gorgeous views over the countryside. Pauline Juillard's soups, *charcuterie*, roast veal or lamb, *beignets au brocciu* in *eau-de-vie*, *pets-de-nonne* (which taste better than they sound) and candied tangerines are made according to her grandmother's recipes. *Menu €40 with as many helpings as you like, plus wine, apéritif and coffee.* No credit cards. *Book well in advance; eves only daily June–Sept, other times Thurs–Sat eves and Sun lunch.*

Le But, Soprano, t 04 95 37 60 92. Not much to look at, but a genuine Corsican institution; like Campo di Monte, there's only one menu (*€36*); sit down and pace yourself to try the many many delicious dishes, wines and liqueurs that appear. *Reservations essential, well in advance. Closed Jan.* On Saturday nights you can boogie some of the excess calories off at the discotheque into the wee hours; see *www.thebut.com* for programmes.

Entertainment and Nightlife

La Conca d'Oro, t 04 95 39 00 46. In Oletta, a real Corsican disco out in the *maquis* next to the ruined Couvent San Francescu. Every night a theme night; the cover charge of €10 includes a drink. *Open summer only.*

remains. It contains a miraculous triptych on wood of the *Virgin between John the Baptist and St Reparata* of 1534, which used to hang in a farmhouse; in 1734, while its mistress was out baking bread, she heard a cry: 'Marie, your child is burning! Save him!' She ran back home and found that a log had fallen from the hearth and the cradle was surrounded by flames. She rescued the baby and fell on her knees before the triptych, and noticed that the Virgin was in tears, which the mother tried to dry with her finger; if you look closely you can see her fingerprint.

Above Oletta, the next village, **Olmeta-di-Tuda**, rises dramatically on the right; further up, the **Col de San Stefano** offers grandiose views over the Golfe de St-Florent and the Conca d'Oro, and a chance to plunge down to the east coast on the D62 by way of a steep, breathtaking schist and serpentine gorge, the **Défilé de Lancône**, high over the Bevinco river.

If you continue south along the D5, however, you'll come to an isolated grassy promontory standing proud against the mountains, topped by the most remarkable Pisan Romanesque church on Corsica, the green serpentine and white limestone **San Michele de Murato** (*c.* 1280), covered in zebra stripes and chequerboard patterns. The proportions are distorted by a bell tower suspended over the porch in the 19th century, but the rest of the church is well preserved, lavishly decorated with sophisticated or naïve reliefs of fantastic animals – snakes, peacocks, sheep – plus planets, stars, a mermaid holding up her forked tail, an awkward Eve already embarrassed by her nakedness as she takes the apple from the serpent's mouth, a man holding a knife and horn, and less churchly symbols – rolls of parchment, cut-off hands, and scissors – believed to represent the law, as in Pisan times the churches doubled as tribunals. The interior is plain in comparison, although it does have a damaged 14th-century fresco of the *Annunciation* (if it's locked, get the key at the *mairie* in Murato).

Murato/Muratu, the most important village of the Nebbio, is another kilometre south. In the **Hôtel de la Monnaie**, a big stone building under the D5, Paoli minted Corsica's first coins, stamped with the Moor's head (each church on the island donated some of its gold and silver treasure to be melted down for the effort). Another of Murato's claims to fame is that the father of Raoul Leoni, elected president of Venezuela in 1963, came from here.

From Murato, the D162 cuts back north to the main road of the Nebbio, the D62. This marks the route of an ancient transhumance trail which edges below the wall of Monte Asto. A picturesque clutch of fortified houses make up **Rapale**, a place that has been inhabited since the cows came home. A large quantity of ashes from Neolithic animal sacrifices, along with pots and inscriptions, were found in a nearby cave, and a path leads up 1.5km northeast of the village to the **Castellari**, a Neolithic fort in cut stone. The ruins of a Roman town identified as Lurinum are 2km north, up another path; while another leads up 2km south through the chestnuts to the ruined green and white chapel of **San Cesareo**, its apse cornice carved with a two-headed dragon.

In **Pieve**, the next village, three schist and granite **statue-menhirs**, similar in style to the one found in Patrimonio (*see* p.223), have been placed in a line-up in front of the church; the tallest stands over 10ft/3m high. At **Sorio**, the next village, the transhumance path continues over Monte Asto to the Ostriconi, through the Bocca di Tenda; the road meanwhile veers north through a canyon to **Santo-Pietro-di-Tenda**, with two Baroque churches joined together by a single bell tower; the one church that's open, **St-Jean l'Evangéliste**, has the most elaborate and elegant Baroque interior in the Nebbio, with a lovely wooden altarpiece. A kilometre north of the village and to the right below the D62 are the ruins of the once impressive late 12th-century Pisan church of **San Pietro**, with more imaginative reliefs, including five enigmatic human faces. A second trail leaves from here over Monte Asto to Urtaca (*see* below), while the road winds down to the D81 towards St-Florent (16km) and the Désert des Agriates.

The Désert des Agriates and the Ostriconi

The Désert des Agriates

West of St-Florent, a 40km bulge in the coast is known as the Désert des Agriates – desert not in the sand-duney sense of the Arabian or Gobi, but in the 'desert island' sense of deserted – a weird, wild, sometimes desolate, sometimes strikingly beautiful rocky expanse of boulders and *maquis*, especially lovely in spring when the *maquis* is in bloom. Yet it wasn't always so. *Agriates* means 'cultivated plots', and from the 16th to the mid-19th century it was famous as 'the breadbasket of Genoa'. The villagers from St-Florent and Cap Corse who planted the wheat would store it in stone huts called *pagliaghji*, which still dot the landscape, and either send it to Genoa or trade it with the shepherds whose flocks occupied the Agriates in the winter. Over the centuries a combination of fires, intensive farming, overgrazing and erosion took their toll, the *maquis* invaded and it was abandoned to the wind and sun, to the wild boar and ambling cows; of the former breadbasket, nary a crumb remains.

In the 1970s, proposals to turn the Agriates into a nuclear test site or an enormous Costa Smeralda-type holiday playground prompted the Conservatoire du Littoral to buy up the coast, and by 1989 the Désert des Agriates was the longest stretch of protected shoreline on the Mediterranean. Which means no paved roads, except for the D81 which passes through **Casta**, the one village in the desert.

Superb beaches are the Agriates' main attraction. The two closest to St-Florent are the silky white sand **Plage de Loto** (or Lodo, or Ludo), stretched between two promontories, and the even more lovely mile-long **Plage de Saleccia**, a tropical dream of soft silver sand on an intensely turquoise sea, backed by a fragrant grove of Aleppo pines planted in the 19th century. In July 1943, the submarine *Casabianca* used Saleccia as the drop-off point for 13 tonnes of arms and munitions for the Resistance, floated ashore over two nights in rubber dinghies. Hollywood later found the beach the perfect location for the D-Day landing scenes of *The Longest Day* (1960), daily transporting John Wayne, Robert Mitchum and a cast of 3,000 here from St-Florent, along with tons of Hollywood bombs – occasionally walkers still find dud shells.

Getting Around

Besides the D81 from St-Florent to l'Ile-Rousse, the only roads in the Désert des Agriates are rutted tracks accessible only by a 4x4 (*see* St-Florent), horse, or by foot.

Two boats, **Le Popeye**, **t** 04 95 37 19 07, and **U Saleccia**, **t** 04 95 36 90 78, each make several return trips daily from St-Florent from June to September for the Plage de Loto and Plage de Saleccia. Places are limited, so be sure to get there at least an hour before departures.

Or hire a horse at the **Relais Equestre des Agriates** in Casta, **t** 04 95 37 17 83.

Tourist Information

Casta: **Syndicat Mixte des Agriates**, **t** 04 95 37 09 86. *Open Mon–Fri 9–4, summer 8–7.*
Lama: **Maison du Pays d'Ostriconi**, **t** 04 95 48 23 90, *www.ot-lama.com. Open Mon–Fri 9–12 and 2–5, July and Aug also Sat and Sun 2–5.* They manage a long list of holiday rentals.

Where to Stay and Eat

Casta ✉ 20217

Le Relais de Saleccia, **t** 04 95 37 14 60, *www. hotel-corse-saleccia.com* (*inexpensive*). A friendly little hotel – the only one, in fact, in the Désert des Agriates, and the closest to the beaches, with big views, a good restaurant, several donkeys and mountain bikes to hire to get down to the Plage de Saleccia. *Closed Oct–Mar.*
Camping U Paradisu, Plage de Saleccia, **t** 04 93 37 82 51 (*inexpensive*). The most isolated campsite on Corsica, shaded with eucalyptus, with a bar and restaurant, and stone bungalows to rent. *Open June–Sept.*
Les Paillers de Ghignu, Plage de Ghignu (for reservations ring the Syndicat Mixte, *see* above; *inexpensive*). Accessible by foot, 4x4 down a rough 12 km track or boat. A dozen restored *pagliaghji*, each sleeping 4 to 6

(bring your own sleeping bag and food). *€10 per person. Closed Nov–Mar.*

Palasca ✉ 20226

Domaine d'Ostriconi, N 197, **t** 04 95 60 53 29, *www.domaine-ostriconi.com* (*expensive*). Near the beach, four beautiful *chambres d'hôtes* furnished with antiques in two 17th-century Genoese houses, with an excellent restaurant, **L'Agriate**, offering dining under the ogival vaults or in the shade of the lemons and eucalyptus. The food – the wine, grains, vegetables and fruit – comes from the owner's farm, which stretches from the Désert des Agriates to the Ostriconi delta: try the kid baked in the oven with honey from the maquis and tender courgette flowers. *Book. Menus €27–37.*
Village de l'Ostriconi, **t** 04 95 60 10 05, *www. village-ostriconi.com* (*inexpensive*). Bungalows, campsite, caravans, restaurant and bar, pool and tennis less than a kilometre from the Plage de Periola, one of Corsica's most striking beaches. *Closed Nov–Easter.*
Ferme-auberge de Petra Monetta, by the intersection of the D81 and N197, **t** 04 95 60 24 88. The name means 'money stone' and there's lots of speculation where this 18th-century posthouse midway between Bastia and Calvi got its name. It fills up with hungry customers who come for the copious terrines, and tender kid and lamb raised on the family farm (*€22 menu*). They also have four simple **rooms** with bathrooms down the hall (*inexpensive*). *Closed Nov–Mar.*

Lama ✉ 20218

Campu Latinu, on the heights of Lama, **t** 04 95 48 22 83, *www.campulatinu.fr*. Lovely restaurant under the oak trees, integrated amid the former agricultural terraces, with fine sunset views by candlelight (*menu corse €27*); they also have five modern **apartments** sleeping 2–6; there's an attractive pool and tennis court in the village. *Closed Oct–April; restaurant closed Mon.*

The Agriates also has a dolmen called the **Casa di l'Urcu** (the Ogre's House) and a nearby cist tomb, in the middle of nowhere (get instructions at Casta's Syndicat Mixte). The story goes that the ogre who lived there was none too popular, and when the locals came to hunt him down he offered to give them the recipe for making *brocciu* in exchange for his life. The locals listened, got the recipe, and then killed him.

The Sentier du Littoral

The only other ways of reaching the beautiful coves and beaches to the west are by private boat (you can hire one at St-Florent) or on foot along the **Sentier du Littoral**. This magificent and mostly level path blazed along the tormented coast by customs officials is ideally done in three days, staying at the campsite at Saleccia and the *gîte d'étape* at Ghignu. The two 1/25 000 IGN maps, 4348OT and 4249OT (available at the newsagent's in St-Florent), are handy if you do the whole thing. Leaving the main path can be treacherous. Because of the danger of brush fires, avoid setting out on windy days; a hat, sun cream and plenty of water are *de rigueur*: like a true desert, the Agriates gets very hot in the summer. And it's wise to arrange for a car to meet you at the Plage d'Ostriconi.

The first stage from St-Florent's Plage de la Roya to **Saleccia** takes about 5½ hours through some of Corsica's most spectacular coastal scenery. The main man-made landmark you come to on the way is the mighty but sundered 16th-century Genoese **Tour Mortella**, which left such a lasting impression on the British (*see* p.218). From here it's another hour to **Lodo** beach; if you start early you can have a swim and catch a boat back to St-Florent. The next stage of the walk, after Saleccia, takes only three hours by way of the delightful white sandy beaches of **Malfalco** and **Ghignu**, the latter with a fresh water source thanks to Corsica's shortest river. The third stage, which takes about six hours, is the hardest, from Ghignu to the striking **Plage de l'Ostriconi** in the Anse de Peraiola. Here juniper-clad dunes under the bare hills offer a stark contrast to the winding lush mouth of the river Ostriconi; if you don't want to walk, you can get there by way of a brief stretch of old corniche road off the N1197 (where people park). From here it's 14km to l'Ile-Rousse.

The Ostriconi

The silent valley of the Ostriconi separates the Nebbio from the Balagne to the west. It now gets a few more cars than before, thanks to the new, relatively straight N1197, 'La Balanina', which provides a fast route not only into the centre of Corsica, but between Calvi and l'Ile-Rousse and Bastia (even if it's much further as the crow flies). Formerly much of this valley was planted with olives; if the Agriates were the breadbox of Genoa, the Ostriconi along with the Balagne was the oil jug, until August 1971, when some 80,000 trees in the valley went up in flames in an afternoon, accelerating a decline that began with the First World War. The now starkly empty lower valley has become the favourite home on the range for Corsica's cows, who like nothing better than standing in the middle of the road, so take care.

In recent years, a local association, the Terrasses de l'Ostriconi, has undertaken the restoration of houses in the valley's villages, at **Urtaca**, but especially at **Lama**, both of which are set high above La Balanina on rocky spurs. Lama, where the restoration work has won prizes, was once home to some of Corsica's richest oil men, and many of their proud 18th-century Italianate houses are now *gîtes*. A former stable in Lama houses an exhibition of old photos of Corsica, and in the first week of August Lama has run, since 1994, a popular film festival devoted to rural themes. The Maison du Pays has maps of local paths: one from Lama to Urtaca in two hours, and another from Lama along an age-old tranhumance path to the summit of **Monte Asto/Astu** (six hours return), offering stunning views over the Balagne and Cap Corse.

The Balagne and the West Coast

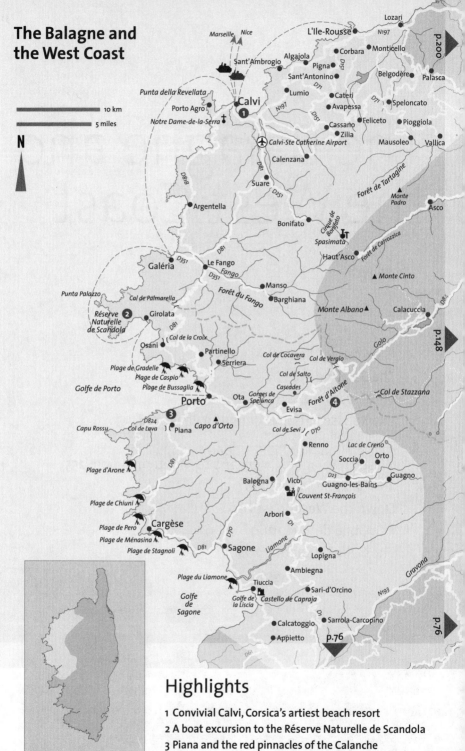

The Balagne and the West Coast

10 km
5 miles

N

Highlights

1 Convivial Calvi, Corsica's artiest beach resort
2 A boat excursion to the Réserve Naturelle de Scandola
3 Piana and the red pinnacles of the Calanche
4 The towering Laricio pines of the Forêt d'Aitone

This is Corsica's northwest quarter, where you could spend your whole holiday and never be bored. Two major resorts, l'Ile-Rousse and Calvi, take advantage of the gorgeous sandy beaches on the north coast, while just inland lies one of the most fertile, beautiful and civilized parts of the island, the Balagne. The name goes back so far that etymologists derive it from the Phoenician city of Balanea, the home of the coast's very first colonists, or possibly from the Greek *balanos*, or acorn, in reference to the acorn-shape of the olive, a tree that the Greeks introduced. Olive oil made the Balagne wealthy, and its charming necklace of sunny *villages perchés* each has a Baroque church to prove it. But head down the west coast, to the Golfe de Porto, and you're in another world, one as savage and elemental as the third day of Creation. Three of Corsica's greatest natural wonders – the Scandola headland, the Calanche de Piana and the Spelunca Gorge – are concentrated here, while just above tower the Laricio pines of Corsica's oldest forest. The Golfe de Sagone further south can seem like an anticlimax in comparison, but it has sandy beaches, Corsica's 'Greek town', and the classic walk up to the Lac de Creno.

L'Ile-Rousse/L'Isula Rossa

The Romans, who knew a good spot when they found one, were the first to settle in this snug port. A cluster of red porphyry islets supplied the name, Rubico Rocega (Red Rocks), and it was busy – in 1989 a wreck full of large storage jars, or *dolia*, from the time of Caligula was discovered off shore. Then barbarians and corsairs took over and Rubico Rocega dwindled – until 1758 when, frustrated by the Genoese entrenched at Calvi, Paoli announced that he would plant 'a gallows to hang Calvi', the gallows, of course, being a new port to export olive oil from the Balagne, which was firmly on his side. Early on, the new town was called Paolina in his honour; when the French took the island, they tried to call it Vaux after their victorious general. But the compelling landmark of red rocks won, and it's been l'Ile-Rousse ever since. Thanks to its three white sand beaches and long season, it is also one of busiest resorts on the island.

Ironically, Paoli's specifically Corsican town is one of the least Corsican today, a place where French, German and Italian tourists outnumber the natives. Like many founding fathers, Paoli chose a grid plan for his town – an alien geometry on an island with very few straight lines. All streets feed into **Place Paoli**, a big and handsome square which, with its huge plane trees and palms, its bust of Paoli and endless afternoon *boules* games and its Greek temple of a covered **market** (open mornings), looks as if it floated here from the French Riviera. Even the coat of arms of l'Ile-Rousse, as of 1814, bears a *fleur-de-lis*, thanks to 50 years of Bonapartist mayors. Yet the streets of the old port, with their peeling stucco and flapping laundry, have a patina of charm, especially in the evening when the restaurants and cafés fill up. Up the causeway, past the waltz of the ferries at the Port de Commerce, the rocky red **Ile de la Pietra** is especially striking at sunset, when it blushes deeply; you can walk up to the lighthouse here for a great view back over town.

Just a mile north of town, along the N197 to Bastia, there's a new **Parc de Saleccia** (*t 04 95 36 88 83; open July–Aug Mon and Wed–Fri 9.30–12.30 and 9.30–8, Sat and Sun*

Getting Around

By Sea
You can get from l'Ile-Rousse to Marseille, Toulon or Nice on **SNCM** and **CMN**; for both, **t** 04 95 60 09 56. **Corsica Ferries**, Agence Tramar, **t** 04 95 60 08 56, go to Savona.

By Train
The **SNCF** runs at least twice daily year-round to Calvi and Ponte Leccia, where you can change for Bastia, Corte or Ajaccio; for information, call **t** 04 95 60 00 50. The same tracks are also used in summer by the much more frequent **Tramway de Balagne** which runs between l'Ile-Rousse and Calvi, stopping at the best beaches or by request.

By Bus
L'Ile-Rousse is linked by **Les Beaux Voyages**, **t** 04 95 65 15 02, weekday mornings year-round, to Calvi, Lumio, Algajola, Ponte Leccia and Bastia. In July and Aug, **Autocars Santini**, **t** 04 95 37 02 98, go twice a day to St-Florent.

By Car and Bike
Car hire: Avis, Col de Fogata (west of the centre), **t** 04 95 60 26 79; **Hertz**, Hotel Isula Rossa, Rte du Port, **t** 04 95 60 01 32.
Taxis: t 04 95 60 26 79 or **t** 06 14 38 33 28.

Tourist Information

L'Ile-Rousse: Place Paoli, **t** 04 95 60 04 35, www.ot-ile-rousse.fr. Open July and Aug Mon–Sat 9–8, Sun 10–12 and 5–7; Sept–June Mon–Fri 9–12 and 3–6. They distribute strada di l'artigiani guides to the Balagne and will book excursions into the Réserve de Scandola.

Sports and Activities

Diving: Book lessons or dives through **Beluga Diving**, Route de Corbara, **t** 04 95 60 17 36, www.beluga-diving.com, or the **Ecole de Plongée L'Ile Rousse**, **t** 04 95 60 36 85, specializing in teaching children from 8 up.
Boat hire: Nautismarine, Av Paul Doumer, **t** 04 95 60 00 73, www.nautimarine.com and **Balagne Rent Boat**, 6 Rue Notre Dame, **t** 06 16 81 53 94, www.balagne-rent-boat.com.
Riding: Centre Equestre d'Arbo Valley, 5km from l'Ile-Rousse in Monticello on the Rte de Bastia, **t** 06 16 72 53 12. By the hour or day.
Cinema: Col de Fogata (N197 towards Calvi), **t** 04 95 60 00 93. Indoor and outdoor, the latter with showings nightly in July and Aug.

Where to Stay and Eat

L'Ile-Rousse ✉ **20220**
***Santa Maria, Route du Port, **t** 04 95 60 13 49, www.hotelsantamaria.com (expensive). Perfectly positioned near the road to the islets, colourful, comfortable air-conditioned rooms with balconies, with a pool in a pretty little garden with sea views.
***La Pietra, Chemin du Phare, **t** 04 95 63 02 30, www.hotel-lapietra.com (expensive). Isolated on the causeway to the big red island; luminous, simply furnished air-conditioned rooms with balconies over the sea, Jacuzzi, and restaurant. Closed mid-Nov–Mar.
Napoléon Bonaparte, 3 Place Paoli, **t** 04 95 60 06 09, hotel.napoleon@wanadoo.fr (expensive). Pink and in a pretty garden by the sea, the first luxury hotel on Corsica, converted in the 1930s from an 18th-century palazzo and home in 1953 to the exiled king of Morocco, Mohammed V, and his son, the late

9.30–8; April–June and Sept–Oct Mon and Wed–Sat 9–12 and 2.30–7, Sun 10–7; closed Tues; adm), a botanical garden in a 17-acre park on a grand old patrician estate created after a fire in 1974 ravaged the ancient olive groves – a few of the old trees survive, with another 100 varieties of olives from around the world. There's a Mediterranean garden, maquis walk, romantic path, olive grove walk, oleander valley, etc.

Around L'Ile-Rousse
The beaches are all jam-packed in July and August, but you may find a bit more room to spread your towel if you head 3km east to a dirt track leading down to the

Hassan II. Although it's gone to seed and been stripped of its three stars, some of the original rooms are fun, if overpriced for what you get; ask to see. *Closed Nov–Mar.*

L'Amiral, Bd Charles Marie Savelli, t 04 95 60 28 05, *www.hotel-amiral.com* (*moderate*). Pleasant shipshape beach hotel, with a nautical theme throughout. *Closed Oct–Feb.*

Splendid, Rue du Comte-François, t 04 95 60 00 24, *www.le-splendid-hotel.com* (*moderate*). Built in the 1930s and well maintained, in an ideal location by the sea, with a garden and small pool. *Closed Nov–Mar.*

Le Grillon, 10 Av Paul Doumer, t 04 95 60 00 49 (*inexpensive*). Simple, 1970s décor but adequate family hotel near the beach with a good restaurant (*menus at €12 and €16*), serving classic French dishes. *Half-board available. Closed Nov–Feb.*

Camping Les Oliviers, Rte de Bastia, t 04 95 60 19 92 (*inexpensive*). A kilometre east of l'Ile-Rousse, 800m from the beach, with decent shade, snack bar and bungalows sleeping four. *Closed Nov–Mar.*

Stella Mare, by the beach along Promenade La Marinella, t 04 95 60 05 76. The excellent chef prepares seafood and meat dishes with savvy and flair: try the *magret de canard* with honey flavoured with asphodel. *Around €28. Open April–Sept daily, rest of year Fri lunch–Sun lunch.*

Le Laetitia, Rte du Port, t 04 95 60 01 90. More good seafood: try the *l'aziminu* (Corsican bouillabaisse). *Around €30.*

Chez Paco, 18 Rue Napoléon, t 04 95 60 03 76. On the ground floor of an old house, with a Spanish touch; start off with a margarita and launch into anything from paella to *bouillabaisse*. Big portions, friendly service, and often open late. *Menus from €17. Closed Jan, and Sun eve in winter.*

A Siesta, by the beach at La Marinella, t 04 95 60 28 74. The place for enormous salads or pizza for lunch, and good seafood while watching the sunset, prepared with an unusual Corsican touch (monkfish with a light chestnut sauce). *Menu at €20.*

Lozari-par-Belgodère ✉ 20226

Auberge A Tesa, t 04 95 60 09 55, (*inexpensive*). 3km south of Lozari beach, on the road to the Barrage de Codole, a modern *auberge* with seven en suite rooms, although it's Marylène Santucci's scrumptious Corsican cooking made from farm ingredients and the herb garden that attracts folks from far and wide. One menu only (*€39*), but massive and all-inclusive from *apéritif* to *eau-de-vie*, with five courses and wine in between. No credit cards. *Bookings essential, but also good value half-board rates. Closed Nov.*

Monticello ✉ 20220

A Pasturella, in the centre, t 04 95 60 05 65, *www.a-pasturella.com* (*moderate*). A charming little inn with a dozen pretty rooms, many with balconies and views. Also one of the best restaurants in the Balagne, featuring the day's catch or *cuisine du terroir*, with the likes of home-made terrine with chestnuts and fig liqueur and lamb with thyme butter (*menus €24 weekdays, €40 on weekends*). *Closed mid-Nov–mid-Dec; restaurant closed Sun eve from Dec to Mar.*

Santa-Reparata-di-Balagna ✉ 20220

Ferme-auberge L'Aghjalle, Rte de Muro, Toro hamlet, t 04 95 60 31 77. Traditional Corsican specialities on a sheep and olive farm immersed in the countryside – *soupe corse*, *sauté de veau*, cheese-stuffed onions and more. *Menus €22. Book. Closed Oct–Mar.*

Plage de Rindara, a big duney beach with a summer snack bar. Further afield, 8km east of l'Ile-Rousse, there's the **Plage de Lozari**, a large white crescent of sand, but again, it's no secret.

The villages in the amphitheatre immediately behind l'Ile-Rousse make for a circuit of about an hour by car. Just 3km from the coast up the D63, **Monticello** is a charming old village in the olive groves, with little cobbled lanes, a pretty *place*, and views down the coast. The ruined Castel d'Ortica above town was built in the 13th century by the Giudice di Cinarca and there are those who think Monticello might have been the birthplace of mystery-man Columbus' mysterious mother, Susanna Fontanarossa, as (unlike Genoa) it does have a place called Fontanarossa, and a ruined chapel dedicated to St Suzanne, who is an unusual saint in these parts.

Drive under the arch in the centre of Monticello to take the scenic 'balcony road' (the D263, although note that it's sometimes closed for part of the day) to **Santa-Reparata-di-Balagna**, an old terraced village built around a Pisan church of the 11th century, its apse still intact, its Baroque front from 1590. St Reparata was the first patron saint of Florence, said to have been introduced to the city in 823 by the same Count Bonifacio who founded the town on the southern tip of Corsica.

The Balagne

The Balagne, the 'Garden of Corsica', extends from the Désert des Agriates in a great swath across the northwest of the island to Galéria on the west coast, but the heart of the region is the hinterland between l'Ile-Rousse and Calvi. Settled by the Romans and Christianized early on, this fertile belt was always a place apart on this pastoral island – some say it was here in Neolithic times that agriculture made its first inroads on Corsica. The depredations of barbarians, Saracens and Barbary pirates forced the

The Olives of the Balagne

In 1898, the Balagne was lovingly described by the traveller Ardouin-Dumazet in his *Voyage en Corse*:

Thanks to the care given to the olive groves, this ample and luminous valley, open between superb mountains, gives an impression of richness like no other place on earth. The two cantons of the Balagne fertile, Belgodère and Muro, are the most beautiful in all Corsica. The sinuous corniche road traced over the flanks of the hills, from Belgodère to Muro and Cateri, is a perpetual enchantment.

The olive trees (the mayor of Belgodère told Ardouin-Dumazet that there were roughly 36 million of them in 1898) were the gold of the Balagne, and treated accordingly; for instance, the trees were never shaken, but during the harvest each morning the women and children would go out and gather the olives from the ground. Three varieties were grown: Saraceni, Genovesi and Sabinacci, the most cultivated and most resistant; the name is said to be, in some mysterious Corsican way, a diminutive of Savelli, a local family endowed with the same traits. Each house had its own press, and in good years each tree produced 63kg of olives. But even when Ardouin-Dumazet visited, the Balagne's olive oil industry was in crisis, challenged by rival oils that sold for half the price, and the fact that the Corsicans, unlike the Tunisians and Provençals, had no industrial presses. Now, just over a hundred years after Ardouin-Dumazet's visit, the landscapes of the Balagne are still beautiful, and, although neglect and fire have destroyed most of the groves, trees up to 800 years old can still be seen here and there. As the demand for quality olive oil grows, farmers are finding it worthwhile to make the liquid gold flow again: a regional irrigation scheme set up in 1971, the olive oil fair in Montemaggiore and the building of new presses are all signs that the great silvery groves are on their way back.

inhabitants into villages where houses huddled together on belvederes high over the sea, skirted by terraces producing olives, wine, oranges, wheat, figs and honey.

The Genoese, who focused on defending the coast at Calvi, were content to leave the feudal lords of the Balagne in peace as long as they didn't interfere in Genoa's plans. Many of these local *signori* were related to the Cinarchesi, and they became among the richest and most influential men on the island. Besides tending their gardens, they built churches, so many over the centuries (especially during the 17th-century religious revival) that the region was called 'holy Balagne'; today their bell towers charmingly punctuate the landscape like a series of mild exclamation marks.

Their feudal ways remained almost unchanged until the 20th century when, as in the Castagniccia, the population of the Balagne plummeted – huge losses in the First World War were followed by the diaspora towards an easier way of life on the coast, on the continent, in the colonies. The national postwar efforts of SOMIVAC and the resettlement of Algerian refugees did little to replant the Garden of Corsica; fires, too, have taken their toll, and the *maquis* has been encroaching a little further each year. What has, however, made a difference are local initiatives, and many of these have been begun or concentrated in Pigna. One result is *A Strada di i Sensi* ('The Road of the Authentic'), set up to make it easy to visit the workshops of craftspeople (*artigiani*), vineyards and local food producers; a booklet with addresses, phone numbers, and opening hours is available from the tourist offices at l'Ile-Rousse or Calvi.

Corbara/Curbara

Piled on the side of the hill, Corbara, 'the key to the Balagne', has a vaguely Moorish air with its hedges of India figs. One focal point is its dusty pink Baroque collegiate church of 1685, the **Annonciation** (*t 04 95 63 06 50; open Mon–Sat 9.30–12 and 3–4; adm to the treasury*). One of the most elaborate in Corsica, the church is known for its triumphant Carrara marble altar and communion table made in Tuscany in the 1750s. But also note the 17th-century plaque with the arms (two lions holding a rose) and story of the village's founder, the Roman knight Guido de Savelli, a follower of the legendary Ugo Colonna. In 816, as a reward for defeating the Saracens, the pope made him Count of the Balagne and he built the **Castello de Guido** on the rock below the village. The nearby citadel, **U Forte**, was begun 400 years later by a descendant. Both were dismantled and ruined by rivals of the Savelli, the castello by a lieutenant of Paoli, U Forte by the Genoese, who thought they should be king of the hill.

One curiosity in Corbara is the so-called **Casa di Turchi**, two doors down from the church, with the Franceschini coat of arms over the door. In 1754, the couple living there were abducted by pirates and taken to Tunis, where several of their children were born, including a daughter, Marthe Franceschini. Mother and Marthe were allowed to return to Corsica, only their ship was captured by pirates again, and they were sold as slaves in Marrakech. The beautiful Marthe, renamed Daouia Lalla (or Davia, as the Corsicans called her), was chosen for the sultan's harem, and eventually became his favourite wife, the queen of Morocco. At her request he allowed her family to return to Corbara; she stayed with her husband and died of plague in 1799. The story has acquired fairytale embellishments over the years, including a magic

The Balagne

5 km
2.5 miles

N

Marseille Nice

L'Ile-Rousse   Lozari
              Monticello
        Corbara   N197
Algajola   Santa Reparata-di-Balagna
Sant'Ambrogio   Pigna   Palasca   N197
        Sant'Antonino   Belgodère
          Aregno
      Lumio   Cateri
Punta della Revellata   Spelon cato
      Calvi   Avapessa   Costa
              Muro Feliceto   Pioggiola
Porto Agro   Montegrosso Cassano Olmi-Cappella
Notre-Dame-de-la-Serra Montemaggiore Zilia   Mausoleo   Vallica
                  Giussani
Calvi-Ste-Catherine   Tartagine
Airport   + Sta Restituta
        Calenzana
                Forêt de Tartagine   ▲ Monte Padro
                          Asco
    Suare

  Argentella
              Cirque de Bonifato
        Bonifato
              Spasimata   Forêt de Caïrozzica
              Haut'Asco
Galéria   Le Fango
        Fango   ▲ Monte Cinto

    Manso Barghiana

amulet marked with the Hand of Fatima. Also in Place de l'Eglise, don't miss the
Musée de Corbara (*t 04 95 60 06 65; usually open 3–6; free*), a delightful collection of
old Corsican things – books, pistols, music boxes, postcards, a mechanical piano –
accumulated over 20 years by a retired baker, Guy Savelli.

Two km south of Corbara, rows of funerary chapels announce **Notre-Dame-de-Latio**
(Madone de Lazio), a charming little white church framed by a pair of palms that shel-
ters a painting of the Virgin famous for having once saved Corbara from a tornado.
A bas relief under the windows of a snake under a star symbolizes the Virgin, the
Morning Star, dominating the serpent of Genesis. Opposite, a narrow road ascends
the rocky slope of Monte Sant'Angelo to the **Couvent de Corbara**, surrounded by olive
groves, with stunning views down to the sea. Built in 1430 as an orphanage by a
Savelli, it was converted into a Franciscan convent, and after damage during the
Revolution the Dominicans restored it in 1857 as a retreat; the church houses several
Savelli tombs. A mule track from the convent leads steeply in about an hour to the
summit of **Monte Sant'Angelo** (1,837ft/56om), looking over the Balagne.

Pigna, the Musical Town

Beautiful old Pigna, a *village perché*, is the guiding light of the Balagne's current
renaissance. Founded in 816 by another follower of Ugo Colonna, it declined so much
after the First World War that most of its pale golden stone houses were ruined and
abandoned by 1964, when local sculptor and musician Toni Casalonga and a handful
of other residents began a co-operative association, La Corsicada, to restore the
houses and start craft apprenticeships. In 1978, La Corsicada founded the influential

Festivals

Festivoce, t 04 95 61 73 13, *www.festivoce.casa-musicale.org*. Pigna's Casa Musicale sponsors a year-round series of concerts (Corsican polyphonies and *chjam' è responde* competitions, medieval music and more) in the Auditorium; dine with the musicians at the Casa Musicale by booking 24hrs in advance.

Where to Stay and Eat

Pigna ✉ 20200

U Palazzu, t 04 95 47 32 78, *www.hotel-palazzu.com* (*luxury–expensive*). In the village, with stunning views towards the sea, a big stone mansion of 1701 that once belonged to the powerful Franceschini family, beautifully restored as *chambres d'hôtes* with 2 suites and 3 bedrooms, bathrooms with old-fashioned tubs and a fine restaurant on the garden terrace (*menu €50, lunch plates at around €25; booking essential; closed Mon*).

La Casa Musicale, t 04 95 61 77 31, *www.casa-musicale.org*. A wonderful 350-year-old house dedicated to gourmet food and traditional music. The restaurant occupies the olive press and has a panoramic terrace with gorgeous sunset views; the menu features the finest *charcuterie*, roast langoustines from Cap Corse, fish grilled on olive wood, lovely vegetables and more (*around €40*). Also *moderate* en suite **rooms** (each named after a traditional Corsican voice). *Restaurant closed Mon in winter; book in summer.*

U Voce di U Comune ('Voices of the Community') to support the traditional music and culture of Corsica. Government grants were given to young artists to live and work in Pigna and other nearby villages. A year-round series of concerts, the Festivoce, fill Pigna's new (2002) auditorium, and the summer concerts, now known as Estivoce, attract singers from all over; you can meet them at the Casa Musicale (*see* box, above).

Today, beyond Pigna's pay car park (many Balagne villages are pedestrian-only), the village is all fixed up, the houses peering over one another's shoulders to catch the famous sunset views. There are interesting **shops** to visit: Scat'a Musica, offering hand-painted music boxes playing traditional Corsican lullabies, some in the shapes of animals or Christian and Moorish figures from the *Moresca* dance (*see* p.30); Ugo Casalonga, a lutanist making traditional *cetere* (Corsican guitars) and harpsichords (*www.arte-di-a-musica.com*); the Casa di l'Artigiani selling crafts from across Balagne; and the Casa Savelli selling gastronomic delights and wines. If it's open, stop to have a look in Pigna's **church**, to see its restored 18th-century organ.

Aregno and its Pisan Church

The D151 continues to **Aregno**, an old village surrounded by citrus groves producing Corsica's sweetest oranges, which are blessed and distributed here on St Anthony's Day (17 January), then kept until they've dried out for good luck. These days, however, the village is investing in a new crop – almonds; in August it holds an almond fair.

By the cemetery is the Balagne's very best Pisan church, the striking 11th-century **La Trinité e San Giovanni**. Its festive façade of grey, ochre and white blocks wears enigmatic sculptures that resemble gingerbread people: the door is framed by a smiling woman (or local lord, according to some) in a long skirt with hands on hips and a naked man holding what may be law texts on his knees: many Pisan churches – San-Michele-in-Murato is another one – originally doubled as courts of law. Above are four blind arches, their five capitals decorated with a strange naïve bestiary, including a number of bears; further up, a smaller arcade is crowned by one of the oddest figures in Christendom: a naked man pulling a thorn from his foot with a mischievous grin. The locals say he symbolizes the month of March. The sides have other animal motifs, and inside are two well-preserved 15th-century frescoes, of *St Michael* pinning the dragon while weighing souls and *Four Doctors of the Church*.

Cateri and Sant'Antonino

Continuing south, just off the D71, at the crossroads of the Balagne, **Cateri**, 'the doors', is an attractive hill village where the little lanes are lined with orange trees. Below the village there's a pretty multicoloured Pisan chapel, **San Cesariu**, and near the centre is the usual 17th-century Baroque church, this one containing paintings by the so-called 'Master of Muscular Angels' and a copy of Veronese's *Judgement of St Sebastian* (the original has been lost, but this is one of five copies that survive). Just west of Cateri is the turn-off for the **Couvent de Marcassu** (1621), the oldest active Franciscan house on the island, built over the ruins of a 10th-century castle. One friar will take you around the Baroque church and sacristry (*t 04 95 61 70 21; open 9–10.30 and 3–5.30; leave a donation*); others serve as priests in the depopulated villages in the Balagne. It has splendid views, and a few rooms on half-board terms; in June 2005 A Filetta recorded their album *Les Chœurs de Médée* here.

One road goes up from Cateri to the Col di Salvi and Montemaggiore (*see* pp.257–8); another ascends, just north of the Cateri crossroads, to **Sant'Antonino/Sant'Antininu**, the most perched of all the Balagne's *villages perchés*. Founded in the 9th century by the Savelli counts of the Balagne and claiming to be even older than Corbara, Sant' Antonino is a web of narrow, winding vaulted lanes and steps (one carved with an ancient nine-men's morris game), tall granite houses and a pair of Baroque churches,

Festivals

Ile Mouvante, t 04 95 65 16 67, *www. ilemouvante.com*. In Sant'Antonino in late June, a two-week-long culturefest.

Where to Stay and Eat

Cateri ✉ 20225

U San Dume-Chez Léon, in the village, **t** 04 95 61 73 95 (*inexpensive*). In a tranquil setting, 7 en suite rooms in a newish building, some with views down to the sea. Also a good family-style restaurant serving big portions, often with *bouillabaisse* on the menu along with Corsican lamb (*lunch menu €16, dinner €24*). *Open all year, but ring ahead.*

Ferme-auberge Chez Edgar, 2km west on the D71 in Lavatoggio, **t** 04 95 61 70 75. A family farm, with a dining room in an old olive press – *prisuttu, soupe corse, sauté de veau aux figues*, suckling pig (by request), and

more. No credit cards. *Menu €32, no wine. Open Mar–Sept eves only by reservation.*

A Lateria, t 04 95 61 71 44. Former dairy (with a great terrace) and now a shop selling local specialities, famous for *fiadone*, perhaps the best in Corsica. *Closed Oct–May.*

Sant'Antonino ✉ 20200

I Scalini, t 04 95 47 12 92. Follow the signs through the village labyrinth to this old family home transformed into an excellent restaurant spread out between three terraces, decorated with mosaics, ethnic furnishings and ceramics, with lovely views down to the sea; the chef has a large olive grove and prepares light, Mediterranean delicacies. *Lunch plates €12, otherwise budget for some €25 without wine.*

La Taverne Corse, t 04 95 61 70 15. Above the village car park, a perfect terrace to enjoy a filling Corsican meal (*€20*) or just a perfect slice of *fiadone* (cheesecake) with a cool glass of muscat. *Closed Nov–Mar.*

all crammed on a rocky pedestal that usually turns an un-Corsican yellow by June. As Corsica's 'Most Beautiful Village', according to the plaques, it also gets many coach parties. Be sure to try Olivier Antonini's unique lemon wine at the **Maison du Citron** (**t** 04 95 61 76 83) down at the bottom of the village, as well as other local products.

Southern Balagne: Cateri to Belgodère

Southeast of Cateri, the D71 follows the rim of the Bassin du Regino eastwards, high over the Regino river and the artificial Lac de Codole. The first village, tiny **Avapessa**, too small to admit cars, is surrounded by olives, and is one of the few places to keep up its original oil press. Two other presses have been started in **Muro**, the next village. Named for the 'Moors', Muro was once a prosperous place, with some 2,000 inhabitants in 1850, where craftsmen worked in the arcaded lanes and three churches served the population, including the ruined 11th-century **San Giovanni**, one of the oldest in the Balagne. The most recent, the big yellow 18th-century **Annonciation**, has a fancy façade arranged in three levels and gives the all-star Baroque treatment to a *Crucifix des Miracles*; if you look at Christ from one side he seems to be in pain, and if you look from the other he seems resigned. The miracle occurred when the Crucifix cried out during Mass in 1730, 'Come and see my martyrdom,' and the face, shining with light, was covered with blood. Although credited with many miracles since, the Crucifix had no power to stop the vault from collapsing in 1778, killing 60 women.

To the east, in a lush setting on the banks of the Regino, **Feliceto/Felicetu** is famous for its pure spring water, its local glassmaker, and AOC Calvi wine, which you can taste in the main square (Domaine Renucci, *t 04 95 61 71 08; open May–Oct*). Along with its other traditions, the Balagne is undergoing a religious revival: in 1990, Feliceto revived its 17th-century confraternity of St Roch, patron saint of flocks and horsemen, whose handsome chapel stands next to the Baroque church. For a brisk hike, you can climb up in an hour to the *falcunaghja*, 'falcon's nest', high over town, where a 19th-century mayor built a house to keep tabs on his constituents (especially the female ones) through a spyglass; bandits later found it a perfect hideout.

Picturesque **Speloncato/Spiluncatu** clings to a Swiss cheese of a rock that gave the village its name, 'cavey'. The most famous hole is the **Pietra Tafonata**, the 'pierced rock', 2km away but visible from just to the left of the hotel in Place de la Libération. This is a 26ft/8m tunnel, though it looks like a pinhole from the square; twice a year (*8 April and 8 Sept*) at 6pm people gather to see Speloncato's private laser show: the sun goes down, then about 10 seconds later reappears in the hole, filling the *place* with a spotlight. As with the *taffoni*, no one is quite sure how much of the Pietra Tafonata is natural, or if any of it was excavated by human hands; archaeologists found Neolithic bits and bobs on the floor in the tunnel floor. The Romanesque church of **San Michele**, with a portal dated 1509, was built over another cave that sheltered women and children in times of danger. Pius IX's chief of police, Cardinal Savelli, was a native of Speloncato; ruling with an iron fist in an iron glove, he earned the whispered nickname *il cane corso*, 'the Corsican dog'. His summer house is now a hotel.

Costa, to the east, has one of the prettiest Baroque churches and campaniles in the area, and an interior decorated with early 19th-century *trompe l'œil* paintings. Next

Festivals

La Montagne des Orgues, t 04 95 61 34 85,
*elizabethpardon@aol.com, http://members.
tripod.com/orgues_corses*. From April to Oct,
the Association Saladini de Speloncato
offers 'pastoral and musical' tours on Tues
and Thurs of the Baroque churches in the
small villages of the Balagne, with an
organist who tickles the ivories of historic
instruments. They also offer tours in the
Vallée de l'Asco and Castagniccia. Book at
least two days in advance; €18 per person.

Where to Stay and Eat

Feliceto ☑ **20225**
★★Mare e Monti, t 04 95 63 02 00 (*moderate*).
One of Jacques Cousteau's favourites: at the
foot of Monte Grossu, a handsome 19th-
century house built by a local Don Juan, with
lovely individual rooms; ask to see the

private frescoed chapel. The owner's son
makes wine and olive oil. Breakfast served
by the pool. No restaurant. *Closed Nov–Mar.*

Speloncato ☑ **20226**
★★A Spelunca, t 04 95 61 50 38, *hotel.a.
spelunca@wanadoo.fr* (*inexpensive*). The
former summer residence of Cardinal
Savelli, now a charming hotel; big comfortable rooms and 19th-century public rooms
around a splendid stair. Bring earplugs for
the church bells. *Closed Nov–Mar.*

Belgodère ☑ **20226**
★★Niobel, t 04 95 61 34 00, *www.niobel.com*
(*moderate*). Just outside the village centre, a
very pleasant Logis de France in a modern
building with stupendous views from the
terrace or restaurant; try pork with chestnuts or lamb roasted with rosemary (*menus
from €17 for lunch, €23 for dinner*). *Closed Jan
and Sun exc in July and Aug.*

east is **Belgodère/Belgudè**, 'fair pleasure', piled over a green valley, although fires have
decimated most of its olive groves. There are grand views from the little square and
even grander ones from the ruined Malaspina castle up the steps. The big Baroque
church here is **St-Thomas** (*key at the Café de la Paix*), which contains a fine painting of
the *Virgin with SS Peter and Marcel* (1595), attributed to two painters from Bastia.
Below Belgodère, the sheer size of the old family mausoleums above the N197 hint at
the village's former wealth; the locals call it the town's 'fifth quarter'.

The Giussani/Ghjunsani Valley

The wildest and most remote part of the Balagne *fertile*, the Giussani runs along the
valley of the Tartagine river in between Corsica's northernmost giants, **Monte Grosso**
(6,358ft/1,938m) and **Monte Padro** (7,851ft/2,393m). Two lofty passes are the only way
into its four lovely villages, where the 170 people who have stayed behind live in a
majestic, arcadian setting of chestnut and oak forests and towering peaks.

The easiest way to see the Giussani is to slip in one mountain pass and out the
other; to visit from east to west starting from Belgodère, head south on the N197 for
6km, then turn right on the D963, the valley's one road. **Vallica**, the first village, enjoys
a stupendous position, looking across to Monte Padro. A nice day's walk from here is
the five-hour trail down to the Tartagine river, with its Genoese bridge, water mill and
swimming holes on the way to Olmi-Cappella. The bridge is believed to have a Roman
base; although the Romans usually shunned the interior of the island (unless slaugh-
tering the Corsicans), they came this way in search of timber to build their galleys.

Olmi-Cappella is the pretty little capital of the Giussani, surrounded by chestnuts,
green pastures, dolmens and Neolithic stone circles. It has a charming 17th-century

Baroque church, **St-Nicolas**, with a little organ of 1808 (*Mme Colombani, the keyholder, lives in Place d'Olmi*). The Battaglini building in the centre is the permanent seat of the **ARIA** (Association des Rencontres Internationales Artistiques) run by actor Robin Renucci, a native of Pioggiola; the association sponsors year-round theatrical workshops and in summer puts on plays in the villages. Stop in Olmi's bar to try the authentic, delicious *canistrelli* biscuits made by Ange-Matheiu Casanova.

Tiny old **Mausoleo/Musuleu**, divided into two by a granite wedge, stands at the entrance to the stunning **Melaja Gorge**, where a twisting road leads to the Maison Forestière in the **Forêts de Tartagine et de Melaja**, with their lofty maritime and even loftier Laricio pines – the name 'Tartagine', in fact, is said to derive from the Carthaginians, who first came to exploit the tall trees for masts. A number of walks start from the Maison Forestière: from a short stroll under the trees, through a three-hour walk up an ancient transhumance path to the beautiful Bocca di l'Ondella, to a challenging hike for experienced hikers to join up with the GR20.

Pioggiola/Pioggiula, the fourth of the Giussani's villages, is also one of the highest in Corsica (3,280ft/1,000m). At other times you may well be serenaded by the bells: Pioggiola's parish church Santa Maria Assunta, with 14, has more than any other on Corsica, and just before 15 August bell-ringers from across Corsica come here for a big mountain ding-a-ling. The church has a big Baroque façade and, inside, a valuable organ of 1844 by local master craftsman Anton Pietro Saladini. A winding road from Pioggiola to Speloncato goes over the **Bocca di a Battaglia** (3,605ft/1,099m) and has the most extraordinary views of all, taking in nearly all the Balagne.

Sports and Activities

Balagn'ane: La Campanella, Olmi-Cappella, t 04 95 61 80 88, *www.rando-ane-corse.com*. Hiking the old-fashioned way, with donkeys carrying your bags (or children). There are a number of routes on offer.

Rencontres Internationales de Théâtre de Corse: Olmi-Cappella, t 04 95 61 91 47, *www.ariacorse.org*. Theatre festival, July and Aug.

Tourist Information

Olmi-Cappella: t 04 95 61 03 02. *Open summer daily 9–6; winter Mon–Fri 9–12 and 2–5.*

Where to Stay and Eat

Olmi-Cappella ✉ 20259
Auberge La Tornadia, 2km west of the village, t 04 95 61 90 93. Under the spreading chestnut trees, genuine Corsican country cooking adapted to modern taste, no holds barred, in a charming rustic inn, complete with rusty farm tools. In the autumn, make a pilgrimage here for the wild mushrooms; any time of the year, the cheese will knock your socks off. *Menu gastronomique, with nine courses, €31. Closed mid-Nov–mid-Mar.*

Pioggiola ✉ 20259
A Tramula, Pioggiola, t 04 95 61 93 54 (*moderate*). Little hotel in a dry stone building constructed by the owner, offering 8 roooms, many with views over the mountains and forests. There's a bar where you can snack on *charcuterie* and cheese, and plans for a little theatre nearby. No credit cards.

Auberge Aghjola, Pioggiola, t 04 95 61 90 48 (*moderate, half-board in July and Aug*). Authentic little mountain hotel with a pool. The restaurant does flavoursome mountain cuisine (*menu €25*).

A Merendella, Bocca di a Battaglia (D63), t 04 95 46 24 28. Simple chalet serving good snacks, simple lunches, grilled meats and crêpes up at the pass. *Closed Dec–Easter; in winter open weekends only.*

L'Ile-Rousse to Calvi: Along the Coast

West of l'Ile-Rousse, the coast is dotted with beaches, holiday developments and private marinas, and in summer the 'Balagne tramway' between l'Ile-Rousse and Calvi stops at them on request. The main resort, **Algajola**, one of six Genoese fortresses that defended the island, is a compact place clustered about the castle of the Genoese lieutenant governor, but the feather in its cap is a mile-long crescent of

Getting Around

Algajola is a stop on the Calvi–l'Ile Rousse *petit train de Balagne*, with up to 9 trains a day in season; you can hail it like a bus if you're on an outlying beach, and buy tickets on board.

Tourist Information

Algajola: Next to the station, t 04 95 60 70 30.

Shopping

L'Astrastella, Lumio, t 04 95 60 62 94. Products made with the essences of the *maquis*. *Open summer Mon–Sat 2–7.*

Where to Stay and Eat

Algajola ✉ 20220

**L'Ondine, 7 Rue A-Marina, t 04 95 60 70 02, *www.hotel-londine.com (expensive; half-board)*. Cushy rooms by the beach, and amenities including a small pool and water-sports. Also one of the best restaurants here, serving Corsican classics. *Closed Nov–Mar.*

**Le Beau Rivage, t 04 95 60 73 99, *www. hotel-beau-rivage.com (expensive)*. Right on the beach, 38 air-conditioned rooms with lovely views; the restaurant has huge bay windows and trendy seafood (*menus from €26; half-board obligatory in season*). *Closed mid-Oct–mid-April.*

**Stella Mare, t 04 95 60 71 18 (*moderate*). Hotel-restaurant near the train station, with 18 refurbished rooms in a garden, over-looking the sea. *Closed mid-Oct–mid-April.*

L'Esquinade, t 04 95 60 70 19 (*moderate*). Simple, tidy en suite rooms by the entrance to the citadel. *Closed mid-Oct–April.*

**Hôtel de La Plage, t 04 95 60 72 12 (*inexpensive*). Opened in 1914 and last renovated about half a century ago, a winsome hotel oozing old-fashioned *pension* atmosphere. Right on the beach, spacious rooms en suite and a restaurant. *Book. Closed Oct–April.*

U Castellu, just behind the castle, t 04 95 60 78 75. In an old cellar or out on the terrace: delicious fresh seafood flavoured with herbs from the *maquis*, a big salad, or a *€21 menu corse. Closed Oct–Mar.*

Lumio ✉ 20260

Le Rocher, Punta di Spano t 04 95 68 74, *www. lerocherdelumio.com (very expensive)*. In a beautiful setting on the beach amid the granite boulders, with views across to Calvi: an excellent gourmet restaurant, serving a seafood and land-food menu (*around €65*) and delightful *chambres d'hôtes* in rich Mediterranean colours; moorings available if you arrive by sea. *B&B available all year; restaurant closed mid-Oct–mid-April.*

***Chez Charles, on the main road, t 04 95 60 61 71, *www.hotel-chezcharles.com (very expensive in Aug, otherwise moderate)*. Stylish pale salmon hotel with a lovely pool, overlooking the sea. The restaurant specializes in sunny, fragrant Mediterranean cuisine, each dish as pretty as a picture, prepared by master chef Olivier Lozac'h; try the *flanc de rouget et risotto en minestrone à la ricotta. Menus from €24 (lunch) to €44. Closed mid-Nov–mid-Mar.*

Camping Panoramique, Rte de Lavatoggio, 2km from Lumio, t 04 95 60 73 13, *www. le-panoramic.com (inexpensive)*. Tranquil site with a pool, games, mobile homes to rent and views over the sea, popular with fami-lies. *Closed mid-Sept–May.*

Le Pain de Sucre, Plage de Santa-Restituta, t 04 95 60 79 45. Excellent, laid-back restau-rant by a small cove (signposted at the bottom of Lumio's hill), specializing in seafood pasta dishes and grilled swordfish (*around €35*). *Closed 15 Oct–15 April.*

golden sand, **Aregno-Plage**. Algajola is believed to be the successor of Phoenician Argha, and in the Middle Ages was ruled by four overweening families whose members, strutting about in their cloaks, were famous for huffing, 'I am one of the four of Algajola!' when passers-by failed to greet them with sufficient respect – the origin of the Corsican expression for the overly proud: '*Pare dei quattro dell'Algajola*', 'He seems like one of the four of Algajola'. In the 1570s, the bishop of Corsica, St Alexander Sauli, spent several years here while spreading the Good Word in the Balagne. At one point, he tried to break up a fight that had erupted in the church (no doubt between the four families) and was socked in the jaw for his efforts.

The Algajolais reckoned that punching out a saint is what brought down divine vengeance in 1643, when 800 Barbary pirates landed and wrecked everything in town. The next year the Genoese built the walls of the citadel, but some 100 years later Paoli founded l'Ile-Rousse and took away much of its shipping business; in the 1790s, Nelson stormed it as a warm-up to the siege of Calvi. Even the '**Paperweight**', a column of granite porphyry, lying in a quarry 2km east of Algajola just off the N197, came from another bit of bad luck: other pillars, such as Paris's Vendôme column, departed smoothly from the quarry, but this 57ft, 300-ton monster, cut in 1837 to support a statue of Napoleon in Ajaccio, was simply too heavy to move.

Further west lies **Sant'Ambrogio**, a little port dotted with pretty coves. Hills of sunlit vineyards and flower gardens surround **Lumio/Lumiu**, the next village west and home town of actress and Marianne-model Laetitia Casta. Pull over to see the mid-11th-century Pisan church of **Santi Pietro e Paolo** (signposted just south of town). Made of peach-coloured stone, it has two grinning bug-eyed lions guarding the door, an apse decorated with circles, lozenges and an onion, and pilasters with stylized palm frond capitals; some believe the stone came from a temple of Apollo, the god of light, and hence the town's name. From the centre of Lumio, an easy path leads in about 45 minutes to the abandoned church and houses of **Occi**. The history of this village is simple: one day the wells dried up, so everyone left.

Calvi

You don't have to look far to see why Calvi has been on the jet-setters' map ever since the Duchess of Windsor wandered here in 1935, followed by the honeymooning Rainier and Grace of Monaco, and Elizabeth Taylor and Richard Burton. The closest Corsican port to the French Riviera, the honey-coloured citadel on its mighty rock forms a stunning backdrop to the attractive town spilling down to a lively palm-fringed port, before petering out in a long crescent of sand that any Riviera town would die for. The snowy peaks hovering on the horizon and strutting members of the élite 2nd Parachute Regiment of the Foreign Legion offer reminders that the rest of the world isn't as warm and cosy, but Calvi doesn't care, and takes on the summer with a near permanent festive atmosphere – helped along by women from all over the world, drawn by the mystique and tattooed muscles of the town's 21st-century Beaux Gestes.

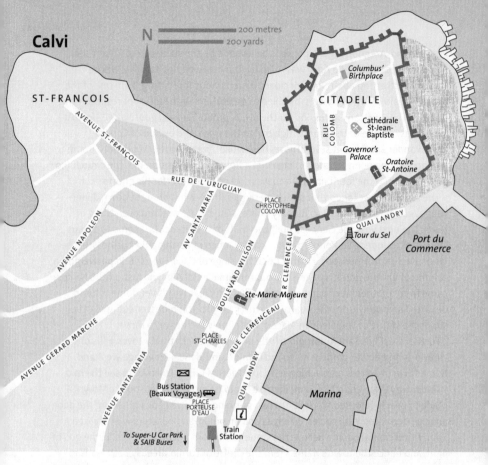

Calvi

N 200 metres / 200 yards

ST-FRANÇOIS

CITADELLE

Columbus' Birthplace

Cathédrale St-Jean-Baptiste

RUE COLOMB

Governor's Palace

Oratoire St-Antoine

AVENUE ST-FRANÇOIS

RUE DE L'URUGUAY

AV SANTA MARIA

AVENUE NAPOLEON

PLACE CHRISTOPHE COLOMB

QUAI LANDRY

Tour du Sel

Port du Commerce

BOULEVARD WILSON

R CLEMENCEAU

Ste-Marie-Majeure

AVENUE GERARD MARCHE

PLACE ST-CHARLES

RUE CLEMENCEAU

QUAI LANDRY

Marina

AVENUE SANTA MARIA

Bus Station (Beaux Voyages)

PLACE PORTEUSE D'EAU

Train Station

To Super-U Car Park & SAIB Buses

History

A busy port in Roman times, Calvi's name derives from the bald (*calvus*) rock that would later provide a base for the citadel. Deserted during the barbarian invasions, it slowly grew back into a small fishing village under the Pisans, before destiny took charge in 1268: during a quarrel between Corsica's warlords, enemies of the Giudice di Cinarca led by Giovaninello de Loreto built a citadel here. The Genoese, already installed at Bonifacio and allied with the bosses of Cap Corse, leapt at the chance to gain a foothold here as well, and granted them a full range of trading privileges. Fourteen years later, after crushing the Pisans at Meloria, Genoa made sure of Calvi's loyalty by settling many of her own people there.

Although Bastia was the Genoese capital, Calvi was their real stronghold in northern Corsica. Although the citadel surrendered to the king of Aragon in 1420 and allowed a garrison to enter, it massacred them as soon as the Aragonese ran into trouble at Bonifacio (*see* p.125). In 1555, the Franco-Turkish allies tried twice to take it, but the first time the Genoese bribed the Turks to fail, and the second time the city was saved when a miraculous crucifix, the *Christ Noir*, was shown to the attackers. Henceforth known as *Civitas Calvis Semper Fidelis*, Calvi remained faithful to Genoa even when Genoa was on the skids, defying Paoli's attempts to take the citadel.

Getting Around

By Air

The Aéroport Ste-Catherine, t 04 95 65 88 88, www.calvi.aeroport.fr, 7km south of town, gets weekly charters from the UK and daily flights on Corse Méditerranée (t 04 95 65 88 60) and Air France (t 04 95 65 88 60) from France. Taxis from the airport are around €18, but note that the airport has no ATM machine.

By Boat

Ferries to Nice and Marseille on **SNCM**, Quai Landry, t 04 95 65 17 77 or t 04 95 65 01 38; their NGVs take about 3 hours. Offices open two hours before sailings. Also slower (5hrs) **Corsica Ferries** to Nice, t 04 95 65 43 21.

By Train

Calvi is linked to Bastia and Ajaccio twice a day, changing at the Ponte Leccia junction, but it's also linked in summer to l'Ile-Rousse and the beaches in between by the more frequent **Tramway de la Balagne**. Call t 04 95 32 80 60.

By Bus

Les Beaux Voyages, Place Porteuse d'Eau, t 04 95 65 11 35, have at least one early-morning bus daily except Sun to Bastia by way of Lumio, Algajola and l'Ile-Rousse. From May to Oct they run direct shuttle buses to l'Ile-Rousse every couple of hours; in July to early Sept they also have five to six buses a week to Galéria, and two buses a day to Calenzana. From mid-May–mid-Oct, there's one **SAIB** bus a day to Porto, t 04 95 22 41 99, departing from the Super U car park to the south of town.

By Car, Taxi and Bike

Car hire: **Avis**, Port de Plaisance, t 04 95 65 06 74, airport t 04 95 65 88 38; **Ada**, airport, t 04 95 60 59 96; **Hertz**, 2 Rue Joffre, t 04 95 65 06 64, airport t 04 95 65 06 64; **Budget**, Av de la République, t 04 95 30 05 05. Or rent a 4x4, Porsche or other fancy car from **Loc'Ago**, Port de Plaisance, t 04 95 47 30 92.

Taxis: t 04 95 65 03 10 or t 04 95 65 30 36.
Bike/motorbike hire: **Loc' Motos**, Av Christophe Colomb, t 04 95 47 31 30, www.calvimoto.com; **Garage d'Angeli**, Place Bel Ombra, t 04 95 65 02 13, garage.dangeli@wanadoo.fr.

Tourist Information

Calvi: Port de Plaisance, t 04 95 65 16 67, www.tourisme.fr/calvi or www.balagne-corsica.com. Open June–Sept daily 9–1 and 2.30–7; Oct–May Mon–Fri 9–12 and 2–6.30. They hire out headsets in English that narrate self-guided tours of the citadel; you may also be able to latch on to one of their tours to get into the Oratoire St-Antoine. They also sell a booklet with maps of six walks around Calvi.

Festivals

Calvi, in its campaign to become Corsica's culture capital, has a full calendar of events.,
Good Friday: Procession of the confraternities, who wind in and out in a granitula spiral.
30 April: The Foreign Legion don dress uniforms to celebrate **Camerone Day**, when in 1863 60 legionnaires held off 2,000 Mexican troops long enough to save the convoy before they were all massacred.
Late May: The **Festival des 3 Cultures**, http://3cultures.free.fr, celebrates France's regions – Corsican plus two from the mainland.
2 June: Traditional celebration for St Erasme.
Last half June: the **Festival du Jazz**, www.calvi-jazz-festival.com, brings in class performers, followed in July by **Calvi on the Rocks**, the island's biggest rock festival, attracting young people from across France.
Mid-June–end Aug: The **Rencontres d'Art Contemporain** is Corsica's only salon of contemporary art.
14 Aug: a huge son-et-lumière and fireworks show called the **Eterna Citadella**.
2 weeks in mid-Sept: The excellent **Rencontres de Chants Polyphoniques** devotes itself to a cappella singing from around the world.

Paoli's revenge came in 1794, when his British allies came to the rescue to dislodge the French who had taken over. Nelson, not wanting to attack the steeply walled citadel full on, sailed right past – then rounded the headland out of sight of Calvi and landed his fleet one by one at little Porto Agro. Everything, including the ships' guns,

Late Oct–early Nov: the colourful **Festival du vent**, *www.lefestvalduvent.com*, celebrates the wind, from high-tech gizmos to kites.

Shopping

The **Marché Couvert**, the ex-Halle aux Poissons, turns into a market of *produits corses* on summer mornings.
Dolce e Savore, Boulevard Wilson, t 04 95 62 78 75. Corsica's finest foods and wines.
A Funderia, Av Christophe Colomb. Foundry making knives, art, *bijoux*, etc.
Atelier di Mammò, Rue Millie, t 04 95 60 59 47. Dolls from around the world.

Sports and Activities

Sea Excursions
Colombo Line, Quai Landry, t 04 95 65 03 40, *www.colombo-line.com* (book at least a day in advance). Trips to the Réserve Naturelle de Scandola and Girolata, and as far as Ajaccio's Iles Sanguinaires.
Locat' Loisirs, t 04 95 60 29 11, *www.locat-loisir.com*. Day-long catamaran trips from Calvi, l'Ile-Rousse and Galéria to Scandola.

Boat Hire
Calvi Marine, t 04 95 65 01 12, *www.calvi-marine.com*. Hires out catamarans taking 6–12 people, with week-long packages.
Calvi Nautique Club, on the beach by the Port de Plaisance, t 04 95 65 10 65, *www.calvinc.org*, hires out sailboats and windsurfs.
Calvi Ski Nautique Club, Plage de Blockos, t 04 95 65 37 54. For waterskiing, wake boards, kayaks, windsurfs or parascending.
Krischarter, t 06 07 24 70 59, *www.krischarter.com*, hires out sailboats.
Tra Mare e Monti, t 04 95 65 21 26, *www.tramare-monti.com*. Zodiacs, motorboats (with or without a licence), scooters and quads, plus offers sailing excursions at Calvi, Galéria and Sant'Ambrogio.

Diving
Very popular in Calvi, whose depths feature an American B-17 bomber that crashed in 1944 just off the citadel as well as the fish-rich waters off Punta della Revellata.
Ecole de Plongée Internationale, t 06 15 51 66 10, *http://perso.wanadoo.fr/epicalvi/plongee*.
Club Plongée Castille, t 04 95 65 14 05, *www.plongeecastille.com*.
Calvi Plongée, t 04 95 65 33 67, *http://plongee citadelle.free.fr*.

Riding
A Cavallu, N197 (near the turn-off for the airport), t 04 95 65 22 22, *http://acavallu.online.fr*. Lessons, excursions, and splashing gallops into the sea. *Open year-round.*

Other
Jungle Jim: A Scimia Calvese, Pinede, t 06 83 39 69 06. Play Tarzan, dangling and walking along aerial walkways with a safety belt. Under 14s must be accompanied by an adult and measure 1.4m (4ft 7in). *Open June–Oct.*

Where to Stay

Calvi ✉ 20260
****La Villa**, Chemin de Notre-Dame-de-la-Serra, t 04 95 65 10 10, *www.hotel-lavilla.com* (*luxury*). Part of the prestigious Relais & Châteaux group, in a garden overlooking the bay, with 34 luminous rooms in an updated version of a Roman villa, where the *dolce vita* reigns under the personal direction of the owner. There are three pools, tennis, fitness centre, hammam, sailing, four-wheel-drive excursions into the mountain villages of the Balagne, and boat excursions to Girolata. It also has **L'Alivu**, one of Corsica's top restaurants presided over by award-winning chef Christophe Bacquié, who concocts light but sensuous Mediterranean cuisine, with an Italian touch; emphasis on seafood and fresh vegetables and heavenly desserts (*menu €70*). Closed Nov–Mar.

had to be unloaded and hauled up the steep rocky slopes to the Col Notre-Dame-de-la-Serra, high over Calvi. The summer heat and malaria took a heavy toll on both sides as 51 days of incessant bombardment were required to reduce the citadel; Nelson lost the sight in his right eye when it was struck by a piece of shrapnel from a shot fired by

****Relais La Signoria**, Rte de la Forêt de Bonifatu, t 04 95 65 93 00, *www.hotel-la-signoria.com* (*luxury*). A 10-minute drive from Calvi, charming and peaceful 18th-century mansion in the middle of a vast park planted with olives, palms and eucalyptus and equipped with a pool, hammam, Jacuzzi and tennis courts. Rooms, furnished with antiques or reproductions, have views over the mountains. The chef in the atmospheric restaurant, t 04 95 65 93 15, makes lovely use of Corsican seafood as well as veal, prepared with vegetables and *girolle* mushrooms in a mytle sauce (*menus €60–75*). *Restaurant open evenings only; restaurant and hotel closed Nov–Mar.*

***Regina**, Av Santa Maria, t 04 95 65 24 23, *www.reginahotelcalvi.com* (*very expensive*). New hotel in the lower town, with a sauna and pool and views of the citadel or mountains; a 5-minute walk to the beach.

***La Caravelle**, Av Christophe Colomb, t 04 95 65 95 50, *www.hotel-la-caravelle.com* (*expensive*). Perfect family hotel close to Marco Plage, a short stroll from the centre; all rooms have terraces with views overlooking a garden or sea; satellite TV, and a restaurant. *Closed Nov–Mar.*

***Hostellerie l'Abbaye**, Route de Santore, t 04 95 65 04 27, *www.hostellerie-abbaye.com* (*expensive*). Classy hotel with sound-proofed air-conditioned rooms, 100m from the beach and town, in the walls of a 16th-century abbey. *Closed mid-Oct–Easter.*

***Le Magnolia**, Rue Alsace Lorraine, t 04 95 65 19 16, *www.hotel-le-magnolia.com* (*expensive*). Near Place du Marché, a charming hotel in a white 19th-century mansion, half buried in an enormous magnolia, with 12 old-fashioned rooms, personalized service and an enchanting garden restaurant, far from the madding crowd; fresh, light and fragrant sea and land food; for dessert, try the roast pear with acacia honey and grilled almonds (*menus €17 and €36*). *Closed Jan and Feb.*

***St Erasme**, t 04 95 65 04 50, *www.hotel-st-erasme.com* (*expensive*). Stylish and comfortable hotel with a lovely pool, a 10-minute walk to town, 5 minutes to the beach. They also have a couple of apartments in a villa, rented by the week.

***Balanéa**, 6 Rue Clemenceau, t 04 95 65 94 94, *www.hotel-balanea.com* (*expensive–moderate*). Friendly hotel in a great location overlooking the marina, with bright sound-proofed air-conditioned rooms. Prices of rooms vary according to the view.

***Grand Hôtel**, 3 Bd Wilson, t 04 95 65 09 74, *www.grand-hotel-calvi.com* (*moderate*). Vintage grand hotel from a century ago, near the port, with many original furnishings, although most of the former genteelly tattered rooms have had a recent facelift and now feature air-conditioning. Fine views over Calvi from the wonderful breakfast room. *Closed Nov–Mar.*

Cyrnéa, N197, 2km from Calvi on the route de Bastia, t 04 95 65 03 35, *www.hotelcyrnea.com* (*moderate*). Welcoming modern hotel with a pretty pool and en suite rooms.

***Hotel Résidence Les Aloes**, Les Aloes, t 04 95 65 01 46, *www.hotel-les-aloes.com* (*moderate–inexpensive; also apartments, for €470 a week in high season*). Opened in the 1950s and still retaining much of its original ambience in a garden setting just above Calvi, a 10-minute walk to the centre; there are pretty views over the town and sea and mountains. *Closed mid-Nov–Mar.*

Casa Vecchia, Rte de Santore, t 04 95 65 09 33, *hotel-casa-vecchia.com* (*moderate–inexpensive*). In a shady garden, with recently renovated motel-style rooms, close to the beach and 15mins on foot to the centre. *Half-board obligatory in July and Aug.*

Les Arbousiers, Rte de Pietramaggiore, t 04 95 65 04 47 (*inexpensive*). Large, pleasant and tranquil hotel with a garden, 1km from the centre (off the l'Ile-Rousse road) but only a 5-minute walk to the beach. *Closed early Oct–April.*

one of his own men. The heir to the fifth Lord Byron was killed in the same siege, leaving the title to his cousin the poet, who would make it famous.

Calvi took a long time to recover. It remained a military town, and in 1962 found itself hosting the Foreign Legion 's parachutists after the war in Algeria. Before then,

Relais International de la Jeunesse U Carabellu, Rte de Pietramaggiore, t 04 95 65 14 16 (*inexpensive*). Four km from Calvi, and a hike up a dirt track from the road. Dorm rooms sleep 3–5, most with views; sheet hire extra. *Closed early Nov–Mar.*

Camping Les Castors, Rte de Pietramaggiore, t 04 95 65 13 30, winter t 04 95 65 14 59, *www.camping-les-castors.com* (*inexpensive*). A good bet for families: campsite in the eucalyptus grove with bungalows, studio apartments, big pool and water park located 800m from Calvi, 300m from sandy beach.

Camping Paduella, 1.3km from Calvi on the N197, t 04 95 65 06 16 (*inexpensive*). Pleasant site in the oaks, pines and eucalyptus; they also rent bungalows. Bookings required. *Closed mid-Oct–April.*

Eating Out

Note that some of Calvi's best restaurants are in its best hotels (*see* above).

Emile's, Quai Landry, t 04 95 65 09 60, *www.restaurant-emiles.com*. For a big night out, book a table at this *haute cuisine* restaurant by the port. *Menus from €30.*

Le Bout du Monde, Plage de Calvi, t 04 95 65 15 41. The owner of Emile's, Théo Luciani, runs this seafood restaurant under the magic spoon of William Berthier, who concocts a host of combinations, such as *rascasse en tartare de guacamole*, that work amazingly well. Excellent wine list too: the Faustine du Comte Abiatucci white comes recommended. *Around €40, lunch plat du jour €14.*

Octopussy, on the beach, t 04 95 65 23 16. Fashionable place right on the sands, to see and be seen, with stunning sunset views over the citadel. Don't miss the *salade de poulpe. Menu €29, open till 2am in summer.*

L'Abri-Côtier, Quai Landry, t 04 95 65 12 76. Superb seafood dishes, but also the likes of fresh *chèvre* and tomato terrine, homemade pasta with morel mushrooms, and lamb tagine. *Menus from €22. Closed winter.*

Le Calellu, Quai Landry, t 04 95 65 22 18. Excellent restaurant by the marina serving only the best of the day's catch, which the owner haggles over every morning from Calvi's fishermen. *Menu €20, but worth splurging for a special fish. Be sure to book. Closed Oct–Feb, and Mon.*

Resto des Iles-Chez Marie, Rte de la Pinède, t 04 95 65 49 89. Come here for a touch of the Caribbean: spicy *€27 menu* and Corsican dishes too, including the speciality, mussels on a skewer. *Closed mid-Jan–mid-Feb.*

U Fornu, Impasse Bertoni, near the marina, t 04 95 65 27 60. Tasty Mediterranean cuisine, including a wonderful seafood lasagne and pasta with boar, as well as hot home-made bread. *Menus at €15 and €20. Closed Nov–early April.*

Cappuccino, Quai Landry, t 04 95 65 11 10. Good choice of pizzas, pastas, salads and a nice house wine. *Around €15. Closed Nov–Mar.*

A Scola, t 04 95 65 07 09. Charming antique shop-cum-tea room in the citadel, opposite St-Jean-Baptiste; besides coffees, 17 kinds of tea and cakes, they do salads, omelettes and a *plat du jour* for lunch. *Closed Nov–April.*

Entertainment and Nightlife

Chez Tao, Rue St-Antoine (in the citadel), t 04 95 65 00 73. Tao's life was the stuff of legend (*see* below). Now his three sons run the cabaret/disco – it's still lovely, with a magical terrace opening on to the Golfe de Calvi. *Open late June–late Sept, from 7pm till dawn.*

L'Acapulco, Rte de Calenzana, t 04 95 65 08 03. The hottest disco in the area – drawing up to 4,000 clubbers on summer weekends, open till dawn. *€10 entrance.*

La Camargue, Vallée al Legno, t 04 95 65 08 70. Popular club drawing a 30–50-year-old clientele, with a piano bar and indoor/outdoor dance floor and pool.

Club 24, Rue Clémenceau, t 04 95 65 08 66. Tiny dance floor but very lively till very late.

however, it had been 'discovered' by a rather unlikely pair: the eccentric Russian Prince Youssoupof, reputedly one of the assassins of Rasputin, and a Tcherkess Muslim named Tao Kereffoff, a White Russian cavalry captain who after the Bolshevik victory got a job as a dancer in a New York cabaret. Youssoupof met Tao in New York, and together they went to Paris, and founded now mostly forgotten fashion houses. Youssoupof bought a house in the citadel of Calvi in the 1920s, and Tao did the same in 1924; reminded of his native Caucasia, he stayed, married a Calvaise, and converted his 15th-century bishop's palace into a legendary nightclub (wonderfully described by Dorothy Carrington in *Granite Island*). Chez Tao gave Calvi an edge unique in Corsica, which Tao's sons, among the biggest promoters of the city's festivals, hope to regain.

The Basse Ville

The bustling Basse Ville, or lower part of Calvi, is now the lively heart and soul of the city. It most postdates Nelson's siege, although here and there you'll find the odd veteran structure. One, on Boulevard Wilson, is big rosy Baroque **Ste-Marie-Majeure** (1774), a focal point but with little to see inside; in adjacent Place du Marché Couvert, the morning **market** sells the products of the Balagne. Boutiques and tourist shops pack Rue Clemenceau, while in little Place St-Charles a charming octagonal pavilion of wood and glass has Calvi's municipal library shoehorned inside.

Below Rue Clemenceau, **Quai Landry** is the favourite evening promenade, a lively café- and restaurant-lined strip overlooking the marina. Along with the locals and tourists, you'll often see Foreign Legionnaires, on leave from their base at Camp Raffali, just southeast of Calvi. By the Citadelle the quay is closed off by the Genoese **Tour de Sel**, a watchtower that did double duty as a salt deposit; on the other end, the train station stands near Calvi's Moby Dick of a **beach**, huge, white and compelling, backed by maritime pines planted in the 19th century to shore up the dunes.

The Citadelle

Bulging high in its girdle of walls and surrounded on three sides by the sea, the citadel owes much of its appearance to the Bank of St George, when it fortified Corsica in the 16th century. If you look at the walls closely, you can still see the scars and even an embedded cannonball from Nelson's siege. The single entrance, Place Christophe Colomb, has the most recent of several monuments to one of Calvi's more tenuous claims to fame – that it was the birthplace of the 'discoverer' of America.

Walk up under the gateway, bearing the city's *Semper Fidelis* motto, and the vast 13th-century Genoese **Governor's Palace** looms ahead; enlarged in 1554 by the Bank of St George, it now does duty as the Sampiero military barracks. Facing the palace, the late 15th-century **Oratoire St-Antoine** (*open only for guided tours, reservations through the tourist office*) is marked by a relief of St Anthony with his pig, flanked by the Baptist and St Francis. Still used by its confraternity today, it has a pair of frescoes of the *Crucifixion* inside. Just up from here, the austere domed **Cathédrale St-Jean-Baptiste** stands at the highest point on the old bald rock. Built in the 13th century, it was badly damaged in 1567 after an explosion in a nearby powder magazine, and rebuilt in 1570 as a Greek cross. The interior has the air of an old curiosity shop; there's a Renaissance baptismal font, a sculpted wooden pulpit of 1752 and on the altar to the right the famous *Christ Noir* or *Christ des Miracles* that frightened the Turks away. The triptych of the *Annunciation* on the high altar is by the 15th-century Genoese painter Barbagelata ('Ice Beard'), a pupil of the Ligurian master, Giovanni Mazone,

.S.
.S.A.S.
.X . M . Y.

This cabalistic pyramid of letters that you may have already spotted around Calvi is Christopher Columbus' signature, which according to his will of 1494 is how his heirs must always sign documents, without ever using their family name. He never explained why, or even what the letters meant. In the same will, he also insisted that his real name (after two decades of using Colon, Colonus, Colomo, Colom) was Colón, a true Colón born of Genoa. But the Colón bit was a lie, and, according to the supporters of the Calvi birthplace, so was the part about Genoa.

Columbus purposely obfuscated his origins to the extent that even his sons had no idea of the date or place of his birth, or the name of their grandparents. In the 18th century, however, when there were no direct male heirs, research into his family produced the following facts: that his real name was in fact Colombo, that his father Domenico was a weaver born in Genoa, and his mother was Susanna Fontanarossa, and that their 'first fruit' was Cristoforo, born around 1451. Calvi was an integral part of Genoa at the time, and on Rue de Fil in the Citadelle there lived a weaver named Colombo. And Susanna Fontanarossa could have been from the Balagne (see p.237). Other evidence pointed out by Calvi supporters is that Columbus took 'Corsican horses and dogs' on his voyage to America, and that his spelling and word usage were always odd, as if he hadn't learned Italian (or Castilian, or Portuguese) correctly.

Hogwash, say the Genoese, who also sniff at Mallorca's, Chios' and Savona's pretensions to Columbus' cradle. But no one will ever really know; the Admiral of the Ocean Sea did a superb job of covering up his tracks. Why? Some say because he was illegitimate and, were it known, he never could have served as a naval officer. Others say he had to disguise his original religion, be it Jewish or Greek Orthodox. In Calvi they say he wanted to hide his Corsican origins because their island had such a bad reputation for insurgency; once he became famous, they say, the Genoese came and took all of Calvi's town records to Genoa to hide the fact. If you read French, you may be convinced by a book by ex-secret agent René Massoni, *Christophe Colomb: Calvais, Corse, Génois* (Nouvelles Editions Latines, 1992).

only you can't get close enough to see it very well. The balcony around the cupola was reserved for the noble ladies, so they wouldn't have to rub shoulders with the people.

The other thing to do in the Citadelle is walk around the **ramparts** for the excellent views, or wander the cobbled streets and stairs. A plaque marks the house where Napoleon, his mother and siblings stayed in 1793 with his godfather Laurent Giubega after being forced to flee Ajaccio, and before sailing to Toulon and destiny. Another plaque indicates the spot of Columbus' possible birthplace – the actual house was destroyed by one of Nelson's shells.

Around Calvi

There are two favourite spots near Calvi, both offering classic views of the bay and the old Genoese town. One is the 2km walk along the peninsula to the lighthouse on

Punta della Revellata, beginning at a car park off the road to Porto. The second is a drive up to the chapel of **Notre-Dame-de-la-Serra** (the road up is to the left, just before the Punta della Revellata car park), which rises out of the granite and *maquis* 708ft over the sea, with a spectacular view over Calvi. The original 15th-century chapel was destroyed in 1794, when Nelson used the terrace for his cannons; the chapel was rebuilt in 1865, and its terrace is now a favourite spot for a picnic.

Western Balagne: Calenzana to Montemaggiore

Southeast of Calvi, **Calenzana** is a village set apart from the rest of the Balagne *fertile*. The ancient Roman town of Olmi, surrounded by fertile fields yet hidden from the sea and passing marauders, it made the Corsican history books on several occasions, mostly recently back in the 1930s and '40s, when the Guerini family of Calenzana were the godfathers of the *milieu* in Marseille, although they would later win medals for their work in the Resistance; some of the village's larger houses belonged to them, their cohorts – and their lawyers. Now Calenzana is known for its wines and cheeses, and as the starting point of the GR20 and the Mare e Monti trail.

A fast road, the D151, links Calenzana to Calvi, only 12km north, although in the 18th century the two towns didn't get along at all: Calvi was faithful to Genoa, and Calenzana was a hotbed of Corsican patriots. In 1732, at the start of the War of Independence, the Genoese, short of manpower, hired an army of 8,000 German mercenaries from their ally, Emperor Charles VI, at the cost of 30,000 florins per month, with the obligation to pay another 100 florins to pay for every soldier killed. Six hundred mercenaries were sent to rout the rebels in Calenzana, only the Corsican General Ceccaldi got wind of their plans and planned a surprise. The Germans marched in without resistance, and the trap was sprung: not only were they ambushed by regular Corsican troops, but villagers on the roofs pelted them with rocks, boiling water, burning torches and, most maddening of all, beehives. As the Germans tried to flee the enraged bees, the villagers caused a stampede of bulls coated with flaming pitch who charged madly through the streets. From this inferno only a hundred Germans survived to tell the tale; the Genoese were left demoralized and wounded where it hurt them most (their pockets), while across Corsica the news was electric: people began to believe they could actually win the fight.

The 500 hapless Germans lie buried in the **Campo Santo dei Tedeschi**, under a bell tower of 1870, a reconstruction of the Baroque original but one nevertheless on the point of collapse. This belongs to the cavernous church of **St-Blaise**, begun in 1691 and finished in 1707, florid inside with polychrome marble and *trompe l'œil* around the altar. Note how the floor slopes, to drain off the water in case of heavy rains.

Calenzana's most famous church, **Santa Restituta**, stands in an ancient olive grove 1km up the D151 towards Zilia; before setting out, pick up the key at the village *tabac* near St-Blaise. Restituta was either a Corsican girl who converted to Christianity or a Christian from North Africa who took refuge at Calenzana. When she was denounced to the governor of Corsica, he ordered the usual kinky Roman torments – she was

Tourist Information

Maison du GR20: Gîte d'Etape Municipal, Calenzana, t 04 95 62 70 08. *Open in season only, Tues 4–9, Mon and Wed–Fri 9–12 and 3–6.* Stop for advice before hitting the trails.

Sports and Activities

Calenzana is the favourite point of departure for the **GR20** (*see* pp.70–72) as well as the beautiful **Mare e Monti** trail (waymarked orange), to Cargèse, a 10-stage walk with *gîtes d'étapes* by way of the bay of Girolata, the Golfe de Porto and the Gorges de Spelunca. **Donkey rides for children:** Fasgianu, by Santa Reparata, Calenzana, t 06 22 34 12 51, *http:// asin.free.fr/fasgianu.htm*.

Shopping

U Fragnu, on the Zilia road, Lunighignano, t 04 95 62 75 51, *www.ufragnu.com*. Great place to pick up a souvenir: olive oils and olive woods, pottery, soaps, sweets, drinks.
Pâtisserie E Fritelle, Rue U Chiasu Longu, t 04 95 62 78 17. Calenzana is famous for the best biscuits on the island, *cuggiuelli*, which are hard and dry but taste great dunked in white wine. They also do delicious hot *beignets* in the morning.

Where to Stay and Eat

Calenzana ✉ 20214
Ferme-auberge A Flatta, t 04 95 62 80 38, *www.aflatta.com* (*expensive*). Some 3km up a rough track from Calenzana, superbly located in an isolated secret wooded valley, with views down to the coast. Five pricey but very comfortable rooms, including a honeymoon suite, and delicious meat and seafood specialities on the menu. *Closed Nov–Mar; restaurant open weekends only out of season.*
Bel Horizon, 4 Place Prince Pierre, t 04 95 62 71 72 (*inexpensive*). A basic hotel but clean, and popular with hikers. *Closed Oct–Mar.*
Gîte d'Etape Comunal, t 04 95 62 77 13 (*inexpensive*). Tidy dormitory beds and breakfasts, designed for walkers on the long-distance paths.
Le Calenzana (Chez Michel), 7 Cours St-Blaise, t 04 95 62 70 25. Good spot for quality Corsican cuisine, including *brocciu soufflé* in the winter and heavenly lamb chops. *Menu €16. Closed Jan and Feb, and Mon in winter.*

Cassano ✉ 20214
Auberge de Calia, just t 04 95 60 57 87. Great place in an old mill for a traditional lunch – limited menu, but all tasty and generous. *Around €25. Open at noon Mar-mid-Dec, eves too in July and Aug.*

stoned and whipped with a bull's penis, thrown in a furnace, torn with iron combs, drowned and survived all until she was beheaded with five other martyrs. Not long after the emperor Constantine converted to Christianity, her relics, along with those of the five other martyrs, were buried here, in what became one of the most famous shrines in Corsica: a primitive Romanesque chapel, rebuilt and added to over the centuries. In 1951, the 4th-century sarcophagus (with six bodies inside) was discovered under the Baroque altar and now lies in the crypt. Made of Carrara marble, it is decorated with bands or *strigiles* and a *chrism* (the symbol of Christ) with figures, possibly of the martyrs, on each end. Most fetching of all are 14th-century frescoes by the altar, illustrating Restituta's story with naïve charm. Also note the unusual font held in a hand, made by a sculptor from Calvi in 1514. Declared the patron saint of the Balagne by John Paul II in 1984, Restituta is celebrated on the weekend after 21 May; her relics are carried to St-Blaise on Saturday night, then returned here with thousands of pilgrims, who finish the day with a giant picnic.

The olives and almond groves here aren't as luscious as before July 2005, when arsonists set a series of fires arond **Zilia/Ziglia**, a village synonymous with the sparkling mineral water bottled here. **Cassano**, next up the road, has an unusual star shaped square in the centre; its pride is a lovely triptych in its Baroque parish church, the *Virgin and Saints* (1505), by a little-known Corsican painter, Simonis de Calvi.

Beyond Cassano is beautiful **Montemaggiore**, set on a promontory with Monte Grosso looming behind. With its ancient olive trees, Montemaggiore does its share towards the revival of the Balagne's economy and hosts an olive oil fair, the *Fiera di l'Alivu*, in July. The views are good here too; some of the best are from the terrace of the outsized Baroque church of St-Augustin, which takes pride in its organ from 1700.

Montemaggiore: The Corsican Don Juan

If you've been to Seville, you may recall that the 'real' Don Juan was named Don Miguel, or more precisely Don Miguel de Leca y Colonna y Magnara y Vincentello, who was born in Seville in 1627. Fewer people, however, realize that he was a Corsican. The Leca were one of the noblest families on the island (*see* p.273), whose lineage, exhaustingly confirmed by both Genoese and Spanish nobiliaries of the time, traced their descent back to the semi-legendary 9th-century Ugo Colonna. Miguel's father, Tomaso Magnara di Leca, was from Calvi; his mother, Jeronima Anfriani Vincentelli, also descended from the Leca, was from Montemaggiore; her family house, the Casa Colonna d'Anfriani, still stands.

Miguel was 14 when he saw Tirso de Molina's play *Don Juan de Tenorio*, the drama that would inspire Mozart's *Don Giovanni* and Byron's *Don Juan*. Miguel was inspired, too: he decided he would become Don Juan in real life. Raised as a Spanish gentleman, handsome and rich, he was irresistible, and he was ruthless, seeking greater and greater challenges, pursuing only the most virtuous women, only to drop them cold after seducing them, often killing their male relatives along the way. He was proud when his contemporaries called him 'Don Juan, the worst man in Seville'.

Unlike Corbara's Sultana Davia of Morocco, Miguel did come back to Corsica in search of his roots, after a fashion. Learning that his father had fathered an illegitimate daughter on an Anfriani cousin before leaving for Spain and that she was being raised by an uncle in Montemaggiore, he decided to outdo the fictional Don Juan by seducing his sister. He was about 20 at the time, and arrived under an assumed name with a letter of introduction from himself, saying he was a close friend of Don Miguel. He courted her, and she fell under his sway and promises of marriage, and was just about to yield to him when he triumphantly declared, 'You are my sister, and you love me, and you are mine!' A good Corsican girl schooled in the horrors of incest, she screamed and woke the house, and after a brief sword fight he escaped.

Don Miguel returned to Seville, as bad as ever, and had just arranged to elope with a nun whose father he had killed when, like a true Corsican, he started having dreams and trances that warned him of his death. Terrified, he repented, and went from the very worst to the very best man in Spain, so pious, benevolent and dedicated to the poor that, when he died in 1679, canonization procedures were begun. The investigations of his life, deposited in the Vatican, were pilfered by Napoleon, and are now in the Bibliothèque Nationale in Paris.

The most charming church in these parts, however, is the Romanesque **San Raniero**; 2km north on a narrow road *(pick up the key at the mairie – for tours of local and normally locked cultural sites, call t 04 95 62 72 78)*. Raniero (*c.* 1161) was a specifically Pisan saint, a big sinner who repented and became a monk, and while the Pisans ruled Corsica their merchants would gather here for a fair on his day, 17 June. The delightful black and white façade has two people and a cross carved on the tympanum, and two masks, one laughing, one furious, under the archivolts on the north side. Inside, the cylindrical font is sculpted with grotesque faces. From here the D151 crosses over the **Col de Salvi,** enjoying a panorama down to the sea, before reaching Cateri (*see* p.242).

The Balagne Désert

In stark contrast with the cultivated terraces of the Balagne *fertile*, the Balagne Désert south of Calvi is ruled by *maquis* and granite. Yet here and there stone walls stand as mute witnesses that this was once a going concern, a few hundred years ago; 90 villages stood here in the 14th century, before the pirates stole the people and a 15th-century epidemic of syphilis followed by malaria decimated the rest.

Since the Balagne Désert was mostly empty, President de Gaulle in the early 1960s announced that he intended to use some of it, around Argentella, for France's nuclear tests. The Corsicans protested vehemently but to no effect, until anti-nuke vigilantes did severe bodily harm to two engineers at Argentella and De Gaulle backed down, having set an unfortunate precedent in Franco-Corsican relations. Nowadays people come to the Balagne Désert for the majestic Cirque de Bonifato and the isolated little resort of Galéria.

The Cirque de Bonifato

The spectacular Cirque de Bonifato, with its spiky pink granite 'needles' and deep green forests of Laricio pines, is one of the first natural wonders along the GR20 after Calenzana, but even non-hikers can have a taste of it by taking the road south of Calvi's airport to the D251 which ends up in a pay car park, near the **Maison Forestière**. From there, backtrack by foot to a sharp bend in the road, for a magnificent view over the trees to the porphyry pinnacles of the **Chaos de Bocca Rezza**, or venture out on a number of walks starting at the Maison Forestière; the most popular (but only if you're fit and have the proper gear) is to penetrate into the high mountain Cirque as far the ruined shepherds' huts at **Spasimata** (*about five hours there and back*), following the river Figarella and a variant of the GR20 and crossing several torrents.

Down the Coast to Galéria

There are two roads from Calvi through the Balagne Désert to Galéria: the quick and fairly dull D81, or the slower D81B, hugging the rugged coast. The latter passes by the way of **Porto Agro,**the little inlet where Nelson landed his troops and dismantled his ships' guns to besiege Calvi. Further south, in the Baie de Crovani, **Argentella** has abandoned buildings and a tall ventilation shaft to recall its silver-mining heyday, and

Tourist Information

Galéria: at the junction of the D81 and D351, t 04 95 62 02 27. *Open May–Oct Mon–Fri 9–12 and 4.30–7.* Good source for hiking info. The nearest **ATM** machine is in Calvi.

Sports and Activities

Diving: L'Incantu, t 04 95 62 03 65, *www. incantu.com*. Besides dives along the coast, they visit the Réserve de Scandola and dive where it's legal, just south of the Réserve.

Hiking: The **Mare e Monti** trail passes through Galéria, but many people come just to do the fourth stage, a demanding but breathtaking 6-hour walk from Galéria to tiny Girolata, where you can spend the night (*see pp.262–3*). From there you can either walk back, or walk to Col de la Croix on the D81 and hitchhike or catch the Porto bus; for details check the Galéria tourist hut.

Where to Stay and Eat

Bonifato ✉ 20214

L'Auberge de la Forêt, t 04 95 65 09 98 (*moderate*). Near the car park. Five cosy doubles and a place to camp. Also a good restaurant with tasty home cooking, and rich boar dishes in the autumn (*around €23*). No credit cards. *Closed Nov–Mar.*

Galéria ✉ 20245

L'Incantu, Rte Calca, t 04 95 62 03 65, *www. residenceincantu.com*. Near the top of Galéria, apartments by the week, sleeping 2–8, linked to a convivial diving centre.

Prices in high season start at €570 for two. *Closed Dec–mid-Mar.*

**Filosorma, t 04 95 62 00 02, *www.corsica-net.com/filosorma* (*moderate, incl. breakfast*). Nice average hotel by the long pebble beach, with sea views. *Closed Nov–Mar.*

*Stella Marina, on the beach, t 04 95 62 00 03, *www.hotel-stellamarina.com* (*moderate*). Modern building with big rooms and terraces, and a restaurant/pizzeria serving succulent grilled seafood. *Closed Nov–April.*

*L'Auberge, t 04 95 62 00 15, *www.corsica-net.com/auberge* (*moderate*). Friendly but fairly basic en suite air-conditioned rooms in the village centre, 150m from the beach; downstairs there is a restaurant (*closed Wed out of season*).

*Sol e Mare, village centre, t 04 95 62 01 44, *www.corsica-net.com/solemare* (*moderate*). Rooms, but primarily known as the best restaurant in Galéria, with big servings of excellent seafood dishes including swordfish carpaccio and stuffed sardines. *Menus from €21. Closed Nov–Mar.*

La Martinella, t 04 95 62 00 44, *http:// martinella.corsica-net.com* (*moderate*). On the road to the Genoese tower, not far from the beach, five of the best *chambres d'hôtes* in Galéria, all with sea views, private terrace and fridges.

Gîte d'Etape Marine, t 04 95 62 00 46 (*inexpensive*). On the Mare e Monti trail, 1km from Galéria, a well-run shelter with dorm beds and a campsite, and a restaurant. Very busy in walking season (spring and September). If it's full, try the a new *gîte*, **Cormoran Voyageur**, t 04 95 20 15 55.

Sole e Mare, t 04 95 6201 44. Come here for big seafood salads and fresh fish caught by the family fisherman. *Lunch c. €15, dinner more.*

a beautiful beach of polished granite pebbles. Overlooking the bay stand the ruins of a large stone palace – once the home of the libertine adventurer Prince Pierre Napoléon Bonaparte (1815–81), the son of Napoleon's brother Lucien, who notoriously shot the journalist Victor Noir in Paris in 1870. His cousin Napoléon III acquitted him, a move that edged Paris another step towards revolt and the *comuni*. This house in Argentella, where he came to live with his wife (who was rejected by the Bonapartes because she was the mere daughter of a foundryman), as well as a fountain in Calenzana, are his chief monuments (his victim Victor Noir did rather better, with a life-sized bronze statue in Paris' Père-Lachaise cemetery that gets constantly rubbed in certain spots by women seeking a happier sex life).

Galéria, at the mouth of the river Fango, is the only real village for miles and miles, and enjoys a certain cachet as the back of beyond. Scattered among the big red rocks, it has a Genoese tower and a small grey pebble beach, but there's another bigger, shingly beach a short walk north where you can skinny-dip. Galéria wasn't always so remote; the ancient historian Diodoros Siculus wrote that its ancestor, Karalis, was founded by the Phoenicians in 570 BC – which makes it even older than Greek Aléria – and it featured on Ptolemy's map. Etruscan and other ceramics have been found near the coast, and in 1992 divers discovered part of a bronze Roman anchor.

The hinterland of Galéria, the Filosorma, is renowned among Corsican trout fishermen, who come to cast their flies on the Fango. The river has its source high on Paglia Orba, and the striking dorsal fin shape of the mountain frequently looms into view as you drive up the **Vallée du Fango** (D351), lined with *maquis* and trees and natural granite swimming holes. Some of the best views are from Tuarelli (at the top of a short path) and from **Manso/Mansu**, with grand views over Paglia Orba and Capo Tafonato from its terrace. The road peters out at **Barghiana**, where you can pick up a 2km path to the **Pont de la Rocce**, for more great views. Beyond lies *mouflon* country.

Down the West Coast

The Golfe de Porto

...a nightmarish menagerie petrified by the will of some eccentric god...
                                                          Guy de Maupassant

When designing the Golfe de Porto, Mother Nature let her hair down, using the primordial lava flows from Monte Cinto to sculpt vertiginous cliffs and pinnacles, splashing them with Fauvist colours and setting them aglow daily in one of the most dazzling sunsets in the Mediterranean. The Scandola headland and the Calanche, her tumultuous masterpieces, are five-star destinations, and inland the grandeur continues in the Gorges de Spelunca and towering Forêt d'Aitone. The only downside to the Golfe de Porto is the sheer volume of visitors who come to partake of its savage beauty; out of season, the peerless rapture is easier to capture and the fiercely narrow *corniche* roads are safer and less crowded.

Porto/Portu

Although the setting is stunning, in the old days Porto was so unimportant that no one bothered to give it a name: it was simply the port of Ota, squeezed under the mountains by the mouth of a river that was also called Porto (officially, though, it's Vaïta). The only permanent building was a square **Genoese tower** of 1549. One of the most picturesque in Corsica, rising from the red rocks, the tower was renovated in 1993, and offers great views of the coast, the sea, and an exhibition on Corsica's defences (*t 04 95 26 10 05; open July and Aug 9–9; April–June and Sept–Oct 11–7; adm*). In the 19th century, a **eucalyptus grove** was planted to dry the marshy river mouth, and the big gum trees are another of Porto's landmarks.

Getting Around

SAIB, t 04 95 22 41 99, has year-round **bus** connections Mon–Sat from Ajaccio and Cargèse to Piana, Porto and Ota; from May–Oct they add a daily service between Porto, Galéria and Calvi.

Autocars Mordiconi, t 04 95 48 00 04, link Porto and the Col de Verghio to Corte (May–mid-Sept, four buses daily exc Sun).

Bike hire: Porto Location, by the supermarket Spar, **t** 04 95 26 10 13, in Porto.

Taxi and minibus: Chez Félix at Ota, **t** 04 95 26 12 92.

Tourist Information

Porto: Place de la Mairie, **t** 04 95 26 10 55, *www.porto-tourisme.com. Open June–Sept Mon–Sat 9–7; Oct–May Mon–Fri 9–12 and 2–5.*

Piana: by the post office, **t** 04 95 27 84 42, *www.calanche.com. Open June–Sept.*

Sports and Activities

Diving: There's absolutely fabulous diving to be had in crystal-clear waters, with plenty of red coral and other wonders. There are three centres: **Centre de Plongée du Golfe de Porto, t** 04 95 26 10 29 or **t** 06 84 24 49 20, *www.plongee porto.com; open Easter–Oct;* **Génération Bleue, t** 04 95 26 24 88 or **t** 06 07 43 21 28, *www.generation-bleue.com, open May–Oct;* **Mediterranée Porto Sub, t** 04 95 26 19 47, *www.le-mediterranee.com; open 15 April–15 Oct.* Reserve in advance for all.

Sea excursions: to the Réserve Naturelle de Scandola, Girolata, and the Calanche de Piana with **Nave Va,** at the hotel Cyrnée, **t** 04 95 26 15 16, *www.naveva.com;* or with **Porto Linéa** on the 12-seater *Mare Nostrum,*

a boat small enough to enter the grottoes (from Easter–Oct, reservations, **t** 04 95 26 11 50). Five firms rent out boats and zodiacs; the tourist office has a complete list.

Canyoning: Corsica Trek, at Les Oliviers, Porto, **t** 04 95 26 82 02. Go down the Gorges de Spelunca or the cliffs of the Golfe de Porto the hard way; also walks and other adventures. *Open 15 June–15 Sept.*

Guided walks: Corse Rando, Serriera, **t** 04 95 10 49 37. Walks with a theme – flora and fauna, legends, etc. *Open 15 April–15 Oct.*

Where to Stay and Eat

Porto ✉ **20150**

Overbuilt with hotels, Porto is the one place on Corsica where you may find a price war raging (except in July and August). If you do come in season, however, avoid the crowds by staying on the outskirts – by the beaches below Serriera or in Piana.

★★Le Colombo, t 04 95 26 10 14, *www.hotelle colombo.com (moderate).* A kilometre from the sea on the Calvi road, a charming hotel with a pretty garden; most rooms (some sleep four) have a sea-breezy, sponge-painted décor and views of the sea and mountains, and TVs. Delicious breakfasts, too. *Closed end Oct–Mar.*

★★★Le Belvédère, La Marina, **t** 04 95 26 12 01, *www.hotel-le-belvedere.com (moderate).* Modern air-conditioned comfort in the cluster of hotels by the port, and most rooms with the promised lovely views.

★★★Le Subrini, La Marina, **t** 04 95 26 14 94, *www.hotels-porto.com (moderate).* Similar to the Belvédère, with views, air-conditioning and friendly owners. *Closed Nov–Mar.*

★★Bella Vista, t 04 95 26 11 08, *www.hotel-bellavista.net (moderate; half-board mandatory in Aug).* Cosy rooms in an older

In the 1950s, after DDT put paid to the malaria that haunted it, Porto began to cater for summer visitors. And cater, and cater, and cater, with about as much forethought as went into its name. Hotels elbow each other for views around the red granite chaos of the harbour and around the straggling, centreless centre. In July and August, Porto verges on the claustrophobic as cars and people queue up every which way, to get money out of the bank wall, to get in the restaurants, the campsites, the shops, the toilets. Out of season, dogs snooze in the road.

granite building with marvellous views, and one of Porto's best and most imaginative restaurants, where the seafood cassoulet or pork roast with myrtle and grilled langoustines go down very nicely indeed (*menus €17–46*). *Open April–mid-Oct and winter weekends.*

★★Le Porto, Rte de Calvi, **t** 04 95 26 11 20 (*inexpensive; half-board obligatory in July and Aug*). Fairly large rooms 1.5km from the sea, but the hotel comes equipped with a rarity in Porto: a good restaurant, with tasty fish and timeless French favourites (*around €22*). *Closed 15 Oct–15 April.*

Le Maquis, in the upper village, Rte de Galéria, **t** 04 95 26 12 19, *www.hotel-du-maquis.com* (*moderate; half-pension obligatory in Aug*). Tranquillity reigns in these six rooms by a trellised garden. The restaurant is one of the best in Porto, serving perfect lobster salads, seafood kebabs in saffron, or fish and meat grilled over herbs from the *maquis*. For an unusual dessert, try the ravioli filled with *brocciu* in chocolate sauce (*menus from €17*). *Closed Nov–15 Feb.*

Camping Sole e Vista, by the supermarkets, **t** 04 95 26 15 71 (*inexpensive*). Immaculate three-star site, shady, on terraces, with fine views over the sea. *Closed Nov–Mar.*

Camping Funtana a l'Ora, 3km on the Evisa road, **t** 04 95 26 15 48 (*inexpensive*). Nice campsite if you have your own transport, with shade and near the river swimming holes. *Closed Oct–15 April.*

Le Sud, on the lane to the Genoese tower, **t** 04 95 26 14 11. At the base of the Genoese tower, a restaurant using only quality local ingredients (lamb with apricots and almonds, or seafood lasagne). *Around €40. Closed Nov–Mar.*

La Mer, overlooking the port and Genoese tower, **t** 04 95 26 11 27. Watch the sun set while dining in a friendly, relaxed setting under the plane trees: seafood (especially the monkfish) prepared with a knowing hand; good desserts too. Not many choices but all are excellent. *Lunch menu €19, dinner €29. Closed Nov–Easter.*

Serriera (Plage de Bussaglia) ✉ 20147

★★★★Eden Park, **t** 04 95 26 10 60, *www.hotels-porto.com* (*very expensive*). Set over the beach, a classy, luxurious hotel and restaurant with air-conditioned rooms and a pretty pool in a palm garden. *Closed Nov–Mar.*

★★★Stella Marina, **t** 04 95 26 11 18, *www.hotel-stella-marina.com* (*moderate*). Solid, reliable hotel near the beach with a pool and restaurant, 300m from the sea. *Closed Oct–mid-April.*

★★L'Aiglon, **t** 04 95 26 10 65, (*moderate; half-board in Aug*). Comfortable rooms in a handsome stone building with a big terrace and views over the valley, less than 1km from the beach. The restaurant serves a good *brocciu* omelette, kid and other traditional fare. *Closed mid-Oct–Mar.*

U Caspiu, Plage de Caspio, Partinello **t** 04 95 27 32 58. In a charming setting overlooking a cove, feast on *bouillabaisse* and freshly caught seafood; try the *civet de langoustes au vin d'orange*. They also do Corsican dishes. *Around €28. Book in the evening. Closed Oct–mid-May.*

Les Galets, Plage de Bussaglia, **t** 04 93 26 10 49. Relaxed beachside restaurant that does good pasta, pizza in a wood oven and seafood – *en papillote, tagines, tartare, etc. Around €25 à la carte. Closed Oct–15 April.*

Girolata ✉ 20147

Le Cormoran, **t** 04 95 20 15 55. Basic dorm rooms for walkers in a *gîte d'étape*, run by a fisherman, who serves the catch for dinner. *Half-board €35. Closed Oct–Mar, but book weeks in advance; you can only stay 1 night.*

Porto's rather exposed pebble **beach**, just over the footbridge from the harbour, drops off quickly and is dangerous when the waves are high. If you can't get in the water, you can at least look at it in the **Aquarium de la Poudrière** (**t** 04 95 26 19 24; *open July–Aug 11–10; April–June 10–9; Sept–Mar 10–6; adm*), where the tanks display groupers, morays, sea horses and the other fauna of Corsica's coasts, especially some of the rarer creatures from the Réserve Naturelle de Scandola.

La Cabane du Berger, t 04 95 20 16 98 (*inexpensive*). *Gîte d'étape* on the beach, with beds in dorms or little bungalows that sleep two, and grilled fish in the restaurant. *Closed Oct–Mar.*

Le Bel Ombra, t 04 95 20 15 67. Come here for fresh grilled fish, fish soup and lobster. *Menu €20. Closed Oct–Mar.*

Piana ✉ 20115

★★★★Capo Rosso, Route des Calanche, **t** 04 95 27 82 40, *www.caporosso.com* (*very expensive*). Incomparable setting over the Calanche and indigo sea, far, far below; the luxurious rooms are large, recently renovated, and there's a big pool. The restaurant has more grand views, with *menus from €24 to €59 for the lobster*. Also bike hire and picnic baskets to take on your excursions. *Closed 15 Oct–Mar.*

★★Les Roches Rouges, t 04 95 27 81 81, *www. lesrochesrouges.com* (*moderate*). Built in 1912 and reeking of faded grandeur and character, with a terrace that enjoys an unbeatable view over the Calanche and gets lively at sunset, as people stop by for a drink. Rooms are large and many sleep up to four (but have no TV or air-conditioning); the Belle Epoque restaurant, with its frescoes, is a historic monument, and serves a delicious *menu at €27* featuring *soupe de poisson*, delicate seafood and a good choice of Corsican cheeses. *Closed mid-Nov–mid-Mar.*

★★Scandola, t 04 95 27 80 07, *www.hotel scandola.com* (*moderate*). Comfy rooms and a restaurant/pizzeria enjoying *the* view. *Closed Nov–late Mar.*

Continental, Place de l'Eglise, **t** 04 95 27 89 00 (*inexpensive*). Simple rooms with well-worn wooden floors and retro charm and toilets down the hall, in an old family home, or there are more comfortable but less atmospheric and pricier rooms in the annexe.

The large garden is an added plus. No credit cards. *Closed Oct–Mar.*

Camping Plage d'Arone, 12km southwest of Piana on the beach, **t** 04 95 20 64 54. Very convivial campsite on a beautiful beach, with a shop. No credit cards. *Closed Oct–April.*

La Casabianca, Plage d'Arone, **t** 04 95 20 70 40. One of the first restaurants to open in the area and a delight, serving seafood salads, pasta and meats, and pizzas in summer. *Around €30. Closed mid-Oct–mid-April.*

Ota ✉ 20150

Chez Félix, in the village centre, **t** 04 95 26 12 92 (*inexpensive*). Double rooms and *gîte d'étape* dorm rooms, and a good barrestaurant with tables on a panoramic terrace, serving solid Corsican favourites – *soupe corse, beignets de courgettes* and old-fashioned chestnut-based desserts (*menu €19 and menus du jour*). Open all year.

Evisa ✉ 20126

★★L'Aïtone, t 04 95 26 20 04, *www.hotel-aitone.com* (*moderate; half-board obligatory in July and Aug*). Spectacular sunset views combined with a choice of rooms (the ones in the newer bit are more comfortable), plus a small pool and playground. The restaurant is good, too, and serves a lovely terrine of boar with chestnuts and fresh trout dishes. *Closed Dec–mid-Feb.*

★★La Chataigneraie, on the road to Porto, **t** 04 95 26 24 47, *www.hotel-la-chataigneraie. com* (*inexpensive; half-board from June–Sept*). Charming granite inn, where the snug little rooms are furnished in pine. The traditional Corsican cuisine in the restaurant makes good use of Evisa's famous chestnuts in polenta (*pulindinu*), in the main courses and desserts (*menus €20*); they'll also pack you a nice picnic lunch. *Closed Nov–late Mar.*

The Coast North of Porto

The D81, the *corniche* road hairpinning over the coast north of Porto, offers magnificent views across the bay to the crimson Calanche and access to three pebbly coves, all of which are more sheltered and better for swimming than Porto. The closest, the **Plage de Bussaglia**, is 5km from Porto, down a sharp left turn. The road then passes under the sleepy villages of **Serriera** and **Partinello**; from the latter, you can reach the

Dragut in Girolata

In the old days, Girolata's day-trippers were pirates. In 1540, the famous Turkish admiral Dragut (in fact a renegade Greek and occasional ally of the French, but a pirate to nearly everyone else in the Mediterranean) anchored here with his fleet, after plundering the island of Capraia and Cap Corse. A Genoese fleet under Giorgio Doria had just missed Dragut at Cap Corse but, knowing it was the pirates' custom to sail against the wind, Doria set off in that direction. He was about to give up the chase when he came across signs of an encampment near the entrance to the Golfe de Girolata. The ashes were still warm. As the first Genoese galley came into sight, Dragut was still dividing up the booty; he at once boarded his ship for a fight, but, after the first cannon shot, the seven other Genoese galleys rounded the bend, and the pirates jumped overboard and ran for it. Doria freed a thousand captives from the holds of the pirates' ships, and they joined in the manhunt, killing many pirates outright. Still, 2,000 were captured, including Dragut, and they were condemned to spend the rest of their days as galley slaves. Three years later, another Greek renegade working for the Ottomans, Khair al-Din Barbarossa, conqueror of Algiers and Tunis, paid Dragut's ransom, and in 1551 he returned to raze Girolata in revenge.

Plage de Caspio. Another 10km of twists and turns leads to the turn-off (D424) at Osani for the best beach of all, the reddish **Plage de Gradelle**, looking across to the Calanche. More stupendous views, over both the Golfes de Porto and Girolata, await from the **Col de la Croix** just above the Osani crossroads. Further up the D81 towards Galéria, the **Col de Palmarella** is a natural look-out over Scandola.

The Col de la Croix is the start of the two-hour, 7km footpath down to the tiny lobster-fishing hamlet of **Girolata**, the last place in Corsica that can only be reached by mule track or sea. The population of eight in the winter rises to all of 30 in summer, although these are overwhelmed in the day by boatloads of summer trippers from Calvi and Porto. Out of season, the only visitors are hikers on the Mare e Monti trail, the occasional yacht, and the fittest postman in France, who hikes this route every day. The landmark is a square 17th-century **Genoese tower** overgrown with cacti and aloes, built after Dragut's return journey to the village.

Réserve Naturelle de Scandola

Created by a volcanic eruption 250 million years ago, the headland of Scandola at Corsica's westernmost extreme is a stunning and savage dreamland of porphyry cliffs eroded by wind and sea into grottoes, organ pipes and pinnacles, the red rock tufted with green *maquis* over a transparent ultramarine sea. Made a nature reserve in 1975, and listed by UNESCO in 1983, its 2,270 acres and even larger underwater expanse are strictly off limits to walkers and divers and can only be visited by boat (excursions from Calvi, Porto, Cargèse, Sagone or Ajaccio). In this scrupulously pure environment flora and fauna flourish: 543 different species of fish swim here, to the great delectation of the ospreys, who were almost extinct on Corsica 30 years ago. The reserve now has 30 nesting pairs, as well as eagles, peregrine falcons and cormorants. Equally rare are the 450 different kinds of algae, and at **Punta Palazzo** you can see a unique white ledge resembling a sidewalk made by one of them, *lythophyllum*, about a thousand years ago, on the rock walls of the 'palace'. The **Baie d'Elbu** to the north is the refuge of Corsica's only free tailed bats (*molosse*), the largest species in Europe.

The Southern Golfe: The Calanche de Piana

Calanche (plural) means 'creeks' or 'inlets', and out of season, when the roads aren't chock-a-block, you would never guess that they were there until you're actually upon them: the first stretch of the D81 from Porto towards Ajaccio rises through typical Corsican coastal scenery, and then you turn a corner and suddenly you're through the looking glass. One of the most awe-inspiring stretches of road in Europe, the next few miles to Piana wind through a corridor of red Gothic monsters, some rising 1,000ft/300m straight out of the sea, pummelled by the elements into spikes, pinnacles and *taffoni*. The story has it that the devil tried to seduce a shepherdess, but she and her fiancé chased him here; in his fury at not being able to tempt the couple, Satan used lightning to sculpt the pair of them in stone, surrounded by a surreal menagerie, guarded by a watchdog – the famous **Tête de Chien**. When all the brouhaha attracted St Martin, a wave rose out of the sea to baptize the infernal creation for the good guys and form the heavenly Golfe de Porto. If you have the luxury to pick and choose, the most enchanting time to do the drive is at sunset, from Piana to Porto.

The Calanche are now a UNESCO World Heritage Site, and in July and August the road, jammed with tour coaches and cars, might as well be in Manhattan at rush hour. For a more leisurely look, take one of the Porto boat excursions, or one of the beautiful *calanche* paths (with sturdy shoes and lots of water), leaving your car in the car park by the Roches Bleues café. The most popular trail, to the **Château Fort**, begins 700m from here, towards Porto (by the Tête de Chien) and leads up to a formation resembling a castle keep with views over the entire bay (there and back takes 1hr 15mins). The *corniche* **walk**, beginning steeply opposite the same café, takes less than an hour. The best views over much of the Calanche, however, are from the old mule track (**Chemin de Muletiers**), once Piana's link to the interior. You can reach it 400m south of the Roches Bleues, by a path from the little oratory of the Virgin.

Piana

At the south end of the Calanche, lovely old **Piana**, balanced on plunging cliffs where the first hotels on this coast were built, somehow manages to be a relatively normal place in spite of the crowds. Most visitors are content to continue a kilometre up the D81 to the **Col de Lava** for the views, but if you aren't in a hurry there are some magnificent sights nearby. A very steep, narrow road, the D624, goes down through a fantastic intense porphyry rockscape to a stepped path leading to the **Anse de Ficajola**, a lovely cove once used as Piana's little port.

Near the top of the D624 (before it descends), the D824 forks left and carries on in a splendid *corniche* along the south coast of the bay towards **Capu Rossu**, the startling pink headland that forms an appropriate grand finale to the Golfe de Porto, rearing up like a pyramid 1,085ft/330m over the sea and topped with a perfectly restored Genoese tower, the **Torre de Turghio**. The path up is a 3hr round trip, but there isn't a lick of shade the whole way and towards the end it involves scrambling through the *maquis*. Not easy, but the views from the tower are truly exceptional; if you bring supplies you can stay the night, as the tower has a working fireplace. As for the D824, it carries on south of Capu Rossu to the **Plage d'Arone** (12km from Piana), a superb beach – sandy this time, although like the others it does shelve off rather quickly – with crystal water, a campsite, a pizzeria and coves for snorkelling nearby.

Piana is also the base for the classic ascent of **Capo d'Orto** (4,245ft/1,294m), the mighty mountain that looms over Porto like Monty Python's hedgehog. The round-trip walk takes about 6hrs, and you need to be fit and have proper boots, and make sure there's no chance of rain, as the path is dangerous when wet. To get to the trail-head, drive 1km north of Piana on the D81 and turn off to the right on to a dirt track until you reach a fork in the road, where you should leave the car. The track on the right picks up the orange waymarked trail after 3km. The last half-hour, marked only by cairns, involves some easy climbing over the rocks; the views over the entire Golfe de Porto are simply ravishing.

Inland from Porto: the Gorges de Spelunca

The natural wonders don't end at the coast. Just above Porto, the river Porto and its tributaries have combined to hew a profound cleft in the granite, the **Spelunca gorge**, as red as a sore throat in places, in others steeped in shadows from snaggletoothed peaks. **Ota**, a handsome stone village 5km east of Porto, is the main base for walks in the area. There's an old saying: *'Ota Ota! attenti à la Cota!'* ('Ota Ota! watch your side!'), and if you look at Capo d'Ota, looming overhead, you can see why: it resembles the Sphinx, ready to drop its giant head on the village. Even worse, the giant rock is said to wiggle to and fro. Fortunately, benevolent monks hold it back with ropes of goat hair in return for their dinner, which the women of Ota dutifully carry up every night. Just ask any child. The same women, or at least their grandmothers, were known for their Ota canal roof tiles, which they used to mould on their thighs.

You can take a stroll around the most beautiful part of the Spelunca gorge from here, or better yet catch a bus or hitch up to Evisa along the D124, with its dramatic views over the gorge, and walk down to Ota along the **Genoese mule track**. This charming three-hour walk (part of the Mare e Monti trail, which you can join by Evisa's cemetery) offers a good idea of how people got around on Corsica for hundreds of years, although the canopy of trees obscures more than the occasional glimpse of Spelunca's towering walls. Along the track are places to bathe, and two graceful Genoese bridges in lush settings, the **Ponte de Zaglia** and the **Ponte de Pianella**, both discreetly restored and listed as historic monuments. A third walk from Ota, an eight-hour trek through the magnificent **Gorges de la Lonca** just to the north, also uses part of the Mare e Monti trail in its circuit, but much of it remains an exercise in map-reading and orienteering skills, only for very experienced walkers.

Evisa and the Forêt d'Aitone

Evisa, 2,700ft/823m higher than Porto, is a beautiful mountain resort reputed for its restaurants and its chestnut groves that yield an AOC nut called *instina*, which are the focus of a very Corsican country festival in November, along with wild mushrooms. At other times, visitors come not only for the Spelunca gorge but for a walk through the magical **Forêt d'Aitone**, which begins just east of Evisa and continues 12km up to the Col de Vergio. This contains Corsica's most extensive and oldest stand of Laricio pines, thousands of which managed to survive the axes of Genoese and French lumberjacks in the 18th and 19th centuries. The giant logs were transported down to Vico and the port at Sagone on what is now the D70, a road known as the Piste des Condamnés for the convict labour used by the French to improve it.

There are several paths into the big trees. From the upper part of Evisa you can pick up the orange-marked Mare e Monti trail through the chestnuts to the Grotte des Bandits and the Cascades (*see* below), an easy family walk of two hours there and back. For an eagle's-eye view over the area, continue 3km up the D84, where a wide lay-by signals the short path to the **Belvédère**, a giant rock over the torrent Aitone, with superb views of the blushing mountains, the Spelunca gorge and the distant sea. Another very popular path to the **Cascades de la Valla Scarpa** (or Cascades d'Aitone) begins another kilometre east, marked by a sign and only a 15-minute walk from the D84. Here the Aitone plunges in cascades over the granite, delving out pools that make perfect if rather chilly swimming holes. If it's too crowded (and in summer it usually is) you can easily walk downriver to find quieter spots.

For longer walks, head another 3km up the D84, where the oldest Laricio pines – mere babies back in the 14th century when the Black Death ravaged Europe – stand

The King of the Mountains

Corsica's most famous bandit, Théodore Poli, was a good citizen until 1817, when he was 20 years old and conscripted into the French army as part of an effort to reduce banditry. Poli was ready to do his duty, but an enemy went to the *gendarmes* and told them he was planning to desert. The *gendarmes* arrested him but, in spite of the chains, Poli escaped, killed his arrester, and swore eternal war on the French police.

Poli was as good as his word. His daring attacks and ability to slip away in the nick of time made him Corsica's Robin Hood. He joined the secret Carbonari society, dedicated to the overthrow of Bourbon France, and attracted considerable support from Corsicans in favour of independence. Making the Forêt d'Aitone his 'green palace', he was joined by the largest gathering of bandits in Corsican history, who elected him Théodore II of Corsica, King of the Mountains. Their Constitution d'Aitone set up a government, whose 'tax collectors' went around to all the wealthy nobles and clergy. Few who refused to pay survived. When the *gendarmes* in Bastia guillotined one of Poli's followers, he captured the executioner, shot him only 300m from the barracks of the *gendarmes*, and still got away. In 1822 the French sent a unit of crack infantry-men against Poli's merry men, forcing them to disperse, so that only a handful remained with him in a mountain cave near Murzo. There were quarrels and killings, and in 1827 Poli was either betrayed by the husband of his mistress, or lured by a beautiful girl into a glade where he was trapped and killed; legend has it that before he died he reloaded his gun and arranged it so that it fired and killed the first man to touch his corpse. His body was displayed for two days in Vico and attracted thousands.

tall and straight like columns seemingly into infinity, the sun filtering in radiant beams through their lofty crowns. The needles crave light and air, and as the tree grows it drops any branches left behind in its shade. The rare *sittelle* (Corsican nuthatch) lives here; an easy 1½hr walk takes in an area where they are often spotted. A more strenuous trail leads in an hour to the **Col de Salto** (4,563ft/1,391 m), from where you can continue for another two hours or so over the treeline to the **Col de Cocavera** (4,839ft/1,475m) for a view that embraces the entire forest and the Golfe de Porto. If you're continuing east to the **Col de Vergio** and the Niolo, *see* p.164; for the Vico road, *see* p.273.

The Golfe de Sagone

If you're approaching from the red granite north and the Golfe de Porto, the Golfe de Sagone to the south seems soft and fluffy. Twice as big, and blessed with sandy beaches, the bay is a favourite for family beach holidays, with Cargèse as the most *simpatico* of the resorts. Inland, the walk to the Lac de Creno is the main draw, along with big helpings of rural Corsica and the vineyards of the Cinarca, the bailiwick of Corsica's medieval hotshots.

Cargèse/Carghjese 'La Grecque'

Within striking distance of Porto (31km), Cargèse becomes more popular by the year, thanks in no small part to its marina and nearby Club Med. Set on a granite promontory, overlooking a coast punctuated by four Geneose towers, Cargèse also has three things that Porto lacks: a choice of safe sandy beaches, architectural character, and Greeks (*see* box, right). The landmarks here are two churches, facing each other on separate heights: the late Baroque **Latin church**, with some fancy *trompe l'œil* inside and a pretty view from its terrace, completed in 1840, and the brightly frescoed **Greek Uniat church**, built in 1870, and complete with bells from the cathedral at Vitylo, brought by the colonists in 1675. There are icons from Vitylo, too: on the left wall, a richly coloured 16th-century *St John the Baptist* painted on Mount Athos, a 13th-century *Epitaphios* (entombment) by the entrance and a *Virgin and Child*, visible behind the iconostasis. In a rare, perhaps unique, spirit of ecumenical harmony, one priest serves both the Latin and Greek churches on a rota basis. There are two processions celebrating the Assumption on 15 August, and others for the two patron saints' days, Spiridion on 12 December at the Greek church, Lucy the day after at the Latin. Cargèse is at its Greekiest at Easter, with the Greek services, candles and cries of 'Christ has Risen!' at Saturday midnight; on Easter Monday an icon is taken out and displayed to the four cardinal points to bless the village, while robed members of the confraternity noisily shoot rifles in the air ('just to make sure Christ is awake').

The most important trump cards in Cargèse's deck are its six beaches. The closest, the beautiful sandy white **Plage de Pero**, 2km north, is guarded by a Genoese watch-tower, Omigna, and another 2km north is the equally pretty **Plage de Chiuni**, where the presence of the Club Med guarantees that you won't lack for company. On 14 December 1942, Captain L'Herminier's submarine *Casabianca* came from Algeria

Corsica's Greeks

In 1675, over 2,000 years after the ancient Greeks founded a colony on Corsica at Alalia, a new colony of Greeks arrived: 730 refugees fleeing Ottoman misrule, all from the village of Vitylo in the Mani, in the southern Peloponnese. They had spent the last 12 years in Genoa, negotiating terms, and the deal suited both parties: the Genoese always needed friends in Corsica, and the Maniots were among the most redoubtable fighters and pirates in Greece. One sticking point was religion – the Greeks were allowed to keep their Orthodox faith as long as they submitted to the pope, i.e. become Uniats (when they promised, they crossed their fingers behind their backs) and changed their difficult Greek names so that the Italians could pronounce them. In return they were allowed to bear arms and to sail in expeditions against the Turks under Genoa's flag, and to buy up land for a small fee in this corner of Corsica.

Their first settlement – they built a circle of five little hamlets – was at Paomia, 4km up in the steep mountains above modern Cargèse. Unfortunately, Vico's shepherds used the same land to graze their flocks in winter, so there was a conflict. Equally irksome to the Corsicans was the Greeks' success: the Mani being extremely rocky and arid, they leapt at the chance to work fertile land for a change, and in no time had built stone-walled terraces for garden plots, clearing the *maquis* to plant olives and vines. To make it worse, the Greeks (many of whom were of the Stephanopolis family, which claimed descent from the Byzantine imperial family, the Comnenes) looked down on their rustic Corsican neighbours and called them 'goat pelts'.

The biggest hurdle in relations, however, was the Greeks' stubborn loyalty to their Genoese benefactors. The shepherds of Vico attacked Paomia in 1715 and 1730, and after a siege the Greeks fled to Genoese-occupied Ajaccio, where they were welcome, while the Corsicans razed Paomia. While in Ajaccio, the Greeks continued fighting for the Genoese with such ferocity that 'May God deliver you into the hands of the Greeks!' became a Corsican curse. When the island passed to France in 1768, many Greeks emigrated to Algeria and founded the village of Sidi Merouan, but the majority stayed and fought for France. In gratitude, the first French governor of Corsica, the Marquis de Marbeuf, gave them Cargèse in 1775. But Corsican mountain-eers burned Cargèse in the French Revolution. Although the Greeks trickled back under Napoleon (by 1804 the population of Cargèse was 1,000, including 300 Corsicans), relations remained strained; when the Greek War of Independence broke out in 1821, many Greeks were keen to go back to the Mani and fight the Turks, but they feared what the Corsicans would do to their families and homes if they left.

Gradually things improved: local Corsicans allied with the Greeks, and by 1830 the shepherds of Vico gave up their attacks. The archbishop of Ajaccio compelled the Greeks to become Uniat. Corsicans moved to Cargèse, and intermarriage and settled times made Greeks into Corsicans. Their Italianized surnames survive, although the language has been forgotten; when Patrick Leigh Fermor visited in 1958 he could find only two women who spoke Greek, and heard them use 17th-century expressions. Even so, identity runs deep here; the population of Cargèse got a boost in 1963, when the descendants of the families who went to Algeria returned, and an even older link was re-established in 1992 when Cargèse and Vitylo were twinned.

Getting Around

Two **buses** a day, and an extra one on Sunday in summer, stop at Cargèse and Sagone on **SAIB**'s Ajaccio–Porto route, t 04 95 22 41 99.

Ceccaldi's buses from Ajaccio to Marignana, t 04 95 21 38 06, provide a link to Vico, Sagone and Tiuccia four times a day, Mon–Sat.

Taxis: Marco Miranda, in Cargèse, t 04 95 24 58 64 or t 06 63 55 83 33, specializes in excursions. Also **Cyril Cortesi**, t 04 95 26 41 09 or t 06 82 02 12 05.

Car hire: Europa, Rue Marbœuf, t 04 95 26 44 50; **Hertz**, petrol station Terrazzoni, t 04 95 26 41 09.

Tourist Information

Cargèse: Rue du Docteur Dragacci, t 04 95 26 41 31, www.cargese.net. Open June–Sept daily 9–7; Oct–May Mon–Sat 9–12.30 and 3–5. **Sagone:** t 04 95 28 05 36, http://ot-vicosagone.com. Open July–Sept Mon–Sat 9.30–12.30 and 3–7, Sun 9.30–1.

Sports and Activities

Sea excursions: Vedettes Nave Va, www.naveva.com, has boats small enough to enter the grottoes, and offers sea excursions to the Calanche de Piana and the Réserve Naturelle de Scandola. In Sagone, reserve at the portside kiosk, t 04 95 28 02 66; in Cargèse get tickets in advance at U Rasaghju Pizzeria by the port, t 04 95 26 48 60.

Horse Riding: Ferme Equestre Muntagnoli, Vico, t 06 08 73 82 19 or t 04 95 26 17 66. Excursions from an hour to 11 days in the mountains, and visits to the lakes.

Where to Stay and Eat

Cargèse ✉ 20130

★★★Les Lentisques, 100m Plage de Pero, t 04 95 26 42 34, www.leslentisques.com (expensive; half-board only in July and Aug). In a quiet setting, 800m from the village, a calm and attractive little hotel with 17 comfortable rooms, including interconnected family rooms. Closed Oct–April.

★★St-Jean, Place St-Jean, t 04 95 26 46 68, www.lesaintjean.com (moderate). Stylish air-conditioned rooms and studios, and a good restaurant that serves both traditional dishes and pizzas and stays open late in the summer. Open all year.

★Bel'Mare, 400m south of the centre, t 04 95 26 40 13, www.belmare.net (moderate). Genial blue and white hotel and restaurant, perched high over the marina; large rooms with sea views from the balconies. The Antonini family, who own it, also rent out a pair of villas near Pero beach. Closed mid-Nov–Feb.

★Thalassa, Plage de Pero, t 04 95 26 40 08 (moderate). Charming, modest rooms on the beach 1.5km from Cargèse, Greek-style with plenty of bougainvillaea. Restaurant open only to guests on half-board terms. Bookings essential. Closed Oct–Feb.

★Le Cyrnos, Av de la République, t 04 95 26 49 47, www.torraccia.com (moderate–inexpensive). In the village, simple rooms in pretty yellow building. They also rent out wooden chalets in the countryside. Open all year.

Punta e Mare, just outside the centre on Rte de Paomia, t 04 95 26 44 33, www.hotel-puntaemare.com (moderate–inexpensive). Quiet, friendly place with basic en suite rooms and studios on a garden, popular with walkers. Closed Jan.

Camping Torraccia, 4km north of Cargèse, t 04 95 26 42 39, www.camping-torraccia.

to drop off the first agents to organize the Resistance on Corsica, along with the vital wireless sets. L'Herminier had been aiming for the Plage de Chiuni but, confused in the darkness, he landed just north at the Golfe de Topiti – a remarkably lucky break, as Italian troops were camped at Chiuni. Other beaches lie east of Cargèse: pretty little **Plage dei Monachi**, 1km east at the bottom of a track, and the **Plage de Ménasina** and **Plage de Stagnoli**, the latter with sugary fine sand.

com. Spread over the terraces of an olive grove near the Mare e Monti trailhead, with some bungalows and a bar, 2km to the beaches. *Closed Oct–mid-May.*

A Volta, behind the Latin church, t 04 95 26 41 96. Pretty sunset views and delicious seafood, with a light Italian touch (*carpaccio* with Parmesan, *daurade aux amandes* with lobster sauce). *Around €35. Closed Oct–April.*

Le Cabanon de Charlotte, by the marina, t 06 81 23 66 93. Informal, friendly little place serving the day's catch (*menus €15–31*) and pizzas in the evenings. *Closed Nov–Mar.*

Sagone ✉ 20118

**Le Funtanella, t 04 95 28 02 49, *www. residence-funtanella.com (moderate).* Set back from the sea behind a lawn with a play area, nothing fancy but a choice of studios, apartments or mini-villas with kitchenettes. *Closed Nov–Mar.*

**Cyrnos, t 04 95 28 00 01, *www.chez.com/ hotelcyrnos (moderate).* Big family-run hotel – restaurant on the beach, linked to a diving centre. *Good €23 menu. Closed mid-Oct–April.*

La Marine, on the Ajaccio road, t 04 95 28 00 03 (*inexpensive; demi-pension terms*). A few rooms in an old-fashioned beach hotel built in 1901, with a decent restaurant, in summer generally full of people who come back year after year. *Closed Jan.*

L'Ancura, Port de Sagone, t 04 95 28 04 93. Restaurant located on the far edge of the beach, serving all kinds of fresh fish and pizzas too. *From €10. Closed Oct–April.*

Tiuccia ✉ 20111

Camping Les Couchants, 5km north of Tiuccia, on the road to Casaglione, t 04 95 52 26 60. Well-kept garden campsite overlooking the sea, with a restaurant and bungalows to rent. *Closed Oct–May.*

U Taravu, t 04 95 52 22 40. An old family-run favourite in an outdated setting, serving

solid Corsican cuisine with style and fresh seafood, including sea urchins in season. *Menus at €25 and €32. Open all year.*

Vico ✉ 20160

U Paradisu, t 04 95 26 61 62, *www.hotel-uparadisu.com (moderate; half-board obligatory from June–Sept).* Maybe not paradise, but a warm welcome, homey atmosphere and pool in a wooded setting; the good restaurant, **Le St-Pierre, features boar *civet*, trout, and *magret de canard* with honey. *Book well in advance for a room.*

Café National, t 04 95 26 60 25. The local rendezvous, with inexpensive pizzas and grilled meats, and live guitar music on Thurs, Fri and Sat.

Guagno-les-Bains ✉ 20160

***Hôtel des Thermes, t 04 95 26 80 50, *www.hotel-lesthermes.com (moderate).* Smart spa hotel with a pool, tennis and restaurant, built by the *département* to bring some people and money into the area. Warm welcome guaranteed. *Closed Oct–April.*

Auberge des Deux Sorru, t 04 95 28 35 14 (*inexpensive*). Simple rooms and good mountain food in the restaurant, with *brocciu* in nearly every dish. *€15 menu du jour.*

Soccia ✉ 20125

**U Paese, t 04 95 28 31 92, *http://monsite. wanadoo.fr/hotel.u.paese.corse (moderate–inexpensive, with breakfast).* Large if somewhat threadbare hotel that gets mostly walkers.

A Merendella, Rte de l'Eglise, t 04 95 28 34 91. Lovely refined cuisine served on tables scattered across a lawn under the trees in the middle of nowhere – good enough to draw diners from miles away. *Daily changing menu, from €16 depending on how many courses you order. Closed Nov–Mar. Be sure to book in summer.*

You can also take an excursion into the region's pre-Greek past, 4km up at **Paomia** – there's a **dolmen** and the **Menhir of Malora or U Scumuncatu** ('the Ex-communicated'), a statue-menhir with a face, helmet (or ears?) and possibly a breastplate, founded in three bits and re-erected at the farm of the finder, Antoine Amédei. Although there are few traces of the first Greek hamlets here, Paomia also has a couple of ruined Pisan chapels, one of which was partly rebuilt by a team of women.

Just outside the centre of Cargèse is one last surprise: the **Institut d'Etudes Scientifiques de Cargèse**, founded in the 1960s and dedicated to High Energies and Particular Physics; run in conjunction with the University of Corsica, it's used year-round for seminars, conferences and courses: see *http://cargese.univ-corse.fr.*

Sagone and Tiuccia

Sagone/Saone, 13km east of Cargèse, occupies the rather melancholy sand-strewn delta of the Sagone river. Although it doesn't look like it, people have lived here since the cows came home: founded by the Romans, it became one of the first bishoprics on Corsica. In the 12th century the Pisans rebuilt its cathedral of **Sant'Appiano**, on the northwest side of the port, with a pair of statue-menhirs embedded in the wall; some think the builders weren't just making use of a handy cut block of stone, but were 'christianizing' the pagan monuments. The cathedral and the rest of Sagone were ruined in the 16th century by the Saracens and, although the Genoese built a tower to warn off future incursions, it never recovered; the bishopric was moved inland to Vico in 1572, and malaria took over. Sagone's lack of charm is compensated by its vast beach of sugar-soft sand, the **Plage du Liamone**. Avoid swimming at Santana beach just south of town, however, where the dangerous currents have claimed lives.

Tiuccia to the south is a modest modern resort 7km from Sagone, with a long strand of golden sand, the **Plage de la Liscia**, as its *raison d'être*. Two Genoese towers frame it on either side, while above town are the lonesome ruins of the **Castello di Capraja**, seat of the ruthless Counts of Cinarca, who claimed to be the heirs of Ugo Colonna and who, beginning in the 13th century with the powerful Sinucello della Rocca, the Giudice di Cinarca, played off Pisa, Genoa, Aragon and rival lords in the Middle Ages to rule the *Dila dei Monti*. From here it's 25km to Ajaccio (*see* p.77).

Inland from Sagone: Vico and Around

Il y a là-bas des matins qui sont comme le premier matin du monde. Les contours des montagnes bleues de la Sposata se détachent sur le bleu du ciel avec une telle préci-sion, une si grande légèreté que le temps semble arrêté là, dans cette lumière touchée par la grâce. Nulle part au monde on ne la trouve, je le sais maintenant; elle est à la fois intense et transparente, irréelle. Le silence alentour, je le connais aussi; on l'entend dans toutes les solitudes, et c'est sur lui que se referme tout amour.

(There are mornings there that are like the first morning in the world. The contours of the blue mountains of La Sposata stand out from the blue of the sky with such preci-sion, such great delicacy that time seems to stop there, in that light touched by grace. Nowhere else in the world do you find it, I know that now; it is at once intense and transparent, unreal. The silence all around, I know that, too – one hears it whenever there is solitude, and it is on it that all love closes upon itself.)

Marie Susini, *La renfermée la Corse*, 1981

Above the Golfe de Sagone, the pitter-patter of cows and pigs and a few road hogs are often the only sound in a collection of villages that hosted some of Corsica's last bandits, a state of affairs that only came to an end (officially, anyway) in 1931, when the French government sent a force of 600 men to 'clean' the *maquis* and disarm the villagers. The most important town is **Vico/Vicu**, an atmospheric, frowning feudal stronghold 13km northeast of Sagone. Vico briefly held the status of Sagone's bishopric before it moved to Calvi in 1625, and it was even more briefly the capital of the *département* of Liamone, in the original division of the island in the French Revolution. It too has its prehistoric monuments, set up on the Col St-Antoine: the 7ft/2m **Statue-menhir d'Apriccani** (or 'de Mérimée' because he was the first to describe it) with a well-defined face, chest and pectorals; the shorter one by its side was rescued from the wall of the cathedral at Sagone.

The big white **Couvent St-François** (*t 04 95 26 83 83; open daily 2–6*), set among the magnolias above Vico, was founded in 1481 by Gian Paolo de Leca. The Leca were among the most powerful of the Cinarca lords, and in the mid-15th century Raffè de Leca, with the support of 22 brothers and cousins, became the leader of the Cinarchesi fight to the death against the Genoese. He won every battle he fought, and even captured the Genoese governor, wheeling him about in a cage until he died of shame and exposure. The Genoese put a thousand-ducat reward on Raffè's head, and in 1456 took the families of his followers hostage, persuading one to betray him. Cornered in his castle, Raffè jumped from the window and broke his legs, so the Genoese captured him alive and brought him to Vico with his 22 relatives, where their throats were cut; Raffè's body was then quartered and each piece sent to a different town in Corsica, while his head was preserved in salt and ceremoniously presented to the senate in Genoa. The inhabitants of Vico managed to hide Gian Paolo de Leca, so he was the only member of the clan to survive the massacre, and the convent was his way of thanking them (he also buried his war chest of silver and ducats in the garden, which the Genoese later found). Since 1836 the convent has been occupied by monks of the order of the Oblats de Marie Immaculée; the church has frescoes, 17th-century chestnut woodwork in the sacristy, and reputedly the oldest crucifix on Corsica, predating the 15th century.

From Vico, the D70 north to Evisa (*see p.266*) is a beautiful 32km drive through century-old chestnut forests, with a pretty 5km detour along the way to **Renno**, a hamlet immersed in orchards and walnut groves. Renno is famous for its old-fashioned fair of St Roch every 16–18 August and for its delicious apples (*pommes reinettes*), sold at roadside stands. Further up, the **Col de Sevi** (3,608ft/1,100m) offers grandiose views down to the Golfe de Porto.

The Lac de Creno

A relatively monotonous road from Vico twists east to **Guagno-les-Bains**, a thermal spa since the 18th century, and recently back in business. Turn left here for Poggiolo and **Soccia**, where a new road continues up to a small car park by a big metal cross, the starting point for the easy two-hour walk to the idyllic little **Lac de Creno**, in the lap of Monte Rotondo, surrounded by Laricio pines. The lake was made by the devil with his hammer; afterwards, he hid in the lake until an old priest and a shepherd prayed so hard that the waters dried up and exposed him, after which he vanished and the waters, now pure, returned. You can also get there on a much steeper path through the chestnuts from **Orto** (east of Poggiolo), a slice of *la Corse profonde* in a stunning setting under Monte Sant'Eliseo. **Guagno** itself, another rough 8.5km east from its spa, has paths linking to the GR20. The birthplace of Théodore Poli (*see* p.267), it also produced the fiery priest Dominique Leca who fought with Paoli, and after Paoli's exile continued his own private war against the French for three years, fighting with a band of guerrilla fighters in the wilds of the Fiumorbo before he was found dead of exhaustion in a cave, clutching a rifle in one hand and a crucifix in the other.

The Cinarca

South of Vico, the narrow D1 winds 8km through the magnificent, lonesome **Gorges du Liamone** to **Arbori**, a beautiful old village in a striking setting, where Raffè de Leca was cornered in his castle. Another 18km of serious driving, will bring you to handsome **Ambiegna**, the first village of the Cinarca, which the French government prefers to call the *pays d'Orcino*. Orcino comes from the Latin *Urcinium*, a wine-exporting stronghold cited by Ptolemy that may have had something to do with the many ogre (*orcu*) legends of Corsica. Famous for the big and often bad barons who terrorized the Genoese from the 13th to 15th centuries (*see* **History**), the Cinarca, some say, still isn't quite tamed; it was only in 1935 that the bandit Spada, the 'Tiger of the Cinarca', was captured and guillotined by the French for killing two *gendarmes* in 1922.

This can all seem light years away from the lush 'garden in the *maquis*' as the Cinarca is known today. A pocket of villages in an amphitheatre above the Golfe de la Liscia and Tiuccia, it made a fortune between the world wars from citrons (*cédrats*), a thick-skinned rustic cousin of the lemon, although these days most have gone wild; and AOC wine is the most valuable crop. There are no great sights here, but **Casaglione**, 3km south of Ambiegna, is proud of a painting of the *Crucifixion* of 1505 in the village church. From here you could back track to pretty **Sari-d'Orcino**, 5km on the D1 from the Ambiegna crossroads; the capital of the Cinarca, Sari-d'Orcino is made up of two hamlets on the slopes of Punta San Damiano and has the area's best-known vineyard, the **Clos d'Alzeto** (*t 04 95 52 24 67, www.closdalzeto.com; open summer Mon–Sat 8–12 and 2–7.30, winter Mon–Sat 1–5.30*), the highest in Corsica and one of the oldest, in the same family since 1820.

From here you can twist around to Cannelle and take the D101 down to **Calcatoggio/Calcatoghju** and its orchards on the main coastal D81 to Ajaccio. In **Appietto** (3km off the D81) the towers still bear rare Arabic inscriptions from the Saracen occupation. From behind Appietto's chapel of San Chirgu, you can walk up in an hour and a half to **La Rocher de Gozzi**, an eagle's nest topped with the ruins of a castle built by the Counts of Cinarca. The area below it on the Golfe de Lava was the stomping ground of another famous *bandit d'honneur*, Nonce Romanetti, 'the king of the *maquis*', who entertained tourists in grand style, selling them postcards of himself covered with weapons and stamped with the postmark 'Romanetti Bandit' since he never learned to read or write, until the *gendarmes* gunned him down in 1926.

Language

Everywhere in France the same level of politeness is expected: use *monsieur, madame* or *mademoiselle* when speaking to everyone (and never *garçon* in restaurants!), from your first *bonjour* to your last *au revoir*.

See pp.49–52 for menu vocabulary.

General

hello *bonjour*
good evening *bonsoir*
good night *bonne nuit*
goodbye *au revoir*
please *s'il vous plaît*
thank you (very much) *merci (beaucoup)*
yes *oui*
no *non*
good *bon (bonne)*
bad *mauvais(e)*
excuse me *pardon, excusez-moi*
Can you help me? *Pourriez-vous m'aider?*
My name is... *Je m'appelle...*
What is your name? *Comment t'appelles-tu?* (informal), *Comment vous appelez-vous?* (formal)
How are you? *Comment allez-vous?*
Fine *Ça va bien*
I don't understand *Je ne comprends pas*
I don't know *Je ne sais pas*
Speak more slowly *Pourriez-vous parler plus lentement?*
How do you say...in French? *Comment dit-on ...en français?*
Help! *Au secours!*
Where is (the railway station)? *Où se trouve (la gare)?*
Is it far? *C'est loin?*
left *à gauche*
right *à droite*
straight on *tout droit*
entrance *l'entrée*
exit *la sortie*
open *ouvert*
closed *fermé*

WC *les toilettes*
men *hommes*
ladies *dames* or *femmes*
doctor *un médecin*
hospital *un hôpital*
emergency room *la salle des urgences*
police station *le commissariat de police*
tourist information office *l'office de tourisme*
How much is it? *C'est combien?*
Do you have...? *Est-ce que vous avez...?*
It's too expensive *C'est trop cher*
bank *une banque*
money *l'argent*
change *la monnaie*
traveller's cheque *un chèque de voyage*
post office *la poste*
stamp *un timbre*
postcard *une carte postale*
public phone *une cabine téléphonique*
shop *un magasin*
central food market *les halles*
tobacconist *un tabac*
pharmacy *une pharmacie*
aspirin *l'aspirine*
condoms *les préservatifs*
insect repellent *l'anti-insecte*
sun cream *la crème solaire*
tampons *les tampons hygiéniques*

Transport

airport *l'aéroport*
aeroplane *l'avion*
go on foot *aller à pied*
bicycle *la bicyclette/le vélo*
mountain bike *le vélo tout terrain, VTT*
bus *l'autobus*
bus stop *l'arrêt d'autobus*
coach station *la gare routière*
railway station *la gare SNCF*
train *le train*
platform *le quai*
date-stamp machine *le composteur*
timetable *l'horaire*

left-luggage locker *la consigne automatique*
car *la voiture*
ticket office *le guichet*
ticket *un billet*
single to... *un aller (or aller simple) pour...*
return to... *un aller et retour pour...*
What time does the...leave?
  A quelle heure part...?
delayed *en retard*
on time *à l'heure*

Accommodation

single room *une chambre pour une personne*
twin room *une chambre à deux lits*
double room *une chambre pour deux
  personnes*
bed *un lit*
blanket *une couverture*
cot (child's bed) *un lit d'enfant*
pillow *un oreiller*
soap *du savon*
towel *une serviette*
booking *une réservation*
I would like to book a room *Je voudrais
  réserver une chambre*

Months

January *janvier*
February *février*
March *mars*
April *avril*
May *mai*
June *juin*
July *juillet*
August *août*
September *septembre*
October *octobre*
November *novembre*
December *décembre*

Days

Monday *lundi*
Tuesday *mardi*
Wednesday *mercredi*
Thursday *jeudi*
Friday *vendredi*
Saturday *samedi*
Sunday *dimanche*

Time

What time is it? *Quelle heure est-il?*
month *un mois*
week *une semaine*
day *un jour/une journée*
morning *le matin*
afternoon *l'après-midi*
evening *le soir*
night *la nuit*
today *aujourd'hui*
yesterday *hier*
tomorrow *demain*
day before yesterday *avant-hier*
day after tomorrow *après-demain*

Numbers

one *un*
two *deux*
three *trois*
four *quatre*
five *cinq*
six *six*
seven *sept*
eight *huit*
nine *neuf*
ten *dix*
eleven *onze*
twelve *douze*
thirteen *treize*
fourteen *quatorze*
fifteen *quinze*
sixteen *seize*
seventeen *dix-sept*
eighteen *dix-huit*
nineteen *dix-neuf*
twenty *vingt*
twenty-one *vingt et un*
twenty-two *vingt-deux*
thirty *trente*
forty *quarante*
fifty *cinquante*
sixty *soixante*
seventy *soixante-dix*
seventy-one *soixante-onze*
eighty *quatre-vingts*
eighty-one *quatre-vingt-un*
ninety *quatre-vingt-dix*
hundred *cent*
two hundred *deux cents*
thousand *mille*

Further Reading

Abram, David, *Trekking in Corsica* (Trailblazer Publications, 2002). Good practical guide.

Boswell, James, *The Journal of a Tour to Corsica* and *Memories of Pascal Paoli* (complete annotated edition, Oxford University Press, 2005). First published in 1768, this was Boswell's first writing success at the age of 29, full of wit and vigour, enthusiasm and insights. His visit made him a great advocate of Corsican independence, and his book was closely studied in the American colonies.

Campbell, Thomasina, *Southward Ho!* (out of print). Written in 1868, a vivid Victorian depiction of Corsican nature that brought down scores of Brits to check it out.

Carrington, Dorothy, *Granite Island* (Penguin, 1984). Originally published in 1971 and simply one of the best and most evocative books about a place ever written. Her *Dream Hunters of Corsica* (Weidenfeld & Nicolson, 1995) is a fascinating account of the *mazzeri* and other eerie traditions; her *Napoleon and his Parents on the Threshold of History* (Viking, 1988) is *the* authoritative account of Napoleon's Corsican years.

Flaubert, Gustave, *Mémoires d'un fou* (Flammarion, France, 1991). In 1840, Flaubert was 19, and went to Corsica as a reward for finishing school; here are his letters home.

Goscinny, René, *Astérix in Corsica* (Orion, 2004). Obelix was there, too – explains where those menhirs came from!

Grosjean, Roger, *La Corse avant l'histoire* (Klincksieck, France, 1966). The most important work by the archaeologist who excavated many of the sites.

Johnson, Paul, *Napoleon* (Weidenfeld & Nicholson, 2002/Penguin, 2006). New critical biography of the prototype for all subsequent totalitarians.

Lear, Edward, *Journal of a Landscape Painter in Corsica* (Harrap, 1966). Originally published in 1870, its wonderfully romantic drawings were another lure for the first English visitors to the island.

Lucarotti, Rolli, *Recipes from Corsica* (Prospect Books, 2003). Excellent recipes and anecdotes by a long-time resident.

Maupassant, Guy de, *Contes du jour et de la nuit* (Flammarion, 1998). Maupassant only spent two months being overwhelmed on Corsica; these are some of the stories he was inspired to write.

Mérimée, Prosper, *Colomba and Carmen* (Kessinger, 2005). When it came out in 1841, *Colomba*, based on a blood feud in Fozzano and the intractable Columba (made young and pretty) caused a sensation. Also see his *Notes d'un voyage en Corse*, written in his capacity as inspector of monuments, reprinted in 1989 by Adam Biro.

Moracchini-Mazel, Geneviève, *Les Eglises Romanes de Corse* (Zodiaque, 1972). Definitive account of Corsica's Romanesque; her *Les Monuments Paléo-Chrétiens de la Corse* (Klincksieck, 1967) is a thorough account of the churches that came before.

Parris, Bill, *The Making of a Legionnaire: My Life in the French Foreign Legion Parachute Regiment* (Weidenfeld & Nicolson, 2004). A British soldier tells what it takes to wear the famous *kepi*.

Pétillon, *L'Enquête Corse* (Albin Michel, 2000). Bestselling comic book in France (and Corsica), poking fun at both Corsican and French attitudes.

Price, Gillian, *Walking in Corsica* (Cicerone, 2003). Good general guide.

Rogliano, Jean-Claude, *Le Berger des morts (Mal'Concilio)* (France-empire, 2001). Novel by bestselling Corsican writer, which inspired songs by Jean-Paul Poletti and a ballet by Marie-Claude Pietragalla.

Silvani, Paul, *Et la Corse fut libérée* (La Marge, France, 1993). Excellent, award-winning account of the Liberation.

Thrasher, Peter Adam, *Pasquale Paoli; An Enlightened Hero* (London, Constable, 1970). Generally considered the best biography of Paoli in English.

Index

Main page references are in **bold**. Page references to maps are in *italics*.

Corsica touring atlas

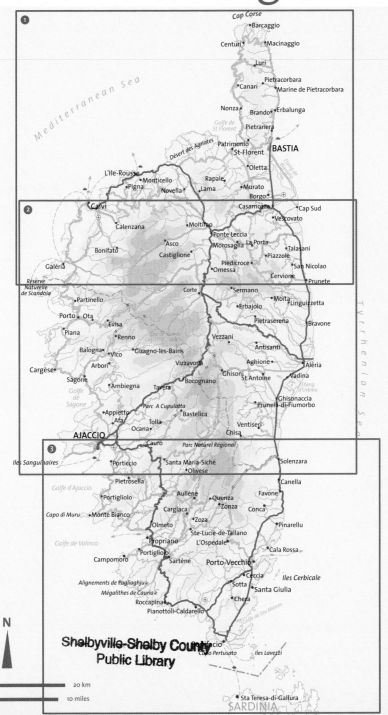

Mediterranean Sea

Tyrrhenian Sea

Cap Corse
• Barcaggio
Centuri• • Macinaggio
• Luri
• Pietracorbara
• Canari • Marine de Pietracorbara
Nonza• Brando• • Erbalunga
Golfe de St Florent • Pietranera
Patrimonio• • **BASTIA**
Désert des Agriates St-Florent•
• Oletta
L'Ile-Rousse• Rapale• • Murato
Monticello• Lama• Borgo•
Pigna• Novella•
Calvi Casamozza• • Cap Sud
Calenzana• • Vescovato
• Moltifao Ponte Leccia•
Asco• Morosaglia• La Porta• • Talasani
Bonifato• Castiglione• • Piazzole
Galéria• Piedicroce• • San Nicolao
Omessa• Cervione• • Prunete
Réserve Naturelle de Scandola
Corte• Sermano• • Moïta
Partinello• • Erbajolo • Linguizzetta
Porto• Ota• Pietraserena• • Bravone
Evisa•
Piana• • Renno
Balogna• Vico• • Guagno-les-Bains Vezzani•
Arbori• Vizzavona• Antisanti•
Cargèse• Aghione•
Sagone• Ambiegna• Ghisoni• St Antoine • Aléria
Golfe de Sagone Tavera• Bocognano• Vadina•
Appietto• *Parc A Cupulatta* Ghisonaccia•
Afa• Tolla• Bastelica• Prunelli-di-Fiumorbo•
Ocana•
AJACCIO Cauro• *Parc Naturel Régional* Ventiseri•
Chisa•
Iles Sanguinaires Porticcio• Santa-Maria-Siché• Solenzara•
Olivese•
Pietrosella•
Golfe d'Ajaccio • Canella
Portigliolo• Aullène• Favone•
Capo di Muru • Monte Bianco Cargiaca• Quenza• Conca•
Zonza•
Olmeto• Zoza• • Pinarellu
Propriano• Ste-Lucie-de-Tallano•
Golfe de Valinco L'Ospedale• • Cala Rossa
Portigliolo•
Campomoro• Sartène• Porto-Vecchio•
Alignements de Pagliaghju Ceccia• *Iles Cerbicale*
Mégalithes de Cauria Sotta• • Santa Giulia
Roccapina• Chera•
Pianottoli-Caldarello•
Golfe de Sta Manza

N

Capo Pertusato *Iles Lavezzi*

20 km
10 miles

• Sta Teresa-di-Gallura
SARDINIA

N

10 km
5 miles

Mediterranean Sea

Plage de Malfalco

Désert

Toulon   Genova   Plage d'
Marseille   Nice   Ostriconi
Savona   Ogliastro   Monetta
                                        N197
Marseille   Nice   Lozari
                           L'Ile-Rousse
Sant'Ambrogio   N197
                           Monticello
              Algajola   Corbara
                  Pigna   Santa Reparata-
Punta della Revellata   di-Balagna
                  Aregno   Sant'Antonino   Belgodère   Palasca
              Lumio   N197
Calvi   Cateri
                           Avapessa   Costa   Speloncato
Notre Dame-   Muro   Pioggiola
de-la-Serra   Montegrosso   Cassano Feliceto   Olmi-Cappella
Calvi-Ste   Montemaggiore   Zilia   Vallica
Catherine   Mausoleo
Airport   Sta Restituta   Tartagine
              Calenzana

Suare

                                         Forêt de Tartagine   Monte Padro   Gorges de l'Asco
Argentella
                                                                              Asco
                           Cirque de   Aiguilles de
              Bonifato   Bonifato   Popolasca
                           Spasimata   Forêt de Carrozzica
                           Haut'Asco
Galéria   Le Fango   Scala di
                                                                Santa
              Fango   Regina
                  Manso   Monte Cinto
                           Bergerie de Cesta

2

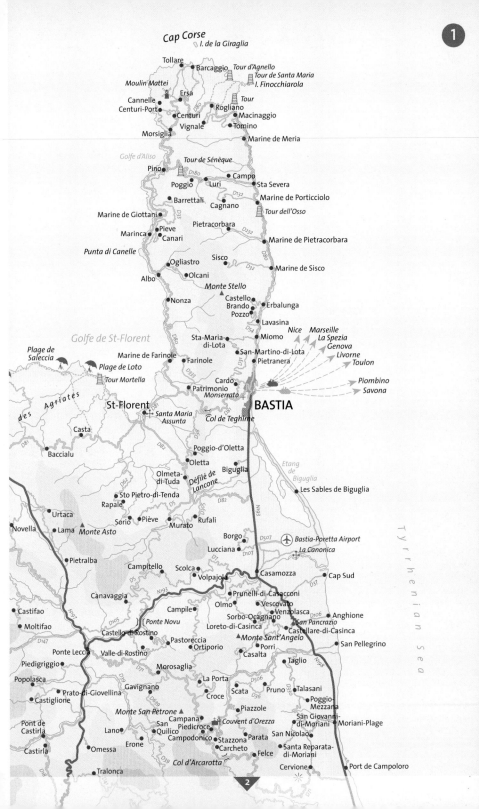

Cap Corse
I. de la Giraglia

Tollare
Barcaggio
Tour d'Agnello
Tour de Santa Maria
I. Finocchiarola

Moulin Mattei
Ersa
Tour
Cannelle
Centuri-Port
Centuri
Rogliano
Macinaggio
Vignale
Tomino
Morsiglia
Marine de Meria

Golfe d'Aliso
Tour de Sénèque
Pino
Campo
Poggio
Luri
Sta Severa
Barrettali
Marine de Porticciolo
Cagnano
Marine de Giottani
Tour dell'Osso
Pietracorbara
Marinca
Pieve
Canari
Marine de Pietracorbara
Punta di Canelle
Ogliastro
Sisco
Albo
Olcani
Marine de Sisco
Monte Stello
Castello
Brando
Erbalunga
Nonza
Pozzo
Lavasina
Miomo
Nice
Marseille
La Spezia
Genova
Sta-Maria-
di-Lota
San-Martino-di-Lota
Livorne
Marine de Farinole
Farinole
Pietranera
Toulon
Golfe de St-Florent
Plage de
Saleccia
Plage de Loto
Tour Mortella
Cardo
Piombino
Patrimonio
Savona
Monserrato
BASTIA
St-Florent
Santa Maria
Assunta
Col de Teghime
Casta
Bacialu
Poggio-d'Oletta
Oletta
Biguglia
Olmeta-
di-Tuda
Défilé de
Lancone
Etang
de
Biguglia
Sto Pietro-di-Tenda
Les Sables de Biguglia
Rapale
Urtaca
Piève
Sorio
Murato
Rufali
Novella
Lama
Monte Asto
Borgo
Pietralba
Lucciana
Bastia-Poretta Airport
La Canonica
Campitello
Scolca
Volpajola
Casamozza
Cap Sud
Canavaggia
Prunelli-di-Casacconi
Castifao
Campile
Olmo
Vescovato
Venzolasca
Anghione
Moltifao
Sorbo-Ocagnano
San Pancrazio
Ponte Novu
Loreto-di-Casinca
Castellare-di-Casinca
Castello di-Rostino
Pastoreccia
Monte Sant'Angelo
San Pellegrino
Ponte Leccia
Valle-di-Rostino
Ortiporio
Porri
Piedigriggio
Casalta
Taglio
Popolasca
Morosaglia
Castiglione
Gavignano
La Porta
Pruno
Talasani
Pont de
Castirla
Prato-di-Giovellina
Croce
Scata
Poggio-
Mezzana
Piazzole
San Giovanni-
Monte San Petrone
Campana
Piedicroce
Couvent d'Orezza
di-Moriani
Moriani-Plage
Lano
San
Campodonico
Stazzona
Parata
San Nicolao
Castirla
Quilico
Erone
Carcheto
Felce
Santa Reparata-
di-Moriani
Tralonca
Col d'Arcarotta
Cervione
Port de Campoloro

Tyrrhenian Sea
des
Agriates

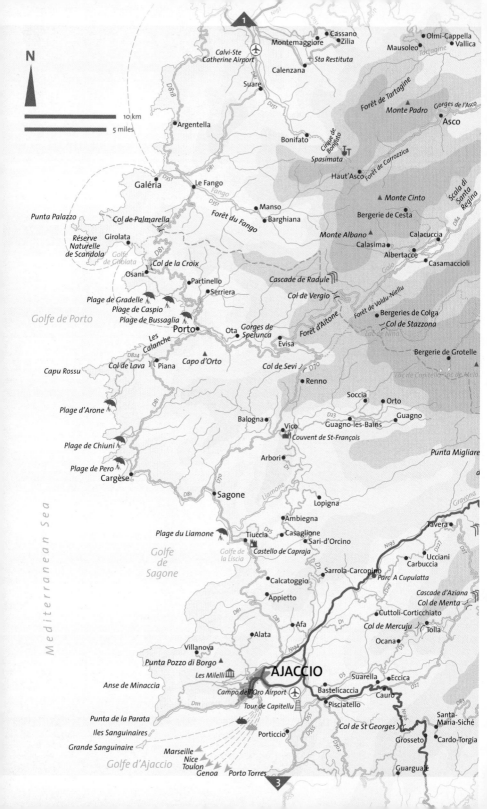

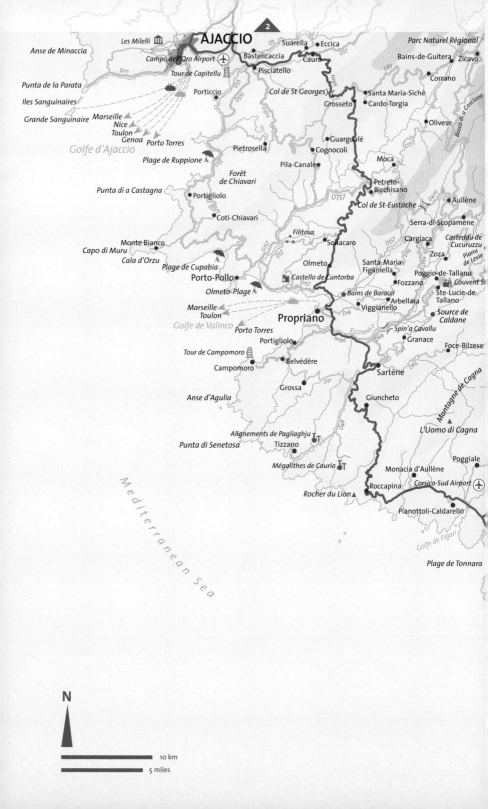

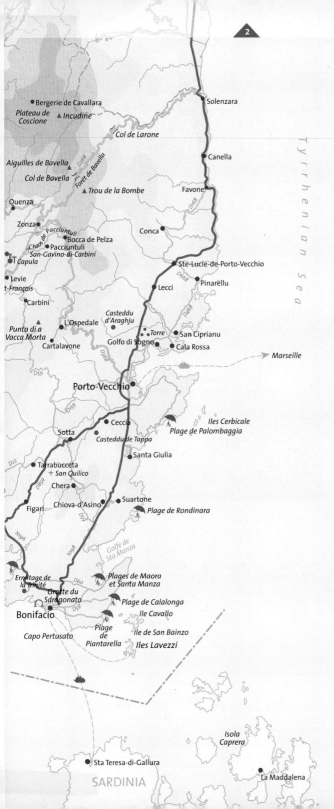

Bergerie de Cavallara
Plateau de Coscione
Incudine
Col de Larone
Solenzara

Aiguilles de Bavella
Col de Bavella
Forêt de Bavella
Trou de la Bombe
Canella
Favone

Quenza
Zonza
Chera de Pacciuntuli
Bocca de Pelza
Pacciuntuli
San-Gavino-di-Carbini
Capula
Conca
Ste-Lucie-de-Porto-Vecchio

Levie
t-François
Carbini
Lecci
Pinarellu

Casteddu d'Araghju
L'Ospedale
Punta di a Vacca Morta
Torre
San Ciprianu
Golfo di Sogno
Cala Rossa
Cartalavone

Marseille

Porto-Vecchio

Ceccia
Iles Cerbicale
Plage de Palombaggia
Sotta
Casteddu de Tappa
Santa Giulia

Tarrabucceta
San Quilico
Chera
Chiova-d'Asino
Suartone
Plage de Rondinara
Figari

Golfe de Sta Manza

Ermitage de la Trinité
Plages de Maora et Santa Manza
Grotte du Sdragonato
Plage de Calalonga
Ile Cavallo
Bonifacio
Capo Pertusato
Plage de Piantarella
Ile de San Bainzo
Iles Lavezzi

Isola Caprera

Sta Teresa-di-Gallura
SARDINIA
La Maddalena

Tyrrhenian Sea

CADOGANguides **FRANCE**

'Amusing comment
and invaluable advice'

Independent